PENGUIN BOOKS

UNLOCKING THE WORLD

John Darwin was until his retirement in 2017 Professor of Imperial and Global History at the University of Oxford. He is the author of *After Tamerlane*, *Unfinished Empire* and *The Empire Project*.

JOHN DARWIN

Unlocking the World

Port Cities and Globalization in the Age of Steam, 1830–1930

PENGUIN BOOKS

PENGUIN BOOKS

UK | USA | Canada | Ireland | Australia
India | New Zealand | South Africa

Penguin Books is part of the Penguin Random House group of companies
whose addresses can be found at global.penguinrandomhouse.com

First published by Allen Lane 2020
Published in Penguin Books 2021
001

Typeset by Jouve (UK), Milton Keynes
Printed and bound in Great Britain by Clays Ltd, Elcograf S.p.A.

The authorized representative in the EEA is Penguin Random House Ireland,
Morrison Chambers, 32 Nassau Street, Dublin D02 YH68

A CIP catalogue record for this book is available from the British Library

ISBN: 978-1-846-14087-7

www.greenpenguin.co.uk

MIX
Paper from
responsible sources
FSC® C018179

Penguin Random House is committed to a
sustainable future for our business, our readers
and our planet. This book is made from Forest
Stewardship Council® certified paper.

In Memory of Jan-Georg Deutsch

Contents

List of Illustrations

List of Maps

Preface

'There are five keys that lock up the world,' declared Admiral 'Jacky' Fisher, grand strategist of the Edwardian Royal Navy: Singapore, the Cape of Good Hope, Alexandria, Gibraltar, Dover. Under Britain's control, they would guard the sea lanes between Europe and the rest of the world and keep them safe from the fleets of any enemy power: a plan soon to be tested to destruction by U-boat warfare. Stationing the British 'Grand Fleet' in the Orkneys completed Fisher's design and sealed the last exit from the North Sea into the open ocean. In this book, we reverse Fisher's image and change most of his places. The nineteenth century was the great age in which the coasts and ports of the world were freed from exclusions and closures; vast continental interiors were unlocked from the seclusion imposed by the costs of overland transport; and rivers whose hazards and currents made upstream traffic a toil (this included the River Seine until the 1840s) were opened by improvement and steam navigation. By the end of the steam century in 1930, regular, scheduled, travel by steamship and railway was possible to almost every closely inhabited part of the world, and so was the exchange of bulky low-cost goods. This was a revolution in world history with whose consequences we now live.

It had been a great technological achievement, the triumph of steam. But it was also a geopolitical trauma. The opening of continents in China, India, Australasia, the Americas, and in North and Central Asia, was consolidated by steam. But the doors had been forced by the armies, navies, settlers, serfs, slaves and indentured labour of the European empires and their American progeny – the settler republics of Anglo- and Hispanic-America and the Empire of

Brazil. Coercive diplomacy, military conquest, and the driving out (or enserfment) of indigenous peoples cleared the way for merchants, administrators, tax collectors, miners, planters, and yeoman or peasant farmers, closely followed by the teachers, priests and missionaries of different religions, the agents of cultural upheaval. By the time that steam was being properly harnessed to the carriage of people and goods over land and sea, a vast new terrain had been annexed to the commercial, administrative and settler empires of the emerging West.

This book had its origins in curiosity about the history of globalization, and of 'steam globalization' in particular. It is framed by a number of key assumptions: that 'our' globalization since 1990 is not unique, but only the latest in a series; that we can best understand its distinctive features by a knowledge of earlier versions; that globalizations are cumulative, but also subject to crises and reversals; that globalizations must be understood not (as we tend to do) as narrowly economic phenomena, but as the conjuncture of technological, commercial, cultural, ideological, geopolitical and environmental change, all of which give them their distinctive character. For what we exchange in globalization is not only goods, but also money, people, ideas, information, habits of consumption – and *biota*: plants, animals and microbes. It is through their complex interaction that the 'quality' of each globalization is formed. It follows logically from this that the catalyst of globalization, its 'regulator' (to use a term from steam technology), is *mobility* – the ease and speed with which things tangible and intangible can cross the wide spaces from one side of the world to the other.

Of paramount interest, historically and today, is the *impact* of globalization: what does it do to the people caught up in its toils, or to those left on its margins? Even to a casual glance, it is clear that it produces winners and losers, often reversing the fortunes of previous winners. Gain and loss might be felt in relative living standards, in cultural self-confidence, and in freedom or not from external domination. At its best it brings an all-round improvement in material well-being; at its worst, it might be a matter of life and death. Much historical debate has turned on the question of why some regions of the world were once prosperous but then sank into deep relative poverty. Just as intriguing is the question of how far globalizations have imposed greater cultural conformity or undermined the coherence of 'traditional' cultures, sometimes with tragic effects. These questions can be asked of any era of globalization, but the focus of this book is on the 'steam century', when the spread and intensity of globalization offers the closest comparison to our own. It is also the period in which the sources and resources available for enquiry are richer than in any previous age.

But the problem remains: how to get to grips with a phenomenon as diffuse and wide-ranging as globalization, properly understood in its complex geometry. Where did it come from? How was it projected? Who were its agents? How was it received by its 'hosts'? How far did it reshape the economies, cultures, politics and demography of the regions in its path? How far was it driven by geopolitics – or violence – as much as by market forces? An obvious place to look was the large maritime cities – port cities – whose spectacular growth was a striking feature of the period. For this, even more than today (when 90 per cent of world trade moves by sea) was a seaborne era in which 'command of the ocean' for mercantile or military purposes was the key to world power. The port city in Asia, Africa, Australasia and the Americas was the entry point through which poured the money, manufactures, ideas and people, as well as the physical force, that flowed out from Europe, and through which it extracted the 'returns' of tribute, raw materials, profits and rents. That was what was supposed to follow when Europe supplied the energy that drove globalization. The world was to be 'unlocked' for the free movement of capital, labour, goods and ideas – transforming and 'improving' hitherto 'backward' or undeveloped interiors along European lines. But did it really happen like that? And how far were Westerners really in control of the changes that globalization unleashed?

The port city was where all the varied agents of globalization encountered a local society. We can see there in close-up the pattern of acceptance or of adaptation and resistance to change; the terms on which inland regions were drawn into the port city's web; and how far it was able to re-shape the culture and politics of its emerging hinterland. But which to choose from the very long list of important port cities? The plan of this book was to select a small group of cities to test the variable impact of Europe-led 'steam globalization' in different locations: in the 'settler world' of Anglo-America; in British-ruled India; and in the connected realm of South East Asia and maritime China, where European influence was more indirect. That left many others in Africa, Latin America, Australia, New Zealand and the Middle East – all of equal fascination – regrettably to be mentioned only in passing. I am also very conscious that those who are expert on the history of the cities I do discuss may feel that I have done them scant justice or overlooked key aspects of their past. I hope that setting them in a comparative frame and highlighting their global importance will do something to compensate. One thing is certain. In the fast-growing discipline of global history, port cities deserve all the attention they can get.

The seeds of this book may have lain in a childhood voyage by Union Castle mailship to Cape Town, the sight and sound of the docks and the bustle of ports before the container-ship era. I have been able to draw on a large and expanding body of scholarship to explore the topics described in this book. But many of the ideas that inform it were knocked into shape by the conversations and activities around Oxford's Centre for Global History. To my colleagues there I owe a great debt of thanks. Early versions of the book's main arguments were inflicted on audiences in Heidelberg, Konstanz, Zurich and Princeton. Two colleagues in particular, James Belich and the late Jan-Georg Deutsch, had to endure more than their fair share of my musings. It is to the memory of Jan-Georg, kindest and most generous of colleagues, that this book is dedicated.

The facilities, stimulation and support that Nuffield College offers its Fellows is unrivalled: I have been very fortunate to enjoy them. As on several previous occasions, I also owe a great deal to the interest and enthusiasm – and sage advice – of Simon Winder at Penguin. Richard Duguid superintended production and Eva Hodgkin gave invaluable help. Cecilia Mackay helped select the images. The maps were drawn by Jeff Edwards.

The lines quoted on p. 182 appear by kind permission of the trustees of the Robert Penn Warren Literary Estate. I am most grateful to Professor John Burt and to Mr Ed Sullivan of Welch and Forbes LLC, for their very courteous assistance.

This preface is written as Britain remains in the grip of its pandemic lockdown. It is a reminder that, as in the steam century, globalization brings not just prosperity but many shocks and reversals. Historians are fond of observing great historical turning points. But, as we're discovering, it's much better not to have to live one's life through one.

John Darwin
June 2020

Introduction:
The Keys and the Lock

Between 1830 and 1930 the world was reshaped by steam. The world's largest economies in China, India, Europe and the Americas were tied together by sea lanes and railways (and increasingly cables) over which flowed people, goods, ideas and money on a scale and with a frequency seen in no previous era. The effect was not just to make the world's different regions easier and cheaper to reach. Steam power also brought with it a radical concentration of commercial, technological and military power without precedent in world history. For much of the century after 1830, access to steam as a new energy source of wide application was largely confined to Europe and the United States, the emerging 'West'. And for much of that century, so it came to seem, the possessors of steam power could reorder the globe. They fashioned a new grid of iron to make their mastery real: empires of settlement, commerce and rule; fleets of steamers for goods, migrants and mail; lines of rail to prise open remoter interiors for occupation and trade. At the hinge of this drive to remake the world as Europe's periphery stood some dozens of port cities, some new, some drastically remodelled to meet the needs of new masters.

Port cities were 'gateway cities'.[1] Unlike the 'classical' city, strategically placed in its agrarian 'province', the source of the surplus on which it depended, gateway cities sprang up on the edge where two different zones met. They were the place to exchange the produce of different economies (and cultures), or where goods were transferred between one mode of transport and another: between ship, rail, wagon, riverboat or (today) aeroplane. Since this often entailed the breaking of bulk into different packets and parcels for onward transmission, the gateway city was home to other services as well: shipping agents, insurers, money-changers and banks, hauliers and draymen, dockers and porters, as well as the merchants and factors whose role was to manage the trade. The gateway city was a vital information exchange, where commercial intelligence about market conditions and consumer desires in the two (or more) zones it sought to connect was gathered, digested and distributed – typically through chambers of commerce, printed 'prices current', or daily encounters in the commodity markets for corn, cotton, rice, sugar, grain, timber, wool, jute or rubber. Inevitably, too, it became the place where political risks were carefully picked over, since war, rebellion or change of regime in its zones of interest might have damaging (or promising) consequences. Indeed, it was a natural extension of commercial concerns to cultivate political influence among its suppliers and customers, and to seek the protection of a powerful ruler or patron.

Of course, not all gateway cities faced out to sea. Only some were *port* cities. We might be tempted to add that not all port cities were to be found on the coast. Inland port cities that faced out over the desert or steppe, uninhabited wastes that had to be crossed, shared some of the character of their maritime counterparts. Saharan oases were founded to serve as regional 'ports'.[2] Damascus and Aleppo in the Levant, Marrakesh and Timbuktu on opposite 'shores' of the western Sahara, Kashgar and Yarkand at the western end of the Gobi, were the destinations for caravans and the 'ships of the desert' that carried their trade. The 'silk route' from China through Inner Asia to the Mediterranean connected a long chain of such inland port cities. In the later nineteenth century, great railway junctions like Chicago (also a lake port) or St Louis (also a river port) performed similar functions: both grew in size with exceptional rapidity. So did Budapest and Vienna, the Chicago and St Louis of south-eastern Europe: both multi-ethnic and strongly Jewish cities stranded after 1918 in fiercely nationalist rump states.

Nevertheless, for most of modern world history it has been the maritime city that has played the largest role in the export and import of cultures and goods between distant locations, if only because movement by sea has almost always been cheaper than carriage over land. For traffic between continents, between Europe and the Americas, and most of Asia and Africa, once the many navigational mysteries were solved, the ship became sovereign. Not until the early twentieth century, when the Trans-Siberian Railway was completed, was another means of travel from one end of Eurasia to the other even conceivable – except to those for whom time had no value. The ocean liner ruled the routes between Europe and most of the world into the 1950s. The age of the globe-facing port city was a long one.

Most port cities had begun as a trading beach where local merchants and shipmen would meet when the trading season began. The timing might be dictated by the winds (in the 'monsoon world' they changed direction almost like clockwork) or by the dangers of sea-going in winter, or by the approach of the harvest – when consumers had the means to buy 'foreign' goods. If a trading beach prospered, it would attract the attention of a local ruler or big man as a revenue source: indeed his protection might be welcome against less regulated predation. For rulers with ambitions or a large court to manage, the beach might become an organized *emporium* to supply exotic goods like silks or ivory that commanded prestige and signalled authority.[3] In early medieval London the king had the right to buy first from a newly arrived cargo.[4] A port city might be founded to further a grand imperial plan (Alexandria, founded in 331 BC, is the most famous example), or grow up as the refuge of traders and fishermen (the origin of Venice). Site was always of crucial importance. A perennial source of fresh water was critical. Reasonably deep and calm water close to the shore, and shelter from the worst of the wind, were other obvious requirements: hence the appeal of an estuary with its up-river access. Across much the world, defence against attack from the sea, or by an inland aggressor, was a vital necessity. To be too close to the open sea would court the risk of a hit-and-run raid by pirates or rivals. A cove-like setting, protected by heights on either side, was often favoured (a typical case is Lisbon). Sometimes the ideal was an island site, where the island was small enough for easy defence, and sea access restricted. Where attack from the land was a menace it might be essential. Tyre on its rocky islet; Venice; Hormuz (at the mouth of the Persian Gulf); New Amsterdam (later New York); Montreal; Bombay; Penang; Singapore; Hong Kong; Lamu, Mombasa, Kilwa and Mozambique (all on the coast of East Africa); Lagos (on the west) – were all of this type. A defensible peninsula with a narrow causeway to land was another alternative: the pattern of Aden, Bushire, Boston, Charleston and Cadiz (Phoenician *Gades*).

There was no guarantee of a port city's success. Its harbour might silt up – a result of cultivation or deforestation upstream. The shoals and sandbanks between it and the sea might shift and obstruct its approach. At worst it might be destroyed by a great storm or earthquake and tsunami – the fate of Port Royal in Jamaica in 1692. It might lose its patron's protection or find that his favour now rested elsewhere. When the East India Company moved its business to Bombay, Surat began to languish. The source of a port city's wealth might dry up, or its production be moved to a distant location. With the loss of New France and the Canada trade in 1763, and the Haitian revolt of 1791, La Rochelle entered a century of commercial contraction.[5] When wild rubber turned into a plantation crop grown in South East Asia, Manaos on the Amazon went into decline. It might lose its hinterland as a result of a diplomatic partition – the misfortune of Freetown with its huge natural harbour.[6] Trade routes might change and bypass old harbours for new: the fate of Galle in Sri Lanka, which had ceded its place to Colombo by the mid-1870s. Technological progress might be the enemy here: bigger ships with a deeper draught that needed more room to manoeuvre; steamships demanding cheap coal; railways that needed access and space for large marshalling yards. How to respond to these threats, and much else besides, was the stuff of port-city politics.

Once a port city was more than a beach, almost every side of its commerce required regulation. Who was to own or control the riverbanks, wharves and jetties where goods were unloaded? Who should decide if new wharves were needed? Who was to pay for them, or for clearing the channels that deeper ships needed? What kind of charges should be imposed on arrivals, and who should decide on spending the proceeds? Who was to safeguard the goods on the quay and ensure the protection of mercantile property? Who would decide how goods should be sold – by private arrangement or at publicly known prices? Who would control the labour supply, since ports needed much human muscle? Who would police the travellers and transients that ports always attracted? Who would ensure their physical and spiritual health, and keep seaborne epidemics at bay? Who would decide whether the port was a 'free' port, or be secluded behind a barrier of tariffs and duties? Who would defend the port against attack from the sea, predators on land, or the interference of rivals? Typically, a patrician elite would emerge to rule the port city and manage its politics. They would have to appease or repress its conflicting interests. But much would depend on their uneasy relations with nearby centres of power, whether magnates, princes or proconsuls. Sometimes the 'prince' would depend on the port and submerge his own interests in its fate. More often he would balance its claims against those of his inland possessions, or (worse still) exploit its resources in some reckless war of expansion. But port-city oligarchies usually needed his backing to maintain their authority, not least when they were threatened by a popular rising against the gross inequalities of port-city society. When improving the port meant incurring fresh debts, imposing new charges or infringing old rights, sovereign approval was especially valuable. Most prized of all was the grant by the ruler of privilege or monopoly in overseas trade.

In fact, a port city's status, and its relative freedom from external control, usually turned on the source of its commercial prosperity. For much of the long period up to the mid-nineteenth century, the most successful port cities were typically *entrepôts*. That is to say they relied relatively little upon the trade and produce of their immediate neighbourhood. Instead, their commercial relations were chiefly with similar ports, and with distant suppliers and customers. Essentially, they were a market and warehouse where goods from abroad were imported and then re-exported, often to other overseas buyers. Their merchants depended upon networks of trust and commercial intelligence with faraway markets and other entrepôt merchants. Geographical location, ease of access to their harbour and a reasonably assured command of a sea lane were critical factors. The size of their mercantile fleet was vital for drawing in trade to their wharves and enlarging the profits of sale and resale. The constant flow of transactions provided far greater liquidity than in agrarian economies, and encouraged the emergence of banks to supply credit and foreign exchange. In favourable circumstances, such entrepôt cities could maintain their autonomy against terrestrial rulers, or purchase their freedom with much needed cash. Where the king was far away, his authority might require a fortified presence. The French monarchy, for example, had to build a fortress in Bordeaux, the Château Trompette (today an open space), to overawe its troublesome citizens.[7] The Tower of London had a similar purpose.

By contrast, a *staple* port existed chiefly to collect and export the produce of the nearby interior, paid for with imports of manufactures and luxuries. Its prosperity depended upon access to the forests, farmlands, vineyards, pastures or mines from which its exports were drawn. Safeguarding its hinterland was a vital priority and its dislocation by war or rebellion a commercial disaster. Hence the interests of a staple port were much more closely aligned with those of the ruler and the landowning elite. It needed their help to keep open the rivers and roads that led to the port, and to discourage rival ports from invading its sphere. Since trade often required the advance of credit to producers, or the holding of mortgages, it was deeply invested in local regimes of labour and property and feared their disruption. While an entrepôt port maintained many connections, and its wealthier citizens might travel quite widely, a staple port was likely to rely on a particular market. Its culture and politics tended to be much more conservative than those of its cosmopolitan counterpart. In practice, of course, many large ports were a mixture of staple and entrepôt. Thus Bordeaux was an entrepôt importing and selling on colonial produce like sugar and coffee, but also a staple for wine.[8] Some might expand from one to the other (as London grew out of being a mere staple for wool), or, having failed as an entrepôt, revert to a staple (Cartagena in modern Colombia, Madras/Chennai, Batavia/Jakarta and Sydney fall into this category). As we will see, the huge growth of commodity trades in the nineteenth century implied a tightening bond between many old entrepôts and the interior economy.

Regardless of the balance of commercial activity, every port city needed plenty of strangers. Its 'foreign' transactions depended on knowledge of faraway markets and products. More to the point, it required trustworthy agents and partners for whom default might spell ruin. Family connection or shared religious allegiance were the best guarantee against commercial defection. A foreign merchant community promised reliable dealings with their kinfolk at home.

Equally, overseas merchants were more likely to trade freely when they could deal with a compatriot, a cousin or a co-religionist. Moreover, outsiders brought expertise, information, fresh ideas and sometimes capital – the vital ingredients of commercial success. A sign of prosperity in any port city was the size and variety of its foreign population: it was a dependable index of the range of its commerce. In all the port cities we explore in this book, commercial vitality was closely connected with the continuous recruitment of expatriate talent (Chinese, Indian, Middle Eastern as well as European) and the networks they brought. Medieval London and Antwerp were colonized by Italians and Hanse from the Baltic; nineteenth-century New Orleans by New Yorkers and French; Singapore by Chinese. In a middling port city like Montevideo nearly three-quarters of its merchants were foreign in the late nineteenth century.[9] Even a declining Red Sea port like Suakin (on the coast of Sudan) had many outsiders. It 'is inhabited to-day', wrote a visitor in 1911, 'by a motley crowd of Jiddans [i.e. from Jeddah], Yemenites, Hadramutians [Hadhramis from South Arabia], Indians, and Abyssinians, whose interests are concerned with other Red sea ports or even with Aden, Bombay, and Mombasa almost more than with the mainland . . . behind them'.[10]

Whatever their origins, merchants had to fit into complex and often quarrelsome communities, where social tensions were sharpened by the two great scourges of port-city life: the volatile nature of commodity trade and the visitations of epidemic disease – worst in tropical or subtropical regions, but also commonplace in Europe and North America until the late nineteenth century. Every port city had a cadre of lawyers to resolve (or inflame) its commercial disputes. It might have a governor and a garrison, and almost always a customs house to collect revenue for the ruler. The shipping interest would be large but not always harmonious. Shipowners, shipbuilders, shipping agents, dock owners, warehousemen, pilots and dock workers rarely agreed on improving the port or sharing the cost. Once railways arrived, they brought with them a new set of interests and a large new workforce. Managers, agents, clerks, engineers, drivers, mechanics, as well as a phalanx of stationmasters, signalmen, cleaners and porters, came to service the terminals for passengers and freight, man the repair shops and marshalling yards, staff the trains and maintain the track. There would be priests and pundits with definite but often conflicting views about the spiritual needs of port-city society and the regulation of its 'floating world' of brothels, gambling houses, taverns and bars that catered for the sailors, boatmen, porters and draymen among the mass of migrant workers who helped to make its population disproportionately male. The combination of wealth and frequent epidemic disease made port cities a magnet for doctors (or those who claimed to be). In Asian ports they might be drawn from different traditions, Chinese and Indian as well as Western. The advertisements in nineteenth-century port newspapers testify to the huge market for cordials, pills and other specifics against local or exotic ailments, for, quite apart from diseases brought in from abroad, the mixture of poor sanitation and a low-lying estuary site often with marshland nearby, made ports unusually prone to a range of complaints.

A more difficult question was how, or whether, to control the arrival of travellers from notoriously 'diseased' destinations, especially those where plague or cholera were thought to be endemic. Typically in the West this was done by quarantine, originally forty days in an isolated *lazaretto*, before the grant of 'pratique' (release or exemption from quarantine), a practice begun in the late fourteenth century and standardized in the Mediterranean. Thus travellers returning to Britain in the 1830s from Greece would spend their quarantine in Malta before resuming their journey, and Britain itself had some twenty-one quarantine stations. Despite a fierce medical debate over whether or not 'contagion' was the cause of diseases like yellow fever or cholera, and merchant hostility to the obstruction of free trade, quarantine was practised in Britain until 1896 and longer elsewhere.[11] Outbreaks of disease were very bad for business and raised the issue of how much publicity they should be given. Port-city journalists and the newspapers they served thus faced a dilemma that went wider than disease. Newspapers were usually owned by mercantile interests or those aligned with them. Part of their role was to trumpet the success of the port and the golden future expected. Their pages were filled with business information and advertisements. Yet they were inevitably drawn into the local disputes that wracked

almost every port city: the need for improved sanitation; for imposing standards on housing; for better policing; for the paving and
lighting of streets: all of which would impose costs on property
owners or infringe their rights. Journalists might rub shoulders with
another influential community. For many port cities by the later
eighteenth and nineteenth centuries (much earlier in some) sustained
a circle of artists, photographers, architects, botanists and other scientists (usually doctors by profession), as well as those with an interest
in the history and ethnography of the nearby interior. Their role was
also ambiguous. They were the collectors, interpreters and purveyors
of scientific or 'useful' knowledge. But – perhaps unconsciously – they
also served in the world beyond Europe to familiarize a new landscape to its colonial invaders, to sharpen their appetite for further
advance, and – implicitly – to assert the primacy of Europeanized
culture.

In a successful port city its great merchant houses were the 'kings
of the castle'. Their leading partners made up its patrician elite. Of
course, their circumstances varied. In European states their wings
might be clipped by dynastic rulers or (later) a nationalist or populist
government. In pre-colonial Asia, they might have to act as 'official'
merchants, like the Hong merchants of Canton, or the factors and
'writers' of the great trading companies – Dutch, English, French, or
Danish. In both cases this often came with the reward of monopoly:
foreign trade was confined to a privileged club. By the mid-nineteenth
century these mercantilist structures had been largely dismantled and
trade was open to the talented, the lucky and the well-connected. In
port-city commerce that meant above all the ability to deal in commodities, for it was the buying and selling of commodities that made
a merchant's and a port city's fortune.

In any transaction the merchant found himself part of a complex
and unpredictable chain of exchange and production. There was huge
variation in the way that different commodities arrived in the market.
Some were the produce of itinerant foragers, hunting, fishing, trap-
ping or tapping, along frontiers of declining returns or (eventually)
outright extinction. Unless the merchant was willing to 'rough it
in the bush', he would depend on an agent or a partner to bargain
his trade goods for ivory, furs, wild rubber or birds' nests with

up-country peoples, and despatch them by trade paths to a river or railhead. To manage the risk of uncertain supply and the costs of collection, merchants sometimes preferred to form a cartel – like the fur-trading companies of the Canadian North-West – or resort to coercion, a practice applied with genocidal effects in the late nineteenth-century Congo. For commodities that depended on cultivators or pastoralists different conditions applied. Here the merchant might deal with smallholding peasants or large landowners and planters, reliant on serfs, slaves or landless labour. He would have to advance credit to meet their needs from harvest to harvest, all the more so if they no longer produced their own foodstuffs. The merchant was at the mercy of a dynamic environment: drought or pestilence could decimate crops and herds, and with them his profit and even his capital. Over-grazing or soil-mining could wreck his supply zone. Epidemic disease could wipe out a workforce or shatter its energy. Or several good seasons, or new production elsewhere, could bring on a glut, driving down prices to ruinous levels. A merchant might have bought dear but have to sell cheap. His overseas buyers might fail, and take with them the credit they owed him. A financial crisis, or the rumour of war, would shrivel the market. Merchants lived on their nerves and by their flow of 'correspondence', reporting the news, predicting the price level.

Commercial success would also depend on a set of interlocking regimes in the agrarian interior. Who had command of the distribution of land or the power to remove its 'uncooperative' residents, like those wedded to subsistence or slash-and-burn agriculture? Was property held individually – to be used as collateral – or collectively by lineages, tribes or caste brotherhoods, unreliable borrowers with nothing to pledge? Was immigrant labour available to open new lands or expand their output, or was it restricted by racial exclusion or the high cost of travel? Was the state willing to pay for internal improvements – the building of canals, railways and roads – or too parsimonious or poor or disorganized to try? Was it willing to free trade from tariffs and duties, and the regulation of prices, or set on maintaining mercantilist rules and a command economy?

It was questions like these that made the port city the vital headquarters for a commodity hinterland. It was above all a factory of prices. For buyers and sellers alike, the larger the marketplace, the better the price information on which they relied. A port city could sustain newspapers and price guides, and (from the 1840s and 1850s) a telegraph office. Dealers and brokers could meet one another.[12] The flow of credits and cash nourished banks and later stock exchanges. Many of the services that were needed by agrarian communities would be domiciled there: doctors, lawyers, educationists, clerics, as well as retailers of clothes, hardware, tools and (in the American South) slaves. But it was also the base from which the mercantile interest could wage its campaigns for 'free land' unrestricted by entail or communal rights, better roads, low tariffs and the free movement of labour; and lobby for protection against piracy, shipping cartels, or an oppressive ruler on their doorstep. Where there was representative government, it was wise to choose a vociferous tribune to champion its claims and chivvy the executive. If not, the ruler's viceroy might be suborned by local patrician inducements to plead in its favour. With luck, and in time, a successful port city might begin to acquire the attributes of a metropolis: not just organizing the market, providing credit facilities and insurance, building a transport system and processing industries, but achieving financial independence by raising its own capital.[13] That was a destiny to which only a few could aspire.

The theme of this book is the part port cities played in globalization. As a term, 'globalization' is most frequently used to describe the economic connectedness between different parts of the world that accelerated dramatically towards the end of the last century: the apparent hyper-mobility of goods, money, information and labour. As often happens, it seemed at first to be a uniquely modern phenomenon, unprecedented and incomparable. A sense of perspective suggests the contrary – that 'our' globalization is merely the latest in a cumulative series of closer encounters between distant parts of the globe.[14] Those encounters, and the connections they forged, went back many tens of thousands of years, to the first migration of *Homo sapiens* out of Africa to colonize Eurasia. Other colonizations followed. Aboriginal societies spread across Australia from its northern 'coast' some 45,000 years ago. The Americas were first settled from

North-East Asia 15,000 years ago, probably in a series of coastal 'hops'. The extraordinary empires of the Aztecs and Incas were among their legacies, and perhaps a lost civilization in the Amazon basin. Madagascar was colonized by settlers from the Indonesian archipelago in the first millennium BC. Between 1000 BC and AD 1250, Polynesian explorers located and occupied all the habitable islands from Fiji to Easter Island, from the Hawaiian islands to New Zealand, in a series of astonishing voyages over the open sea.[15] They may even have established some form of contact with the west coast of the Americas long before Europeans appeared in the Pacific.[16] Long-distance trade networks appeared in the Bronze Age (3000 BC to 1000 BC). After 1000 BC the use of coinage, the formulation of law codes, the provision of credit for merchants and the emergence of 'mega-empires' (Neo-Assyrian, Achaemenid, Hellenistic, Mauryan, Han and Roman) encouraged the growth of long-distance commerce (including the slave trade) across much of Eurasia.[17] The pre-conditions for a globalized world were put in place early on.

Global connectedness has thus had a very long history. But within that history we can see phases and periods when connectedness grew stronger, more intense and wide-ranging, and those when it appeared to slow down or even retreat. It is possible to argue that the term should be reserved for the period after 1492, when the Americas were 'annexed' to the rest of the world; or that, properly thought of as a purely economic phenomenon, it was delayed until the late nineteenth century when a genuinely 'global' economy came into existence. In fact, both these alternatives seem unduly restrictive, if for two different reasons.

Globalization is best understood as the long-distance exchange of people, goods, money, technologies, ideas, beliefs and *biota* – animals, plants and (less visibly) microbes. It long pre-dated the voyages of Columbus, or, for that matter, the European 'discovery' of Australasia. It was certainly true that the 'Columbian Exchange' which brought American plants, diseases and silver to Eurasia, and sent back the Old World's animals, infections, conquistadors and slaves, dramatically modified the inter-continental connections between Asia, Europe and Africa.[18] It was also true that both goods and people moved round the world on an unprecedented scale in the late nineteenth century, and that a global economy, superficially similar to that of our times, had appeared by 1914. But both these great accelerations built on older foundations and on previous phases of global connectedness. And both must be understood as something wider and more complex than merely new patterns of trade. They embodied, in fact, a new set of cultural, demographic, geopolitical and ecological relations, as well as those that were shaped by technology and commerce. Indeed, it is easy to see that, at almost all periods of history, the scope for commercial exchange has been shaped by the cultural preferences of consumers, the distribution of populations, the physical power to force open markets, and the ease (or not) with which different natural environments could be 'tamed' and exploited. The history of globalization must be sought in the intricate interplay between these various components and in the conjunctures they formed in different parts of the world. Global connectedness has always been uneven (and remains so today): favouring now one region, now another; constantly creating new cores and peripheries; and shifting the balance of power, wealth and cultural self-confidence across the continents.

The catalyst for globalization (and the source of its limits) can be found in mobility – the relative ease of movement around the world and across its huge inland spaces. In the earliest times, the domestication of horses, camels and other draught animals, and the invention of the wheel, had extended the range of overland transport, just as the sail and navigational experiment had over the sea. In the early modern era (c.1400–c.1750) improvements in ship design and navigational technique enabled Columbus and Vasco da Gama to pioneer new shipping routes and bring many more coastlands into touch with each other. But overland movement remained costly and slow, largely restricting the traffic in bulk goods to interior waterways and their immediate surroundings. In the mid-1770s Adam Smith compared the cost of sending goods by road or by sea between Edinburgh and London in the sailing-ship era. 'Six or eight men', he concluded, '. . . by the help of water carriage, can carry and bring back in the same time the same quantity of goods . . . as fifty broad-wheeled waggons, attended by a hundred men, and drawn by four hundred horses.'[19] This was still an 'eotechnic' age,[20] in which the energy needed for movement came from wind and current, supplemented by human and animal muscle. These constraints of energy supply dictated not only the volume and speed (and therefore the cost) of traffic on land and sea, but also the routes that that traffic must follow. Overland transport demanded forage and water for humans and animals. Except where they were freely available, this imposed sometimes tortuous diversions to seek the necessary 'fuel'. In the vast arid world it favoured the use of grassy savannahs or a chain of oases; in the temperate world, the avoidance of dense woodland as much as mountain or marsh. At sea, ships sought the wind and a favourable current and selected a course that would maximize both. To reach East Asia from Europe, they followed the trade winds towards the coast of Brazil before turning east, and, once past the Cape of Good Hope, kept far to the south where strong westerlies blew before turning north to pass between Sumatra and Java. This was the route pioneered at the turn of the sixteenth century with world-changing consequences. Both routes and time-keeping depended on the seasonal change of winds and currents, dictating the sequence of landfalls and ports to which goods might be carried and where produce was exchanged. The result, across much of the world, was a patchwork of coastal and inland economies, cultures and polities, where coastlands far apart might have more regular contact with each other than they had with their nearby interiors.

As long as this was the case, global connections depended on a long chain of port cities maintaining their place in the circulations of people and goods. How far those connections could penetrate inland before they were crushed by the barriers of distance would vary enormously. In the chapters that follow, we can see how this pre-modern calculus was transformed by a revolution in mobility. By the mid-nineteenth century, the application of steam power in shipping had brought directness and regularity to long-distance sea voyages, with major savings in time. Later in the century, large iron- or steel-hulled steamers making frequent round trips, brought a massive expansion in shipping capacity, and a radical change in the economics of migration and the carriage of bulk cargoes. But the real revolution lay in the impact of steam on interior spaces. Steamboats on rivers extended the reach of port cities upstream – where in the past a fast-flowing

current had made that impracticable – and thus the sphere of commercialized agriculture and seaborne influence in continental societies.
They encouraged recourse to the canalization and control of 'unreliable' waterways like the Seine or the Elbe. They opened the great
rivers of Asia and Africa, the Indus, Ganges, Irrawaddy, Mekong,
Yangzi, Congo, Zambezi, Nile and Niger to the crowd of European
explorers, adventurers, merchants and missionaries – and sometimes
to European armies, navies and gunboats. In 1885 a flotilla of twenty-
six steamboats carried 10,000 soldiers of Britain's Indian Army 400
miles up the Irrawaddy to Mandalay and brought down the last king
of Burma in a matter of days.[21]

But the greatest engine of change was the steam locomotive. Like
rivers of iron, railways 'opened' the land, ending the historic dependence on water for the transport of goods. The line of rail, its outgrowth
of branch lines, and the telegraph wires that usually followed, promised (or threatened) the lightning conversion of the realm of the
hunter, the herdsman or the subsistence farmer into a landscape of
cash crops, close cultivation, alien settlers, wire fences and debt: in
few places more swiftly than in late nineteenth-century Argentina.[22]
The impact on lifeways might be no less dramatic.

We will see in later chapters how far this could reach in Asian societies. In older slave-and-settler communities a change in their external
connections could produce a sweeping adjustment in everyday habits.
In the sailing-ship era it became common for homeward-bound
Portuguese Indiamen from Goa and Macau to call at Brazil's great
harbour at Bahia to exchange porcelain, cloth and oriental luxuries
for Brazilian gold and diamonds as well as bringing with them trees
and plants like breadfruit, mango, oil palm and coconut. Brazilians
cultivated 'oriental' habits: clapping hands at the doorway to announce
arrival; sitting cross-legged on the floor; using the parasol as a sign of
status; the seclusion of women; the taste for mantillas and shawls and
bright-coloured clothing.[23] A French traveller in the 1830s found that
even rich planters had almost no furniture and slept in hammocks or
cots rather than beds.[24] In the second half of the century, with steam
navigation and new markets in Europe, and the end of the old sailing
route to the East, European lifestyles swept all before them. Heavy,
dark European-style clothes and stove-pipe hats became de rigueur

for the respectable classes – in the tropical heat 'a vivid act of self-martyrdom'.[25] Local foods were disdained in favour of imports. Walnut, apple and pear trees were planted to recreate Europe in America. The enthusiasm for the products of Europe extended to furniture, art, music and courtesans. 'With trains, sanitation in the cities, gas-lighting . . . The European workman, the white artisan, the foreign technician became as necessary as the air for breathing.'[26]

Yet the reach of steam globalization was far from universal. Nor of course could its impact be uniform. If eotechnic technology constrained movement to certain limited pathways, so did the complex of steam, coal and iron that followed on after. Steam-shipping, even more than the sailing ship, preferred certain 'trunk routes', partly because the shortest distance to the next port of call meant a saving in coal. Dallying in byways, costless to a sailing ship, was a profit destroyer. The need to refuel at frequent intervals dictated a voyage from coaling station to coaling station – and the choice was further constrained by a preference for large coaling ports where the supply was unlimited and the price most competitive. As 'liners' sailing on fixed routes ('lines') to fixed schedules became increasingly standard for mail and passengers, and even for cargo, the tendency became stronger, and it was reinforced by the 'channelling' effect of the Suez and Panama canals (opened in 1869 and 1914 respectively). By the late nineteenth century, the choice of port of call also bowed to the need for an ever deeper approach, ever more rapid refuelling and modern cargo-handling facilities – amenities that only a large and well-funded port could afford. The result was a hierarchy in which clusters of secondary ports depended on the service from a major port city.

A similar kind of channelling applied to the railway. Railway builders avoided sharp turns and kept to easy gradients: less than 3 per cent was considered advisable.[27] They preferred river valleys or open plains. Unless they were built for non-commercial purposes, their routes sought out regions where a cash crop (or mineral) would repay the enormous fixed costs. Notoriously, most railways of the extra-European world extended inland from a port to a favoured supply zone but provided no 'sideways' links. In effect, they formed corridors that carried port-city influence to a particular tract, but left much of

its hinterland to the traffic of caravans, carts, mule-trains or porters.[28] The main exceptions to this rule could be found in Europe and
the United States, where, not by coincidence, global connectedness
was more intense and widespread than anywhere else in the world.
As late as 1930 three-quarters of the world's railway mileage could be
found in North America and Europe.[29] Over most of the globe, as in
the Australian wheat lands, fifteen miles from the railway was considered the limit of profitable cultivation.[30] But it was the combination
of steamship and railway (or river steamer) that created a 'hub': where
sea lanes and inland routes converged. The telegraph and submarine
cable further strengthened the trend.[31] It was the port cities that
offered the critical junction between the two modes of steam that
were to grow most rapidly, and became the forward bases for Europe's
globalizing endeavours in the long nineteenth century.

It is easy to take globalization for granted as the inevitable perme-
ation of modernity's forces into 'backward' or pre-modern regions.
We are often encouraged to think that its effects are bound to be
liberating – from poverty, superstition, xenophobia, serfdom or
slavery. We might expect its promoters to be ardent proponents of
freedom: free trade, free land and free labour. We might imagine its
natural corollary to be a geopolitical regime respectful of law, self-
determination and the overriding value of peace. However, the
argument of this book is that globalization has taken different forms
in different periods of history, and that no single formula holds good
for them all. The 'steam globalization' of 1830–1930 was strikingly
different from globalizations before and since. But how different, and
in what ways? Part of the answer is set out in the following three
chapters. Part of the problem in framing an answer is that steam globalization had such a variable impact, a result not just of geographical
differences but also of the way that it changed over time. Moreover, it
must be understood as a cultural and geopolitical, as much as commercial, phenomenon. This is just as true of the century of steam – the
main focus of this book – as of earlier periods in world history.
   The best way to grasp the variations and limits of steam globalization is to see it at work in the port-city societies that were to serve as
its springboards into continental interiors. Their histories allow us to

see in more detail how the 'global' combined with the 'local': how external agents, technologies and military power overwhelmed, co-opted or adapted to the commerce and culture of those they met on the shore. What were the circumstances in which a particular haven grew into a port-city hub? Was it merely commercial good fortune or were other forces decisive? How large a role in expanding its commerce was played by outsiders or by local entrepreneurs? What kinds of trade goods allowed port merchants to attract new inland buyers? How did they build a return traffic of produce that commanded a market? Where did they find the credit and capital to drive into a hinterland? How important to their trade was the arrival of railways, and who could pay for their building? Who provided the labour force to man its transport and docks or expand the inland production of profitable commodities? What kind of polity did the port city become and what kind of relations did it have with those who ruled the interior? Could the port city become the kernel of a new nation state, or was it condemned by its location on the edge of a continent to be seen as half-foreign? In short, how far was a port city able to transform its interior into a fully commercial economy of consumers and producers, 'Europeanizing' their economic behaviour, and tying them permanently into a global economy of which Europe was the centre? And could it remake the politics of inland societies to resemble the ideal (if not the reality) of the European nation state: ordered; law-bound; the guardian of property; committed to 'moral and material progress'?

Underlying these questions, perhaps, was the murkier issue of whether port cities could serve as the agents of a cultural transformation. While other urban centres might be under the sway of monarchs or aristocrats, soldiers or priests, and act as the headquarters of governments and armies, the business of port cities was trade and exchange. In the nineteenth-century West their culture and ethos was avowedly commercial and capitalist – a world of buying and selling, profit and loss, credit and debt, wages and work. They embodied the values of individual self-interest, free from the old obligations to lineage or family; the systematic pursuit of profitable knowledge; a religious observance that was austere and respectable; a deference to property and commercial success rather than to caste, descent or the aura of holiness. Of course, mercantile societies in the world beyond Europe were ruled by distinctive conceptions of moral and social prestige, some more compatible with European notions than others. They owed their protection – and their allegiance – to different kinds of regime. The question became how far Europe's steam globalization, with its technological glamour and wealth-creating power, would succeed or fail in Europeanizing the cultures of those it drew into the networks and bridgeheads of the new global economy.

For much of world history, port cities have been synonymous with the concentration of wealth and economic opportunity, usually in contrast with the poverty and oppression of rural society. They offered escape from the deadening routine of agricultural life, the demands of landlord, lineage, caste and commune, the fear of harvest failure and famine. But port cities, like all urban communities, had travails of their own, not least the constant assault of both endemic disease (the product of overcrowding, poor sanitation and the omnipresence of animals), and those borne by strangers that were even more deadly: plague and cholera were the most feared of these. Their economic well-being was easily disrupted by warfare, blockade, shipping losses or the breakdown of supply routes. Commercial contagion – spread by financial default, a fall in demand, crop failure or regime change – was an ever-present danger. Nowhere else, perhaps, was the consumption of news (and rumour) so voracious.

Port cities could accumulate great wealth, but their foundations were fragile. Yet the century of steam was for most a golden age of prosperity. Why was that possible, and what were the limits on port-city fortunes in earlier times? To answer those questions, we need first to peer back into previous centuries – to begin at (or near) the port city's beginnings.

PART ONE

Making Global Connections

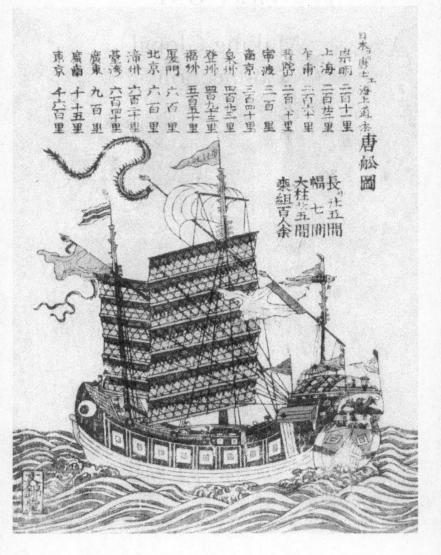

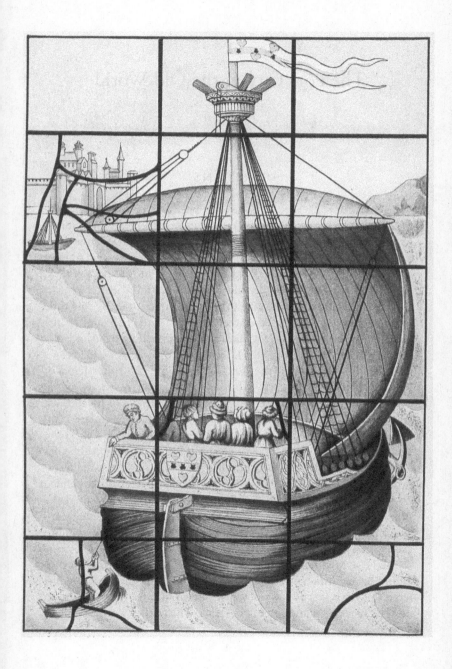

I

The Port City in the Old World

ORIGINS

Long-distance trade across the sea has been a part of world history for at least five thousand years. Perhaps its origins lay in the demand of the rulers of the first urban societies for exotic or prestigious commodities not available locally. The Mesopotamian cities seem to have traded with those of the Harappan civilization in the Indus Valley, perhaps via 'Dilmun' (usually identified as Bahrain) in the Persian Gulf from some point in the late third millennium BC. By this time ships were regularly sailing between Egypt and the Lebanon to buy cedar wood, following the circular route prescribed by wind and current via Crete and the coast of Libya.[1] Before 2000 BC, expeditions were being sent through the Red Sea from Egypt to the 'Land of Punt' (probably in modern Yemen or Eritrea) in search of ivory, ebony, aromatics and spices of ritual value.[2] A period of breakdown and chaos ensued at the end of the Bronze Age. But soon after 1000 BC coastal city states appeared, first Phoenician then Greek: Tyre, Sidon, Carthage, Cadiz, Piraeus, Corinth, Byzantium and Marseilles among them.[3] Tyre was a forerunner in connecting the Mediterranean from East to West. Built on an offshore island, it depended on the mainland for food. But its maritime commerce secured the protection of the Neo-Assyrian Empire (935–612 BC), which had captured Babylon, near modern Baghdad, and opened a trade route to the Persian Gulf. Phoenician merchants from Tyre and Sidon crisscrossed the Mediterranean. They founded Carthage in c.814 BC to guard the narrows between Sicily and North Africa. By Homer's time (c.700 BC) Greek cities were appearing around the Mediterranean and the Black Sea, and in North Africa. The port city as a source of

4

wealth and power was becoming a dominant feature of the classical world.

Meanwhile a larger maritime world had emerged around the Indian Ocean, which stretched from the East African coast to the South China Sea. Evidence of traders from India reaching Africa extends as far back as 1900–1300 BC.[4] By 500 BC Broach (Bharuch), at the mouth of the Narmada on the west coast of India, was a major entrepôt for Indian grain, timber, textiles and metal being sent to markets in the Persian Gulf, Red Sea and Mediterranean. By 100 BC knowledge of the seasonal rhythm of the monsoon winds, blowing north in summer, south in winter, had helped to disseminate the influence of Indian innovations in textiles, metallurgy and the science of astronomy and navigation all around the Indian Ocean.[5] The Roman conquest of Egypt in 31 BC turned the ports of Alexandria and Berenike, on the Red Sea, into the conduits through which Indian goods poured into the Roman Empire, while fabrics, gemstones, frankincense, copper, wine and slaves were sent to India in exchange.[6] At the other end of Asia, the conquest of South China in 220 BC had brought Qin and Han rule to hot, humid and malarial Lingnan and the Pearl River delta with its port at Canton (Guangzhou) – perhaps to be seen as a northern extension of tropical South East Asia.[7] Although Chinese silk seems to have reached the West overland by the second century BC, maritime trade between China and the Mediterranean only really began in the first century AD.[8] At around this time, too, the famous manual for Romano-Egyptian merchants, the *Periplus of the Erythrean Sea* (now dated to AD 40–70), describes a network of ports linking the Mediterranean and Red Sea to the Malacca Strait and beyond, and a seaborne commerce that was largely managed by Indian merchants.[9] If by AD 250 Eurasia had been bound together 'in a single global system', as has recently been claimed,[10] maritime trade and its overland counterpart had provided much of the glue.

Port cities and the empires they served could rise and fall, to be (in Kipling's phrase) 'one with Nineveh and Tyre'. The Han Empire fell apart after AD 220 and China was not reunited until the late sixth century. The Roman Empire in the West broke up after 476 and with it much of the urban network north of the Mediterranean. By the early seventh century, the Eastern Roman (or Byzantine) Empire was locked in a three-way struggle with the Sassanids in Persia and the insurgent force of Islamic Arabia. How far these disruptions affected the flow of maritime trade is unclear, although it seems certain that the dense overseas trade within the old Roman Empire was badly affected by its political breakdown.[11] Port cities could be sacked or destroyed by their rivals – the fate of Carthage and Corinth at the hands of the Romans. They could be swallowed by sand, silted up by mud, devastated by plague (perhaps the fate of once-prosperous Berenike, a ghost town by 550)[12] or boycotted by foreign merchants, the reaction of Arab and Persian traders to the massacre of Muslims at Canton in 878. In the harsh environment of the Red Sea and Persian Gulf and along the coasts of India with their fierce winds and monsoon rains, urban prosperity was a war against nature, and long-term survival unlikely. Nonetheless, by about AD 1000 we can see four great transformations which converged to create a vast Afro-Eurasian trading network that was to last up to and beyond the age of Columbus and Vasco da Gama.

IN THE OLD WORLD OF EURASIA

The first, and perhaps the most important, of these was China's 'medieval economic revolution'.[13] From the 700s onwards, China experienced a remarkable phase of economic expansion. There were several ingredients and, as is often the case with economic transitions, China's florescence is best explained as the effect of their fusion. Geographically, the striking feature was the southward movement of population and agriculture into the warmer, wetter lands below the Yangzi: this 'was the dynamic driving force behind an era of economic revolution'.[14] The adoption of wet-rice cultivation allowed for two or more harvests a year and permitted a much larger population. Ethnic Han Chinese colonized wider and wider areas of (modern) South and South-West China, spreading the practice of intensive cultivation and commercial exchange. Political unification under the Tang (AD 618–907) and Song (AD 960–1279) dynasties provided stable conditions for the schemes of water control and canal-building that increased agricultural production and promoted inter-regional trade. Greater commercial integration reduced reliance on locally produced food and encouraged specialization and the division of labour – the vital condition, as Adam Smith famously argued, for improved productivity and material progress. Thus, in the Song era, the reclaimed land close to the mouth of the Yangzi, near the new market town of Shanghai (founded *c.*1024), began to specialize in the production of raw cotton, drawing its foodstuffs from the rice-growing countryside further west.[15] In this more dynamic setting a series of scientific and technical innovations spurred China's advance. The adoption of woodblock printing helped diffuse knowledge (among other things) of new agricultural methods. Higher-yielding rice seeds were propagated. Coal was used to smelt iron ore and increase the production of iron goods. The gun was invented in the mid-thirteenth century. Paper money was adopted to meet the shortage of coin. Lightly taxed and effectively governed through the cultural assimilation of its gentry elite to the Confucian 'civic religion' focused on the 'heavenly mandate' of the emperor, China had become a wide zone of growing prosperity and technological adaptation, a model and a magnet for the rest of Eurasia.

The result was a growing demand for Chinese manufactures, the sought-after items of elite consumption elsewhere in Eurasia. Chinese silk and porcelain were top of the list. Copper and iron goods, sugar, rice and books were also exported. In turn, Chinese consumers increased their own demand for exotic goods from other parts of Asia, especially the forest and marine produce of South East Asia: camphor, ivory, tin and gold from Sumatra; rattan and rare timbers from Borneo; exotic birds and sandalwood from the eastern islands of the Indonesian archipelago. China's seaborne trade with the *Nanyang* ('Southern Ocean') prompted the appearance of a series of maritime states in South East Asia: Funan, in the Mekong delta, from the first to the fifth century AD; Champa, looking out over the coastal sea lane to China from what is now central and southern Vietnam, from the seventh to the tenth century; Srivijaya, in southern Sumatra, between the ninth and the thirteenth centuries, controlling both the main highways through the Indonesian archipelago, the Sunda and Malacca straits. Ayutthaya (near modern Bangkok) and Malacca (now Melaka) were to follow in the fourteenth and fifteenth centuries. These states were the commercial hinge between China and the trading zones to the west in the Bay of Bengal and the Arabian Sea – the two great divisions of the Indian Ocean. From the tenth century onwards, India, like China, had experienced an expansion of trade and agrarian settlement in the Indo-Gangetic plains, Bengal, the peninsular Deccan and along the south-east coast in the deltas of the Godavari and Kaveri.[16] Forest-clearing and town-building reflected a rising population, perhaps triggered, as in China, by the 'medieval climate anomaly' that brought more rainfall and more reliable harvests.[17] Sugar, cotton and indigo were cultivated as 'cash crops'. Gujarat and the Konkan on the west coast of India traded extensively with the Persian Gulf and the Abbasid Empire (c.750–1258) with its capital at Baghdad. Abbasid silver flowed into west Indian ports to buy pepper, pearls, textiles and gemstones.[18] But by the tenth century, the increasing traffic with China through South East Asia favoured the Coromandel coast along the Bay of Bengal, and the rise there of the Chola (or Cola) Empire. It seems likely that the Cholas invaded Sri Lanka in 993, and attacked Srivijaya in 1025 to expand their commercial network and to control, if they could, all the trade routes between India and the Middle East and between India and China.[19]

Far away to the west, in Latin Christendom, a similar pattern could be seen: rising population, the extension of cultivated land, the growth of towns and trade, and the steady colonization of northern and eastern Europe (the reverse of the southward movement to be seen in China). Here, too, a key part of the explanation may lie in the more benign climate that ruled from the tenth to the late thirteenth centuries, bringing warmer weather and a longer growing season.[20] As the lords of the land grew richer, they spent more freely on the products of artisan labour in the towns and the luxuries, delicacies and prestige goods supplied by long-distance trade.[21] Europe, like China, enjoyed a 'medieval economic revolution'. The increasing urban population demanded grain and wine, stimulating a grain trade from the Baltic and Sicily, and a wine trade from Gascony, Andalusia, the Greek islands and elsewhere – and the shipping to transport them. By the thirteenth century a commercial boom was in full swing, lubricated by the influx of silver from Germany, Bohemia and Sardinia.[22] The rise of 'court cities', made possible by the growth of centralized monetary revenues (peripatetic courts that depleted their revenues in the course of their travels were no longer necessary), added a further twist to the rise in consumption. By the twelfth and thirteenth centuries, cloth manufacture was firmly established in Flanders and Tuscany, drawing its wool from England and Spain as well as more locally. For spices, pepper, silks, fine cottons, and other items from China and India, Europeans went to the markets of Syria and Egypt, or to the emporia on the Black Sea. The wealth of Venice, Amalfi and Genoa was built on this trade.

This far-reaching web of commercial exchange was loosely organized into a number of overlapping circuits of trade: between East and South East Asia; between South East Asia and India; across northern Eurasia between the Black Sea and China (the 'Silk Road'); linking India, Egypt, Persia and the Fertile Crescent; between the northern, eastern and southern coasts of the Mediterranean; and, at the far end of the world, the north European trades that stretched from the British Isles to the Baltic and from Norway to France with their forward connections to the Mediterranean and Near East.[23] Of these, the most important, perhaps as late as the 1400s, were those that were centred on the Islamic lands of the Near and Middle East: in the Umayyad Caliphate and (after AD 750) its successor the Abbasid Empire with its eastern frontier in what is now Afghanistan; and Fatimid (969–1171), Ayyubid (1171–1250) and Mamluk (1250–1517) Egypt. This was no accident. From the eighth century onwards the Islamic Middle East experienced a 'golden age' of high wages and living standards (perhaps not to be exceeded before 1800), technical innovation, especially in irrigation, the introduction of new food and industrial crops, and new commercial practices in credit transfer and shipping contracts – a productivity leap that may have been triggered by rising real wages in the wake of the 'Justinian plague' of AD 541–2.[24] It was here that the city-based civilization of Antiquity – largely demolished in northern and western Europe – continued to flourish. Cities were the strongholds of the new Caliphal Empire with its capital at Damascus. The ruling elites continued to live in cities and (more importantly) to spend there. They could do so because the Arabs inherited the tax system of the Byzantine Empire, drawing the surplus from country to town – perhaps the crucial condition for preserving a monetized economy and the commercial apparatus that depended upon it. The trade routes through the Persian Gulf and the Red Sea that linked the

Mediterranean and the Indian Ocean survived and thrived. In Egypt, whose agrarian economy, based on the Nile, was uniquely robust, a centralized government and revenue system had especially deep roots: indeed Egypt was, and long remained, the keystone of the Near Eastern economy. The Arab conquest of Persia enhanced the importance of the Persian Gulf, and Basra (founded in AD 638) became the great Abbasid emporium serving their capital at Baghdad, an enormous city with a population of more than one million. By the early eighth century, the lightning advance of Arab imperialism had created a wide 'Islamicate' sphere – with a shared Islamic religion and culture – that extended from Spain to Afghanistan. Across this vast realm, Muslim traders, scholars and those in search of military or bureaucratic employment could move with comparative freedom. Its slave trade sucked in labour from sub-Saharan Africa and Slavic northern Europe. Gold was drawn up from the African interior to the Mediterranean coast and thence to Egypt, enlarging the stock of precious metals for manufacturing money. By the 900s, the East African coast, too, was becoming Islamized, and its Muslim port of Kilwa was supplying ivory, amber, slaves and gold to the markets of the north. Arab seafarers and merchants colonized the west coast of India, and Arabs and Persians made their way to Canton. Jewish bankers and merchants, tolerated under Islam as a 'people of the book', played a key role in the all-important trade with India, first in Baghdad then in Cairo, and some made their way to settle in the ports of India's Malabar coast.[25]

Of course, we should not exaggerate the smoothness and stability of this commercial regime. It was subject to shocks and upheavals. The occupation of Baghdad by Seljuk Turks in 1055 disrupted the Persian Gulf trade with India, wrecking Basra. Much of this trade now moved to Egypt. From the 1060s, the Frankish advance into the Mediterranean culminated in the First Crusade of 1099 and the invasion of Palestine. The advance of the Mongols, invading Persia in 1216 and sealing the fate of Baghdad and the Abbasids in 1258, inflicted further damage on the cities and trade of the Islamic heartland, and strengthened its pastoral and nomadic elements against urban life and the 'sown'. Soon after 1300, if not earlier in some places, a general recession set in across this 'semi-global' Eurasian economy. Its causes are disputed. It might have been sparked by a 'Malthusian' crisis as a growing population pressed up against the means of subsistence and diminishing returns afflicted the agrarian economy. The 'medieval warm period' in Europe gave way to the 'Little Ice Age', shortening the growing season and reversing the gains of previous centuries – just as a 'Big Chill' had wiped out the cotton economy and its urban florescence in eleventh-century Persia.[26] Colder conditions affecting Central Asia may have lain behind the shift of plague-carrying fleas from wild rodents to more 'domestic' rats, whose journey westward along the 'Silk Road' (as non-paying passengers on mercantile caravans) reached Europe and the Middle East by the late 1340s.[27] Bubonic plague – the 'Black Death' – whose first violent onslaught was followed by repeated visitations, inflicted drastic population decline, perhaps by as much as 50 per cent, while sparing animals and other forms of wealth. Its effects may have been felt most deeply in Egypt, where agricultural production was peculiarly dependent on a large labour force.[28] Elsewhere the pandemic may have served to raise wages and encourage labour-saving innovation. But it was more than a century before populations in Europe and the Middle East began to recover. India seems to have been relatively little affected.[29]

In China meanwhile, the Mongol conquest in the thirteenth century caused widespread devastation, especially in the north, triggering a savage population fall from 120 million people to between 65 and 85 million.[30] In the mid-fourteenth century, the overthrow of the Mongols (to be replaced by the Ming) inflicted further calamities: agriculture collapsed as rural communities fled violent disorder or were cut down by famine.[31] Unusually cold weather may also have been a factor.[32] The urgent priority of the first Ming emperor was to restore rural order and limit mobility. Overseas travel and trade were closely restricted.[33]

By the 1450s, as Eurasia began to recover, its economic configuration was beginning to change. One of the most striking features was the growing prosperity and commercial integration of north-west Europe. A vital corridor of exchange now extended from southern England through the Low Countries, southern Germany and the Rhône Valley into the dense urban network of northern Italy with its two great ports at Venice and Genoa. The Islamic Middle East, once the source of high-value exports to Europe, was now more likely to buy Europe's cloth than sell its own, to welcome European merchants and shipping rather than send forth its own. But the region, and Egypt especially, remained the key entrepôt for the exchange of goods between Europe and Asia, overland or by sea. Its merchants and sailors traversed the Red Sea, the Persian Gulf and the Arabian Sea to bring the delicate fabrics and spices – pepper above all – that Europeans craved.

At the other end of Eurasia, Ming China had made its remarkable experiment with a seaborne imperialism in the voyages of Zheng He. Seven naval expeditions between 1402 and 1433 extended China's commercial and military power from the *Nanyang* into the *Xiyang* ('Western Ocean'), as far as Calicut, Hormuz, Aden and the East African coast, exacting tribute and trade and demanding the fealty of local rulers. One of these voyages brought a giraffe back to China. After 1422, this great maritime drive seemed to peter out, although Zheng He made one final voyage in 1431–3 as far as Hormuz, Mecca and Mogadishu, dying on the return trip.[34] Cost was the most likely reason for this loss of interest: some 217 large ships had been built or ordered at the shipyards of Nanjing. The Ming were also in the throes of their move to Beijing (the 'northern capital'), another hugely expensive enterprise. This was not the end of Ming China's overseas activity, but it signalled a shift of priorities away from the *Nanyang* and *Xiyang* towards the secular struggle to defend the Middle Kingdom against invasion from Inner Asia. Indeed, the shift to Beijing acknowledged the brutal reality that dynastic survival required the Emperor's presence at China's northern gateway.

China's manufactures remained in demand but in many ways it was India that was now at the centre of the Eurasian economy, forming the pivot of long-distance trade. India's great advantage lay in its abundant supplies of raw cotton. By the fifteenth century, Indian cotton goods were becoming the most widely traded goods across the Old World. What lay behind this was the remarkable sophistication of Indian artisans in the weaving and finish of cotton fabrics, through printing and painting and the application of dyestuffs to produce a range of appealing patterns and colours. Cotton weaving was carried on in many different parts of India – in Bengal, the Coromandel, the Malabar coast and Gujarat. It catered for a variety of different markets, favouring different kinds of fabric, finish and colour. Specialization rather than concentration was its hallmark.[35] Commercially, Indian producers benefited from the long-established connections between India and its markets and customers to the West and East, and from the ubiquity of Indian merchants as far west as Aden, as far east as Malacca. India was becoming the workshop of the world, a position it held from the fifteenth century until the mid-eighteenth century.

On the eve of the voyages of Columbus (in 1492) and Vasco da Gama (1497–8), a distinctive pattern of globalization had emerged across Afro-Eurasia. India and cotton may have been its driving force. But this was also a segmented world of distinct – if linked – trading spheres. Merchants could rarely despatch their goods from one end of Eurasia to the other, even if that was where their market lay. Distance and uncertainty were too great and time was the enemy of their limited credit. Instead they might send (or often accompany) their goods to one gateway port – Alexandria, Aden, Calicut or Malacca – where they would be sold and sent on their way to the next place of exchange. Even then it might take a whole season to reach Malacca from Gujarat, and the merchant had to wait for the winter monsoon to make the return trip. Seasonal winds (the monsoon above all) and currents would govern the pace, and sometimes the direction, of commercial activity. In most ports, indeed, there were frenzied trading seasons alternating with periods of somnolence. Across Eurasia, a wide variety of technologies had evolved: in navigation and weaponry; in the production of textiles, ceramics and metalware; in the use of water and wind power for milling, pumping, grinding and crushing; in building huge structures in wood and stone; and in the harnessing of animal power to supplement human muscle. This was complex technology that mainly depended upon wind, wood and water, but no single technology was dominant, in the way that steam became in the nineteenth century. Specialization between many different locations rather than centralization in one or two was the rule in most kinds of manufacture, especially cottons. India's cotton goods may have found many markets, but they did not replace or supplant local textile production so much as supplement or combine with it – quite unlike the machine-made cottons of the nineteenth century that swept all before them. Thus a global division of labour existed to a certain extent. Indeed, India and China, not

Europe, were still the suppliers of high-value consumer goods. The flows of money (in gold or silver) passed from West to East as payments (not investment) and not from East to West.

This was also a world in which quite different forms of political economy coexisted. In China, the imperial regime eschewed public debt and exacted low taxes but undertook extensive responsibility for the management of waterways and flood control, promoting agrarian colonization and providing public granaries. In the rice economies of Monsoon Asia, the sheer productivity of rice agriculture, and the surplus it earned, relieved their rulers from dependence on debts and financiers – and thus from the kinds of capitalism that arose elsewhere.[36] In the vast landscapes of 'Saharasia', from Morocco to southern India, where desert and steppe intersected the zones of settled agriculture, 'post-nomadic' regimes based on horse-borne mobility (and its military dividend) ruled (often peripatetically) over agrarian subjects, who were taxed and conscripted to meet the needs of their wars. Far to the west in Europe, also the scene of dynastic wars of expansion, princes and city states had already come to depend upon public debts and loans, and the bankers and financiers who kept them afloat in exchange for tax-farms, monopolies or mineral concessions, like the silver-mine 'farm' in the Tyrol that the Fuggers received from the Habsburgs.[37]

It was also a mobile world in which slave labour was dragged from the Slav lands and Africa towards the Middle East. But, in general, intra- rather than inter-continental migration was the rule: Han colonization of South and South-West China; Arab colonization in North Africa and (on a limited scale) as far east as Central Asia; regional migrations (impossible as yet to quantify) in sub-Saharan Africa; the settlement of Turkic peoples in Anatolia and northern Iran; the eastward advance of German-speaking settlers in Europe. The great Mongol invasions may have been led by a warrior elite but seem to have relied upon armies of local (often Muslim) allies.[38] But Mongols, and other 'world-conquerors' like Tamerlane, habitually conscripted and relocated skilled specialists and artisans, taking them hundreds if not thousands of miles from their homes.[39] The capture and destruction of cities (Baghdad was one of many examples) led to the dispersal or enslavement of those who survived. The Turkic invasions in northern India, spearheaded by the sultanate of Delhi, set off a wave of secondary migrations into southern India.[40] The vast extent of the Islamic world from Morocco to Java, with its tradition of pilgrimage and the extraordinary range of Muslim mercantile activity (as far east as coastal China), offered innumerable frontiers of opportunity to Islamic travellers and scholars. The best known of these, Ibn Battuta (1304–69), wandered for twenty-five years between Tangier and Beijing, relying upon his prestige as a *qadi* or jurist to provide support or employment on the way.[41] India especially attracted Muslim soldiers and literati from the Arab lands, Central Asia and Persia, seeking their fortune in the conquest-states of the subcontinent: India was the medieval 'America' of the Islamic world. Above all, the great corridor of the Arid Zone, with its dromedaries, horses and oxen – and the grasslands to feed them – promised (relatively) easy overland access across a vast part of Eurasia.[42]

In such a fluid world there was bound to be much cultural traffic. Mongol prestige had encouraged the widespread adoption of the regalia and pretensions of the Mongol courts and khans. (After 1260 the Mongol Empire was divided between Yuan China, the Ilkhanate centred on Iran and Iraq, and the Jochid – often called the 'Golden Horde' – and Chagatai khanates in Central Asia.) Mongol-style robes remained the apparel of royalty.[43] The Mongol imperium had facilitated overland contact with China, whose porcelain was envied, desired and copied all across Asia, just as its silks were the byword for sophistication and wealth. Chinese techniques in the visual arts – especially the production of ornate manuscripts – were also widely borrowed.[44] The expansion of Islam diffused Arab and Persian cosmologies, scripts and literatures across a vast swathe of Eurasia from Spain to China. Ideas about agronomy, medicine, astrology or the qualities of certain foods and drugs travelled from one end of the 'known world' to the other. On the other hand, there were certain obvious limits to such cultural exchange and diffusion, even among those wealthy enough to have access to artefacts, knowledge and consumer goods from distant regions. The most important of these were imposed by the barriers of language, script and religion – for even Islam fell short of universal appeal. With the growth of vernacular languages and literatures, notably in Europe and South Asia (probably stimulated by the pressure of Islamized culture),[45] further defences were erected against cultural diffusion. The role of intermediaries, translators and brokers became more and more vital in diplomacy, business and scholarship. Diasporic communities – like Jews and Armenians – whose networks and connections straddled cultural frontiers and whose 'outsider' status was recognized by both sides – specialized in these roles and profited from them, often at the cost of mutual mistrust and victimization. And just as in later times, many cultural imports were modified and 'domesticated' for local consumption, and their foreignness all but obliterated.

In reality, of course, the shape of Old World globalization was subject to the demands and constraints of geopolitical forces: the distribution of political power across Afro-Eurasia. By the 1450s, the age of Eurasia's 'world-conquerors', based on the military power of the steppe, had passed. Tamerlane had died in 1405, and his short-lived empire broke up. Ming expansion had been checked, on land and sea: the Vietnamese had thrown off Chinese rule in 1426 and absorbed Champa (today's southern Vietnam) in 1471. The rest of mainland South East Asia was divided between half a dozen or more ruling powers. After 1400, Malacca dominated the petty port states of Sumatra and the Malay peninsula.[46] In the Indian subcontinent, where Tamerlane had savaged the Delhi sultanate, its most powerful state, dominion was shared between numerous regional polities, Hindu and Muslim. Further west, the Ilkhanate (Iran and Iraq) had broken up into several successor regimes, while the Mamluk Empire, uniting Egypt and Syria, made Cairo the true capital, political and cultural, of the Islamic Near East. Ottoman expansion, symbolized in the capture of Constantinople in 1453, seemed at this stage to be directed towards the Crimea in the north (where Ottoman rule was imposed in 1478) and the Balkans in the west. There it encountered the sea empire of Venice, built to protect its Levantine trade routes: Negroponte in 1209; Crete in 1211; Corfu (to guard the entrance to the Adriatic) in 1386; Cyprus in 1489; and a scattering of key points in the Greek archipelago. Venice contested the sea lanes to the east with Genoa, which held the island of Chios, a great entrepôt, from 1346 to 1566, and a commercial depot at Kaffa in the Crimea, where the Genoese bought slaves from the Caucasus for export to Italy. To the west, the Genoese competed with the Catalan kingdom of Aragon, united with Majorca since 1343, and a major sea power in the western Mediterranean.[47] In northern Europe the gradual consolidation of dynastic states in England and France was a crucial development. In eastern Europe the Jagiellons had united the vast realm of Poland-Lithuania, stretching from the Baltic to the Black Sea, in the late fourteenth century. The Habsburgs were on the march with their empire-by-marriage, adding Burgundy and the Low Countries in 1477 (and most of Spain by 1516) to their central European possessions. But in the later Middle Ages there had been no dominant power in Europe. Along the Baltic and North Sea coasts, in southern Germany and northern Italy, city states had largely preserved their autonomy or, like the Hanseatic League, forged commercial empires of their own.

Across the whole breadth of Eurasia, and along the north and east coasts of Africa, fragmentation and competition, not the consolidation of great states, was now the rule. The result was a 'mixed economy' of empires (that of the Ming was much the most powerful), dynastic states (frequently wracked by internal struggle), city states and 'harbour principalities' (like Malacca or Calicut). Just as important was the free-for-all at sea. Here the retreat of the Ming, renouncing the maritime primacy that Zheng He's voyages had promised, was of enormous significance. No other ruler had the power to control the South China Sea, then (as now) one of the great marine highways of the world. None of its littoral states could hope to exert naval command over the vast expanse of the Bay of Bengal, the eastern arm of the Indian Ocean.[48] The same was still truer of its western arm, the Arabian Sea, with its Arabian, Persian, African and Indian coastlines. Europe's 'narrow seas' were much more readily contested. The Mediterranean, English Channel, North Sea and Baltic saw fierce competition both commercial and strategic. But even here, the means to impose a command of the sea were lacking. None of the sea powers – not even Venice – was strong enough to drive its rivals into port or strangle them by blockade.[49] But after 1500, some, or all, of this was to change.

SLOW BOAT FROM CHINA

In these relatively benign conditions a necklace of port cities helped to bind the Old World together, from the Sea of Japan to Europe's Atlantic outposts in Iceland and the Azores. Although Nanjing on the Yangzi had been the base for Zheng He's voyages, for most seaborne merchants from the Middle East, Quanzhou in South East China (Marco Polo's 'Zaitun') was the furthest destination. 'The port of Zaitun is one of the biggest in the world, nay . . . it is the biggest of all ports,' wrote Ibn Battuta, who was there in the mid-fourteenth century.[50] For others Canton was the place to buy Chinese porcelain and silk in exchange for cargoes from Egypt, India and South East Asia. Here since the Tang era (AD 618–907) or before could be found merchants from all over the Indian Ocean, usually living in their separate quarters within the city. Trade was closely regulated by the imperial authorities, but foreigners were governed by their own laws and headmen.[51] Although direct voyages between China and Indian Ocean ports were not unknown, it became increasingly common for the traffic to and from China to break its journey in the ports of South East Asia, so that the South China Sea formed a distinct maritime zone. For Chinese merchants and settlers, this 'Asian Mediterranean' had long been a sphere of commercial expansion and influence. The South China Sea, with its own wind patterns, channels, shoals and reefs, demanded special expertise from captains and crews. Indeed, several port towns had evolved in South East Asia to serve both the local and the transit trades, including those of Srivijaya, long the dominant power in the archipelago. By the late fifteenth century, however, the most important were Ayutthaya, near modern Bangkok, and Malacca, on modern Malaysia's west coast.

Ayutthaya had been founded in 1351, probably by Chinese. It became a favoured trading partner of the Ming, exchanging local 'exotics' for China's ceramics and silks. It attracted Mons, Tais and Khmers from the surrounding interior, as well as Arab, Persian, Chinese and Indian merchants. It sent fish, rice, copper, lead, tin, gold, ivory and rubies to Malacca and received opium, cloves, textiles, carpets, cowries, camphor and slaves in return. The need to control its supplies from the hinterland pushed Ayutthaya towards an inland empire in the Chao Phraya Valley, while competition with Malacca drew it westward towards the Indian Ocean, absorbing Tenasserim (in modern Burma) by the 1460s.[52] The Dutch who visited the city in the early 1600s reported Ayutthaya 'as great a city as London' (containing perhaps 200,000 people) with stone walls, wide straight streets, and a palace complex with gilded buildings and towers.[53] But as the centre of long-distance trade, Ayutthaya could not match Malacca. Malacca was founded around 1400 by a rebellious prince from Srivijaya in southern Sumatra. It owed its fortune to the winds: it was where 'two monsoons met'. Junks sailing from China late in the year on the north-east (winter) monsoon could reach the Straits of Malacca and then return home in the following summer on the south-west (summer) monsoon that blew from May. Zheng He's fleet made the voyage from Malacca to China in less than two months in 1433.[54] Four hundred years later a fast sailing ship might do the same trip in under a month, although six weeks was more common.[55] But to sail on from Malacca to the west coast of India would mean a tedious delay for the next winter monsoon, as well as waiting for the next summer monsoon to return, stretching the round trip from China to India to two years. It made more sense for goods to change hands from one set of merchants to another. Hence Malacca became the natural entrepôt where cargoes from the Indian Ocean would be trans-shipped for the onward journey through the South China Sea, and where Chinese goods would be exchanged for Indian and Middle Eastern ones.

Malacca lived entirely by trade, above all the commerce in pepper, for which both China and Europe had an insatiable demand. It lay on two banks of a river, hemmed in by the dense forest which came down to the sea: it was said that tigers roamed its streets at night. But by the late fifteenth century it had a population of some 120,000. Its ruler, the Sultan, extracted a large customs revenue and also engaged in trade on his own account. Tamils from Coromandel, Gujaratis, Javanese and Chinese were the main merchant communities: each lived in its own *kampong* or quarter and was governed by its own *shahbandar* (or port king). Muslim Gujaratis, who commanded the trade from Egypt and the Persian Gulf, were the most powerful group: it was their presence that had made Malacca a centre of

Islamic influence in South East Asia.[56] If it had not been for its swampy and unhealthy location, remarked a Portuguese visitor in the following century, it might have been a much bigger city than it was.[57] From Malacca, a merchant might sail north to Bengal or west to the Coromandel. But if bound to Egypt or the Persian Gulf, his next port of call would likely be Calicut on the Malabar coast.

Unlike Malacca, Calicut drew only modest advantage from its coastal site. Like other ports on the west coast of India, it could be easily reached by ships from the Red Sea and Persian Gulf on the South-West Monsoon, perhaps in as little as ten to twelve days from Muscat.[58] But since the Malabar coast was extremely hazardous from May until early September (when, in later periods, insurance policies forbade any call at its ports), it was best to arrive at the tail end of the monsoon. Calicut itself offered little shelter, and in bad weather ships scattered to take refuge in neighbouring rivers and creeks. Its rise to prosperity arose from the destruction of nearby Kollam (Quilon), and the decision of its Hindu ruler, the *Zamorin* or 'Lord of the Sea', to welcome Muslim merchants with open arms. By 1343, when Ibn Battuta visited, it was the main port on India's south-west coast and the great entrepôt for trade between China and the Middle East. Arab sailors and merchants, usually Hadhramis from southern Arabia, intermarried with locals to create a creole population of Muslim *Mappilas*. Since ritual purity precluded Hindu merchants from overseas travel, Calicut's trade was largely in the hands of Arabs, *Mappilas* and, later, Gujarati Muslims. The town itself hugged the riverbank and the shore. It had no walls. A mile inland, separated by coconut plantations, stood the ruler's palace. Beyond lay the estates of the Hindu notables, spread over the coastal plain that produced the pepper and ginger from which much of the city's wealth and fame derived.[59] It was to Calicut that Vasco da Gama made his epic voyage in 1497–8. Already, perhaps, it was in decline, with its harbour silting up, soon to be replaced by Cochin and its lagoon to the south.[60]

From Calicut, a merchant might have made his way home to Gujarat further north. But if his base or his market lay in the Middle East, his next port of call would be Hormuz, at the mouth of the Persian Gulf, or Aden, near the entrance to the Red Sea. Hormuz was a waterless island, an odd choice perhaps for a mercantile city. Its origins lay in the decision of the Arab ruler of nearby Quaysh Island, an older entrepôt, to move to Hormuz, which was bought for the purpose. The kingdom of Hormuz, as it became known, practised a vigorous brand of commercial imperialism. It conquered Bahrain (the source of its food and water) and extended its hegemony on both sides of the Gulf, and over the coast of Oman. Its rivals were stifled. The trade with the Iranian plateau and the head of the Gulf at Basra fell into its hands. The city itself had perhaps 50,000 people at the end of the fifteenth century (many fewer outside the trading season). Persians, Arabs, Baluchis and Gujaratis dominated its commerce: usually there were around 400 foreign merchants in the city trading in silks, pearls, jewels and spices. Twice a year merchants from Damascus and Aleppo came with overland caravans to Basra and sailed down the Gulf to Hormuz. There they could buy textiles, spices and rice from China, South East Asia and India. The Gulf region itself exported comparatively little: dates and some wheat, but especially horses – much sought after by rulers in India, where horses were difficult to breed. This was a challenging if profitable trade requiring considerable logistical skill. The balance was made with specie.[61] As at Malacca and Calicut, the custom house was a key institution, reflecting the close attention of the ruler to the revenues it earned.

Hormuz was the real hub of Persian Gulf trade and the maritime highway to the Levant and its ports. Zheng He had made Hormuz his destination in five of his seven voyages to the west. It was no accident that it was an early target when the Portuguese invaded the Indian Ocean in the early sixteenth century: they attacked the city in 1507 and imposed their control in 1515 – hoping to throttle the trade through the Levant in favour of their own seaborne traffic round the Cape of Good Hope. Hormuz had long had a rival in Aden, a rival too strong to subdue by the methods it had used against its competitors in the Gulf. Aden was a much older city and had been a major emporium since at least the ninth century AD. Like Malacca or Calicut, its location was crucial. It lay at the western edge of the monsoon route to and from India and enjoyed easy communication by sea along the East African coast.[62] But the sea route to Egypt via the Red Sea was a different matter entirely. The Red Sea was notorious for its reefs and shoals. Northerly winds prevailed, so that shipping coming south to Aden had to wait until April

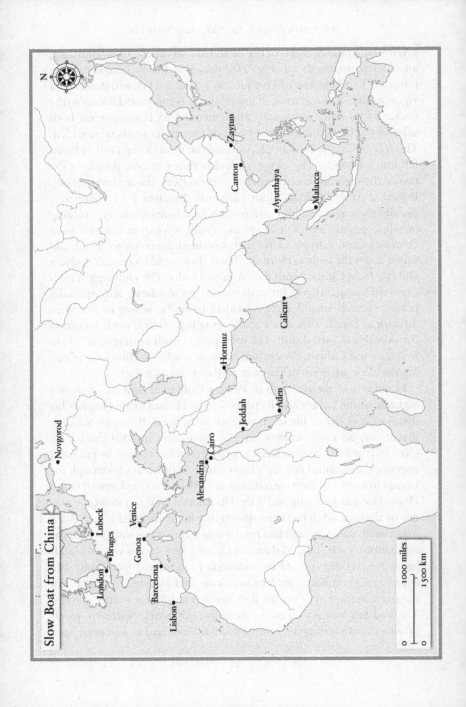

Slow Boat from China

Novgorod

London
Bruges
Lubeck

Venice
Genoa

Barcelona

Lisbon

Alexandria
Cairo

Jeddah

Aden

Hormuz

Calicut

Zaytun

Canton

Ayutthaya
Malacca

N

0   1000 miles

0   1500 km

to make the return voyage north, and often sailed only as far as Jeddah (the port for Mecca), from where goods were taken to Cairo by caravan overland. Thus cargoes arriving from India from October onwards on the winter monsoon would wait until the following spring to be shipped to Egyptian and Mediterranean markets; while return freight from Cairo would arrive in Aden at the end of July to catch the late summer monsoon to the west coast of India (when that coast had become safe).[63] Like Malacca, Aden was a child of the winds, the source of its wealth. It was, said one enthusiastic commentator, the 'anteroom of China, entrepôt of Yemen, treasury of the West, and mother lode of tradewares'.[64] It was the obvious place to exchange goods from the Mediterranean with those from India, avoiding a long and risky two-year round trip for the merchant. It had a safe harbour, though one prone to heavy winter seas – the off season for trade. Perhaps just as important, it was well defended. Its landward approach was via a narrow causeway: its shoreline was guarded by crenelated walls. 'The strongest city ... ever seen on level ground,' marvelled one visitor in 1503; 'extremely beautiful', proclaimed another.[65]

Unlike Hormuz or Malacca, Aden was not a free state, although its location may have given it considerable autonomy. The Rasulids of Yemen, in origin a Turkic clan, had ruled there, but in the late fourteenth century their influence had waned in favour of local clans and warlords. The traveller sailing up the Red Sea passed into the realm of the Mamluks, the slave-soldier caste who ruled Egypt and Syria and whose victory over the Mongols in 1261 had made them the most powerful and prestigious of the Islamic states. After 1400, however, the Mamluk Empire faced growing pressure from the north as the Ottomans pushed towards Syria, while its domestic economy had been dislocated by the huge fall in population that had followed the Black Death. The effect was to make the Mamluk sultans more determined than ever to exploit the spice trade (in pepper especially) that passed through Cairo and Alexandria on its way to Europe. Cairo was the Mamluk capital: they had made its great citadel, looming over the city, the centre of their power.[66] Cairo was also the hub of the spice trade. It was here that the caravans from Jeddah or Aqaba delivered their cargo of pepper, to be sold on and sent down the Nile (a voyage of seven days or so) for shipment from Alexandria.[67]

Alexandria was Egypt's principal port. Its eastern harbour (for Christian shipping; the western harbour was reserved for Muslim shipping) was the only one suitable for the larger cogs, or fat-sided sailing ships, in which Mediterranean trade was increasingly carried. By contrast, Rosetta and Damietta, at the mouths of the Nile, were very dangerous in summer when northerly winds met the Nile's flood waters.[68] Alexandria marked the northern boundary of the Indian Ocean world in whose commerce Muslims were dominant, and the southern limit of European mercantile influence. By the late 1400s, much of the walled city was decayed or in ruins, the result in part of the shrinking of its hinterland and the decline of its industries. But if the city decayed the port had flourished, and urban settlement shifted north of the walls to fringe the harbour.[69] For the Mamluks, Alexandria was a frontier city facing the infidel and the *dar al-harb* – the abode of war. After the devastating raid by the Lusignan king of Cyprus in 1365 (designed perhaps to benefit his own port city of Famagusta), the city was refortified and Cairo's control reinforced. But it was also the marketplace for both Christian and Muslim merchants. Venetian, Genoese and Catalan traders came to the city to buy eastern goods, spices above all. The Mamluk sultans welcomed their presence – indeed had come to depend more and more on their purchases to finance their state, not least its increasingly costly slave imports.[70] They made strenuous efforts to maintain the canal that linked Alexandria to the Nile and the trade from the south.[71] They allowed the Venetians, the Genoese and others to maintain consuls – to settle their private disputes and deal with the Mamluk officials – and to operate the *fondacos* that served as warehouses and accommodation for the visiting merchants. In fact, it was the Venetians who dominated the spice trade. But they had to deal with the Sultan's official merchants and to buy a set quantity of pepper at the Sultan's price. It was an arrangement that suited both sides, although not without periodic tension. The Venetians found it wise to keep an agent in Cairo to get the latest information on the traffic up the Red Sea and across the desert to the Mamluk capital.[72]

This was partly because the spice trade between Venice and Alexandria was closely regulated by the Venetian authorities. Galleys, not the slower cogs, were used to bring back the precious pepper. They were dispatched each year in early September to arrive in Alexandria four or five weeks later. There they landed their cargo of woollens, furs, wax and copper, supplemented by copious amounts of bullion, in small boats since the eastern harbour had no quays. An elaborate etiquette governed the movement of goods from the harbour to the Customs House nearby, and from there to the two Venetian *fondacos* behind it.[73] Venetian merchants enjoyed exceptional privileges in Egypt: they were exempt from the discriminatory rules applied to other Christians and could travel freely in the Mamluk dominions.[74] But Venice insisted that the *muda* – the annual purchase of pepper and spices – should be completed in twenty days, allowing the galleys to return home before Christmas and before the shipping season closed with the onset of winter. At the Customs House auctions and in their purchases from the Sultan's official merchant, the Venetians carried off each year some one and a half million pounds of pepper.[75]

On leaving Alexandria, the seaborne traveller entered a new maritime world that stretched from the Black Sea, through the Mediterranean and into the Atlantic, and through the North Sea and the Baltic as far as 'Great Novgorod', the fur-trade capital of Eurasia, with its tribute-empire extending deep into the Arctic. If the Mediterranean remained the 'hub', partly because of its intense connectivity (driven in part by the uncertainty of food supply),[76] and partly because of its close links with the monsoon world and its trade, Europe's maritime zones now formed a connected whole. After 1300, Mediterranean shipping, both galleys and cogs, routinely made its way north to England and the Low Countries, perhaps drawn initially by the demand for grain – a bulk commodity – in a period of uncertain harvests in northern Europe.[77] It was a maritime world very different from the vast expanse of the monsoon oceans. Its rhythms were less regular. The variety of sea conditions was much greater, demanding a wide range of navigational techniques. The indented shoreline of the European 'peninsula' favoured the proliferation of ports and port cities. So did the extreme fragmentation of territorial sovereignty. The ecological pressures that threatened the survival of ports in South Asia were felt less intensely. But Europe also benefited from a common, religion-based culture, much as Islam had become the common currency of most merchant life in Asia.

In the late fifteenth century, Venice was the greatest of Europe's port cities.[78] It dominated the eastern Mediterranean. It was the first European state to have a permanent navy. It was the largest market for Asian goods in Europe, for pepper and spices above all. Its commercial connections spanned the continent. Its rise and rise showed the extraordinary wealth and power that a port city could accumulate without the protection of empires or the backing of kings. From its obscure beginnings as a refuge of boatmen, it had depended on trade for every essential: most of all for its grain and the timber for fuel, shipbuilding and the wooden piles on which the city was built. It had crushed its nearby competitors by force and freed itself from early dependence on the Byzantine Empire to become a sovereign state ruled by its Doge and Senate. Its commercial fortune was made by its favoured location as the Mediterranean's most northerly gateway to central and northern Europe with easy access by sea to the consumers and products of the Levant, the Black Sea and (as we have seen) the Orient. Securing that fortune required more than mercantile *nous*. Venice was as famous for its system of government as for its commercial success. It was a rule-bound regime that favoured custom and contract, encouraged social solidarity and reflected a pragmatic materialism. It funded the constant war against silt to keep the port open; paid for the Arsenal that sustained its sea power; purchased the grain that fed the (potentially) troublesome poor; and steered the Machiavellian diplomacy by which Venice exploited the clash of great powers.[79]

In fact, the fusion of commerce and politics had made Venice much more than a city of traders. Venice in the fifteenth century had a huge commercial fleet of some 45 galleys and over 300 sailing ships of 100 tons or more. Its great galley fleet turned the Adriatic Sea into a Venetian lake, excluding its rivals and protecting its shipping. Galleys were costly to build (a burden assumed by the state) but fast and manoeuvrable in shallow coastal waters. Hired out to merchants, and organized in convoys, they drove down the costs of insurance and guarded the huge sums of bullion that the Levant trade demanded. Merchant galleys relied mainly on sail but their 'auxiliary engine' of oarsmen assured greater regularity and speed, and helped to defend valuable cargo against pirates or rivals. As the Byzantine Empire contracted, Venice extended its grip on the Aegean archipelago from Corfu to Cyprus. These were the way stations for its galleys in an age when sailors preferred to stay in sight of land and tie up for the night – a practice that feeding and watering a large crew of oarsmen made all the more necessary. There were also plantations that produced cotton, wine, sugar and raisins for the market in Venice. For Venice was an empire not just a port city, with outposts and colonies as distant as Tana, from where (on the Sea of Azov) its merchants dealt in the overland traffic from Central Asia and China – until the Ottoman capture of Constantinople closed the Black Sea to Christian shipping. Venice practised a form of what became known as 'mercantilism': shipping in the Adriatic and its colonial possessions had to sell their cargoes in the city – to the profit of its merchants and its public finances, since every transaction carried with it a tax. Indeed, finance was the secret of Venetian success. Venice's gold ducat was the dollar of the age. Its citizens were encouraged, and sometimes compelled, to lend to the state, with a dividend secured on its revenue streams – the so-called *Monte*.[80] At the Rialto – the city's commercial hub – could be found bankers and bills, for exchange and credit, and that precious commercial commodity, news. 'What news on the Rialto?' asks Shakespeare's Salanio in *The Merchant of Venice*. For a constant stream of traders and travellers passed through the city, including the pilgrims from all over Europe who embarked there for Palestine on the pilgrim galley to Jaffa; they brought information and rumour as well as hard news.

Powerful as it was, Venice was not without challengers. Ragusa (modern Dubrovnik) on the Dalmatian coast had evaded its grasp by the mid-fourteenth century, skilfully playing off its links with the Papacy against the rising power of the Turks and maintaining an extensive trade inland as well as by sea. But the real rival was Genoa. Like Venice, Genoa had crushed its nearest rival, in this case Pisa, by the late thirteenth century. Like Venice, Genoa depended on trade and profited from the traffic between northern Europe and the Levant, the Black Sea and beyond. Like Venice, it established colonies and trading posts, including Kaffa (modern Feodosia) in the Crimea and Chios in the Aegean. Corsica became its colony. And like Venice, it recruited much of its labour and talent from outside, from those drawn to the city by the promise of wealth. It maintained a large mercantile fleet, including the war galleys that had threatened Venice itself in 1379. Before 1300, Genoese shipping was already passing through the Straits of Gibraltar, reaching England and Flanders, and Genoa was a nursery of navigational skill and technical innovation.

Genoa was not simply a second, less powerful, less stable and less independent Venice, constantly wracked by political conflict, periodically falling under outside control.[81] Its commercial system was notably different, more individualistic and opportunistic than Venice's, and much less reliant on the support of the state.[82] But the real difference could be found in the precocious maturity of Genoese banking. The most remarkable feature was the rise of the Casa di San Giorgio, the bank into which all Genoa's tax revenues were paid, and which assumed control of Genoa's extensive colonial possessions in the Mediterranean and Black Sea while they lasted in Genoese hands. The Casa managed the state's public debt (until 1805) and also served as a deposit bank. It funded the vital improvements in Genoa's port and managed the *Portofranco* – Genoa's free port area.[83] This huge income stream, and the financial network it bred, laid the foundation for Genoa's pre-eminence as a prime source of credit. Across the western Mediterranean and in the colonization of Madeira and the Canaries, Genoese merchants and money were the indispensable catalyst of commercial expansion.

Genoa's great rival in the western Mediterranean had been the Catalan port city of Barcelona. Catalan merchants (as we have seen) were active in the Levant and also in North Africa – taking advantage of the favourable current which carried shipping southward past the Balearic Islands to the ports of the Maghreb.[84] Barcelona merchants lacked the wealth and political freedom of their Venetian and Genoese counterparts. Their commercial success was really dependent on the ruthless maritime imperialism of the Catalan kingdom of Aragon, with which Barcelona had been united since *c.*1150. Majorca (the centre of a prosperous Arab commerce) and the Balearics had been conquered by 1235, clearing the way for Barcelona's advance. In the following century Sicily, Sardinia and (briefly and unsuccessfully) Corsica were added to the Catalan dominions. After an inconclusive struggle with Genoa, the Aragonese Crown extended its reach into the eastern Mediterranean, briefly acquiring the Crusader dukedom of Athens. In 1442 it captured the city of Naples, rounding out its domination of southern Italy. By the mid-1400s, however, the effects of the Black Death in Catalonia and the loss of trade in the eastern Mediterranean with the triumph of Ottoman power combined with the insatiable ambitions of its royal house to impose an unbearable strain on Barcelona, which collapsed into civil war and commercial decline. Royal power could make – and break – a port city.

By contrast, Lisbon, on the Atlantic coast of Iberia, showed how royal privilege and patronage could be turned to solid commercial advantage. A seaborne traveller, beating through the Straits of Gibraltar against the heavy inflowing current from the Atlantic, entered the sphere of Lisbon's ambition. Until 1147 Lisbon had been an Islamic city, looking south to the Maghreb and Muslim Andalus. The Christian reconquest of the Algarve, and the beginnings of regular traffic through the Straits of Gibraltar, made the wide Tagus estuary a natural port of call for voyages from the Mediterranean to northern Europe. Portuguese kings, endowed with a meagre hinterland, made Lisbon their capital and gave it the monopoly of grain and other commodity imports. Foreign merchants and sailors (especially Genoese) clustered there, making it by the mid-fifteenth century a laboratory of ship design, cartography and navigational technique. Already in 1415 Lisbon had been the base for the Portuguese conquest of Ceuta, the Moroccan fortress overlooking the Straits of Gibraltar, perhaps partly inspired by hopes of diverting the flow of African gold. Much more productive (at least in the short term) had been the colonization of Madeira – 'Timber Island' – from the 1420s, a source of much needed timber, grain and, most profitably, sugar. The Portuguese would have liked to annex the Canaries, known to European sailors from the mid-fourteenth century but settled by Castile from c.1400. By the 1430s they had begun to colonize the Azores, some 800 miles to the west, and one of the mysterious groups of islands (like the mythical 'Brazil') that tantalized medieval cartographers. Flemish settlers arrived in the 1450s to grow wheat and sugar. In the 1460s, the Cape Verde islands were Lisbon's southern outpost: here Genoese merchants brought in slaves from the Black Sea to work its sugar plantations.[85] Already Portuguese sailors were hunting for the fabulous kingdom of Prester John, and prospecting for gold on the Guinea coast. By the 1480s they were building a fortress on the coast of modern Ghana. In less than a decade Bartolomeu Dias had rounded the Cape of Good Hope.

To most of the Venetian or Genoese merchants who passed through Lisbon this maritime empire held little interest. They were en route to the great mart of the north. Bruges in Flanders had attracted regular visits from Italian merchants from the thirteenth century. It had grown up as the centre of the great wool-turned-cloth trade in Flanders. A fortunate flood had opened a channel to the North Sea coast, soon improved by a canal. With its riverine links south (to France) and east (to the Rhine), Bruges soon attracted merchants from all over Europe. Since Italian merchants and shipping went no further north, it became the place to exchange their silk, alum, dyes, wine, fruit and spices for goods from the Baltic: furs, fish, wax, honey and grain. The volume of business required credit and the scale of long-distance trade needed bills of exchange, as well as insurance: so Bruges became the 'financial capital' of northern Europe – Italian banking houses could be found there. It was the site of northern Europe's first *bourse* – which took its name from the square outside the tavern of the innkeeper Beurs – though the first purpose-built *bourse* appeared later, in Antwerp.[86]

Like most prosperous port cities, Bruges owed its importance to something much more than commercial convenience. It gained protection and privilege from its sovereign, the Count of Flanders, who upheld its 'staple' – the rule that all goods coming up its canal must be offered for sale in the city – and strangled competitors. Foreign merchants – perhaps as many as 400 in the mid-1400s – controlled Bruges's long-distance trade. They enjoyed wide freedom – in Venice foreign merchants had to live in the compound of their 'nation' – but were required to deal through local 'hostellers' who provided accommodation, brokerage and credit. The locals did not have it all their own way. The Count's interests lay in promoting the largest volume of trade, not in feather-bedding the patricians of Bruges. So he intervened to force equal treatment for foreign merchants in the courts and restrict the fees that hostellers could charge. Yet, favoured as it was, Bruges was not invulnerable. Its route to the sea began to silt up. Nearby Antwerp's began to improve as the channels in the Scheldt shifted their course, favouring the western over the eastern channel and easing the passage to its quays. Antwerp lay across the main north–south route in the Low Countries. It enjoyed close links with Cologne – the great entrepôt on the Rhine, connecting the south German cities with the trade of the Baltic – and drew many German merchants to its markets.[87] Foreign merchants began to relocate there from Bruges. But the crucial blow was political. When the Low Countries passed to the Habsburgs, they favoured loyal Brabant over disloyal Flanders. In 1484 Maximilian as regent ordered all foreign merchants to leave Bruges for Antwerp – and most followed his orders. In the century that followed, Antwerp became 'the undisputed commercial metropolis of the Western World'[88] – until it too fell victim to political catastrophe.

Only the most curious of Mediterranean merchants would have pressed on from Bruges. Indeed, there was little profit in doing so. He would not have lingered in Amsterdam, still a small player in seaborne trade, but would have gone first to Hamburg, famous already for its vast production of beer, and then overland to Lübeck on the Trave. He would have found himself now in the commercial realm of the Hanse, the great merchant league that was centred on Lübeck. Lübeck had a long prehistory as a 'trading beach'. It lay at the Baltic end of the portage across the isthmus of Holstein, long preferred by merchants to the dangerous sea route round the Skaw at the tip of Jutland. It was founded as a 'German' city in 1143, perhaps as part of the medieval colonization of the north and east. Lübeck's early fortune was made from salted herring: it lay between the great herring fishery off the south-west coast of Sweden and the saltworks at Lüneburg, forty miles to the south (herring had to be salted or smoked within a day or so to prevent decomposition).[89] But it rose on the tide of the long-distance trade between the Baltic and the North Sea: Lübeck was the pivot of a commercial axis that stretched from London and Bruges in the west to Reval (modern Tallinn) and Novgorod in the east. Lübeck's merchants might have dreamed of becoming the Venice of the North. In reality, their scope was much more restricted. They were hemmed in to the north by the powerful kingdom of Denmark (for much of the thirteenth century Lübeck was part of the Danish Empire). The Baltic trade in furs, wax, fish and grain could not sustain the grandeur that was Venice: the value of Venice's trade with Egypt and Syria alone in the 1490s was at least double Lübeck's total, and Baltic trade was perhaps a tenth or less of Mediterranean trade.[90] Nor could Lübeck exert domination over the trading cities nearby: Danzig (then also a German city), with its wide Polish hinterland, soon matched it in wealth; so did Hamburg, once Lübeck's 'outer harbour' on the North Sea.[91] Instead Lübeck became the recognized head (from 1418) of the Hanseatic League of German merchant cities.

The League may have begun as a means of resolving commercial disputes. Its membership grew to include some seventy towns, with perhaps one hundred or more lesser confederates. It reached as far as Cologne, the Rhineland metropolis. Its growth reflected in part the weakness of monarchical power in medieval northern Germany. But it was also a form of collective defence for the German ports on the Baltic against the threat of Danish expansion. The League's commercial importance lay in securing trading privileges for all the citizens of the member cities: exemption from (or reduction of) duties and dues; the right to re-export unsold goods; prompt restitution in the case of theft; safeguarding his property if a merchant died abroad.[92] Its commercial diplomacy was backed by the threat of a boycott, and by piracy against rival shipping. In English port towns like Boston in Lincolnshire or King's Lynn in Norfolk, the League occupied premises on the best trading sites.[93] It also maintained four great *Kontore* – commercial agencies where German merchants could live and trade, and where they enjoyed a form of diplomatic immunity from local jurisdiction: in Bruges and London (to which we come shortly) as well as in Bergen, the centre of the League's profitable trade in protein-rich stockfish (sun-dried cod from the Lofoten Islands), and Novgorod – the end of the line. In Bergen the *Kontor* served as a German colony, with artisans and craftsmen as well as merchants living in or around its premises (still to be seen) on the 'German quay'. In Novgorod the *Kontor* housed the German merchants and exercised close control over the lucrative fur trade.

Hanseatic merchants long dominated trade between the Baltic and North Sea, but by the later fifteenth century Lübeck and the League were in relative decline. Dutch merchants and shipping moved into the Baltic. Monarchical power was on the rise: in 1426 the Danish king began the infamous Sound tolls on shipping passing through the Kattegat between Denmark and Sweden.[94] The Tsar of Muscovy annexed Novgorod in 1478 and the *Kontor* collapsed soon after. The Hanse faced more competition from the prosperous south German cities and powerful bankers like the Fuggers. The Hanse response was defensive: excluding foreign merchants from trade in Lübeck and Danzig, and resisting the use of credit.[95] Neither may have helped much. Lübeck and Danzig stagnated.[96] The great exception was Hamburg, a reflection perhaps of a deeper force at work – the rising importance of Atlantic trade by 1500, soon to carry all before it.

Our seaborne traveller might have turned aside after Bruges and sailed west not east, up the Thames to London. London was a Roman foundation, abandoned at the end of Roman rule in Britain. It revived as a beach market half a mile upriver as Saxon 'Lundenwic', on the site of today's Covent Garden. The Viking invasions had driven it back to the shelter of the Roman walls by *c.*900.[97] By 1000 it had a bridge across the Thames, making London the key to communications in south-eastern England. Perhaps for that reason it replaced Winchester as the English capital. The Normans built the White Tower (part of what became the Tower of London) to protect the city and assert their control over it. Its trade and revenue became a key royal asset.

London's importance derived from its command of an extensive riverine hinterland that included much of southern and eastern England; its role as the political and administrative capital, attracting tax revenue, the court and the high-spending elite; its protected but accessible site on the tidal Thames; and, above all, its location opposite Flanders, the commercial and industrial heartland of medieval northern Europe. On the eve of the Black Death in 1348, London had a population of some 80,000, making it one of Europe's largest cities. A century later, that had fallen quite sharply, but by the early sixteenth century London was ten times as wealthy (by the yardstick of tax assessment) as its nearest English rival, Norwich.[98] London's trade was heavily concentrated on Flanders, initially through the export of wool. By the fifteenth century the export of cloth, manufactured across southern Britain, had become its great staple. The striking expansion of English trade attracted many foreign merchants, mainly Italians (from Florence and Genoa) and Germans (from the Hanse ports). By late medieval times London had come a long way from its trading-beach origins. Now the river was lined with specialized quays trading in wine, salt, grain, fish, spices, timber and firewood. The bank had been filled up with merchants' premises, so that access to the river was confined to narrow alleys and lanes.[99] London merchants and shipping, pushing into the Baltic and the Mediterranean, increasingly challenged the dominance of Italian and Hanse merchants.

Like other port cities, London profited from the mingling of commercial success and political fortune. For the English Crown, the customs revenue it drew from London and the loans it could raise there (often from foreign merchants and bankers like the Florentine Bardi and Peruzzi) made the city an enormously valuable asset. By the same token its discontent was also exceptionally dangerous, especially when labour unrest or anger at price rises coincided with wider political upheaval in England. London was granted a degree of self-government by the Crown and paid for it in taxation, a stream of 'gifts', and payments for the grant of monopolies and commercial privileges.[100] Among the most valuable of these was the right granted to 'freemen' (the small minority with full citizenship) to trade throughout England exempt from the tolls and charges usually imposed on outsider merchants. It was a privilege that allowed London merchants to penetrate – and then suffocate competition from – successful outports like Southampton.[101] London merchants profited from the military contracts occasioned by royal ambitions in Europe, and from their effective monopoly over the export of cloth. But the Crown also exerted its power to protect foreign merchants from the xenophobic violence (and mercantile jealousy) that broke out periodically in London and elsewhere: foreign merchants and the financial assets they commanded were far too valuable to be driven away. In the late fifteenth century there were some 3,000 'aliens' in London, both merchants and craftsmen – for London was also a major manufacturing centre with many wealthy consumers.[102] Time and technology were also its allies. As sailing ships became more manoeuvrable, the difficulty of navigating from the Channel around the North Foreland and up the Thames estuary became much more manageable (to Southampton's great loss), and the rising importance of Atlantic trade and fisheries enhanced London's location at the crossroads of north–south and east–west trade in Europe.

PORTS AND PATTERNS

In the port cities of pre-Columbian Eurasia we can see many of the features (as well as some of the challenges) that were to shape the history of later port cities. Politically, they occupied an ambiguous position. Some, like Malacca, Hormuz, Venice, Lübeck and Hamburg, enjoyed sovereignty or its equivalent. In the case of Malacca, this might have been helped by distance from a major power; Hormuz, Venice and the Hanse cities used naval power to assert their claims. But perhaps the majority were subject to inland rulers, near and far. The attitude of these rulers varied considerably. For the Zamorin of Calicut, or the Portuguese king, 'their' port was a critical asset, the principal source of their wealth and power. They welcomed foreign merchants and (where they could) enhanced the prospects of the port's maritime trade. The Counts of Flanders (sovereigns of Bruges), the English Crown and the Mamluk sultans in Cairo were also keenly aware of what their port cities could offer, and mixed privilege with rules that constrained the protectionist instincts of the local merchant elite. By the fifteenth century, half the income of the English Crown came from trade. However, where inland rulers were distant, or preoccupied with overland routes and vulnerable frontiers, indifference (as in India) or active disengagement from maritime concerns (as in Ming China by the 1430s) was the pattern. But perhaps common to all these 'external' rulers were the limits on the degree of control they could exercise – because they depended on the commercial and financial collaboration of the merchants, because customary freedoms were dangerous to challenge, or because rule at a distance meant relying on agents who themselves were subject to local influence. Indeed, almost all pre-modern rulers suffered from a deficit of coercive power, usually only available in short bursts before dissolving in the face of rebellion or bankruptcy.

But how cosmopolitan were these Old World port cities? Almost everywhere their trade depended on the presence of foreign merchants: their absence was a death knell. All across Eurasia, long-distance trade was sustained by merchant diasporas – Chinese, Arab, Persian, Gujarati, Jewish, Greek, Italian (Venetians, Florentines, Genoese) and

German. Merchants sent their sons or nephews abroad to buy and sell, or travelled themselves to accompany their goods. They needed local contacts (ideally co-religionists) to supply market information, offer hospitality, provide arbitration in case of dispute, and safeguard their property in case of disaster or death. Hence many a port city contained foreign quarters or colonies, whose 'captains' or consuls dealt with the local authorities. Typically, foreign merchants were required to buy from and sell to their local counterparts and were barred from retail trade. Their movements were often restricted – though there might be little incentive to travel inland – and confiscation, expulsion or worse was a constant anxiety. Anti-alien feeling, religious or commercial in origin, orchestrated by rivals or ignited by rumour, was an ever-present danger. If the ruler was careless, or himself at odds with the foreigners, calamity might follow. Of course, the threat that foreign merchants might leave in a body and boycott the port imposed some restraint. Xenophobia was often moderated by the ease with which foreign merchants could acquire a local identity by inter-marriage or royal favour, and by the extent to which within both Christendom and Islam codes of ethics and religious observance prescribed common rules of behaviour and notions of justice. A form of customary sea law governed maritime trade and the relations of captains and crews in the Mediterranean (Rhodian sea law) and northern Europe (the Rules of Oleron). Even across the major cultural borders, merchant self-interest made mutual trust and square-dealing a condition of commercial success.[103]

The jewel in the crown of port-city commerce was long-distance trade. But we might be tempted to ask what contribution that made to the economic transformation of their regional hinterlands, or to the wider diffusion of capitalism. The answer is far from clear-cut. Long-distance trade represented barely a fraction of economic activity in a world that was still overwhelmingly rural. Most trade was local or regional, and conducted in a vast number of inland market towns. Even seaborne trade was typically short-distance and coastal, ferrying grain, timber, fish or salt between nearby locations. Port-city harbours were cluttered with this maritime traffic, and the boats and barges that plied in their estuaries. But if long-distance trade was modest in volume, the profits it made could sometimes be huge. By one calculation a kilogram of pepper was sold (to its European consumer) at up to thirty times the price paid to the grower, and for twice the price paid by the Venetians in Alexandria.[104] Nor was the outlay economically trivial. What Europeans paid for their spices each year would have purchased the grain to feed one and a half million people.[105] But perhaps the significance of long-distance trade lay as much in the institutions and habits it fostered as in the wealth it created. With turn-around times of a year or more, merchants needed good information and to maintain careful records. Correspondence and book-keeping were vital; some form of insurance was essential. Filling a ship required merchants to devise partnerships between themselves and the shipmasters. Where goods crossed the boundary between monetary systems, they had to master exchange or make use of the banks that sprang up to manage it. It was no coincidence that Italian business methods set the standard for the rest of Europe.[106] Nor that the demands of long-distance voyaging (between China and South East Asia or between the Mediterranean and North Atlantic) were the forcing-house of navigational skill and improved ship design.

But were the Old World port cities so many cradles of capitalism? The usual criteria for the presence of capitalism include secure property rights, the ability to enforce contracts, a more or less free market for both goods and labour (which might be slave labour), and states willing and able to act in their support. Long-distance trade and the shipping it needed were prime users of capital, and practitioners of capitalism. But port-city merchants had little taste for free trade or the integration of markets. Nor did their profits depend only (or even chiefly) upon entrepreneurial skill. The aim of the merchant was to secure a monopoly – what economists call 'rent-seeking behaviour' – by grant from the ruler or the forceful suppression of all competition. Fortunes were made by lending to kings and receiving their bounty. In much the same way, port-city communities tried to restrict the activity of commercial outsiders as far as was practicable. Where they could they created wider zones of exclusion by territorial expansion (as did Genoa, Venice and Ayutthaya) or building 'informal' empires of commercial pre-eminence (Genoa again and also Hormuz). They were helped by the fact that much of the Old World was seamed with multiple jurisdictions (within as much as between states), conferring different privileges and imposing different taxes and tolls. It has been persuasively argued that breaking these down and widening the market (the essential precondition for the division of labour and 'Smithian' or pre-industrial growth) was the work not of merchants but of rulers intent on centralizing authority.[107] The argument can be applied to China, precociously centralized and bureaucratized. Where that was lacking, or where the defenders of privilege were too deeply entrenched, markets remained narrow and growth stagnated.

As all this suggests, Old World port cities favoured 'globalization', though of a peculiar and limited kind. But they also faced challenges that threatened prosperity or even survival. Pandemic disease was a major scourge, typically killing half the urban populations in its path – although its long-term effect (in Europe at least) was to raise living standards, consumption and trade. Keeping ports open required a constant battle against silting, or, in Alexandria's case, to keep open its route to the Nile. Changes in ship design and manoeuvrability favoured some ports over others or demanded a costly upgrade in harbour facilities. Domestic politics – the favour of rulers – could take away privilege as well as dispense it. Social order was precarious and depended on the skill of patricians in appeasing the discontents of lesser merchants, shopkeepers, artisans and the labouring poor – all the more dangerous in periods of dearth or other calamity. But perhaps the greatest dangers of all were geopolitical. Predation by rulers was much less of a hazard than the ambition of rulers and the wars it set off. Trade was disrupted; ports might be razed (the fate of Southampton in 1338); disorder and violence at sea raised the cost of insurance or drove shipping away. Without a maritime hegemon, or the cooperation of sea powers, piracy (licensed or not) was endemic wherever the narrowing of sea lanes afforded rich pickings.

This then was the Old World of port cities. 'Pre-Columbian' globalization fell short of the Americas, and, for that matter, Australasia. But over the previous two millennia it had created a matrix of navigational techniques, mercantile skills, habits of consumption, colonizing practices and cultural prejudices into which the Americas were to be more or less forcibly integrated. With how much success and with what unexpected results we will see in the chapters that follow.

2

Columbian Prelude

'The discovery of America, and that of a passage to the East Indies by the Cape of Good Hope, are the two greatest and most important events recorded in the history of mankind. Their consequences have already been very great . . .'. This was Adam Smith's verdict in *The Wealth of Nations* (1776), parroting the views of the Abbé Raynal in his *Histoire des Deux Indes* (1770).[1] Together with Vasco da Gama's voyage round the Cape of Good Hope to India in 1497–8, Columbus's discovery of a viable sea route to the Caribbean *and back* in 1492 had opened the way for direct navigation between the Americas, Europe, Asia and Africa. By 1513 the Portuguese had arrived on the south coast of China, by way of Sofala in East Africa (1505), Goa (1510) and Malacca (captured in 1511). In 1553 they acquired Macao as a trading station on the China coast. They had already established themselves in north-east Brazil, a convenient port of call (because of wind and current) for ships on their way between Lisbon and the Orient. When the cultivation of sugar was brought there from Madeira, slaves began to be shipped across the South Atlantic from Angola, henceforth a 'sub-colony' of colonial Brazil: Luanda was founded as a Portuguese settlement in 1575. Meanwhile, in 1571, the Spanish crossed the Pacific and founded Manila in the Philippines to attract merchants from China with the lure of silver from Mexico and Peru. By the late sixteenth century, then, a new network of global sea lanes ran in parallel to the old overland trade between Europe and Asia, while seaborne merchants from Europe tried to cut their way into the dense mercantile traffic around the Indian Ocean and the South China Sea. The foundations had been laid for what we might call the 'Columbian globalization' of the era between 1500 and 1830.

In fact, as we have seen, Columbian globalization was itself the culmination of a longer history of global connections between the western end of Eurasia (and North Africa) and its eastern edge overlooking the Pacific. In pre-Columbian Eurasia, the trade between Rome and China, the astonishing speed with which Islam was spread from western Arabia to the borders of China, and the diffusion of technologies, games (like chess), literary styles, tastes in luxuries like ivory,[2] spices, gemstones and silks,[3] and the use of precious metals as coins, were all made possible by skeins of commerce and contact lost in Eurasia's deep 'half-global' history.[4] Thus the demand for Chinese manufactures that Columbus was hoping to buy, the navigational know-how he expected to use, and the crusading ethos which the Spanish took to the Americas, were the cultural, technical and political legacy of western Europe's long engagement with the civilizations of China and Islamic Eurasia. Globalization might come in phases, and exhibit moments of acceleration and deceleration, but it was also cumulative – drawing upon, adapting or reinventing an inherited suite of technologies, routes, cosmologies, commercial institutions, cultural tastes and ideas of prestige. What makes each phase historically distinctive is the novel set of conditions – in commerce, technology, geopolitical power, environmental change or the spread of disease – that favour new routes over old, new habits of consumption, new notions of space, new targets for migration, new spheres of religious belief and new ideologies.

COLUMBIAN GLOBALIZATION

Columbian globalization was, first of all, an extraordinary enlargement of Europe's long-constrained place in the world. European merchants, first Portuguese, then Dutch, then English and others, monopolized the new long-distance sea trade around the Cape to Asia. European states – Spanish, Portuguese, Dutch, French and English – turned the New World (or those parts they could reach) into an annexe of Europe. Was Columbian globalization merely the prelude to the expansion of Europe – a common enough view? It was certainly true that the extraordinary terms on which Europeans entered the New World hugely magnified its impact on their economies, cultures and societies. Had they found what they expected – peoples willing to trade and organized in states on Old World lines – the European conquest and colonization of the Americas might have been delayed for centuries (as it would be in Asia), if it had happened at all. Instead, the sensational triumphs of the conquistadors, the legend (and reality) of inexhaustible plunder, the vast windfall of bullion, and the stimulus given to Atlantic navigation encouraged the practice (and enthroned the ideology) of colonization and maritime trade as the high roads to wealth and geopolitical power. Atlantic imperialism transformed European understanding of the shape of the globe and induced a remarkable new cartographic culture.[5] Europe could now be imagined as the crossroads of the known world, not as its periphery. It created a huge new theatre for missionary enterprise and religious expansion, and (before long) a refuge for dissenters. American produce – sugar especially – encouraged new kinds of consumption.[6] American space became the target for migration, and its settler societies a place for social experiments, not always benign. It was in the Americas that Europeans really discovered their addiction to plantation slavery.

Yet it would be wrong to suppose that the global effects of the new oceanic geography were felt only or primarily in Europe. The transfer of food and industrial crops, like sorghum, rice, sugar cane and cotton (and the technologies that went with them), over long distances and across climate zones had long been a feature of Old World agriculture. Bananas were brought from Indonesia to East Africa by Malay seamen sometime after AD 300 and rapidly spread across the African continent. New crops modified local ecologies and increased populations. But the 'Columbian exchange' after 1492 injected an extraordinary range of prolific new food crops into Eurasian societies, to be adopted there at astonishing speed.[7] Sweet potatoes, peanuts and maize were all established in China by the mid-sixteenth century, and are usually credited with part of its huge population rise from 160 million in 1700 to 350 million a century later,[8] although the cultivation of maize did not expand dramatically until 1750–1820.[9] Manioc (cassava) from Brazil became a staple food crop in tropical Africa, as did maize. Indeed, the adoption of maize to support a relatively dense population may well have been the crucial factor in the emergence of the powerful Asante Empire in the West African forest belt after 1600.[10] We might even speculate on the link between the population growth that New World crops promoted in Africa and the reverse flow of slaves that crossed the Atlantic.[11]

In the sphere of trade, the global impact of the Americas was just as striking. The American colonies, north and south, became the source of plantation crops, some brought from Eurasia, like sugar, coffee and indigo, others, like tobacco and cacao, indigenous to America. Produced with slave labour, they quickly supplanted the older suppliers in Europe and the Middle East, undercutting a whole chain of Old World producers and traders. But the most valuable 'dividend' the Europeans drew from America was its wealth of silver, around three-quarters of which was exported to Europe, or directly to Asia. Silver expanded the monetary base of Europe's economies – and paid for its wars. But from *c.*1600 more than 40 per cent of the silver sent to Europe was then transported east to Asia.[12] In Asia, where silver was scarcer, its price was higher, offering a handsome profit just for shipping it there. But the real significance of this bullion trade was to allow Europeans to buy Asian goods on a far grander scale than before, since Asian demand for Europe's own products had never been large. In 1660–65 the English East India Company sent some 40,000 kilograms of silver to the East: by the 1750s this figure was ten times as great.[13] European consumers could now indulge their appetite for Chinese porcelain and silks and for fine Indian cottons, while Chinese and Indian producers responded eagerly to this buoyant new market. Porcelain from Jingdezhen, and increasingly tea from Fujian, poured out through Canton (Guangzhou), the leading entrepôt of the South China coast. Indian muslins and calicoes flowed westward from Gujarat, the Coromandel and Bengal, much of it in the ships of the East India Company.[14] Slaves in the Americas were clothed in Indian cottons.[15] Silver became the principal currency of global trade and by some calculations China consumed between one-half and two-thirds of what was mined in Mexico and Peru between 1500 and 1800, much of it sent directly across the Pacific to Manila.[16] It was Chinese demand that helped to make Spanish America so valuable.

What had begun to emerge after 1600 was a new global pattern.

Columbian globalization had drawn America, Europe, India, South East Asia and China into a great circulation, enlarged the scale of Asia's trade with Europe and its colonies, and turned western Europeans into the main carriers of long-distance seaborne trade. European-rigged ships enjoyed a curious advantage: while they were slower in a following wind than Chinese junks, they could make better headway *against* the monsoons that governed the wind system in the Indian Ocean and South China Sea.[17] Much of Asia's regional or 'country trade' remained in local hands, except for the share that was taken by the Dutch East India Company (VOC), from whose Asian headquarters at Batavia (Jakarta) spread a fan-shaped commerce with some twenty-eight 'factories' (i.e. commercial agencies), from Mocha in Yemen to Nagasaki in Japan.[18] In the eighteenth century a lively trade sprang up between Madras (modern Chennai) and Manila, sending Indian cottons (for onward sale in Spanish America) in exchange for American silver. Columbian globalization had made India and China into the workshops of the world. It also fuelled the mass transfer of African slaves to American plantations (more than eight million between 1519 and 1800). Indian textiles were among the products that Europeans sold in exchange to African slavers:[19] by the 1730s Indian cottons made up between two-thirds and three-quarters of the goods sent out by the Royal African Company to West Africa.[20] It favoured more modest migration by Europeans to the Americas (some 1.4 million between 1500 and 1783), and by Chinese to South East Asia, where Chinese labourers cultivated the new sugar fields in the *Ommelanden* round Batavia.[21] It was a powerful stimulus to new notions of comfort, consumption and luxury in both East and West: Indian fabrics transformed European taste in clothes and drove popular fashion, reshaping the continent's material culture.[22] Columbian globalization was also a powerful vector of Eurasian and African diseases (a grim litany including measles, smallpox, malaria and yellow fever) that killed millions of Native Americans who lacked the immunities – this was their share of the 'Columbian exchange' – and helped spread the plague that struck again and again in the seventeenth and eighteenth centuries.

Above all, perhaps, it transformed the maritime world. The seaborne circulation of goods and people dictated by wind and current, and their seasonal variants (especially the monsoons), created new ports of call, and new kinds of proximity. The clockwise movement of winds in the North Atlantic governed its sea lanes. The Caribbean became the great crossroads for shipping from Europe to the Americas, and hence the main cockpit of Europe's colonial rivalries. North-east Brazil was contested by the Portuguese and the Dutch partly because (for both) it lay on their wind-ruled sea routes around the Cape of Good Hope to South East Asia. Ceylon (Sri Lanka) lay on the junction between the Bay of Bengal and the Arabian Sea and was coveted by the Portuguese, the Dutch and later the British. The Asian headquarters of the VOC at Batavia guarded the Java Strait, the main entrance from Europe into the South China Sea and the sea road to China. The Cape of Good Hope, which had been regularly visited by European shipping to the East,[23] became the guard house between the Atlantic and Indian oceans, and was occupied by the VOC in 1652 as an outpost of its East Indian empire. And while European exploits have tended to grab the historical headlines, the new opportunities brought by long-distance seaborne trade and by the European mercantile presence in Asia and Africa were eagerly taken up by Africans, Chinese and Indians – as slavers, merchants, shipowners and -builders, or producers. Trading diasporas, old and new, moved into the new middleman roles that oceanic commerce now offered: Armenians, Hadhramis and Jews among them. Across much of South East Asia, Chinese merchants became the favoured partners of the Dutch East India Company, and asserted their commercial pre-eminence with Dutch support.[24] Once the Qing eased their restrictions on overseas trade in the mid-1680s, Chinese junks from Amoy (Xiamen) and Canton carried Chinese manufactures to Siam (Thailand) and the Indonesian archipelago in return for rice and exotics like sandalwood (for ritual, medicine, cosmetics and coffins) and coral.[25]

Yet we should not mistake this busy scene for a world of free movement or cosmopolitan values. Nor should we suppose that the volume of commercial exchange was constantly rising. Just as in our times, trade was subject to periods of depression and disruption. The declining supply of American silver in the mid-seventeenth century, the upheavals in China that followed the dynastic change from Ming to

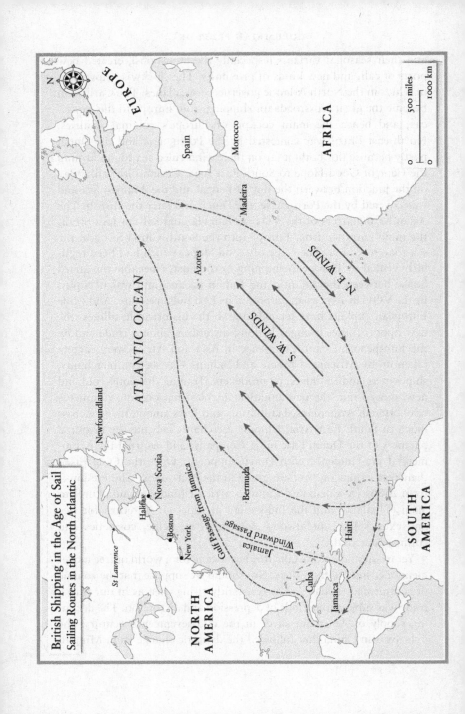

British Shipping in the Age of Sail
Sailing Routes in the North Atlantic

EUROPE

AFRICA

Spain

Morocco

Madeira

N. E. WINDS

Azores

ATLANTIC OCEAN

S. W. WINDS

Newfoundland

St Lawrence

Halifax

Nova Scotia

Boston

New York

Gulf Passage from Jamaica

Bermuda

NORTH AMERICA

Jamaica Windward Passage

Haiti

Cuba

Jamaica

SOUTH AMERICA

N

0   500 miles
0   1000 km

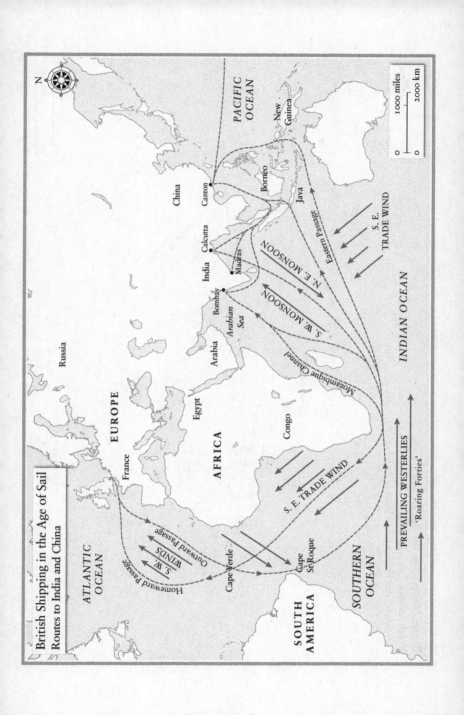

British Shipping in the Age of Sail
Routes to India and China

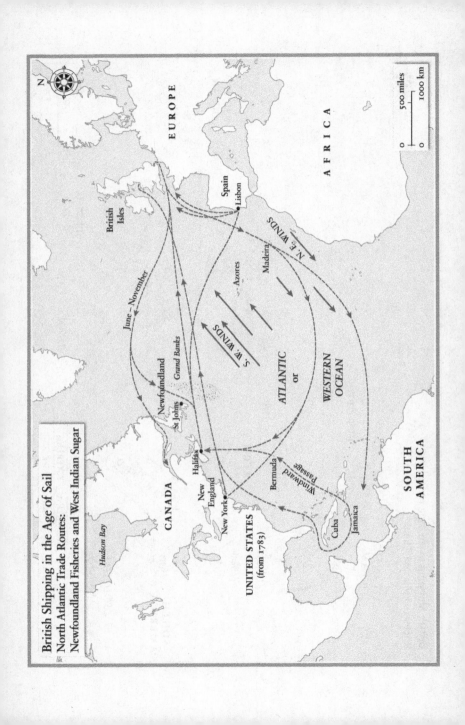

British Shipping in the Age of Sail
North Atlantic Trade Routes:
Newfoundland Fisheries and West Indian Sugar

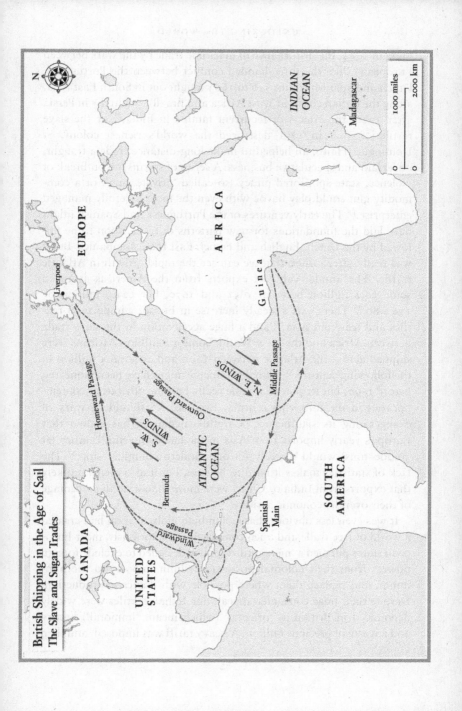

British Shipping in the Age of Sail
The Slave and Sugar Trades

Qing in 1644, the disturbance of maritime trade by the wars between Europeans (like the three-handed conflict between the Portuguese, Dutch and Spanish from 1640 to 1663 fought out in South East Asia, along the Indian coast, in West Africa and Brazil),[26] anarchy in Persia after 1720, the effects of recurrent famine in India,[27] or the slave revolution that in 1791 destroyed the world's richest colony, St Domingue (Haiti), all helped to make long-distance trade a fraught, uncertain and speculative business. A series of storms, an outbreak of violence, state-sponsored piracy (so-called 'privateering') or a commodity glut could play havoc with even the most carefully managed enterprise.[28] The early ventures of the Portuguese and Spanish might have laid the foundations for new patterns of trade, soon to be followed by the Dutch, English and French East India companies. But it was really after *c.*1690 that we can see the rapid growth in Atlantic traffic. The annual value of exports from the Americas averaged some £6.2 million between 1651 and 1670, but £21.9 million by 1761–80.[29] There was a steady increase in Europe's imports of textiles and tea from Asia,[30] and a huge acceleration in the slave trade between Africa and the New World. Some 1.8 million Africans were shipped across the Atlantic between 1600 and 1700; 6.4 million in the following century.[31] Global commerce might have been pioneered before 1690, but its potential scale really became obvious to contemporaries in the following century. Even so, we should be wary of exaggerating its significance. Careful calculation has shown that Europe's yearly imports from Asia in the late eighteenth century (at 50,000 tons) would scarcely fill one modern container ship.[32] The lack of statistics makes it hard to be sure, but it also seems unlikely that exports from India or China were more than a small percentage of their overall economic activity.

It was even less obvious that Columbian globalization had created a world of free trade and open competition. Notoriously, most European states pursued a 'mercantilist' policy designed to exclude foreign powers from their colonial possessions, limit imports to the minimum, and replace them where possible with domestic production. Despite their huge consumer appeal, fine Indian textiles were widely denounced in Britain as 'oriental' (which meant 'immoral') luxury and a waste of precious bullion. A heavy tariff was imposed, and then followed by prohibition. The import of Indian cottons was banned from the domestic market in France between 1686 and 1750.[33] Most European experts believed that overseas trade was a predatory zero-sum game in which one country's gain was another's loss, and that the key to real economic well-being still lay in the highly unpredictable grain harvest. Nor were Europeans unusual in imposing the limits and exclusions on external trade that Adam Smith was to denounce so vehemently. On the other side of the world, Tokugawa Japan closely restricted all external contact to Dutch and Chinese merchants – admitting the Dutch only to a commercial keyhole in Nagasaki harbour and after 1708 limiting the number of Chinese junks allowed to land there to thirty a year.[34] The Qing emperor relaxed his ban on China's foreign trade in the 1680s, but Europeans were only allowed to trade in the southern port of Canton and then under close supervision, a system tightened up in 1757. In their turn, the 'official' European companies in Asia struggled to maintain their monopoly over Asia's trade with Europe against 'interlopers' from home. West African rulers were careful to keep their European clients pinned to the coast to preserve their control over the supply (and price) of slaves. India was unusual in being more open to traders from abroad, perhaps because the decay of Mughal authority after 1700 had thrown up new commerce-friendly or commerce-dependent regimes around the South Asian coast.

As these restrictions suggest, contemporary opinion, whether European, Asian or African, was far from convinced that globalization (not a term contemporaries would have used) was desirable. As late as 1811, the idea that foreign goods offered Japan any benefit was contemptuously dismissed by Tokugawa officials: 'Our countrymen wish to carry on no commerce with foreign lands,' they told a captured Russian, 'for we know of no want of necessary things.'[35] The Chinese emperor's retort, when the Macartney mission of 1792–3 (sent to open diplomatic relations between Britain and China) presented him with examples of Western ingenuity, is well known: 'I set no value on objects strange or ingenious, and have no use for your country's manufactures', ran his message to George III.[36] Africans might have bought Indian-made textiles as well as their own, but they demanded patterns and colours that fitted local tradition and mixed imported cloth with the local product.[37] Imported textiles might have added to the sartorial range of African consumers, but they showed no desire to dress like Europeans, preferred the loincloth for men, and preserved the distinctive cut, shape and style of previous eras.[38] But it was in western Europe, where global commerce had made the largest impact, that mistrust of its course and consequences was most forcibly expressed.

In part, this arose from the feeling that the promise of commercial expansion had been throttled by the brutal ineptitude of European conquest and the resort to monopoly. Trade with the New World, argued Adam Smith, would have been much larger without the destruction of its most advanced civilizations (a reference to Mexico and Peru), just as trade with Asia had been stifled by the prohibitions on private traders.[39] The large slave populations of the Americas could consume very little: it required codes and laws to compel slave owners to provide even a minimal ration of clothing.[40] The discontent was not merely commercial. Like other writers in Europe, Smith denounced the cruelty and injustice that marked Europe's commercial relations with the rest of the world, and for which one day a price would have to be paid.[41] To social critics in Britain, the extraordinary wealth brought home by 'nabobs' from India after 1757 threatened the rise of a plutocratic elite with 'oriental' tastes and morals, and the corruption of politics. In much the same way it was the fear that the practice of slavery would pollute British society at home (a fear dramatized by the famous Mansfield judgment in 1772 declaring slavery 'odious' and making its status unenforceable in Britain) that stimulated a rising tide of anti-slavery feeling by the 1780s, despite the huge commercial importance of the slave trade and slave labour.[42] Columbian globalization, on this view, rewarded the privileged few and was the enemy of freedom, morality and a balanced economy.

In France, where in his widely read *Histoire des Deux Indes* (1770) the Abbé Raynal had chillingly forecast that a great slave revolt provoked by European brutality would shatter the pivotal role of the Caribbean in world trade,[43] the critique was even more virulent. France's Atlantic trade had grown rapidly in the eighteenth century (indeed more rapidly than Britain's). Her colony of St Domingue was a source of vast profit. Ports like Bordeaux, Nantes and La Rochelle thrived on the traffic in sugar and slaves. Raynal's attack had been essentially moral. But fear that global commerce would undermine France's power and the French state was also pervasive. Montesquieu had pointed out in his hugely influential *Spirit of the Laws* (1748) that the rise of oceanic trade had created new forms of mobile mercantile wealth that threatened the power and prestige of great territorial monarchies – like France.[44] The great example was Britain, France's main rival in commerce and sea power. Montesquieu was sanguine: Britain's commercial collapse would come sooner or later.[45] The powerful school of Physiocrats that formed round François Quesnay and his *Tableau économique* (1759) was more urgent. A commercial state, argued Quesnay, was precarious and unstable. Merchants were fickle and without real allegiance. Their business was vulnerable to competition and attack. Their wealth was invisible and could not be mobilized for the public good. 'Their assets consist in dispersed and secret credits . . . mobile and moneyed wealth is not available to the sovereign.'[46] Moreover, they were able to exercise far too much influence and had turned Britain into a 'warehouse state'. France must be saved from such a fate. The only true basis for national wealth and well-being was agricultural production: 'a large state should not abandon the plough in order to become a carrier'. The programme of the Physiocrats was to wrench France back towards the stability promised by an agricultural state, avoid the recourse to vast public debts (the British model), and keep mercantile influence in its proper place. The revolt of Britain's American colonies in 1775 seemed to prove their point. With its gross dependence on trade Britain would be plunged into bankruptcy and social revolution, predicted Turgot, the French finance minister.[47]

Yet commerce, what we might call 'globalization', could also be seen by European thinkers as the source of moral and social progress. 'Commerce,' said Montesquieu, 'is a cure for the most destructive prejudices . . . Commerce has . . . diffused a knowledge of the manners of all nations: these are compared one with another and from this comparison arise the greatest advantages.'[48] David Hume's view was similar: 'a kingdom that has a large import and export, must abound more with industry . . . than a kingdom which rests contented with its native commodities'.[49] The criticisms advanced by Smith,

Raynal (whose team of research assistants included Denis Diderot) and the Physiocrats reflected their belief that it was the *form* that Columbian globalization had taken that made it morally repellent, economically wasteful, politically destabilizing and inherently conflictual. 'Commerce,' said Smith, 'which ought naturally to be, among nations, as among individuals, a bond of union and friendship, has become the most fertile source of discord and animosity.'[50] There was indeed plenty to suggest that the competition for world trade was the trigger for incessant 'colonial' wars, in the Caribbean, North America, India, South East Asia and West Africa. In the Seven Years War of 1756–63 the British had besieged and captured Quebec, Havana, French Pondicherry in southern India and Manila: a colonial 'world war'. Columbian globalization had encouraged the growth of great maritime empires, with slavery at their heart, and turned the local geopolitical rivalries of the European states into a global phenomenon. The result was to burden their trade and populations with the huge overhead costs of fleets and armies and the defence of far-flung trading stations. The saving grace was that, as late as 1750, across much of the world the Europeans' presence was either confined to the coast or meekly dependent on the fiat of Asian or African rulers.

In fact, Columbian globalization had left intact or even strengthened many of the polities of Asia and Africa that had shared in the increase of trade. In the 1750s few seemed vulnerable to a European takeover. The Ottoman Empire had been pushed back from central Europe by the Habsburgs, but there was little sign of any headlong retreat from eastern Europe and the Balkans, while the North African states, from Morocco to Egypt, still acknowledged their allegiance to the Sultan in Constantinople. The Black Sea was still an Ottoman lake. Almost nowhere in Africa did European influence extend beyond a few coastal 'factories', except in Angola, where mixed race *pombeiros* traded for slaves.[51] In India, Mughal power was in decline, but its successor states in Bengal, the Maratha Confederacy, Hyderabad or Mysore looked far too strong to fall victim to the puny military power that the French, British, Dutch or Portuguese could deploy in South Asia. Mainland South East Asia had been convulsed by war between the Burman and Siamese empires: neither looked remotely vulnerable to European encroachment. In

China, the Qing Empire was more secure than ever, having conquered Xinjiang ('Chinese Turkestan') in 1759 and crushed the age-old threat of invasion from the steppe.[52] The Emperor Qianlong's contemptuous dismissal of Macartney's embassy in 1792–3 was a mark of his confidence that China's 'prosperous age' was far from over. And while Macartney might jeer that the Qing Empire resembled a rotting man-o'-war, only the wildest of fantasists would have dreamed of trying to steer it with a new (European) captain and crew. Japan, occasionally visited by storm-driven ships, was too dangerous for Europeans to visit, except for the handful of Dutch merchants licensed to stay at their factory on the tiny artificial islet of Deshima at Nagasaki.

PORT CITIES IN THE COLUMBIAN ERA

For all its limitations, this new global regime had a transformative impact on the scale and reach of Eurasia's port cities, and created the space for new 'colonial' port cities in the Americas and Asia. In Europe, the most obvious change was the end of the old commercial primacy of the Mediterranean ports. With direct access by sea to India, South East Asia, China, the Americas and the 'slave coasts' of West Africa, Europe's Atlantic shore, from Hamburg to Cadiz, became a vast landing stage for the trade of the world. Cotton textiles, silks, ceramics, sugar, tobacco, tea, coffee, chocolate, and a mass of smaller luxury items like diamonds, coral and the rich scarlet dye cochineal, supplemented the older staples of timber, grain, salt, fish, wine and spices. European consumers, at least those with disposable incomes, responded eagerly to the new goods on offer, refashioning their diets, clothes and leisure habits to display their wealth, indulge their sweet tooth or dull their aches and pains – part of the appeal of tobacco. Chocolate (as a drink) reached Spain in the 1590s and spread quickly through Europe after 1600. The first London coffee house opened in 1652, and the first tea and chocolate houses in 1657.[53] Sugar and tobacco became cheap enough to become mass-consumption goods by the late seventeenth century. Indian-style textiles and Chinese porcelain were the hallmark of wealth, sophistication and comfort.

Europe's port cities expanded rapidly to supply these new commodities and arrange their distribution. After capital cities like Paris or Madrid, port cities grew fastest in population: between 1500 and 1700 more than half doubled or tripled their populations.[54] The global scale of their trade piled new functions onto those they inherited from the pre-Columbian past. Now they had to finance and manage mercantile ventures at a far greater distance and with far longer turnaround times – the challenge that prompted the rise of great corporations like the English East India Company and its powerful Dutch counterpart, the VOC. In Lisbon and Seville, rulers established new institutions to control their Asian and American trade and, with mixed success, to enforce a royal monopoly. As American trade shifted gradually from its initial reliance on the extraction of silver towards the cultivation of cash crops, sugar above all, a new plantation economy demanded facilities and 'factors' to provide credit, take goods on consignment, and purchase supplies for the planters and their workforce.[55] The rapid conversion of the plantation workforce from indentured whites to African slaves – as happened in Barbados between the 1640s and the 1660s[56] – was symptomatic of one of the most extraordinary (and, in retrospect, horrifying) aspects of the Americas' integration into the global economy. In fact, the Spanish and Portuguese had already turned to African slaves to work their New World plantations and mines by the mid-sixteenth century; by 1640 nearly 800,000 had been brought to Brazil and Spanish America (which took much the larger share).[57] This reflected both the difficulty of recruiting (or enslaving) Native Americans (already decimated by disease) and the belief that African slaves – wrenched from home and kindred – would make more docile labourers than Europeans, resistant to the savage regime of the sugar plantation. For the English, the success of slave plantations in Brazil was all the evidence they needed.[58] The working life of imported slaves was appallingly short, cut down by disease and the brutal conditions of plantation labour. Hence a vast business sprang up to finance their purchase and replacement and arrange the barter goods (usually Indian textiles) and ships that were sent to the slave coasts, from where slaves were despatched to buyers in the Caribbean and mainland America. The ships sent to West Africa to trade for slaves formed part, and quite a large part, of the swiftly growing merchant fleets that sailed out from Europe (around 15 per cent of British tonnage by the late eighteenth century). Europe's shipping tonnage has been estimated at some 225,000 tons in 1500, at 1.5 million tons by 1670 and at some three million tons a century later; and the number of ocean-going seamen as up to 100,000 by the later seventeenth century.[59] Ships were expensive to build (they were the single most expensive capital good in the pre-modern world), and required a complex supply chain of highly specialized equipment. They had to be crewed, freighted and insured, loaded and unloaded. Ship-owning, ship-building and maintenance, ship-broking (the hiring of ships), and the recruitment of ship labour, sometimes from remote locations, were among the most dynamic elements of port-city economies.

A successful port city required something more than a favourable location and a vigorous mercantile class. Just as in earlier times, protection and privilege were vital. Merchants lobbied fiercely to win the support of the state for their overseas ventures, or to obtain a 'charter' that would exclude their home-grown competitors from a lucrative trade. They had to fend off – or try to exploit – royal demands for more customs revenue: winning the 'tax-farm' to administer the customs might be the high road to riches or the low road to bankruptcy. In an age of intense rivalry between Europe's maritime states, merchants had to reckon with the costs of commercial disruption and loss as their ships were picked off by enemy navies or by officially sanctioned 'privateers'. The demand for naval protection was high on the agenda of port-city politics.[60] They might hope to profit from their sovereign's needs for loans, supplies and shipping in time of war: victory would bring a handsome dividend. For all these reasons, commercial success was at least partly dependent upon the political and geopolitical environment in which a port city existed. Where its business class had ready access to the ruling power, or enjoyed close relations – through marriage or commercial partnership – with the governing elite, there was some guarantee that dynastic ambition would be moderated by economic self-interest. But it was equally true that if its ruler failed by ill-luck or bad management to defend his subjects' commercial interests abroad, a port city's prospects would soon start to pale. The shortcomings of Spain's sea power, and the inability to protect the potentially lucrative monopoly over its American trade, were a constant lament of Spanish commentators after 1700.

We can see these preconditions at work in Atlantic Europe's leading port cities after 1600: Amsterdam and London. Amsterdam had profited from the commercial ruin of Antwerp, the victim of Spain's failure to destroy Dutch independence and Dutch control over the mouth of the Scheldt, Antwerp's outlet to the sea. Amsterdam grew with sensational speed from a population of 50,000 in 1600 to some 220,000 by 1675, a growth made possible (as in all pre-modern cities) by a flood of in-migration, much of it from Germany. Its commerce-friendly republican government smiled on the creation of a Bourse for the trading of commodities and shares, and an exchange bank for foreign transactions, and granted a trading monopoly in Asia to the Dutch East India Company (VOC) and to its (less successful) Atlantic counterpart, the West India Company (WIC). Dutch naval power was deployed against Sweden to keep open the Sound and preserve Amsterdam's commercial pre-eminence in the Baltic. A huge merchant fleet carried much of the traffic between northern and southern Europe. Much of England's trade with Europe passed through the city since Dutch merchants had the credit, the contacts and the commercial expertise to outmatch any rival. Low import duties made the Netherlands the most open market in Europe. With its old staple trades of grain, fish and timber from the Baltic and the North Sea – much of it exported to southern Europe via Lisbon – its 'exotic' imports from Asia and the Americas, its easy access to the Rhineland and southern Germany, its manufacturing industries in textiles, beer, soap and sugar refining, and its tolerance of religious dissenters, including Portuguese Jews, who played a leading role in finance, Amsterdam became the queen city of Atlantic Europe. It was also the 'great staple for news', Europe's information capital. By the early seventeenth century, printed newsletters, 'prices current' and tables of interests were all readily found there. Amsterdam was the 'post office' for mail all over northern Europe. Mapmakers waited on its quays for homecoming ships.[61]

Yet commercial supremacy was never secure. By the late seventeenth century, the Dutch advantage in the carrying trade was under pressure as merchants elsewhere bypassed Amsterdam and mercantilist rules favoured local shipping over Dutch. Caught between the landward threat of France and the maritime challenge of Britain, the Republic lacked the power to impose its commercial and maritime interests. It lost its North American colony to England in 1664, and the attempt to seize the north-east of Brazil from the Portuguese for the sake of its sugar was also a failure. By the 1730s, if not earlier, British trade was greater than Dutch and no longer depended on Dutch intermediaries.[62] British sea power enforced the 'navigation acts' to exclude Dutch carriers from Britain's trade with the Americas, Asia and Africa (though not with complete success).[63] By the mid-eighteenth century, Britain's merchant fleet had overtaken that of the Dutch.[64] England's turn to protection in the 1690s encouraged manufactures and the export of finished goods, damaging the Dutch export economy. London now came to rival Amsterdam. It was a much larger city – nearly three times the size with almost 600,000 people in 1700. It dwarfed England's other ports and was more than twenty-five times the size of the next largest, Bristol.[65] It dominated foreign trade, receiving some 80 per cent of English imports. Compared with Amsterdam, its domestic market was much wider. It was the centre of a much more extensive transatlantic empire (including the great sugar trade from the Caribbean), and re-exported its produce to consumers in Europe. It was the headquarters of the East India Company whose fast-growing trade in South Asian textiles proved much more profitable than the VOC's reliance on spices. As the capital of a larger and increasingly centralized state, London benefited from the spending of government, court and landed aristocracy. It acquired the same institutions that had made Amsterdam an efficient place to do business: a Royal Exchange, a Post Office, the specialized coffee houses for correspondence and contacts with different markets abroad.[66] A sign of its growing importance was the presence of ever more Dutch and German merchants, drawn by the need to make contracts in London. Nevertheless, through the eighteenth century, Amsterdam remained Europe's main centre for foreign exchange, where merchants could settle their foreign currency bills, and its main source of loans. Dutch bankers invested heavily in foreign government stocks, not least in Britain, where they held some 40 per cent of

Britain's public debt in the 1770s.[67] Not until the catastrophe of French conquest overwhelmed it at the end of the century did Amsterdam finally cede pride of place to its cross-Channel rival.

Both Amsterdam and London depended – with varying success – upon their governments and navies to guard their commercial empires against European rivals, and if possible to enlarge them. Although much of their business lay within Europe, the global scale of their commerce was a catalyst of prosperity and created new kinds of investment, new patterns of consumption, and new institutions through which to collect and distribute information and news. But perhaps the most striking new feature of Columbian globalization was the appearance of colonial port cities. Merchants from Asia and Europe had long been used to living in enclaves, quarters, kampongs and *fondacos* where they enjoyed a degree of licensed autonomy under the local ruler. The Venetians and Genoese had built trading outposts on the Black Sea, precariously dependent upon their neighbours' goodwill. The conquest and settlement of the New World marked a radical change. Here Europeans established new urban settlements not on sufferance but by right of conquest or 'discovery' and applied the institutions and laws of their European homelands. By the mid-seventeenth century a skein of settler port towns ran down the east coast of North America from Quebec (founded 1608) in the north, through Boston (1630), Dutch New Amsterdam (1624 – English New York from 1664), to Jamestown (1607) in Virginia. By the end of the century they had been joined by Charleston (1670) in the Carolinas and Philadelphia (1681) on the Delaware. In the Caribbean, where the English, French, Dutch, Danes and Swedes as well as the Spanish had acquired island colonies, most were served by small coastal settlements: among the largest were Bridgetown in Barbados and Port Royal in Jamaica, captured by the English from Spain in 1655. Of the port cities the Spanish had founded – Havana, Vera Cruz (the gateway to Mexico), Cartagena, Portobelo in Panama, Lima (actually eight miles inland; its harbour was at Callao) and Buenos Aires – Havana and Lima were the most substantial. Recife, Salvador and Rio de Janeiro on the Brazilian coastlands, all founded before 1600, were the nerve centres of Portugal's American empire.

These New World port towns performed a wide range of functions.

They were the beachheads from which Europeans ventured into the vast inland interior of mainland America. They were the funnel through which supplies and manpower arrived from their homelands. They were expected to defend the claims of their founders against rivals and predators: a key factor in their siting. The French soon moved their Canadian base from Tadoussac in the St Lawrence estuary to Quebec, because that was where the river narrowed to a cannon shot. Everywhere their forts and defences faced out to the sea – the main source of danger. It was the vast fishing grounds of Newfoundland's 'Grand Banks' that had drawn Europeans across the North Atlantic by c.1500. But it was trade rather than settlement that encouraged a presence on the North American mainland. The fur trade had drawn the French into Canada, and the Dutch to the Hudson. Trade with the Indians had been the original motive for the landing at Jamestown. But once settlement grew, port towns expanded to meet the needs of settler communities for local manufactures and imported goods. They managed the sale of their export commodities (tobacco from the Chesapeake, rice from Carolina) and housed the clergymen, lawyers, surveyors and doctors who regulated the colony's spiritual, legal and physical health. In the Caribbean, where the plantation economy had created extraordinary wealth by the later seventeenth century, port towns grew rich on the traffic in sugar and slaves and the conspicuous consumption of the planters and merchants as well as the lawyers and doctors on whose ministrations they depended. On the south-east coast of Brazil, in Pernambuco and Bahia, sugar and slaves were likewise the spring of urban prosperity; further south still it was gold (from the 1690s) that made Rio's fortune.[68] Colonial port towns were also in most cases the colony's capital, the seat of the governor and his petty court of functionaries, and usually the station for such military force as the governor commanded. They could serve as the base for undeclared warfare and illicit trade. It was from Port Royal in Jamaica that the British tried to subvert Spain's vast imperium by piracy and privateering, and by the contraband trade on which Jamaica's prosperity was originally based.[69]

The Spanish pattern was different. Spain's trade with the Americas was a monopoly officially vested in a handful of merchant houses in

Seville and later Cadiz (whose elegant old town reveals its eighteenth-century prosperity), and organized in an annual convoy across the Atlantic, the *Carrera de Indias*, divided between Portobelo at the Panama isthmus and Vera Cruz on the Mexican coast. In Spanish America, two principal *consulados* or merchant guilds were licensed to deal with this imperial trade, in Mexico City from 1592 and in Lima from 1613. Their role was to manage Spanish-American trade on behalf of the Crown and safeguard the revenues that helped to sustain its solvency.[70] The main commercial wealth of the empire lay not on the coast but in the silver mines of the interior plateaux in Mexico and Peru to which Vera Cruz and Lima (equidistant between Panama and Potosí) gave access. Merchants from Mexico City made their way to Vera Cruz in time for the arrival of the *flota* from Spain – which after 1640 was much more spasmodic than regular. The *galeones* to Portobelo, the rendezvous for the merchants from Lima, became just as intermittent, sailing only seven times between 1690 and 1739.[71] In reality, a huge proportion of Spanish-American trade was technically 'contraband', carried on by Dutch and British merchants from their Caribbean colonies, taking advantage of the flimsiness of Spanish control over the long Atlantic coastline of South and Central America. The Pacific coast may have been less vulnerable to smugglers, although Lima and its port Callao were heavily fortified against the threat of attack from the sea. Indeed, the Lima *consulado* retained official control over almost all the trade of Spanish South America: not until 1770 was Buenos Aires allowed direct dealings with Europe.[72] It seems likely, however, that much Spanish-American commerce was really internal, supplying the dozens of mining centres with food and locally made manufactures. Yet Spanish America remained a rich prize for Spain's European rivals. Havana (founded and then relocated 1515–19) on Cuba's north coast, with its magnificent and well-fortified harbour overlooking the Florida Strait, had originally served as the assembly point for the home-bound *Carrera*. It became the dockyard and supply base for Spanish shipping in the Americas and the great naval stronghold guarding the entry to the Gulf of Mexico and Spain's American empire.[73] It was its strategic importance that made Havana a prime target to be captured by the British in 1762 – but returned a year later at the Peace of Paris in 1763.

The New World port towns and cities were thus vital agents of the European conquest and the Columbian globalization to which it gave rise. As transatlantic trade (including the slave trade) grew rapidly after 1700, their size and importance increased in proportion. Charleston's population quadrupled in the course of the century, New York's tripled between 1740 and 1790.[74] Towns like Charleston, Kingston and Bridgetown ceased to be mere 'shipping points' and themselves produced goods and services for local consumers.[75] The freeing of Spanish and Portuguese trade in the 1770s brought a 'commercial revolution' to Iberian America. But the Columbian world brought constraints as well as opportunities, setting the limits to port-city growth. The 'Columbian exchange' of animals, crops and diseases between the Old World and the New devastated the indigenous populations of the Americas, requiring a very long period of recovery. The reliance on slave or servile labour in the Caribbean and much of the American mainland further depressed consumer demand and the growth of internal trade. It also discouraged the migration of free labour, skilled and unskilled, from Europe. On the North American mainland, Native American peoples, aided by the rivalry between the British and French, largely confined the white settlement zone to the coastal plain, east of the Appalachian Mountains, between one hundred and two hundred miles wide. The prevalence of plantations and vast landed estates – the *latifundia* of Spanish America – was a further barrier to free white migration. The range of products for which there was a market in Europe was wide, but, except for sugar, tobacco and silver, the volume was small. Away from the waterways, only silver and a few luxury items could bear the cost of overland transport. And although Atlantic communications improved across the eighteenth century, trade and exchange were constantly disrupted by wars and rumours of wars – the result, as Adam Smith pointed out, of commercial as well as dynastic rivalry. Atlantic wars, the outgrowth in part of dynastic conflict in Europe, filled almost half the years between 1700 and 1763.

Colonial port cities could also be found in the 'Monsoon World' of maritime Asia. Scattered between the Red Sea and Japan were Portuguese, Spanish, Dutch, British, French and Danish 'factories' or trading posts, usually on the fringe of an older Asian port city. In a handful of cases, the European presence had become more entrenched, a permanent fixture in the Asian landscape: Goa, Pondicherry, Madras (modern Chennai), Manila and Batavia (modern Jakarta) were the grandest. Madras, on India's south-eastern or Coromandel coast, was founded in 1639 as the Asian headquarters of the English East India Company. It was the depot for the purchase of the Indian cottons that had become the Company's staple import from Asia, the prime source of its profits.[76] Madras lacked a harbour and its road-stead was dangerous in the winter monsoon. The East Indiamen anchored offshore and sent passengers and freight through the surf to the beach in small boats. 'White' Madras was a fort ('Fort St George') housing the Company's warehouses, the homes of the governor and the Company staff, and the minuscule garrison. Even including the garrison, the European population numbered only a few hundred, and many of them were Portuguese, Jews and Armenians. Outside its walls lay the more spacious residences of the richer Europeans, and the much larger 'Black Town' with its huge Indian population (per-haps over 300,000 by 1700), trading, weaving and labouring under the eye of the Company. Technically, the Company paid a rent for its lease of the city and its environs, and was careful to defer to the suc-cessive regional overlords, Golkonda and the Mughals. Superficially, Madras and its poorer twin, Bombay, acquired from the Portuguese in 1661, resembled the English colonies in the Americas, importing English law, religion and social customs. In practice they were com-pany towns in which no question arose of representative institutions even for those who were not employees but 'free merchants' trading within Asia, and where the law was what the Company's courts said it was.[77] By the mid-eighteenth century, Madras had become the embattled citadel of the Company's armed struggle with the French East India Company, based to the south in Pondicherry. Diplomacy and strategy now became its business, as much as buying and selling. It was from Madras that Robert Clive set out in late 1756 to restore the Company's claims in Bengal and Calcutta, and take revenge on Surajah Dowleh, the Nawab of Bengal, who had driven it out. The ironic result would be to turn Calcutta, not Madras, into the commer-cial, administrative and political capital of the British in South Asia.

In the Columbian era, Batavia on Java was the 'Queen of the

Orient'. Founded in 1619 by the VOC to command the passage between the Indian Ocean and the South China Sea, it was built as a fortress. For much of the seventeenth and eighteenth centuries it was the capital of a marine empire that stretched from the Red Sea and the Cape of Good Hope in the west to Nagasaki on the Sea of Japan. It was the base from which the Dutch enforced their monopoly over the spice trade of the Indonesian archipelago, driving out their competitors, like the tenacious Portuguese, who clung on wherever local rulers would give them protection.[78] Most of all it was the great eastern emporium to which the 'country trade' of Asia (intra-Asian trade as opposed to trade between Asia and Europe) was to be drawn: cottons from India, pearls and gold from the Persian Gulf, rice from Siam, aromatic woods and tin from the Malay peninsula and islands, copper from Japan, tea, silks and porcelain from China. The Dutch relied on their network of 'factories' to assemble the produce that would attract the 'junk trade' from Amoy, bringing the high-value goods they could send home to Europe, and, increasingly, to pay for their purchases of tea at Canton.

Batavia was laid out like a city in Holland with a grid of canals, and was surrounded by a ring of forts against the threat of attack from Java's interior. But, as in most of Europe's Asian port cities, its European population was a small minority amid Chinese, Javanese, Balinese and Bugis. Of the 70,000 people who lived in the city and its immediate hinterland in 1700, only 6,000 were Europeans.[79] Slaves from Malabar, Bengal, Sumatra and the Celebes (Sulawesi) made up half the population.[80] Indeed, over the seventeenth and eighteenth centuries between 200,000 and 300,000 slaves were brought to Batavia.[81] A community of mixed-race Mestizos arose – as elsewhere in Asia – from the unions of European men and Asian women. But, while the VOC relied on the continuing migration of sailors, soldiers, officials and clerks from Europe, Batavia's commercial success really depended on the presence of Chinese merchants, the great trading class of the South China Sea. Batavia became, in effect, 'a Chinese colonial town under Dutch protection'.[82] By the early eighteenth century thousands of Chinese had come to live in and around the city as traders and farmers, growing sugar in the reclaimed marshlands that lay south of Batavia. Chinese tribute and taxes helped pay the costs of defending Batavia. Chinese merchants administered the Company's tax-farms. Just like Manila (the model the Dutch may have copied), Batavia was a European fortress with a Chinese population.

By the mid-eighteenth century, the Dutch were on the defensive in Asia, facing competition from the British and French. Batavia itself passed through a major crisis when Chinese farmers revolted against the falling price the Company paid for their sugar. Fearing their own overthrow, the Dutch massacred some 10,000 Chinese living in the city. The Chinese returned: by 1800 some 100,000 again lived in and around Batavia. But the city itself was in commercial decline. From the 1730s on it was swept by devastating epidemics of malaria – perhaps the result of the deforestation and water pollution that sugar production had brought. The 'junk trade' from Amoy, the vital element in Batavia's trading economy, began to dry up as Chinese merchants and shipmasters preferred to frequent the 'free' ports and harbours of Siam and around the straits of Johore and Malacca. Worse still, the VOC now bought its tea direct from Canton and not through Batavia.[83] British 'country traders', based in India, undercut the Dutch East India Company in the nearby archipelago. The Company made up the shortfall by selling Indian opium in South East Asia.[84] Batavia itself looked increasingly inward as the Dutch presence on Java turned towards territorial dominion after 1740[85] – a change dramatically symbolized at the end of the century when the old city was abandoned in favour of a healthier site inland.

In Madras, Batavia and the other port cities that the Europeans had established in Monsoon Asia, commercial activity was largely concerned with the 'country trade', partly to pay for the goods bought for consumers in Europe, partly because its profits were vital to meet the costs of the Europeans' presence: their forts, shipping, garrisons and conspicuous consumption of both Asian and European luxuries. Quite unlike the pattern in the Atlantic world, Europeans were able to piggyback on a vast indigenous 'semi-global' network of trade and go into partnership with highly sophisticated indigenous merchant communities. Hence for much of the Columbian era their Asian port cities looked much less like bridgeheads, poised to assert an interior hegemony, than fortified factories, precariously perched on the rim of Asian states. And while Indian cottons were still a powerful magnet

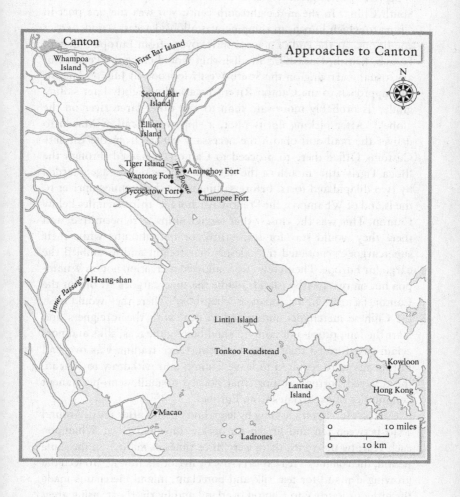

Approaches to Canton

drawing European merchants to the subcontinent's ports, in the mid-eighteenth century much the most remarkable of Asia's port cities was also one of its oldest: Canton in South China.

Served by three great rivers, Canton was the emporium for much of South China. In the mid-eighteenth century it was the one port in China to which European shipping was allowed access – under strict conditions. At the end of a six-month voyage from Europe a Dutch, French, British, Danish or Swedish ship would enter the Pearl estuary, usually arriving on the South-West Monsoon in July or August. The approach to the Canton River, remarked a slightly later sailing guide, 'is probably more safe than to any other large river on the globe'.[86] After picking up its pilot, a ship would call at Macao to deliver the mail and obtain the necessary licence from the Chinese Customs Office there to proceed to Canton. It passed through the 'Boca Tigris' (the 'mouth of the tiger'), a mile-wide passage guarded by two dilapidated forts, before sailing some thirty miles upriver to the island of Whampoa, the 'Yellow Anchorage' thirteen miles below Canton. This was the closest that foreign ships were permitted; and there they would stay for some three or four months while their supercargoes negotiated the sale of their freight and assembled the cargo for Europe. Their crews were allowed recreation not on Whampoa but on two nearby islands, while the supercargoes set off for the Canton factories in a sampan or 'chop-boat'. There they would meet the Chinese merchants authorized to deal with the foreigners and start the long process of sampling and buying the teas, silks and porcelain that formed their main business. Once trading was over, all Europeans were required to leave Canton and withdraw to Macao, the decayed Portuguese port that housed a small, semi-permanent community of expatriates from Europe.

Canton's foreign trade grew by leaps and bounds after 1700. Around 1740 between ten and fifteen European ships arrived at Whampoa each year; by the 1770s there were three times as many.[87] In the same period, the volume of tea exports rose by five or six times.[88] To feed the growing demand for tea, silk and porcelain, inland merchants made the arduous journey to Canton overland and by riverboat, using great convoys of porters (some 30,000 were employed for this traffic), and returning with salt, cottons and furs. In Canton all business with foreigners was supposed to be transacted by officially nominated 'security merchants' – the Hong merchants – one to each foreign ship. They were responsible for meeting the dues and customs that foreign shipping had to pay, and for ensuring that foreign ships and crews complied with the rules. As the scale of trade grew, the Hong merchants came to depend more and more on the credit advanced by foreign merchants: indeed, some foreigners arrived as passengers not to sell goods but to lend money at interest. For Canton was a remarkably safe place for foreigners to trade and lend. While written contracts were rare, few Chinese merchants dared to default for fear of official disapproval and the sanctions that followed. In fact, far from discouraging foreign trade or harassing foreign merchants, the 'Canton system' was designed to minimize friction, avoid the direct intervention of government, promote competition between local merchants and – above all – stimulate trade as a source of imperial revenue.[89]

Yet, for all its efficiency, Canton's trading regime was gradually approaching a crisis by the late eighteenth century. Part of the difficulty lay in the crowd of 'country traders' drawn to the port: they were much harder to manage than the European companies. Smuggling and other forms of illicit trade were harder to police. After 1765, when the British East India Company gained control of Bengal, its opium, sold at auction by the Company in Calcutta, became the great staple of 'country trade' commerce with China – despite the Qing ban on its import. To some outside observers, the solution lay simply in throwing open Canton to become a 'free' port, dismantling the apparatus of official controls. But the problem lay deeper. At its heart was the growing weakness of the great Canton merchants, the Hong. The trades that they dealt in were brutally competitive and profit margins were low. The European companies imposed a 'truck' system, forcing them to buy the goods they brought in before accepting their exports – a rule that often inflicted a loss, or pushed them deeper in debt to foreign creditors. Repeated conflicts in Europe led to sudden reductions in the movement of shipping and the collapse of foreign demand. In combination with the heavy burden of official and unofficial exactions imposed by the Qing state, the result was to cripple their reserves of credit and capital, so that bankruptcies were frequent. Far from creating a great merchant class to exploit foreign trade and parry the influence of outsiders in China, the 'Canton system' ended by dragging the Qing state into precisely the confrontation it had sought to avoid. For the moment, however, that prospect was only a cloud on the distant horizon.

THE COLUMBIAN CRISIS

It was not just at Canton. By the late eighteenth century, Columbian globalization was reaching its crisis. At its root lay the consequences, unintended and unpredicted, of the cultural, political and geo-political effects of ever-wider commercialization. The dangers of a commercialized culture and values had been the stuff of Cassandras since time immemorial: it was against this tradition that David Hume had directed his praise for commerce as a civilizing force. The argument against commerce was usually moral: in a world ruled by wealth (especially mercantile wealth), virtue and honour would go to the wall. Without rules against luxury, usury, a free market in property, or the dilution of elites by vulgar 'new money', the pursuit of enrichment and conspicuous display would destroy social deference and religious authority (the vital adhesives of under-policed societies), wreck the solidarity of lineages, castes and classes, and create the conditions for social war. These anxieties were felt even more strongly in China than in Europe. But there were other side effects that the Cassandras (and Hume) overlooked. In a fiercely competitive world, states and rulers could rarely disdain the revenues that commerce would yield, or the loans that merchants and financiers could offer. It was hard to exclude or escape their influence, or to deny their claim on military help if they were threatened by rivals abroad. Even in China, where the Qing carefully avoided recourse to public debt, the state still relied on the cooperation of merchants (especially grain merchants in periods of famine), and devolved its relations with the Europeans at Canton to a guild of approved traders. In Bengal and southern India the new Indian regimes that shrugged off Mughal control became more and more dependent on the profits and revenues that flowed from the links between Indian merchants, bankers and cloth-makers, and the European companies entrenched at the coast.

The greater the volume of trade, the larger the interests at stake, the louder the voice of those for whom any interruption of business spelt loss or ruin. And the more likely it was that new centres of power would spring up to destabilize the old and to reflect the changing distribution of social influence and wealth.

Thus commercialization could be the trigger for geopolitical change, or deepen its impact. In Asia the most dramatic example took place in India, where commerce and geopolitics interacted spectacularly. Under assault from the Iranian warlord Nadir Shah and his Afghan allies, the Mughal imperium in northern India had collapsed by the mid-1750s. Meanwhile, the rising Anglo-French competition for trade and influence in southern India began to hasten the shift from a commercial to a military posture by the Europeans at the coast. The East India Company began to build an army. But the turning point came when the Nawab of Bengal, mistrustful of the Company's influence and ambition, seized its main factory at Calcutta and imprisoned its staff (in the infamous 'Black Hole'). In earlier times the Company could have done little. But now it had an army at Madras and a seasoned commander, Robert Clive. It had the support of the Royal Navy in the Bay of Bengal. Most of all it could exploit the frictions and divisions in the Nawab's regime, the result in part of Bengal's rapid commercial development. At the battle of Plassey in June 1757 it was the desertion of the Nawab's key allies that won the day for the British. Clive and the Company pressed home their advantage. They turned Bengal into a puppet regime and then, de facto, into a Company-ruled province.[90] Within a few years the Company had extended its military power up the Ganges as far as Awadh. It inherited a buoyant tax income and quickly recruited a large army to match. It was not yet the master of India: formidable rivals like the Marathas and Mysore stood in its path. But it now commanded much of India's trade with Europe: the textile weavers of Bengal had become its subjects and were forced to accept the prices it offered. The Company typically paid 25 per cent below market price.[91] It controlled India's richest province, and the source of India's most valuable export – Bengal opium, a Company monopsony from 1773. It was, said Clive without exaggeration, a revolution, and one whose full impact in Asia was soon to be seen.

In the Atlantic world, the economic grievances of Britain's American colonies may have played their part in inciting revolt, but it was the size and strength of their commercial economies that sustained their resistance against Britain's naval and military power – and attracted the backing of France, Spain and the Dutch. The motive for French intervention was to reverse the humiliating defeats of the previous decade, including the loss of New France in 1763, restore France's Atlantic position and vindicate its claim to hegemony in Europe. But as it turned out, French success was a mirage. The British lost their thirteen mainland colonies in 1783, but not the bulk of their trade. Their naval power survived the French challenge. But French public finances slid into bankruptcy, and French politics into revolution. The financial collapse that Turgot had predicted for Britain was inflicted on France. It was the astonishing mobilization of France's domestic resources after 1792, the appeal across Europe of its revolutionary message, and Napoleon Bonaparte's military genius that transformed France's turmoil into a vast geopolitical struggle, in effect a world war.

Napoleon's first aim was to restore and enhance France's continental supremacy. But he was also determined to make it secure by breaking Britain's empire of trade, the secret of its naval and financial power and its lever of influence in continental affairs. His expedition to conquer Egypt misfired: it was seen by the British as a move towards India and was destroyed by Nelson's victory in the battle of the Nile in August 1798, cutting Napoleon's army's supply lines to France. His campaign between 1801 and 1803 to recover St Domingue (Haiti) from its black freedom fighters and rebuild the Bourbon's lost American empire fared no better: the French army was devastated by disease, the usual fate of Europe's military expeditions in the Caribbean. In disgust Napoleon sold off France's claim to the North American interior for what now seems like a song (at three million pounds it was equivalent to less than 10 per cent of the British government's annual revenue at the time): this was Thomas Jefferson's Louisiana Purchase of 1803. Napoleon's project now was a closed continental system in Europe to exclude Britain's trade, smash its economy, and ease the conquest of the bankrupted island. Nelson wrecked his hopes of invasion at Trafalgar in October 1805 by destroying the French and Spanish fleets, though not Napoleon's drive to be supreme in Europe. But by 1812 the draining struggle to enforce his economic system drove the emperor into the catastrophic advance on Russia. Defeat and abdication in 1814, and a brief second coming in 1815 that ended at Waterloo, brought what Europeans afterwards called the 'Great War' to an exhausted close.

A hundred years later, the end of another 'great war' was widely seen as the onset of Europe's decline in the world. The results of the earlier struggle were strikingly different. Napoleon's huge effort to seize the fruits of Columbian globalization, or, at least, to deny them to Britain, had set off a whole series of geopolitical explosions. His occupation of Spain in 1808, rudely dethroning its Bourbon king, created a crisis of legitimacy in Spanish America, where creole patriots demanded the right to self-rule. By the 1820s Spanish rule had collapsed across the Central and South American mainland, now, like Brazil, thrown open to British trade. The Louisiana Purchase signalled a colossal expansion of the American Republic, the most dynamic component of the Atlantic economy, and a great annexe of Europe. France's subjugation of the Netherlands prompted the British to capture the Cape of Good Hope on the route to India and China, and occupy Java. Java was returned at the peace: the Cape was retained, with its turbulent hinterland. Napoleon's failed occupation of Egypt hastened the rise of a new regime in Cairo: the over-mighty viceroy Mehmet Ali, who set out to free Egypt from Ottoman rule, and build a new empire in Sudan and Arabia. The impact in India was no less dramatic. Fear that the French might stage a return, or ally with the East India Company's most dangerous enemies, drove its man on the spot, the governor-general in Calcutta, into a ruthless forward policy. At enormous cost, but with London's approval, the Company defeated Mysore and then the Marathas, the great military powers of the Indian subcontinent. By 1820 the Company was paramount in India. It had already become the indispensable auxiliary to British power in the world, its sword arm in Asia. Its cocktail of opium and military power, the growing army of European merchants busy in the 'country trade' (between India, South East Asia and China), and the profits to be made in the tea-for-opium trade at Canton, were (or should have been) an unmistakable portent:

commercialization was bringing geopolitical crisis to China's door-step. Qianlong might have been able to wave Macartney away: his successors were not to be so lucky.

Already by the late eighteenth century Columbian globalization had served to strengthen and enrich the economies of north-west Europe more than anywhere else – those of Britain, France and the Netherlands most of all. Their commercial growth had begun before their trade beyond Europe had become significant, but it was super-charged by the 'inter-continental trade boom' of the seventeenth and eighteenth centuries.[92] Both Britain and France experienced an excep-tionally rapid expansion of their foreign trade: in the British case, trade with their American colonies made much the largest contribu-tion.[93] Shipping and the Atlantic fisheries, the export of metal goods and textiles, the refining and re-export of sugar (which France came to dominate), were among the many sources of stimulus that the trades with the Americas, Africa and Asia supplied. This was also the period in which the countries of north-west Europe vastly enlarged their stocks of knowledge about the rest of the world: cartographic, navigational, commercial, ethnographic and botanical. European sailors, soldiers, settlers, merchants and missionaries had marked out the lines of further advance into the world beyond Europe, even if, as yet, they lacked the means if not the motive to pursue their ambitions. But after 1780 many of the constraints that had held them in check began to fall away.

Indeed, between 1780 and 1820, much of the older landscape of Columbian globalization began to dissolve. The global triumph of British sea power, Britain's deliberate acquisition of key naval sta-tions on the route to India and China (the Cape, Mauritius and Ceylon with its great harbour at Trincomali – which the British had been eyeing since the 1780s – and the East India Company's new port at Singapore), its new imperium in India, the crushing of France as a colonial power, the end of Spain as a great mercantilist empire, and the rise of white-settler power on the North American continent: together they transformed the geopolitical conditions that had long governed the relations between the Asian states and Europe, and Europe's colonization of the American New World. In the British case in particular, the mercantilist rules and restrictions that Adam

Smith had lamented now became obsolete – though the political struggle to abolish them lasted for decades; the costs of empire had fallen; and the chance to push further and deeper into the half-closed markets of Asia and Latin America were all but irresistible. Geopolitical change was the crucible. But another, deeper, transformation was already under way.

3

Steam Globalization

'It is useless for men to stand in the way of steam-engines,' declared the American critic Charles Francis Adams Jr.[1] Between 1830 and 1930 much of the world was reshaped by 'steam globalization'. Steam was a 'general-purpose technology'. It was applied to manufacturing, mining and construction, and above all to transport and communications. It enabled the large-scale shift from wood to iron and steel in machinery, tools, locomotion and shipping. With its junior partners, gas and electricity (vital for the telegraphic revolution), it remained the dominant technology for more than a century and the great unifier of distant parts of the globe. Measuring steam capacity (oddly) in 'horse power' became a prime index of material progress.

Like other globalizations before and since, steam globalization imposed a distinctive hierarchy in global relations. Steam power placed a premium on cheap and accessible supplies of coal as well as the means to distribute it easily. Its application to manufacture and transport favoured those parts of the world where high wages encouraged both the resort to machinery and the location of industry near supplies of cheap labour – a vital convenience offered by steam. Geological good fortune and the precocious development of an integrated commercial economy combined to give Britain and north-western Europe an extraordinary lead in the application and development of the new technology, closely followed by the United States. Thus steam globalization, by its very nature, was lopsided, favouring one corner of the world and its North American annexe over all the rest. The 'great divergence' in economic performance between north-western Europe and the most prosperous regions in Asia, perhaps already under way before 1600, and clearly visible by the late eighteenth century, became all but irreversible. A new (and inequitable) global division of labour was entrenched, and with it a new cultural hierarchy.

There were many contradictions and paradoxes. 'Globalization' implies a free-trading, free-moving world in which economic efficiency is the key to wealth and power. But steam globalization was also an age of empire in which coercion distorted commercial relations and economic rewards. For at least half a century it coexisted profitably with slavery in the Americas and elsewhere. It helped to release a tidal wave of migration but also enforced new kinds of racial exclusion. It favoured cosmopolitanism but was conscripted by nationalism as well as imperialism. It was the catalyst of mobility – but a mobility constricted by technological limitations as well as politics. It represented universal modernity, but in practice produced different kinds of modernity in different parts of the world.

Port cities were the great agents of steam globalization. They expanded to meet its demands and exploit its opportunities. They were the beachheads from which its influence – commercial, technological and cultural – was expected to penetrate the interior regions behind them. How far it did so, and on what terms and conditions, we shall see in the chapters that follow. For port cities were also a frontier where seaborne trade, ideas and migrants commingled with inland peoples and cultures. They were the vanguards of modernity to some, a godless source of disruption to others. Their relations with the property and labour regimes of inland communities were ambiguous at best – bearing both the promise of profit and the threat of subversion. Their merchant elites inhabited the rackety world of commodity trade with its booms and busts, speculations and frauds. They required the protection of rulers and governors for whom inland politics or global anxieties were usually more pressing. In this uneasy setting each port city formed its own amalgam of the global and local, and devised its own version of 'steam modernity'.

COLUMBIAN LEGACIES

Columbian globalization had created many of the openings of which steam took advantage. But its overall shape had been very different.

For most of the Columbian era after 1500 the great Asian monarchies of the Ottomans, Safavids, Mughals, Ming, Qing and Tokugawa had looked impregnably safe from European domination, and European intruders (where they were not privileged guests like the Jesuits at the Qing court, or the mercenaries scattered across South and South East Asia) were closely controlled or confined to the coast. In the vast interior of North America, the geopolitical rivalry of the Spanish, French and British helped Native Americans to restrict the area of European settlement north of Mexico to the eastern edge of the continent. The European presence in sub-Saharan Africa was minuscule, and mostly to be found in slave-trading 'factories' or in the Dutch 'refreshment station' at the Cape of Good Hope. Before the first of Captain Cook's voyages in 1768–71 the South Pacific was a cartographic blur. Columbian commerce was similarly constricted. It brought Asian manufactures and luxuries, mostly cotton cloth, silks and porcelain, and increasingly tea, to Europe in exchange for a smattering of European products and rather more specie. It drew silver, sugar and tobacco across the Atlantic and sent back metal goods, cloth and a wide assortment of consumer items, including wine and spirits. Everywhere it carried the heavy burden of mercantilist regulation, limiting what could be sold where and in whose ships it could be carried, and bore the costs and risks of incessant maritime warfare. Buying and selling, or financing the purchase of, African slaves lay at the heart of this Atlantic economy, as did the apparatus of control and coercion that slave labour required. Technologically, this was a world held together by wind, wood and water – indeed Europeans have been described rather wittily as 'water-borne parasites'.

As we have seen, between 1750 and 1815 a wave of geopolitical convulsions dissolved many of these features of the Columbian world. But this was not yet a world made safe for globalization on European terms. Within Europe itself deep tensions prevailed. French ambition remained a constant source of unease, fed by the Orleanist revolution of 1830, French interference in Spain, and fear that the break-up of the Kingdom of the Netherlands would turn the newly formed Belgium into a French client state. The prolonged crisis of Ottoman survival between 1830 and 1841 threatened a strategic revolution in the eastern Mediterranean and brought Britain, France and Russia into a tense triangular stand-off.[2] Russia's expansion in the Caucasus confirmed its designs on Iran and Central Asia. In India, the Company state and its vast sepoy army kept nervous watch on the surviving princely states, on Ranjit Singh's powerful Punjab kingdom, and the turbulent Afghan frontier beyond. Its fragile hold on Indian allegiance lent a paranoid intensity to fears of Russian intrigue and Islamist plotting and prompted the fatal adventure of the First Afghan War in 1839–42.[3] In the late 1820s the Dutch faced fierce resistance in the prolonged Java war at the heart of their South East Asian empire. The commercial penetration of China, spearheaded by opium, shuddered to a halt in the 'Opium War' of 1839–42: how far the 'treaty port regime' prescribed in the Nanjing Treaty would 'open up' the Middle Kingdom was uncertain at best. Across the Atlantic, the newly independent Latin American republics were mostly too distracted by internal conflict and frontier disputes to open their borders or liberate their trade.[4] In the United States, despite the ruthlessness of settler imperialism, it took until the late 1830s to push the Indian nations beyond the Mississippi, and build the 'cotton kingdom' in the American Deep South.

In other ways too, steam globalization was indelibly marked by its Columbian inheritance. The imperial claims staked out before 1800 remained deeply embedded in the ruling mentality of the European powers. Imperial rivalry continued to shape their diplomatic relations. France and Spain might have lost much of their empires, but not the appetite to keep what was left and add what they could. For Britain and Russia, the defeat of Napoleon had been, among other things, a great imperial triumph, a licence to enlarge the colonial possessions of an earlier period. However, 'steam imperialism' had to take account of the uneven development of its Columbian version. In the Ottoman Empire, Morocco, Egypt, Oman, West Africa, parts of South East Asia and Japan, local regimes had exploited the changes of the later eighteenth century to build greater resilience to a European takeover. Here, as in China, Europeans were forced to rely at best on the 'capitulations' regimes devised in earlier centuries: the right to enjoy (in selected enclaves) exemption from local taxation and judicial authority. Meanwhile, the Asian merchant diasporas on which Columbian commerce had depended so heavily became more indispensable than ever. On the Indian subcontinent, the vast extension of British over-rule from its original bridgehead in Bengal had largely relied on local resources and manpower. The inevitable concessions that this 'collaboration' required drastically hobbled the scope of British initiative. The Raj from the outset was a makeshift affair that excluded any major reshaping of Indian society. In their settler colonies, the British similarly found that the wide degree of self-government conceded early on could not be retracted and must indeed be enlarged if a settler revolt was not to be risked. Settler mistreatment of indigenous peoples, the racial exclusion of immigrant 'others', even the recourse to protection and tariffs, proved beyond London's control.

Nor was this all. While free trade and 'free labour' had become the mantra of part of the mercantile world – in Britain above all – they were far from supreme. Slavery and forced labour survived across much of the world. Slave labour in the Americas supplied the raw materials – cotton especially – on which industrial capitalism in Europe built its global ambitions. Indeed a 'second slavery', the direct progeny of industrialization, was forged in the shadow of steam.[5] Even where slavery and serfdom were abolished, the social and economic systems they had fashioned retained much of their force, and the free movement of labour was closely restricted. Free trade was resisted across much of Europe and in the United States ('the system nominally called "free trade"', declared the American statesman Henry Clay, '. . . is a mere revival of the British colonial system')[6], and it was often enforced elsewhere only by the presence of gunboats. Two residues of the Columbian age softened the triumphalist edge of steam globalization. The first was the libertarian message of the European Enlightenment. Exported willy-nilly to the non-European world, it was the warrant for political, religious and racial equality, and contradicted the claim that European rule embodied European values. 'Un-British rule in British India' became the slogan of Indian nationalism. The second was the evangelical revival of the late eighteenth century and the missionary and humanitarian commitments to which it gave rise. Between these and the agents of Europe's commercial and colonial expansion, relations were frequently tense if not openly hostile. Missionaries and humanitarians typically saw their role as protecting indigenous peoples from unscrupulous traders, land-grabbing settlers and the slavers and ne'er-do-wells that frontier regions attracted. They offered visions of global fraternity in which commerce deferred to the claims of Christianity and 'civilization'.

The result was to leave important elements of the Columbian world embedded in the new age of steam. The drastic incompleteness of European empire-building still left much room for manoeuvre and bargain in the non-European world. It was still possible for Afro-Asian polities – like Egypt – to use commercial power to strengthen their states. On the other hand, in many places steam globalization arrived in imperial guise – most obviously in India – where European imperialism had fashioned a firm foothold long before 1800. There was also the unfinished business of slave emancipation, which whetted the European appetite for other varieties of coerced labour, like the 'indentured' workers from India and China bound to strict labour contracts and subject in practice to a 'new system of slavery'.[7] Settler colonialisms were already well-entrenched in the Americas, Australasia and, more marginally, southern Africa. Steam globalization would offer them new resources for rapid expansion, and enable them to shrug off much of what was left of imperial control, though not their dependence on migrants and investment from Europe. By contrast, the universalist messages of the European Enlightenment and missionary Christianity had both been forged in a pre-industrial world, and were in key respects out of sympathy with the coercive and colonizing tendencies of steam-age imperialism. The revolutionary belief in the common descent of all human beings and of their potential for equality, asserted in William Robertson's *History of America* (1777), was reinforced by Christianity.[8] European intellectuals corresponded enthusiastically with their counterparts in Bengal;[9] and European missionaries denounced what they saw as the degrading encounter of crude settler communities with the unspoilt indigenes whom they hoped to convert. But the 'noble savage' and schemes of universal enlightenment faced formidable enemies in the new era of steam.

STEAM POWER

Before 1830, steam power had made only a modest contribution to the emerging pattern of global relations. Until the crucial improvements pioneered by James Watt in the 1770s, steam engines were notorious for their extravagant use of fuel and were mainly employed in pumping water from coalmines in Britain, where fuel (often 'waste' coal) was virtually free. Between 1775 and 1800 Watt and his business partner, Matthew Boulton, designed and erected some 400 stationary steam engines for a variety of purposes – for pumping and waterworks as well as driving machinery. By the 1780s, Watt's engines and those of much older design, like the Savery and Newcomen engines (less efficient but much cheaper to build), were being used for pumping water, boring cannon, grinding corn and powering lathes. In the next decade they were being employed for spinning, calico-printing, as well as in iron foundries.[10] In Cornwall, where tin and copper mines created a large demand for pumping, Richard Trevithick's high-pressure engine competed strongly with Watt's low-pressure model.[11] Soon after 1800 there may have been several thousand steam engines in Britain (a French calculation in 1810 suggested 5,000 in Britain but only 200 in France). But the costs of coal and of erecting the cumbersome structure that the engines required greatly limited their appeal. In the fifty years after 1775, Boulton and Watt received only sixty-two orders from the European continent.[12] Even in Britain the role of steam in advancing industrialization had been tiny.[13] Until the 1830s more energy in the cotton industry had come from human muscle than from steam.[14]

The year 1830 was a turning point. By that time the potential of steam power for shipping had already been grasped. Robert Fulton's *Clermont*, a steamboat powered by a Boulton and Watt engine, had started service on the Hudson in 1807; the steamboat *Comet* was launched on the Clyde in 1812; and by 1822 an iron paddle steamer was at work on the Seine. In 1829 Robert Stephenson's steam locomotive the *Rocket* showed how Boulton and Watt's engine could drive wheels on rails to provide a (more or less) reliable mode of traction on land. The following year was the first in which the power generated by steam in Britain equalled that by the waterwheel, hitherto the prime source of mechanical energy. Thereafter, the advance of steam was rapid. It began to be used more widely in manufacturing, especially in cotton weaving, although even there the final displacement of handlooms was delayed into the 1850s.[15] Improvements in engine design and manufacture reduced steam's running costs, especially its consumption of coal. The result was a huge expansion in the supply of steam power. Measured in 'horsepower' (the standardized measure of output devised by James Watt in 1783), the amount available in Britain increased twelvefold from 620,000 in 1840 to 7.6 million by 1880. Comparable increases from a much lower starting point occurred in France (from 90,000 to three million), Germany (from 40,000 to 5.1 million) and Belgium (from 40,000 to 610,000). Even Russia, where steam had been very slow to take off, had reached a figure of some 1.7 million by 1880. In the United States, where steam had been applied early on to riverboats and railways, steam horsepower rose from 760,000 in 1840 to 9.1 million by 1880.[16] Indeed, it was striking that for most of the century steam power was used mainly for transport. As late as 1888, railways and steamships accounted for around 80 per cent of steam horsepower, except in Britain, where industrial demand predominated.[17]

Across most of the world the adoption of steam lagged well behind Europe and the United States. The main exceptions were found in British dependencies. One hundred and fifteen steam engines were imported into the British West Indies and put into sugar mills between 1803 and 1825.[18] In British North America, a steamboat service on the St Lawrence River linking Montreal and Quebec was pioneered in 1809 and firmly established by 1820.[19] The first railway in Canada followed in 1836. The first stationary steam engine arrived in Australia in 1813; local assembly of steam engines began in the mid-1830s and by 1840 some forty were in service. They were widely used for pumping in the Ballarat goldfields by the 1850s. The first Australian railway began operations in 1856, between Melbourne and its outport.[20] In India, the main impetus came from the East India Company, the subcontinent's ruling power. By the 1820s it was using imported steam engines for dockyard pumps, irrigation, a cannon foundry, printing, a mint and a sawmill.[21] By 1832 it had ten steamers on the

Ganges working the 1,000-mile route between Calcutta and Allahabad,[22] although the first railways had to wait until the 1850s. Meanwhile, the Company had launched a regular steam service from Bombay to Suez to carry its mails (and some passengers) via Egypt to Europe in 1830.

The anglophone bias in the spread of steam beyond Europe is revealing. While the basic principle of steam power was simple, its efficient application was much more demanding. Constructing a stationary engine was a highly skilled task. Its components, especially the boiler, cylinders, pistons and tubes, had to be made from suitably durable materials and (crucially) engineered with precision – a task best performed with other (steam-powered) machine tools. A steamboat or locomotive engine required a further range of expertise in the mechanics of the drive system, whether paddles or wheels, if the engine was to deliver the requisite horsepower. Designing the engine, whatever its use, assumed familiarity with a particular tradition of technical drawing that was noticeably absent in China. Even to maintain and repair an imported engine would require the services of a trained mechanic and a regular supply of components. Until the 1860s and beyond, Britain was the main reservoir of both skills and materials and the flows of knowledge and manpower reflected its commercial and colonial connections. Of course, these were not insuperable difficulties for countries that lacked a British connection. But they faced another constraint. For the adoption of steam power required both a benign commercial environment in which its expected benefits outweighed its obvious costs and a favourable ideological climate. Steam power was not just a technology adopted by cold calculation: it became a passion that bordered on mania. For perhaps thirty years faith in its promise (especially in Britain) far outran its performance. It is hard to think of anyone in the early railway age, concludes a recent study, who destroyed more shareholder value than the great engineer Isambard Kingdom Brunel.[23] Belief in steam power, and the willingness to pay for it, was as much a cultural as a commercial phenomenon – a point to which we will return in a moment.

Against this background, it is hardly surprising that the spread of steam technology in the Ottoman Empire and China should have been slow. For the Ottoman government in the 1820s and 1830s, defence mattered most. It began buying steamships in the late 1820s and was even constructing its own by the late 1830s. But the need to keep up with technical progress elsewhere soon forced it to abandon local dockyard production and buy 'off-the-shelf' instead.[24] Civilian use of steam power was also very limited. Steam engines were being used for silk production in Salonika in the 1820s, for cannon and rifle factories in the 1830s, and for an iron and steel foundry in the 1840s. But by the 1850s, many of these had failed against foreign competition, and the Ottoman exhibition of 1863, showcasing foreign technology, was the first sight of steam power for many local industrialists.[25] In China the challenge proved even greater. The first steamship visited Canton in 1828, but local observers assumed that it was driven by the heat of the fire, not by steam. The steamship *Nemesis* (after a disaster-plagued voyage from Britain) played a key part in the First Opium War, dragging British warships up to Canton and Nanjing.[26] It was closely watched by Chinese officials. But without the engineering tradition to understand its components or the method of technical drawing to convey its mechanics, the steam engine's workings remained a puzzle.[27] After 1842 foreign steamships became a more familiar sight along the China coast, and a foreign-owned shipyard in Shanghai had installed steam engines, lathes and planes by the 1860s. However, the first Chinese-built steamship (in 1868) was a failure, and the Qing government, like the Ottomans, gave up the experiment in home-grown technology in favour of foreign suppliers, with all the disadvantages attendant upon technological dependence.

Why did steam power matter so much? In part, at least, because it supercharged the growing divergence between the West (strictly north-west Europe and the United States) and the rest of the world in geopolitical power and economic performance. Steam supplied a source of mechanical power which (in time) hugely enhanced the penetration of the West and its agents into other parts of the globe. River steamers, railways and eventually ocean steamships brought inland regions that had once seemed inaccessible within reach of European businessmen, missionaries, diplomats and settlers – or made them seem so. They supplied the means for the application of force beyond Europe on an unprecedented scale and with tantalizing economy. Troopships and gunboats driven by steam were now weeks not months away from almost any conceivable target. The logistics of expeditionary warfare – always its greatest challenge – became decisively easier. Steam transport facilitated the dramatic increase in Europe's demographic presence all round the world, in the temperate 'neo-Europes', but even in places like India where permanent settlement was ruled out. It encouraged Europeans to conscript 'subaltern' populations of Indians and Chinese as the indentured labour for their tropical colonies. As the carriers of both mail and passengers – adventurers, traders and tourists – steamships and railways enlarged the supply of new information about hitherto 'remote' places, albeit often distorted by self-interest or fantasy: a feverish appetite for Eldorados and treasure, lost worlds and private empires, was one of the consequences.

Yet this expansionist impulse might have receded quite quickly had not steam power also equipped it with manufactures and machinery whose commercial attractions and scientific prestige proved highly seductive. Foremost among the manufactures was cotton cloth, perhaps the most widely traded commodity since medieval times. Steam-powered looms (there were some 250,000 at work by 1850 in Britain)[28] gave British producers a decisive advantage over artisan competition, especially where, as in British-ruled India, handloom weavers enjoyed no tariff protection. By the late 1850s cotton goods, (cloth and yarn) together with woollens and linen, made up well over half of Britain's total exports, and had increased three times in value since 1820. Between 1850 and 1885 the speed of looms, and hence their productivity, grew by some 50 per cent,[29] and cotton goods exports had nearly tripled again by 1913. The application of steam power was just as important in metalworking and engineering – the machine-making industry. Steam supplied the energy for an increasingly sophisticated range of machine tools for drilling, boring, grinding, milling, pressing and cutting metal, so that machinery could be built from standardized and precision-made parts.[30] Demand from railways, steamships and metal machinery stimulated the enormous increase in the production of iron (which grew fourfold in Britain between 1830 and 1855), and the mid-century experiments in the large-scale production of steel, which became the metal of choice in railway construction by the 1880s. This British pattern was closely paralleled by industrial development in Belgium and somewhat later in Germany, where chemicals and electricity assumed a distinctive importance.

Steam power had prompted a restless search for an ever-wider set of industrial applications. It was the leading edge in what had become a culture of systemic innovation.[31] A striking example can be found in the animated discussion in 1870 of possible improvements in steam navigation.[32] Steam catalyzed the application of other technologies. The telegraph line largely owed its adoption to the need to match the speed of the steam locomotive. Steam's insatiable hunger for coal encouraged the use of coal-produced gas as a source of energy and especially of light – improved lighting was a vital convenience in an industrializing world, extending the day's work into night. But steam contributed something else that accelerated the economic divergence of the industrializing world. Industrialization in Europe, and especially in Britain, might have begun on widely dispersed sites or in favoured pockets where water power was abundant. But by the 1830s and 1840s it was becoming concentrated in industrial regions, typically located close to one of the larger coalfields scattered liberally across Britain and (less prolifically) in northern Europe. Typically, also, those regions began to specialize in particular manufactures – cotton textiles, woollens, metal goods or shipbuilding. It was steam that made these 'agglomerations' possible, and agglomeration was a, perhaps *the*, vital element in the acceleration of growth and industrial innovation. When factories clustered together, so did the reservoirs of skilled and unskilled labour on which they depended. Indeed steam, unlike water power, made it possible to locate factories where population was densest.[33] Tinkering improvements and the spread of 'best practice' were much more likely where a large number of enterprises faced similar problems, and engineers could move easily from plant to plant. Infrastructure – like gas lighting – was cheaper to install. Repairs and maintenance were cheaper. Supplies of raw materials or fuel were imported more easily, and usually more cheaply, where a large concentrated market for them had come into being. A sophisticated commercial apparatus to buy raw materials and sell finished products developed more quickly where the demand for its services had reached a critical level. Information was cheaper and commercial behaviour more easily monitored. Agglomeration might even have helped to adjust the workforce to the strains of urban industrial life – if at a terrible cost in disease and privation. The classic example was the cotton industry in Lancashire.[34]

Except in northern Europe and the north-eastern United States (where steam only came to dominate in manufacture after 1865), the most widely felt effect of steam power was through railways, river-boats and ocean steamships (we turn to oceanic transport in the next chapter). From early beginnings in the 1830s, the world's railways grew rapidly over the century to reach a total of over 600,000 miles by 1907. Of course, this mileage was distributed very inequitably. A third of it lay within the confines of Europe. More than two-thirds of the lines in the Americas were in the United States. In Latin America, Argentina (13,673 miles), Mexico (13,612 miles) and Brazil (10,714 miles) were far ahead of the rest. Of the 56,000 miles in Asia, some 30,000 were in India, and a further 8,000 in Russian-ruled Asia, including the notorious Trans-Siberian Railway. China, which had almost no railways in 1890, had laid some 4,000 miles by 1907. Iran had just 33 miles. In Africa, South Africa with over 7,000 miles, French-ruled Algeria and Tunis with 3,049 miles, and Egypt with just over 3,000 miles, took the lion's share of the total of 18,516 miles.[35] These huge disparities are not hard to explain. Railway-building was for most societies a prohibitively expensive undertaking without the aid of outside capital. The enormous upfront costs had to be met – for track, bridges, stations, signalling, locomotives, rolling stock, fuel depots, as well as skilled and unskilled labour – before any revenue could be earned. Typically, it might take eight years (often punctu-ated by financial crisis) before a line made a profit. Hence, almost everywhere, railways required the support of the state, and the elites who controlled it. In Britain and elsewhere, legislative sanction was needed to secure rights of way against recalcitrant landowners. In many parts of the world the speculative nature of railway enter-prise demanded a subsidy from the state, through land grants along the line of rail (common in the Americas), a guaranteed return on the capital raised (the pattern in India), and by the conferment of monopoly to protect the investors. In France, the state bought the land on which the tracks would run. Even so, railway construction consumed a vast proportion of the capital invested beyond Europe after 1870: of British foreign investment by 1913 (then around half the world's total), more than 40 per cent had found its way into the construction and operation of overseas railways.[36] Over 70 per cent of Latin American mileage was foreign-owned in 1913.[37]

But how important were railways in opening up the landlocked interiors of the world beyond Europe and drawing them into a global economy in which bulk products (like grain) were traded and prices converged? Railway promoters were confident they had solved the problem that had restricted commercial prosperity since ancient times: the extortionate cost of inland transport. This became a cliché in the age of steam. In recent times there has been less agreement. It has been vehemently argued in the American case that, far from being indispensable to economic growth in the nineteenth century, even in 1890 the vast United States railway network contributed less than 2 per cent of the country's national product by savings on the cost of alternative forms of transport.[38] Against this startling claim, one response was to ask how much it would have cost to build the roads and waterways that would have been needed instead.[39] Another was to show that removing all railways in 1890 would have reduced the value of United States agricultural land by some 60 per cent, with a knock-on effect on output and population growth.[40] On a wider view, what made the United States unusual was its exceptional endowment in navigable waterways, where steamboats achieved a huge reduction in transport costs: by some 60 per cent on the Mississippi and Ohio rivers before 1850.[41] Where navigable waterways were lacking, the contribution of railways was far more significant. In India, where navigable rivers were largely confined to the north, the economic (or 'social') savings that railways contributed have been estimated at five times the American level[42] and the reduction of transport costs at up to 80 per cent. Across much of Latin America, navigable rivers were scarce and interior roads catered for pack animals not carts. Here railways reduced the cost of overland transport by as much as thirteen times, produced social savings of as much as 25 per cent of GDP, and were indispensable to the growth of an export economy.[43] The African scene (where railways were far rarer) would have been similar.

Of course, much depended upon the shape and management of the railway networks that emerged. In India, where the colonial regime was obsessed with security, many lines were built for strategic rather than commercial reasons, and some perhaps as much for private gain as for public benefit.[44] Grand 'trunk routes' were all very well, but what mattered to farmers and peasants was the building of branch lines to bring the railhead as close as possible. Density as much as mileage was what they needed. Just as crucial was the burden of freight charges that the railway companies imposed, which made all the difference to the farmer's income, especially when prices were volatile. 'Railway rates' were always a burning issue, most of all where the company enjoyed a monopoly. This is brilliantly captured in fiction in Frank Norris's *The Octopus: A Story of California* (1901). 'Can we raise wheat at a legitimate profit with a tariff of four dollars a ton for moving it two hundred miles to tide-water, with wheat at eighty-seven cents?' demands one its characters.[45] By their nature as large corporations, the giants of most local economies, railway companies wielded enormous political influence and were often suspected (not unfairly) of having politicians in their pay. Politicians' willingness to load the state with debts and guarantees, or to proffer huge land grants to keep the railways profitable, aroused widespread resentment. In India, the large debts accrued by the government's support for railway investment and its building programme fuelled the complaint that wealth was being drained out of India for the profit of capitalists in Britain. Railways could also be built to enable a port (or even a state) to capture the trade of a long-standing rival (or a neighbouring territory), with geopolitical as well as commercial effects. In many parts of the world the arrival of a foreign-owned railway was equated with the threat of foreign domination: it sparked the 'rights recovery' movement in China after 1900 that helped precipitate the revolution of 1911. Almost everywhere the spread of railways brought with it 'railway politics', and what was often lamented as the corrupting contagion of 'railway influence', what one cynical observer called 'railway morals'.[46] But not the least of steam's transforming effects was on the ways in which people imagined the world.

STEAM CULTURE

Visions of universal peace and progress, and the means to achieve them, had preoccupied the thinkers of Europe's eighteenth-century enlightenment. The application of reason, the assault on superstition, the systematic dissemination of useful knowledge, the freeing of the individual from 'feudal' obligations, would open a new era in human society. It was in this tradition that Adam Smith had attacked the 'mercantilist' restraints on trade. The French Revolution and its Napoleonic culmination (vividly expressed in the *Code Napoléon*) diffused the idea that the state and its institutions must be rationally organized to achieve their purposes, including material well-being. Together the Enlightenment and its revolutionary sequel, further reinforced by Benthamite utilitarianism, provided much of the inspiration for the European liberalism of the long nineteenth century.

The ideas of the Enlightenment had been formed in a pre-industrial age. But by the 1820s they began to be fused with an exuberant sense of technological possibility that derived above all from the excitement of steam. A new 'steam culture' began to make its appearance. James Watt was celebrated not only as an engineering genius but as a cultural hero, and not just in Britain. Statues and monuments began to appear. A statue was raised in Westminster Abbey. Meanwhile the capacity of steam power to transform the world was ever more widely acknowledged. In *The Steam Engine, Steam Navigation, Roads and Railways*, first published in 1827, the influential scientific popularizer Dionysius Lardner proclaimed that Watt's invention had called 'new pleasures into existence' and made 'former enjoyments' available to those who could not have hoped to share them. Nor, he added, had the effects of steam been confined to Britain: 'they extend over the whole civilized world; and the savage tribes of America, Asia, and Africa must ere long feel the benefits . . . of this all-powerful agent'.[47] By 1840 his rhetoric had become even more florid. 'Streams of knowledge and information,' he declared, 'are kept flowing between distant centres of population, those more advanced diffusing civilisation and improvement among those that are more backward. The press itself . . . has had its power and influence increased . . . by its union with the steam engine.'[48] The manifesto of the newly formed Institution of Civil Engineers proclaimed (in 1828) that 'civil engineering is the art of directing the great sources of power in Nature for the use and convenience of man'. The most important object of civil engineering, it went on, 'is to improve the means of production and of traffic in states, both for external and internal trade'.[49] Novelists were quick to take up the theme. Jane Webb's *The Mummy*, published in 1827 but looking somewhat further ahead, imagined the Egypt of the twenty-second century in which 'steamboats glided down the canals . . . whilst iron railways intersected orange groves . . .'[50]

The fusion of utopian ideas and visionary engineering inspired the followers of the Marquis de St Simon (1760–1825), the so-called St Simonians. St Simon was an early proponent of a Panama canal. Prosper Enfantin (1796–1864), a banker who converted to St Simonianism (and the cult of free love), went to Egypt in 1833 to urge the building of a Suez canal. For Enfantin the canal was a means to restore the spiritual and material union between East and West, a St Simonian obsession. The ruler, Mehmet Ali, mindful of British hostility to anything that might enlarge French influence in Egypt, would have none of it. The project was abandoned in 1836, but Enfantin's scheme lodged in the mind of a youthful Ferdinand de Lesseps, then a consul in the country. Another St Simonian, Michel Chevalier (1806–79), a former mining engineer who became the editor of the St Simonian organ *Le Globe*, was even more ambitious. He looked forward to the time when a traveller could leave Le Havre in the morning and embark the same evening on a steamer for Algiers or Alexandria.[51] In his *Système de la Mediterranée*, published in 1832, the Mediterranean was to be the 'marriage bed' (*lit nuptial*) of Occident and Orient, drawing its peoples together and reinvigorating a stagnant East. That required the Mediterranean itself to be unified politically and morally by a vast network of railways linking its ports and waterways. Great trunk routes would run from Frankfurt to Budapest, Belgrade, Sofia and Constantinople. Others would drive east towards Russia, awakening the 'somnolent Slav races',[52] and from Scutari (opposite Constantinople) to the Persian Gulf, with branches to Smyrna (Izmir), Tehran and Cairo. Chevalier imagined a future in which Europe 'would extend itself' into Asia through Russia in the north, Turkey in the west and the British Empire in the south. It may have been no coincidence that his son-in-law, Paul Leroy-Beaulieu, was the author of *De la colonisation chez les peuples modernes* (1874), proclaiming the economic necessity and civilizational benefits of colonial expansion.

For Chevalier himself, railways were the instrument of peaceful coexistence and he became, by extension, an ardent free trader. His greatest achievement was the Anglo-French free trade treaty of 1860, concluded in part to defuse the tension between the two countries. His negotiating partner on the British side was Richard Cobden, the foremost champion of free trade in Great Britain. Like Chevalier, Cobden saw free trade as the great preventive of war through the ties of mutual dependence, and denounced the reactionary influence of an aristocracy fed on the profits of military service, aggressive diplomacy and imperial rule. In 1836–7 he toured the eastern Mediterranean largely by steamship, and rejoiced at the growth of a Europeanized Alexandria through which Egypt's cotton was sent to the West.[53] Cobden, like Chevalier, expected free trade and steam power to promote liberal politics as well as commercial growth. 'Not a bale of merchandise leaves our shores,' he proclaimed in 1835, 'but it bears the seeds of our intelligence and fruitful thought to some less enlightened community . . . Our steamboats . . . and our miraculous railroads . . . are the advertisements and vouchers for our enlightened institutions.'[54] This was steam as the instrument of moral and cultural power, the decisive weapon in the peaceful conquest of the non-Western world.

Steam reshaped culture in other, more immediately practical ways. It transformed the economics of printing. The first commercial steam-printing machine was commissioned by *The Times* in 1814 and its wider adoption was initially slow. But by the 1850s steam presses were being used for newspapers and book publishing in Europe and America and in other parts of the world. The cost of books and other print products fell dramatically. The printed word became an everyday commodity and the range of information that was cheaply available rose astronomically.[55] Steam navigation brought the prospect of a frequent and reliable mail service between Europe, the Americas and Asia. This was seized upon by James MacQueen, a sometime Caribbean planter turned shipping entrepreneur. In 1838 he published his *General Plan for a Mail Communication by Steams between Great Britain and the Eastern and Western Parts of the World*, which argued that Britain's commercial interests made rapid and frequent mails essential. MacQueen's tract laid out in detail, and with costings, how such a service might work. It caught the public mood. By 1840 the British government had accepted the obligation to subsidize steam navigation across the Atlantic (the Cunard line), to the Caribbean (the Royal Mail Steam Packet Company), and to India and East Asia via Egypt (the Peninsular and Oriental Steam Navigation Company – P&O). In 1849 MacQueen's Royal Mail Steam Packet Company won a further contract to carry mail between Britain and Brazil.[56] The implications were not lost on commercial interests in New York. In April 1852 William Henry Seward warned his Senate colleagues that 'England ... is completing a vast web of Oceanic steam navigation, based on postage and commerce that will connect all the European ports, all of our ports, all the South American ports, all the ports of Asia and Oceania with her great commercial capital.' Postal foreign connections, he told them, were 'auxiliary to commerce, to immigration, to political influence and power'.[57]

A timetabled mail service (that also carried passengers) enabled information – in the form of private, commercial and official correspondence, as well as newspapers (an increasingly important item of mail) and books – to flow with predictable regularity and in much greater volume from one side of the globe to the other. It now made more sense for newspapers in all parts of the world to feature monthly or bi-monthly reports from a 'foreign correspondent' or news from 'home'. Travelling celebrities like Charles Dickens, Anthony Trollope or Mark Twain could recount their adventures to the news-reading public in something close to 'real time'. Fashions, whether literary, intellectual, or in dress, spread more quickly. The sense of distance diminished, and the immediacy of events far away (depicted in journals like the *Illustrated London News*, first published in 1842) became more pressing. But we should not exaggerate. It still took forty days for news of the great Indian rebellion of 1857 to reach London, even with the help of a telegraph line from Trieste.[58]

By the 1840s and 1850s, indeed, the telegraph line and submarine cable were providing an express, if costly, alternative to surface mail. Britain, France, Germany and the eastern United States acquired overland telegraphs during the 1840s and Britain and France were linked by submarine cable in 1851.[59] Long-distance overland lines needed frequent relay stations to maintain transmission, so that the first telegraphic link between London and India in 1865 required five to six days to deliver a message. Long-distance submarine cables posed a greater challenge: despite several previous attempts, the first successful Atlantic cable had to wait until 1866. Of course, telegraph and cable technology were based upon electricity not steam. But the demand for the telegraph had been hastened by the arrival of the railway, and laying submarine cables would hardly have been practicable without the steamship, let alone the mobilization of capital that steam industrialization had encouraged. By the 1870s a combination of overland and submarine lines linked Europe to North America, the Middle East, India, China, Japan, Australia, the Caribbean, South America, as well as East and South Africa. The times for transmission began to fall rapidly, from thirty-seven hours between London and India in 1870, to thirty-five minutes between London and Bombay by 1900.[60] News agencies, like Reuters and Havas, exploited the potential of the telegraph to supply more or less 'instant' news.[61] By the 1890s, as George Parkin, a leading campaigner for (British) imperial federation, remarked 'a new nervous system has been given to the world. The land telegraph and submarine cable ... have revolutionized the meaning of the terms "geographical unity" and "geographical dispersion" ...'.[62] The barrier long remained cost and the great cable companies like Sir John Pender's Eastern Extension Company would be roundly denounced for extortionate charges and exorbitant profits.[63] William Henry Seward, when American Secretary of State, despatched a characteristically prolix telegram through the new submarine cable to his envoy in Paris: the bill was three times his own annual salary.[64] By 1900, however, there were thirteen Atlantic cables carrying some 10,000 messages daily[65] and by 1904 the price per word on the Atlantic cable had fallen from $10 in 1866 to 20 cents.[66]

These new forms of mobility laid the foundations for a networked world. Jules Verne's *Around the World in Eighty Days* (1872) might have been fictional but it was not unimaginable. The timetables for trains and ships on which Phileas Fogg depended already existed. Verne himself came from a family of shipowners and navigators, and his story was larded with convincing details. *Bradshaw's Railway Guides*, first published for Britain in 1839, were extended to continental Europe in 1847, to India in 1864 and the Ottoman Empire by 1872 – and Fogg relied on his *Bradshaw*. From 1874 the Universal Postal Union established the principle of a uniform flat rate for mail to any part of the world, ending the need for payment in each jurisdiction through which a package might travel. By the 1890s a system of standardized time zones (originally necessitated by long-distance train travel) had been widely adopted around the world, although mainly for transport systems rather than everyday purposes.[67] To an extent inconceivable in 1800, the world had become an accessible place, even to those of modest means, unadventurous disposition, or a preference for 'armchair travel' from the comfort of home. Yet the results of this great cultural shift were contradictory.

One powerful effect was the re-imagining of distance. Regularity and predictability dissolved (and in some cases reversed) the sense of remoteness. By the 1930s, Prague was less than twenty-four hours by rail and sea from London, while New Zealand was six weeks away by sea. But that did not stop Neville Chamberlain from saying of Czechoslovakia that it was a 'far-off country of which we know little' – a phrase he would not have dared use of New Zealand. The idea of a global 'Greater Britain', unified by ties of culture and race, depended on this new conception of distance, as did similar dreams of a 'Greater France' or 'Greater Germany'. The idea of a 'Greater Britain', first aired by Charles Dilke in 1869, was promoted in J. R. Seeley's widely influential *The Expansion of England*, published in 1883. The sense (not just in Europe) of Europe's global centrality, its role as the motor of the world's 'moral and material' progress, was hugely reinforced. The scope for the commercial exploitation of what had only recently seemed 'remote corners' of the world in Asia or Africa became more immediate and its appeal more readily disseminated to an often credulous public. This was a world in which tycoons like Cecil Rhodes or the Belgian King Leopold could flourish through the black arts of publicity. But it was also a world in which the reverberations of distant crises (in China or southern Africa) threatened the fragile equilibrium of Europe's own power politics. The result, by the 1890s, was a feverish mood that combined imperial opportunism and geopolitical anxiety. Steam technology and its electric 'control system' was dividing the globe between a handful of 'world states', and the decisive moment (so it seemed) was approaching. These fears and hopes drew on what was perhaps the deepest and (as it turned out) most durable element of the West's steam culture: the belief that command of its (steam-based) technology confirmed its possession of a permanent cultural, evolutionary and racial superiority over the non-Western world.

Ironically, at the very time when this Europe-centred triumphalism was becoming explicit, its limits and weaknesses were becoming more obvious. Lardner and Cobden had assumed that steam would make the world 'flat': amenable to the West's (liberal) institutions and habits. But steam could energize other cultures as well. The spread of steam printing and a subsidized mail service into the world east of Suez gave local guardians of indigenous culture the weapons they needed to mobilize wider support against the threat from the West. Newspapers and pamphlets could be printed in Calcutta (in Persian) or Singapore (in Arabic) for faraway readers. Bombay's Muslims could strengthen its claim to be the religious and cultural metropole of a wide maritime zone from the Persian Gulf to Zanzibar.[68] Religious and linguistic identities from Egypt to Japan received a powerful and timely transfusion of cultural self-confidence. Steamship and railway made religious pilgrimage cheaper and easier, most obviously in the case of the *Haj* to Mecca. Returning pilgrims, *hajis*, freshly imbued with orthodox practice and exhilarated by a sense of religious fraternity, enjoyed great social prestige at home. They supplied the network of 'activists' who would purify the faith, mobilize the faithful, and reinforce their solidarity against the insidious temptations of other faiths and cultures.[69] Steam and print endowed the *Umma*, the worldwide community of Islamic believers, with a new infrastructure to meet the challenge of Western modernity. Buddhists and Hindus could and did exploit them as well.

This cultural resistance to the West could also draw upon an influential critique thrown up within steam culture itself: the argument that steam-driven machinery had dehumanized work, turned its workforce into wage-slaves, and condemned them to live in the insanitary, coal-blackened slums described by a host of appalled observers and by no one more vividly than Friedrich Engels in *The Condition of the Working Class in England*, published (in German) in 1845. Whether sexual morality, family life, or religious observance, let alone social cohesion, could survive in this bedlam was fiercely debated in Victorian Britain. A powerful tradition in radical politics urged a return to rural self-sufficiency, to give every worker 'three acres and a cow'. The romantic medievalism championed by William Morris rejected factory production in favour of the individual craftsman. Only by emigration to the non-industrial Arcadias of Canada, Australia and New Zealand, claimed the historian James Anthony Froude, could Britons be redeemed from the stunted and volatile mass that industrialism had created.[70] The genius of Mahatma Gandhi turned this depiction of the steam-machine world into a compelling manifesto against British rule in India. 'It is not the British people who are ruling India,' he declared in 1909, 'but it is modern civilization, through its railways, telegraphs, telephones ... The railways, telegraphs, hospitals, lawyers, doctors, and such like have all to go ... Machinery is the chief symbol of modern civilisation; it represents a great sin.'[71] In his *Hind Swaraj* (1909), Gandhi insisted that Indians could only recover the moral self-reliance required for self-rule by rejecting the industrial civilization on which British authority depended.

THE WORLD THAT STEAM MADE

By the later nineteenth century a new world had emerged, fashioned by steam and by those who commanded its power. The pattern of global exchanges had become strikingly different from that of the Columbian era. This was not just a matter of volume and value, although their growth was extraordinary. Between 1860 and 1913 the value of world trade increased from some £1.5 billion to £4 billion in 1900, and then doubled again to £8 billion by 1913.[72] It was the type of exchange that was radically different. North-west Europe had become the workshop of the world. It poured out a stream of manufactured goods for markets in Asia, Africa and the Americas, as well as in its own non-industrial hinterlands. Textiles, machinery, metal goods (rails, kettles, needles, cutlery, spades, hoes, ploughshares), firearms (a profitable trade), clocks and other instruments, chinaware, soap, candles, furniture and toys from Europe's factories, foundries and workshops displaced the products of local artisans elsewhere in the world by their huge differential in price or by their novelty. By 1899 all but 2 per cent of the world's manufactured exports came from nine Western countries.[73] The return flow of goods reflected northern Europe's new hunger for raw materials and foodstuffs: cotton, wool, timber, leather and skins, silk, hemp, jute, grain, sugar, coffee, chocolate, tea. Europe had become not only the most industrialized but also the most urbanized part of the world. In western Europe the share of the population living in towns of more than 10,000 people rose from some 10 per cent in 1800 to nearly 30 per cent by 1890.[74] (China's figure in 1890 was less than 5 per cent.) It had also become a vast exporter of people. The numbers are startling. In the 1850s some two million people left Europe as emigrants. In the 1870s the number was more than three million. In the 1880s nearly eight million. In the first decade of the twentieth century, the number exceeded eleven million.[75] Most of these went to the Americas, and a much smaller proportion to Australia and New Zealand; but together they were enough to increase vastly the share of the world occupied by Europeans. These figures were matched, if on a more modest scale, by the migration of Asians. Indians and Chinese travelled, usually as migrant or 'indentured' labour, to parts of Latin America, the Caribbean, Mauritius, Natal, Burma, Malaya, or Fiji and, until excluded, to Australia, New Zealand and North America. To a far greater extent than in any previous age, this was a world on the move, a world in which trade and commercial exchange penetrated more deeply and sucked in more people than ever before.

What had made this possible? In part, as we have seen, the mechanization of production had brought down the cost of manufactures in Europe wherever steam power could be applied. Yet the new pattern of world trade would not have developed so far or so fast without the revolution in transport that steam had induced. Railways, steamboats (of particular importance on the North American continent) and steamships were a major cause behind the drastic fall in the cost of moving goods across the world, which declined on average by some 50 per cent between 1870 and 1913.[76] This was of crucial importance not so much for the carriage of Europe's manufactured exports as for the return shipment of bulk goods – grain, raw cotton, wool, timber – with which customers in the rest of the world paid for their purchases of European goods. Nor would producers of raw materials have been willing to risk specializing in cotton, silk, coffee or tea for the European market (increasing their productivity, income and buying power) without the assurance that their own need for foodstuffs would be met by regular supplies from more distant food-growing regions, now linked by steamship or rail. Without the vast movements of people (and their labour) that steam had made possible, neither production nor consumption, and the trade that they generated, could have grown at such speed. Telegraph and cable played their part. Price information (a major element of telegraph traffic) could now be transmitted quickly and easily, and commercial decisions adjusted more readily, reducing the risk and inefficiency of long-distance trade. Already in the 1860s one Liverpool firm was spending the large sum of £1,000 a year on telegrams to the East.[77] The telegraph guided the movement of shipping to where demand was greatest. It facilitated – and cheapened – the transfer of credits and debits on which trade depended so heavily, helping to level out interest rates across the world.

But something more was required than a new technology. Steam transport demanded the mobilization of capital on a far larger scale than previously in peacetime. Railway-building in Britain had needed a manic level of enthusiasm (what economists call 'irrational exuberance') on the part of the investing public. The owners of railway shares had to be confident that (unlike most commercial transactions) an income stream would continue into the indefinite future, making railways as 'safe' as landed property. Railway-building abroad, and the parallel infrastructure of docks, harbours and urban utilities, needed a new leap of faith. It had to be funded by the great export of capital, since local wealth was rarely available to meet the expense. Investors in Europe usually preferred to entrust their savings to enterprises in settler countries, the United States above all, where commercial arrangements were familiar and the law offered some (but only some) protection against theft and fraud. British investors happily bought shares in Indian railways because there the (British) government of India guaranteed them a 5 per cent dividend against the revenues paid by Indian taxpayers. Nevertheless, in many parts of the world, railways were built where there were neither settlers nor rule. Europeans, with the British in the van, acquired large and valuable properties, to be owned and managed from Europe, on a scale hugely greater than in any previous era. Moreover, to make them profitable, they had to deploy a wide-ranging influence in the host countries concerned. They had to recruit labour – to build their railways and work their mines and plantations. That was not easy since control over manpower was always of great interest to the local elite. Hence the import of indentured 'coolies' was a common recourse. Railway companies were anxious to protect their investment by securing land grants and monopolies, and to ward off any pressure to lower their rates.

Then there was the question of expanding their traffic and remitting a profit. Both required the transformation of the local economy, to produce the staples that the world market would buy. Both required the extension of credit on a much larger scale. Growers who specialized needed credit to carry them from harvest to harvest. They had to be creditworthy, which implied the ability to pledge their property and a mortgage law to enforce it. Creditors needed a network of agents to sort good risks from bad. Exchange banks sprang up in almost every port to lend to agents and dealers, and to manage the transfer of funds to and from lenders abroad. But everything depended upon the export of staples to Europe. From the income these earned investors and lenders 'at home' could extract interest and dividends, while the producers (with luck) were left with enough to buy the imports they coveted. But commercial advance required almost everywhere the subtler penetration of cultural and political influence, coopting the local ruling class into modernizing the state.

The most striking examples of these processes at work could be seen in the Latin American states after c.1850. In Brazil, British merchants assumed a dominant role in the export of coffee, Brazil's great staple. British steamship companies supplied the main links with Europe and even entered Brazil's coastal trade. British capital and expertise constructed the main railway from the coast to the coffee district behind São Paulo. But all this required close links with the Brazilian elite, who were attracted to the prospects of agrarian wealth and to the promise that British-style modernity would help to unify what was still a loose-limbed and regionalized Brazilian state.[78] In Uruguay, where the railways, docks, tramways and banks were all British-owned, British ranchers led the wire-fencing of the plains and the modernization of pastoral farming, now focused on the British market. By 1890 the Uruguayan president could remark – perhaps a little dolefully – that his position was really that of 'the manager of a great ranch whose board of directors is in London'.[79] In Argentina, where British capital was also omnipresent, British-owned banks, like the Bank of London and South America, supplied credit, British merchant houses managed *estancias*, and much of the infrastructure of railways and utilities was owned and managed by British companies. Here, too, the local elite had grasped the benefits of adapting the law to this new commercial environment, and the social appeal (to large landowners at least) of aping the lifestyle of European aristocracies.[80]

Meanwhile the telegraph, mail and the greater ease of travel offered investors and creditors greater assurance that their funds and property were in safe hands. But the intricate links between the export of commodities and the flow of credits and capital encouraged an unprecedented degree of commercial and financial centralization in world trade. That central role was filled by London, the queen city of the steam age.[81] London was first and foremost a great marketplace for produce from all over the world, with free entry for most goods after 1850.[82] A merchant who consigned a cargo of tea or timber, sugar or sago, ostrich feathers or wool, from some distant port could be sure of a sale (the great exception to London's supremacy was raw cotton, for which Liverpool was the main mart). Buyers in Europe who wanted such goods could be sure to find a ready supply there. A great commercial apparatus existed to hire and fill ships, arrange marine insurance and manage the sale of the imported commodities. The London houses that did this forged close connections with overseas merchants through constant correspondence and (often) personal ties, cemented by visits or even by marriage. It was a natural extension that they should serve as the conduit through which credits were advanced to overseas partners and their clients and customers.[83] Because London received savings from many parts of Great Britain, credit was rarely costly or scarce. It was only a short step for some merchant houses to specialize in the provision of funds and then to act as the intermediaries for borrowers abroad seeking foreign investment from London. Investment like trade depended above all upon information and agents, local knowledge and trust.

The huge volume of business that passed through London was the best guarantee that goods and money were more cheaply available there than elsewhere in Europe, and information more plentiful. That helps to explain why, by late in the nineteenth century, a large proportion of world trade was financed through London without being landed in its docks. For similar reasons London was the source of around half the world's foreign investment in 1913, although a considerable part almost certainly originated elsewhere in Europe and was merely invested *through* London. London was the vast clearing house of the new world economy that had emerged in the 1860s and 1870s. Its primacy was buttressed by three vital props and a geological bonanza. The first was the widespread use of the 'sterling bill' – a credit note ultimately redeemable in London – for commercial exchange across much of the world (the role filled today by the US dollar). By 1913 some two-thirds of the sterling bills in circulation financed trade between third parties outside Britain.[84] The second was the rapid growth of the London Stock Exchange to mobilize capital in Britain and elsewhere for export abroad. By 1914 one-third of all quoted securities around the world were being traded in London.[85] The third was the remarkable stability of the gold-backed pound, which attracted foreign savings and encouraged the adoption of the so-called 'gold standard' – fixing currencies to a quantity of gold and promising the conversion of paper money into gold on demand – around the world. That would hardly have been possible without the colossal increase in the supply of gold from gold rushes in California, Australia, New Zealand, South Africa, the Yukon and Russia. Between 1801 and 1850 – before the great gold rushes – some 38 million fine ounces of gold were produced. Between 1851 and 1900 that figure rose to 336 million, and to 477 million between 1901 and 1925.[86] Silver production, too, also grew hugely, much of it from the American West. Indeed, the flood of gold and silver – both widely accepted as money in different parts of the world – was itself a powerful stimulus to trade and exchange after 1850.[87]

It is easy to see why the idea of free trade and an open door to the markets of the world was so popular in Victorian Britain. It had produced, so it seemed, the great wave of commercial and industrial prosperity that set in after 1850. Its champions insisted that free trade was the universal prescription for commercial success – for poor and rich countries alike. 'Few better securities for continued good-will can be devised than the mutual benefits the cotton trade affords,' wrote a mid-Victorian commentator.[88] It was the only means by which poor countries could attract credit and capital, advance from subsistence farming to cash-crop production, and fund railways and other infrastructure improvements. Its benefits would 'trickle down' from the landowning rich to the landless poor. Moreover – this was Richard Cobden's claim – it would encourage the rise of 'commercial classes' who favoured peace and interdependence and displace aristocracies whose archaic values were a prime cause of war. 'The battle-plain is the harvest-field of the aristocracy,' he declared, 'watered with the blood of the people.'[89] The diffusion of knowledge, increased personal freedom, the decline of autocracy and the spread of representative government: together they made up what for many Victorians was the meaning of 'progress'. The precondition for them all was universal free trade – what we would call 'globalization'. It stood to reason that those who opposed it had malign motives at best: to safeguard their privileges, exploit the poor, preserve retrograde values or defend superstition, idolatry and fanatical religions.

There was, of course, a darker side to the new global economy that steam had helped to create. Commercial integration brought contagion as well as contact. Mass movement by steamship and railway could spread diseases at lightning speed. The nineteenth century saw successive epidemics of cholera in Europe's port cities from the 1820s onwards.[90] Russia alone experienced six pandemics in the course of the century.[91] The increased number of pilgrims travelling to Mecca, and crowded together in insanitary conditions, created a large new 'disease pool' carried to the borders of Europe and then taken home by returning *hajis*. In 1866 an 'International Sanitary Conference' at Constantinople, attended by delegates from sixteen states, ruminated on the problem and agreed that cholera was being spread from India. 'The disease was propagated by man with a speed proportioned to the amount and rapidity of his emigration' was the sage conclusion. It demanded the inspection of ships leaving India and insisted that the disruption of trade through Egypt might be necessary to keep cholera away from the Mediterranean ports.[92] As immigrants poured into American ports, they offered a new host population to the 'saffron scourge' of yellow fever, which made repeated and devastating visits for the rest of the century.[93] At the end of the century, plague, endemic in India and parts of China, made an unwelcome return to many Eastern ports, including Australia's,[94] and spread as far as Paraguay and Brazil.[95] Commercial contagion could be just as disruptive. Once commercial centres were bound together by close ties of credit, any upset in its supply or price had repercussions that swiftly crossed continents. Wars and the rumours of wars, threatening the movement of shipping or increasing its cost, had a similar impact. The telegraph carried information at a convenient new speed: but it could spread financial panic just as quickly.

In fact, it was far from obvious that global free trade could promise a steady ascent in material prosperity – at least not for everyone. 'Trickle down' might mean just a trickle, and economies could stagnate as well as grow. Despite the fortunes being made there by the export of guano (a widely used fertilizer), most of Peru's population remained at subsistence level through the nineteenth century.[96] In Colombia by the 1880s foreign demand for its exports had been too erratic to sustain economic growth; no new middle class had appeared.[97] The global market, especially in major commodities like cotton or sugar, was chronically vulnerable to speculative booms and busts. Tropical and subtropical commodities (cotton, sugar, coffee, tea, tobacco and rubber) spread to new zones of cultivation – and new competitors. Slave-grown sugar in Cuba wrecked the trade of the other 'sugar islands' where slaves had been freed. Tea grown in Ceylon (Sri Lanka) and Assam gradually replaced China tea in the

British market after c.1870. Malayan rubber plantations replaced Amazon and Congo 'wild' rubber after 1900. Almost every tropical and subtropical economy tried its hand at cotton. Overproduction at one end (a bumper harvest), a drop in demand at the other, could bring a violent price fall, shipwrecking dozens of firms, starting a 'run' on the rest and threatening the banks on which they relied.

Reliance on foreign capital could be just as risky. As many borrowers beyond Europe discovered to their cost, the interest on their loans could prove dangerously high. A decline in their tax revenues or commodity prices could push them into default, for which the punishment might be a form of 'financial protectorate' imposed by the great powers – the fate of Egypt and the Ottoman Empire in the 1870s[98] – that handed over control of domestic finances to a board of foreign bankers and officials. Similar debt administrations were imposed on Tunis, Greece, Serbia, Morocco, the Dominican Republic and Liberia before 1914.[99] Adopting the gold standard and its rigid currency discipline might be seen as the warrant of financial stability, and the best way to keep open the flow of credit and capital for countries developing at high speed – like Argentina and Brazil in the 1890s. But the gold standard also brought risks. If London and Paris raised their bank rate to check inflation and draw in more gold, smaller economies on the 'periphery' saw their gold reserve contract, and their money supply shrink: depression would soon follow – and perhaps even rebellion.

Nor should we assume that London- or Paris-based capitalism was always benign, or that the capital raised there was invariably put to constructive purposes.[100] We now know much more about the financial malpractice that came with the phenomenal growth in foreign investment. Much of the capital raised in London, especially for mining, never reached its nominal destination, but was used for financial speculation or buying out rivals.[101] Mining prospectuses were notoriously fraudulent and samples of ore routinely 'salted'. A favoured technique of 'company-makers', as was observed at the time, was to divide up an enterprise once its capital had been raised, hiving off its assets into a separate 'subsidiary' and leaving the investors with an asset-free 'shell'.[102] This was particularly useful when unwary outsiders had a claim on the profits. It was no accident that the rapid expansion of the London Stock Exchange in the decades before 1914 inspired growing alarm about the new class of 'plutocrats' and the dubious source of their wealth.[103] In France, the Third Republic (*La République des camarades*) acquired an unsavoury reputation for financial corruption.

There was much less awareness of, perhaps even general indifference to, the impact of globalization on developing (what Western contemporaries called 'backward') countries. Where conditions were favourable, capital and free trade could raise living standards, hasten urbanization, expand the middle class, and bring greater stability to hitherto fractured states. This was the hope for commodity-led growth in Latin America especially. But much depended on who had control over land and labour. On the African continent this was particularly problematic. With the partition of sub-Saharan Africa in the 1880s and 1890s, new colonial regimes were created. Where no settlers arrived, a common practice was to grant 'concessions' (for mining, plantations or wild-rubber harvesting) to European entrepreneurs with no question asked about how they would find the labour they needed. This was the practice in French Equatorial Africa, the German Cameroons and Portuguese East Africa (Mozambique).[104] Its very worst features were seen in the so-called 'Congo Free State', the private empire of King Leopold II of Belgium.[105] The scale of atrocities was sufficient to create a huge scandal at the time. In regions where white settlers moved in (Kenya, the Rhodesias – modern Zambia and Zimbabwe – and, much earlier, South Africa), land was taken by force and labour conscripted by outright coercion or the device of a poll tax to be paid in cash. In the mines, conditions for labour were exceptionally harsh, punishment beatings commonplace and the death rate (five times higher than in contemporary Britain) appalling.[106] In the Americas, slave labour survived into the 1860s in the United States, and into the 1880s in Cuba and Brazil. In all these cases, slavery or serfdom was the corollary of free trade. Where indigenous populations were merely excluded, rather than incorporated as serf labour, and placed on 'reserves', displacement and dependency bred demoralization, alcoholism and social disintegration. 'The Anglo-Saxon,' wrote a shrewd late Victorian, 'has exterminated the less developed peoples with which he has come into competition even more effectively than other races have done in like case; not necessarily indeed by fierce and cruel wars of extermination, but through the operation of laws not less deadly and even more certain in their result.'[107] Thus across much of the world, globalizing capitalism revealed itself as essentially predatory, and alarmingly free from social restraint or moral anxiety in what were grossly under-governed colonial regimes. A minority of critics, with humanitarian or missionary connections, sought to raise the alarm. But to most contemporaries in the West, even thoughtful observers, the sufferings inflicted on indigenous peoples – if reported at all – seemed merely to be the 'collateral damage' incurred on the march to 'moral and material progress'. After all, they reasoned, shedding the bonds of primitive tribalism was bound to be painful. The fate of so many indigenous societies was thus to become 'morally invisible', necessary casualties in the forging of a new world economy. Indeed, it was widely expected that some indigenous peoples at least would simply die out when confronted by 'progress'.[108]

Steam globalization, like earlier versions, was the product of a geopolitical as much as a commercial regime. It was profoundly shaped by the global distribution of power. As we saw at the start of this chapter, one of the legacies of the Columbian era was an imperial mentality among the great powers of Europe. The facilities that steam offered for the projection of power sharpened their appetite for imperial as well as commercial expansion. Railways and steamships and an array of new weaponry (eventually to include repeating rifles and machine guns) lowered the cost and risk of armed intervention far from home. In the maritime world the lead was taken by Britain. Britain was best placed to take advantage of the end of the 'mercantilist' rivalries that had dominated the Atlantic world before 1800. Its sea power was second to none and its commercial fleet much the largest in the West. Its rivals had been driven from the seas in the 'Great War' of 1793–1815. By the 1830s industrial production at home had made the search for new markets beyond Europe a matter of urgency. Already in the 1820s London had negotiated treaties of navigation and trade with the new republics in South America to gain access for British merchants and protect their civil rights – with mixed success.

Under Lord Palmerston as foreign secretary (1830–41), the duty of government 'to open and secure the roads for the merchant' was acknowledged explicitly.[109] In 1838 a free trade treaty was forced on the Ottoman Empire and Egypt – its nominal dependency. In 1842 the Qing government in Beijing was forced to open five 'treaty ports' to foreign merchants and limit its tariffs to a nominal 5 per cent.[110] The 1858 Treaty of Tianjin wedged the door open even wider. In 1855 an Anglo-Siamese treaty imposed free trade on Siam (modern Thailand). In 1858, alongside Russia, the Netherlands and the United States, London secured a treaty port in Japan at Yokohama, and soon after the promise of free trade.[111] In all these (eastern) places, foreign merchants enjoyed an exemption from local jurisdiction and taxes. These were one-sided arrangements (there was no reciprocity) that reflected the disparities of physical power.

The British enjoyed another grand asset: their rule over India. It was the main base from which they could exert their power over the vast maritime realm between the Cape and Japan, from Suez to Yokohama. Soldiers sent from India were the vital auxiliary to the 'gunboat diplomacy' deployed in East Asia and across the Indian Ocean world. The Great Rebellion of 1857 had been a massive crisis that took nearly three years to suppress. The East India Company government was abolished (though not its administrative machine in India) in favour of closer control from London. The size of the pre-Rebellion all-British garrison was more than doubled in size and that of the old Indian army cut down by half. The effect, after 1860, was that the Indian taxpayer met the ordinary costs of some two-thirds of Britain's professional armies: the large (all-British) garrison in India – around 70,000 men – and the separate British-officered Indian Army 140,000 strong.[112] On India, too, the British enforced free trade, so that it became the largest customer for their largest export, cotton cloth. Once the foot-dragging East India Company was pushed aside in 1858, the Indian government promoted railway-building with a will, with the aim of transforming the subcontinent into a producer of staples: raw cotton, wheat, indigo, jute – and opium. India's overseas exports, much of which went to markets other than Britain, earned foreign currency that was then remitted to London to pay the 'Home Charges' – the 'rent' India paid for its British garrison; the interest on its large railway debt; and the cost of the pensions paid to British officials and soldiers. India's foreign earnings, drawn on in this way, made a key contribution to Britain's balance of payments, and thus the strength of the pound sterling.[113]

The British led the way but they were not alone. For much of the nineteenth century, France also pursued a combination of formal and informal empire: in the Mediterranean and North Africa; in sub-Saharan West Africa; and in South East Asia. Despite much jostling and an occasional revolt (as in 1840 and 1898), France broadly accepted its status as the junior partner to Britain in a 'global condominium'.[114] German aspirations to global influence by the 1880s were a complication, but not – apparently – fatally so until 1914. The United States, secure in its sphere (and even more so after 1898 with the removal of Spain from the Caribbean), also seemed willing to acknowledge British leadership at the global level so long as its special status in the western hemisphere was conceded.[115] The 'odd man out' was Russia, advancing overland across North Asia and largely impervious to seaborne coercion. For the British in particular, with their uneasy Raj, its open north-west frontier, and their long, exposed, sea corridor from Gibraltar to Bombay, any Russian advance towards the Dardanelles, Persia, the Gulf, Afghanistan or Tibet was a strategic nightmare in the making. Russia's ambitions in the Pacific and for influence in China were signalled in the Treaty of Aigun in 1858 (by which China conceded control over the Amur Valley) and the founding of Vladivostok ('Sea-Cucumber Cliffs' was its Chinese name) in 1859–60. 'England displays its power with gold,' remarked the Russian viceroy in the Caucasus at mid-century. 'Russian which is poor in gold has to compete with force of arms.'[116] But even Russia accepted the need for a working relationship with Europe's maritime powers and its ruling elite adopted the same ethos and values used by western Europeans to justify their imperial expansion.[117]

The result was a regime of 'competitive co-existence' by which all the main European powers sought to advance their non-European interests without recourse to an open war between themselves. This caution was rooted in their refusal to risk the balance of power in Europe for the sake of colonial gains: hence the only conflicts fought over colonial issues were those between Spain and the United States and Russia and Japan. The consequences of this prudential restraint were far-reaching. The ideological solidarity of the European states was striking: no great power repudiated the morality of empire or urged the case for racial equality. There was general agreement that it was legitimate to intervene in states which failed to keep order and protect the lives and property of foreigners. All the great powers accepted the freedom of navigation on the high seas and, by mid-century, the limitation of territorial waters to a cannon shot from shore – conventionally three miles.[118] Under their pressure, the two great gateways to South America, the Paraná and Amazon rivers, were opened to all shipping (in 1853 and 1866–7); and China's Yangzi after 1862. They shared, if not without friction, the privileges of extraterritoriality imposed on the Ottoman Empire, Morocco, Egypt, Persia, Siam, China and Japan (until 1899), and allowed their extension to other Western states, including some South Americans. But the most striking evidence of their grudging cooperation was the 'peaceful' (not of course to the indigenous peoples) partitions of Africa, the Pacific and South East Asia. Even in Africa, where the 'scramble' between an assortment of European adventurers, entrepreneurs, filibusters, career-building army officers and visionary sub-imperialists (the most famous being Cecil Rhodes) was fiercest, ministers in Paris, Berlin and London sought lines of partition, mainly to soothe importunate lobbies at home and restrain the headstrong 'men on the spot' before rivalry led to an irreparable breach. It was partition diplomacy, not imperial design, that allowed much of tropical Africa to be ruled on a shoestring with minimal governance. The price of this cost-cutting convenience was paid by subject populations in exploitation and abuse at the hands of European settlers, traders and miners in what was, for the most part, an administrative vacuum.

By the end of the century, this extraordinary geopolitical regime had helped to establish a globalization largely on European terms. It became a commonplace that the world was now a 'closed system': there were no new 'empty lands' left to occupy; the frontiers had been reached. The future in 1900 seemed to belong to a handful of 'world states' dividing the globe into overlapping spheres of influence. The non-Western world seemed destined to remain indefinitely in forms of tutelage or economic dependence. There was little reason to think that Afro-Asian resistance could disrupt the domination of the colonial powers: the one great exception was Japan, whose sudden ascent to (almost) great-power status after victory over Russia in 1905 amazed Asian onlookers and alarmed Europeans.

Indeed, some of the most virulent critics of capitalist imperialism were resigned to the fact that the imperialist states would always find ways to settle their differences.[119] Yet to an extent largely hidden from contemporary observers, this imperial geopolitics turned out to contain an enormous – and fatal – flaw. It was the unfinished business of partition diplomacy on Europe's own doorstep that threatened the stability of its continental politics. It was the failure to manage the collapse of Ottoman rule in the Balkans that ignited the explosion of 1914 and was – eventually – to destroy the global regime on which steam globalization had depended so heavily.

Such was the outward shape of the Victorian globe. But, as we shall see, this global perspective dissolves on closer inspection into a complex landscape of acceptance, adaptation, resistance or even revolt. It was in the world's port cities and in the 'back countries' behind them that the struggle to impose the West's 'steam modernity' had really to be waged.

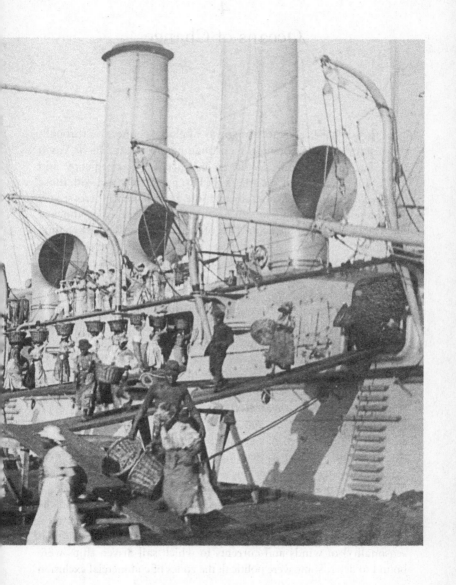

Coaling Ship at Suez. Women and children did much of the work, all of it deployed by hand; hours were long and conditions perilous in the service of commercial exchange.

4

Oceans of Change

That the sea has been a great highway of global connection through-out history seems an obvious fact. Long before Columbus or Vasco da Gama, the sea connected the great concentrations of people and wealth in the 'monsoon' coastlands of East and South Asia with those on the coastlands of Europe, through the great terrestrial crossroads of Middle Eurasia – the modern Middle East. Once Europe annexed the Americas, they too became part of a maritime network stretching around the world, to slave markets in Africa and silver-buyers in Asia. Today, when some 90 per cent of world trade is carried in ships, it is clear that our globalized economy depends to an extraordinary extent upon this seaborne traffic. The sea, we might conclude, has been the vital instrument of our globalizations, old and new.

Yet to imagine the sea as merely a highway is to miss most of its importance in history. 'Highway' suggests a broad stream of traffic moving between two destinations. The sea was never like that. In many parts of the world, it was more like a dense web of sea paths criss-crossing each other, linking a myriad of ports, roadsteads and trading beaches. Even these left much of the watery globe empty of all human activity, a barren and terrifying desert. More to the point, communication by sea has always been subject to changing condi-tions that have helped to determine the shape and scope of global exchange in any particular era. Some of those conditions have been physical or environmental: the configuration of continents that for long forced direct navigation between Europe and Asia around the Cape of Good Hope, and made Cape Horn the storm-lashed gate-way to the Pacific coast of the Americas; the peculiar geography (and seasonality) of winds and currents to which sail-driven ships were bound to defer. Some were political: the zones of commercial exclusion enforced at various times by the Portuguese, Spanish, Dutch, French and British; the close restraints upon maritime access imposed by Chinese, Japanese or Ottoman rulers. Some were the product of disorder and violence: the naval warfare that convulsed the early modern Mediterranean, the eighteenth-century Atlantic and much of the early twentieth-century world, making fortunes for some, inflicting great loss upon others; or the pirate zones that flourished in the seventeenth-century Caribbean, around the coasts of North Africa (until the 1820s), and in the Persian Gulf and the South China Sea. And some derived mainly from the limits of technology and maritime knowledge, or the commercial appeal of certain commodities – precious metals, luxury fabrics, foodstuffs and drugs. At any particular time this maritime cocktail of environment, technology, commerce and politics favoured some routes over others, some ports over others, some trades over others. It pulled some places together and pushed others apart.

The pattern was rarely settled for long. The advance of maritime knowledge, new shipping technologies, a new order at sea, a change of regime on land, or novel consumer demands could alter, perhaps radically, the global distribution of shipping and naval power, the preference for sea lanes, the choice between ports, the links between places. We can see these great shifts at work across the length of world history. In our own day, the container ship has transformed the economics of sea transport (and thus the scale of commercial globalization). The slower transformation from the sailing-ship world to the world of the steamship across the nineteenth century was no less consequential.

THE SAILING-SHIP WORLD

The art of navigation with sails may be at least seven thousand years old. The oldest image of a sailing ship dates from some time before 3100 BC.[1] However, reliance on wind, current and tide imposed certain distinct limitations on oceanic navigation. The most obvious was time and time-keeping. While certain sea passages could offer a high degree of predictability (depending on season), most seaborne travellers had to reconcile themselves to delays caused by contrary winds or (worse still) periods of calm that might last for weeks.[2] Escaping from the English Channel against the prevailing westerlies was often a struggle – one reason why Plymouth became a key naval base, reducing the risk of warships being trapped further east in the Channel. Sailing times depended on favourable winds and the help of currents, but also demanded a circuitous route to find the wind and maintain steering way. Wind and current also determined the sequence of ports at which a sailing ship called, affecting their access to news and their place in the regional hierarchy of ports of call.[3] The weeks and months needed to accomplish a journey later completed in days by a steamship or in hours by plane imposed extra costs, not least the necessity of carrying large quantities of water, food and fuel in case of unexpected delay. They also increased the likelihood of encountering bad weather on some part of the voyage. Nevertheless, as we will see later on, the sailing ship remained the great carrier of freight from one side of the world to the other until late in the nineteenth century.

We should keep in mind, of course, that the sailing ships engaged in long-distance voyages across thousands of miles made up only a fraction – perhaps a minute fraction – of all the sailing craft afloat. In any harbour, around the barques and brigs and other fully rigged ships, or the large junks and *pralas* of the eastern seas, would have clustered dozens if not hundreds of much smaller craft, plying in estuaries and deltas, or along nearby coasts in the short-haul navigation called *cabotage*. Here could be seen an almost infinite variety of hull shapes and sailing rigs. Large numbers of sailing craft were also engaged in fishing or other maritime foraging, like the harvesting of pearls in the Persian Gulf. While larger sailing ships embodied a considerable investment and carried cargoes that depended on credit and capital, many smaller ships were closer to being part of a marine 'subsistence economy'. The cost of the ship would be modest and its navigational equipment exiguous. Their crews would depend less on wages than on the right to trade small amounts of goods between a series of landfalls. Their lives would be spent in toil at sea, much as the land-bound peasant or labourer spent his in his fields. This way of life, brilliantly depicted in Alan Villiers's account of the dhow trade between the Persian Gulf and East Africa,[4] was probably typical of much of the maritime world in Asia and Africa before 1900.

By the later nineteenth century it was becoming easy to think of the world's oceans as a single space, offering unrestricted access to every port in the globe. 'The one and continuous ocean,' remarked the influential English geographer Halford Mackinder in 1904, '. . . is . . . the geographical condition of ultimate unity in the command of the sea . . .'[5] 'The sea is the world's great medium of circulation,' wrote the American admiral Alfred Mahan, urging a more active naval policy upon Washington in 1893.[6] The atlases of the day displayed globe-spanning sea lanes, and tables that listed the days required to travel from Europe (forty-seven days from London to Wellington in New Zealand). Much of the knowledge that had made this possible was laboriously accumulated in the hydrographic surveys in which the Royal Navy took the lead: its hydrographic department was established in 1795, and by 1829 Francis Beaufort (of the 'Beaufort Scale') was in charge. The main purpose of the voyage of HMS *Beagle* (1831–6), which carried Charles Darwin round the world, was 'to survey the shores of Chile, Peru and some islands in the Pacific'.[7] In fact, Darwin's famous *Journal* was first published as the third volume of the official *Narrative of the Surveying Voyages of HMS Adventure and Beagle between the Years 1826 and 1836.* In the 1840s surveys began of China's coastal waters, Sir John Franklin was sent on his doomed expedition to search for the North-West Passage, and a series of ships were despatched to survey the Great Barrier Reef (a famed shipping hazard since the time of Captain Cook) and the Coral Sea to the north of Australia (taking Thomas Huxley as its naturalist).[8] A whole library of Admiralty charts and 'Pilots' supplied detailed soundings and descriptions of coastlines and harbours made available to commercial shipping – a venture complemented by the beginnings of deep-sea oceanography, an American specialism.[9]

For the steamship, the sea was mainly an element through which to force its way on the shortest route between two ports. The sailing-ship world was quite different from this. It required an intricate knowledge of winds and currents in all their seasonal variations, the signs of storms and squalls that could arrive without warning, the hazards of coasts and landfalls, often poorly recorded on available charts, the risk of attack by pirates and predators, the location of water and food supplies in case of delay, and the prospects of a profitable cargo in an age before telegraphic communication. One result was the appalling death rate suffered by sailing-ship seafarers: by one calculation more than one hundred and fifty times that of contemporary factory workers: the age of sail was 'an age of mass death'.[10] For the sailing ship, the sea was less 'one continuous ocean' than a set of distinct 'seascapes': in which climatic, geopolitical and commercial conditions combined with physical configuration to create a series of unique maritime environments. Each one was to change – in some cases dramatically – between the 1830s and the 1870s.

The three eastern seas were ruled by the monsoon, blowing northeast towards Inner Asia in summer and south-west in winter: the South China Sea that connected China, mainland South East Asia and the vast Indonesian archipelago with its more than twenty thousand islands; the Bay of Bengal (colloquially 'the Bay'); and the Arabian Sea or western Indian Ocean with its Indian, Arabian and East African coastlands. Except for a few local steamers and the subsidized mail boats, running from Suez to Bombay and Calcutta and by the mid-1840s onwards to China, this remained the realm of the sailing ship deep into the 1870s, even after the opening of the Suez Canal in 1869. European- and American-owned shipping controlled the long-haul trades between the Afro-Asian coastlands and Western ports. But old commercial ties between the Middle East, East Africa and India, and between India, South East Asia and China, survived and flourished. These and the complexity of navigation, especially in the Red Sea, the Persian Gulf and Indonesian archipelago, largely uncharted until well into the century, favoured local ships and shipmen. Chinese junks, with their great square sails stiffened by bamboo, continued to sail from Amoy (Xiamen) in Fujian to buy rice in Cochin-China (today's southern Vietnam) and Siam (modern Thailand), and the forest and marine products of the archipelago: sea slugs, pearls, tortoiseshell, sharks' fins, camphor and ebony. Bugis *prahus* (or *proas*) from Makassar in Celebes (Sulawesi), with their lateen sails and distinctive tripod masts, traded between the islands, collecting this produce: the naturalist Alfred Russel Wallace used them in his travels in the 1850s.[11]

Indian-owned ships from Kathiawar in western India carried cottons to East Africa in exchange for ivory and also slaves – a trade that lasted into the 1840s.[12] Lateen-rigged dhows, baggalas and booms from the Persian Gulf and Oman carried dates and salt to East Africa, bringing back ivory, slaves and mangrove poles to the wood-starved Gulf. With a favourable wind, a baggala could sail from Muscat in Oman to Zanzibar, the great entrepôt of East Africa, in a fortnight.[13]

But if older patterns of shipping and trade continued, political change was dramatic and rapid. By retaining Cape Colony and Ceylon (Sri Lanka), both seized from the Dutch in the wars of 1793–1815, as well as Mauritius (taken from the French), the British ensured that no European rival could challenge their maritime primacy in the seas east of Suez. Piracy (a serious problem in the South China Sea), not naval war, now became the main human threat to merchant shipping.[14] The 'opening' of China after 1842 turned the South China Sea into a corridor not just to Canton and Amoy but to Shanghai, North China and even Japan, where 'opening' began in 1858 with a treaty port at Yokohama. By 1860, with the suppression of the 1857 rebellion, British rule was paramount across the whole Indian subcontinent, and the end of the East India Company *raj* created a new colonial regime (answerable to a cabinet minister) that was much more responsive to London's (and Lancashire's) commercial interests. In a series of wars, Burma was absorbed piecemeal into British India: Arakan and Tenasserim in 1826; Pegu with what became the great port at Rangoon in 1852 and the remainder of Burma in 1885. Teak, rice and (later) oil became its staples. Siam (another great rice producer) was opened to free trade in 1855. The Persian Gulf became all but a (turbulent) British lake from the 1830s onwards.[15] The British seized Aden and the gate to the Red Sea in 1839, and had turned the Omani sultans of Zanzibar into reluctant clients from the 1840s with the forced abandonment of their profitable slave trade. Even so, in the 1880s, vast tracts of East Africa, Arabia, South East Asia and inland China remained well outside the direct control of the European empires and their commercial outriders.

The Atlantic was a different world entirely. The North Atlantic lay at western Europe's front door. It linked two continents whose populations and wealth were both growing rapidly. The population of the

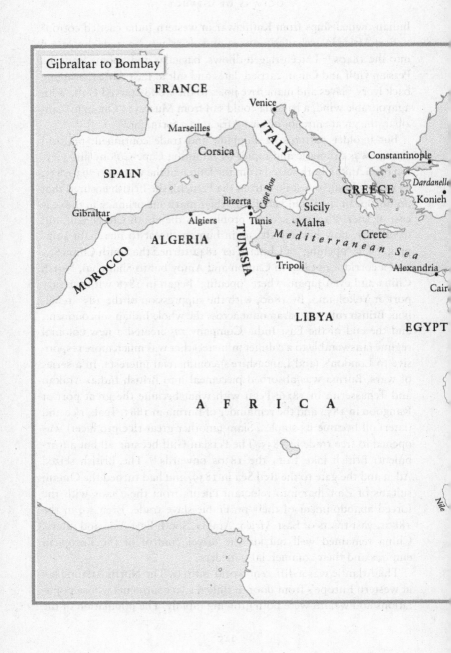

Gibraltar to Bombay

FRANCE

Venice

Marseilles

Corsica

ITALY

SPAIN

Constantinople

Dardanelle

GREECE

Gibraltar

Bizerta

Cape Bon

Sicily

Malta

Crete

Konieh

Algiers

Tunis

MOROCCO

ALGERIA

TUNISIA

Tripoli

Mediterranean Sea

Alexandria

Cair

LIBYA

EGYPT

AFRICA

Nile

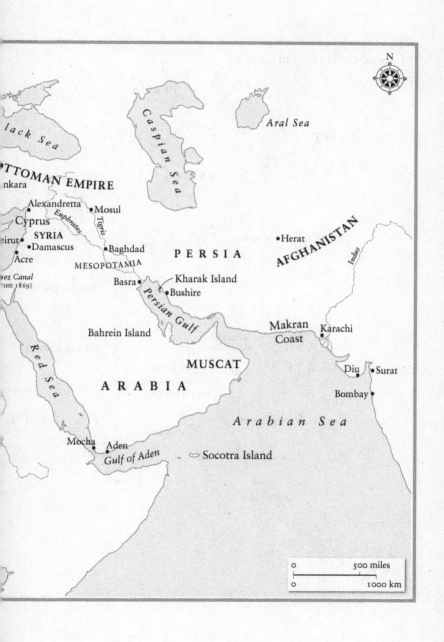

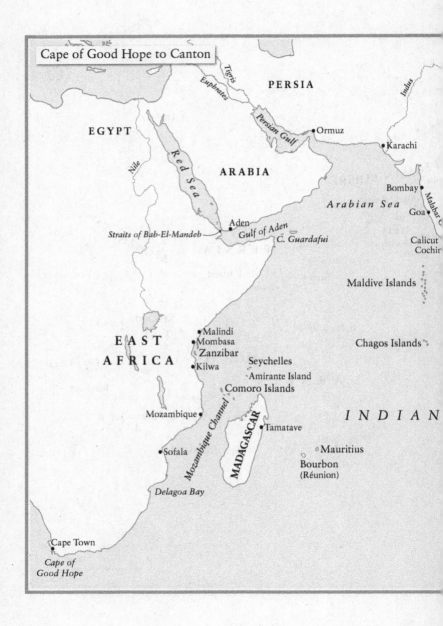

Cape of Good Hope to Canton

PERSIA

Tigris

Euphrates

EGYPT

Indus

Persian Gulf

•Ormuz

ARABIA

•Karachi

Nile

Red Sea

Arabian Sea

Bombay•

Goa•

Malabar C.

Aden•

Straits of Bab-El-Mandeb—

Gulf of Aden

C. Guardafui

Calicut

Cochin

Maldive Islands

E A S T

•Malindi

•Mombasa

Zanzibar

•Kilwa

Seychelles

•Amirante Island

Chagos Islands

A F R I C A

Comoro Islands

Mozambique•

Mozambique Channel

MADAGASCAR

•Tamatave

I N D I A N

Sofala•

○Mauritius

Bourbon

(Réunion)

Delagoa Bay

Cape Town•

*Cape of
Good Hope*

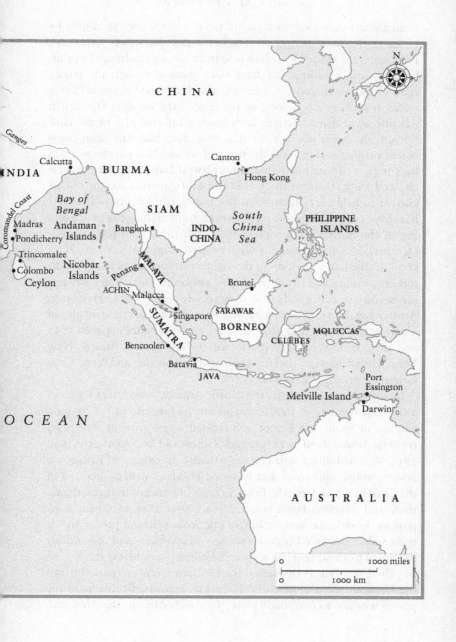

United States increased from 3.9 million in 1790 to over 31 million by 1860; in the same period the combined population of 'Germany', France and the United Kingdom rose from some 55 million to 95 million. European sailors had long since pioneered its main sailing routes.[16] Sailing directly westward was 'uphill' work: at ten to twelve weeks it took twice as long as the homeward voyage. The North Atlantic was ruled not just by its westerly winds but also by the Gulf Stream, the great ocean river that flowed up the American coast before turning east towards the British Isles and Norway. Its warmth kept the seas around Britain and north-west Europe ice-free in winter, and shipping from the Caribbean and America sought out its current to help carry them east. But the North Atlantic was also a hazardous sea, perhaps the most hazardous of all major seas. Ice and fog in the north, hurricanes in the south (from mid-July to mid-October), and a tempestuous winter tested ships and seamen. Yet a dense traffic had grown up in the eighteenth century to carry sugar, tobacco, timber and (from the 1790s) cotton to Europe in exchange for textiles, metal goods and increasingly immigrants. Hamburg, Amsterdam, and especially La Rochelle and Bordeaux, had all played a part in this trade[17] But after the wars and blockades between 1793 and 1815, London and Liverpool took the lion's share. Boston, New York, Philadelphia, Charleston, Kingston, Havana and Vera Cruz were their principal partners.

In the 1820s and 1830s, the North Atlantic was emerging from a strategic revolution. Rebellion and war had destroyed the Atlantic empires of Spain and France and created a fast-growing American republic whose land area expanded threefold between 1790 and 1850. War had also confirmed the Atlantic supremacy of British sea power, whose squadrons and bases (at Halifax, at Bermuda and in the Caribbean) underwrote Britain's huge investment in transatlantic trade and shipping. For a hundred years after 1815, merchant shipping in the Atlantic was strikingly safe from war and predation – a remarkable interlude between two ages of conflict – and only mildly disrupted by the Union blockade of Southern ports during the American Civil War (1861–5): over 90 per cent of attempts to pass through the blockade were successful.[18] For all its benefits, British maritime power was not to everyone's taste. To slaveholders in the American

South (with their eyes on what had happened in Haiti) the British crusade against the slave trade and slavery was at best an outrage, at worst an incitement to slave rebellion at home. 'England [is] our great rival in peace, and chief foe in war,' raged the oceanographer (and Virginian) Matthew Maury in 1843. 'England has hedged us in at the South, with a chain of islands and military posts and naval stations ... Not a stitch of canvass can leave the Gulf but by [her] leave.'[19] Maury was right to insist on the importance of American shipping. By 1860, America with some 2.5 million tons of ocean-going vessels (to Britain's 4.5 million tons) was Britain's chief commercial rival at sea in the Atlantic and in the eastern seas, far ahead of France, Norway and the Dutch. 'The time is not distant,' President Polk told Congress in 1847, 'when our ... commercial marine will be larger than that of any other nation in the world.'[20]

A vast amount of shipping in the North Atlantic was devoted to the coastal or local traffic of the British Isles, north-west Europe, the American mainland and the Caribbean.[21] London, the great entrepôt of Atlantic Europe, maintained a large trade with Hamburg and other continental ports. Transatlantic traffic by the mid-nineteenth century was dominated by the cotton and corn sent from American ports, largely carried in American ships: of the 4,000 ships employed in Britain's trade with the United States in 1860, American-owned vessels outnumbered the British by two to one.[22] Two-thirds of the trade in and out of New York was in American ships.[23] However, the really striking feature of North Atlantic shipping was not just its volume but the frequency and regularity of sailings between Europe and North America. So-called 'packets', offering a regular service for passengers, mail and high-value goods, had been tried in the early eighteenth century as a wartime experiment, but soon abandoned as too expensive in peacetime.[24] But from 1818 the Black Ball line in New York supplied a packet service to Europe and by 1834 no fewer than nine packet lines and forty-six ships (some up to 1,000 tons) connected New York with London, Liverpool and Le Havre. West-bound packets from Liverpool could now reach New York in thirty-six days, and a mere sixteen with an easterly wind behind them. East-bound packets could reach Liverpool in seventeen days.[25] From 1821, New Orleans was linked to New York by packet, and

packets increasingly carried bales of cotton as well as mail and passengers.[26] On both Atlantic shores a network of coastal packets had
spread out from the main transatlantic ports by the 1820s and 1830s.

Up to the late 1860s, sailing ships remained the main carriers of
transatlantic cargo. Indeed, it was not until 1874 that a large fall in
the number of sailing ships was noted in New York.[27] But the volume
of mail and passenger traffic, and the manageable length of the crossing, had encouraged the extension of steam from its coastal or
short-haul beginnings. The year 1838 was an *annus mirabilis*. The
first transatlantic steam crossing was made by the *Royal William*, a
Canadian-built ship. Then in rapid succession, the *Sirius* and Brunel's
Great Western arrived in New York to great excitement. Within two
years, Samuel Cunard's paddle steamers supplied a steam packet line
between Boston and Britain. As yet, however, their vast consumption
of coal, and the space it consumed, made steamers uncompetitive for
the carrying of bulk goods, and reliant on subsidy (or mail contract)
to be profitable. If this technological revolution was partial at best,
a commercial revolution was more far-reaching. Between 1849 and
1851 Britain abandoned its two-hundred-year-old navigation laws
restricting trade with Britain to British-owned and British-manned
ships, and opened the way for 'third-party' carriers to bring produce
from Europe or the British colonies into British ports. The effect was
electric. Hamburg, long dismissed as an outport of London ('Hambourg est une ville anglaise,' said Napoleon), swiftly doubled its
fleet.[28] British shipowners began to fear the threat from the rapidly
expanding American merchant marine. They were saved by a cata-
clysm. The American Civil War swept much of America's fleet from
the seas. Fear of Confederate raiders and the spiralling cost of insurance led to the sell-off or disposal of much of America's deep-sea
shipping.[29] By the time that the war ended the North Atlantic had
moved on. There the march of iron and steam had begun in earnest.

The South Atlantic stretched from the Caribbean to Cape Horn,
from Brazil to West Africa. For more than three centuries it had been
above all a slave-trade ocean, shipping millions of slaves from West
Africa to the plantation economies of North America, the Caribbean
and Brazil. The trade survived deep into the nineteenth century,
despite the formal bans imposed by Britain (since 1807), the United

States, France, the Netherlands, and, with great reluctance, Spain and Portugal. Indeed, the ban remained a dead letter wherever local enforcement was lacking. With barely a dozen ships to police the whole South Atlantic, the British campaign to choke off the slave trade was ineffective at best. In the late 1830s more than 125,000 slaves were illicitly landed in Brazil alone (some on the beach at Copacabana) in a traffic employing some hundreds of ships. It was not until the 1850s in Brazil, and the 1860s in Cuba (these two plantation economies were the main markets for slaves), that the trade was gradually strangled.[30] The South Atlantic had also long been the sailing ship's highway to the East: the optimum route from Europe followed the trade winds from the Canaries to the coast of Brazil before turning south-east toward the Cape of Good Hope and the Indian Ocean. In the eighteenth century, the British had hoped to use Rio de Janeiro as a base for their naval operations in India and returning East Indiamen regularly called at the island of St Helena for water and food.[31] Shipping for the west coast of the Americas and American ships bound for China sailed south to Cape Horn (rounding the Horn could take a month against contrary winds): this traffic grew rapidly with the discovery of gold in California in 1848, and made Valparaiso in Chile the great entrepôt of the South American west coast.[32] The South Atlantic was also the return route for ships from Australia, racing across the Pacific along the 'Roaring Forties' before rounding Cape Horn and turning north towards Europe.[33]

By the mid-nineteenth century, however, shipping was being increasingly drawn to the South Atlantic by the promise of trade with Brazil, Argentina and Uruguay. All three had been 'opened up' to British merchants by the end of Spanish rule and by Portugal's acute dependence on Britain once Napoleon had invaded the Iberian peninsula in 1807. Rio de Janeiro, Brazil's capital, was already a large and wealthy city, with a magnificent harbour – so easy to enter that no pilot was needed.[34] It had boomed on gold in the eighteenth century. By the 1840s and 1850s it was booming on the export of coffee produced in its near-hinterland in the Paraíba Valley. Between 1820 and 1849 its population had more than doubled from 86,000 to 205,000 (of whom half were slaves). It became the world's largest coffee mart, and handled more than half Brazil's foreign trade. Over much the same period Buenos Aires too had doubled in size to reach a population of over 90,000. It had prospered mainly on the export of livestock and hides, as Argentina's ranching frontier extended deeper into the pampas.[35] The 1850s and 1860s saw, in both countries, the adoption of commercial codes that opened the way to joint-stock companies, the chartering of banks and provision of guarantees or subsidies for railway-building. And in both Rio and Buenos Aires, foreign – especially British – merchants largely controlled their export trades.[36] By the 1850s, the arrival of a steam-packet service had further strengthened their commercial links with Europe and North America.[37]

The South Atlantic after 1815 was free from the rivalries of the mercantilist age. But its politics were complex. Much of this complexity arose from the struggle over slavery and the slave trade. On Africa's Atlantic coast this had drawn the British government into grudging intervention ashore, first to provide a safe haven for liberated slaves at Freetown in Sierra Leone,[38] and then to discourage local rulers, preferably by treaty, from allowing slaves to be sold and exported. In many places on the West African coast the export of slaves was the main source of both wealth and tax revenue: in Dahomey, in Lagos (the chief port in the Bight of Benin) and in Portuguese-ruled Angola among others. One reason for Lisbon's reluctance to agree a complete ban was the fear that its colonials in Angola would declare independence or transfer their allegiance to independent Brazil, their main slaving partner.[39] Mounting frustration at the failure of policing (and mounting pressure from abolitionists at home) pushed London into imposing a change of regime at Lagos (where slave exports peaked in the late 1840s)[40] in 1851, and full-scale annexation ten years later – the prelude, as it turned out, to creeping expansion in what became southern Nigeria. No more easy to deal with was the extreme reluctance of Brazil's ruling elite of planters (*fazendeiros*) to cut off the constant resupply of slave labour on which their prosperity depended (the life expectancy of imported slaves was appallingly low). Indeed, they suspected that British abolition was really a ruse to enrich their own colonies at Brazil's expense, and to turn West Africa into a second Brazil under British control. Official connivance in slaving was brazen. Then in an astonishing escalation British warships entered Brazil's harbours in 1850 and

1851, seizing or sinking vessels carrying slaves or fitted out for slave voyages.[41] Local enforcement followed swiftly, but slavery itself survived until 1888.

Nor were these three South American states – Brazil, Argentina and Uruguay – as yet stable polities with definite boundaries. All three were the scene of intermittent civil wars, the result of the strong regional identities of the colonial period and the primitive state of overland transport. The appetite for expansion was strong. Argentina's attempt to annex Uruguay (the 'Banda Oriental') in 1828 was thwarted by British intervention. An Anglo-French blockade in the 1840s forced Buenos Aires to abandon its drive to control the Paraná, the great river road into the continental interior. Brazil, Argentina and Uruguay fought a series of wars over command of the river, the easiest route (before railways) into Brazil's own hinterland. These culminated in the gruelling struggle between Brazil, Uruguay and Argentina on one side against puny Paraguay on the other, which lasted from 1865 to 1870. But by that date, indeed, the consolidation of the three victor states (Paraguay was devastated) under effective central governments had been largely achieved, and their 'modernization' as commodity producers for Europe and North America was well under way.

The Pacific was the last great maritime frontier of the nineteenth century. Its vast extent, parsimoniously scattered with island landfalls, had discouraged outsiders, who confined themselves to traversing its width, often, like George Anson in 1742, with little real idea of their exact location.[42] Captain Cook's great voyages and the occupation of Botany Bay in 1788 were a turning point. So too was the advance in the 1770s of Russians from the north and Spanish from the south into the Pacific north-west of continental America. At almost the same moment it was learned that sea-otter fur from the coast of modern Alaska and British Columbia would command a high price in Canton; the first modern trans-Pacific trade route was created.[43] In the 1820s and 1830s the Pacific became a vast hunting ground for whales and seals, for whose oil and skins a large market existed, attracting fleets from New England and Britain. Honolulu in Hawaii (a 'crossroads' of the north-east and south-east trade winds) became the whalers' main base; the Bay of Islands, in New Zealand's

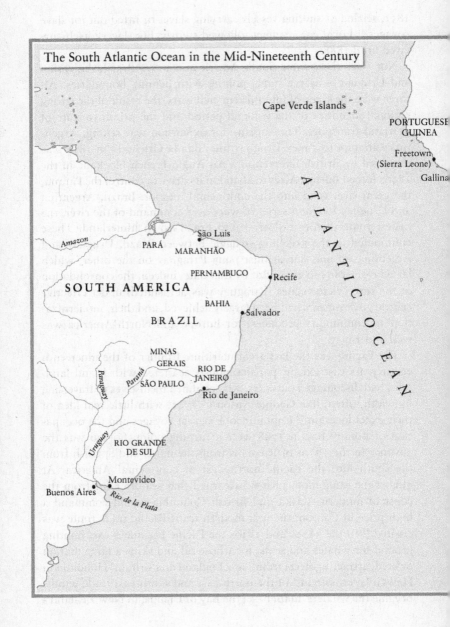

The South Atlantic Ocean in the Mid-Nineteenth Century

Cape Verde Islands

PORTUGUESE
GUINEA

Freetown
(Sierra Leone)

Gallina

ATLANTIC OCEAN

Amazon

PARÁ

São Luis

MARANHÃO

PERNAMBUCO

Recife

SOUTH AMERICA

BAHIA

Salvador

BRAZIL

MINAS
GERAIS

RIO DE
JANEIRO

SÃO PAULO

Rio de Janeiro

Paraguay

Paraná

Uruguay

RIO GRANDE
DE SUL

Montevideo

Buenos Aires

Rio de la Plata

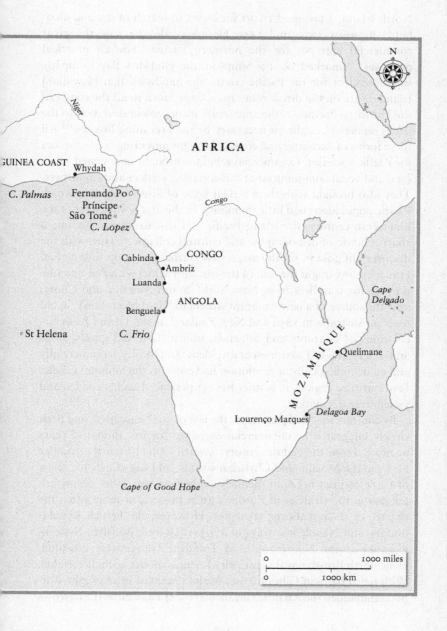

North Island, a favoured resort for crews in search of sex and alcohol.[44] Between 1820 and 1850 Honolulu also became the great commercial entrepôt for the northern Pacific. 'For all practical purposes,' remarked George Simpson, the Hudson's Bay Company superintendent for the Pacific coast, 'the Sandwich [i.e. Hawaiian] Islanders are on the direct route from Cape Horn to all the coasts of the Northern Pacific . . . the apparently inconvenient deviation to the left is rendered . . . almost necessary by the prevailing breezes.'[45] All these forms of exchange and contact brought unwitting consequences for Pacific societies. Commercial relations brought new vested interests, and vocal communities of missionaries, settlers and sojourners. They also brought with them a tidal wave of diseases against which Pacific populations had little immunity. In the first few decades of the nineteenth century, the Island Pacific and its eastern rim became a charnel house of demographic and cultural collapse.[46] Then with the discovery of gold in California, a new traffic sprang up linking San Francisco (overnight the hub of the eastern Pacific) with Panama (the portage for travellers from New York), South America and China, now the source of a new emigrant stream to 'Gold Mountain'.[47] Gold finds in Australia in 1850 and New Zealand in 1860 drove fresh circulations of migrants and minerals, information and goods, ships and their crews. Environmentally, demographically, commercially and epidemiologically, a revolution had come to the 'remote' Pacific. Few maritime regions in history have experienced such a sudden and violent transformation.

By contrast the Mediterranean, the last of our 'seascapes', had been closely integrated by commercial exchange for five thousand years or more. From the eighth century onwards it had been the frontier between the Muslim and Christian worlds, and sometimes the scene of fierce conflict between them. No other sea was more deeply entangled in the rivalries of Europe's great powers, or more often the theatre of their seaborne struggles. However, the French Revolutionary and Napoleonic wars of 1793–1815 were decisive. Nelson's victories at the Nile (1798) and Trafalgar (1805) were crushing. Henceforth British naval superiority became almost unchallengeable. With naval bases at Gibraltar and Malta (annexed in 1813), the British commanded the Atlantic entrance to the sea as well as the narrows dividing its western and eastern halves. The Grand Harbour at Valletta became the base of their Mediterranean fleet, the citadel of their naval hegemony.

The result was the consolidation in the first half of the century of an 'Anglo-Mediterranean order': a new geopolitical and commercial regime.[48] It required agile diplomacy, as well as naval coercion. But at the end of the twenty-year Eastern crisis from 1821 to 1841 its main elements were in place. The Ottoman Empire had survived, by the skin of its teeth, against the double assault by Russia and its rebellious viceroyalty Egypt. It remained the guardian of the sea gate between the Mediterranean and the Black Sea, and the landward approaches to the Persian Gulf. Egypt, which had at one stage bid fair to be a new eastern empire over Anatolia, the Arab lands, the Persian Gulf, Sudan and Crete (and, London feared, the cat's paw of France), was penned back to the Nile Valley. A small Greek kingdom had emerged. France had embarked on the conquest of Algeria, but its ambitions in the eastern Mediterranean (if they existed) had been checked. Above all, the Straits Convention of 1841, the charter of this new regime, forbade the passage of warships through the Straits in peacetime – sealing Russian sea power into the Black Sea. The vital corollary to this geopolitical architecture was the Convention of Balta-Liman, imposed in 1838 on the Ottomans, and by extension on Egypt, still technically part of the Ottoman Empire.[49] Its terms were drastic. Their command economies, which included state control over markets and (in Egypt) a state monopoly over the sale of raw cotton, were to be wound up. Their internal commerce would be opened to foreign merchants, hitherto forced to deal through local agents. And a strict upper limit was placed on the tariffs they could impose. Free trade had come to the Near East.

Mediterranean trade had always combined the exchange of regional commodities with an 'oriental' traffic, brought overland to Levantine ports or through the Red Sea and Egypt. After 1815 the Mediterranean shared in the general expansion of global trade, but in very particular ways. Firstly, its coastlands became more productive, perhaps because a drier and warmer climate allowed the cultivation of land abandoned in the early modern 'Little Ice Age'.[50] Secondly, a new agrarian order made Egypt into a prime producer of cotton, drawing it into a nexus of dependence on the finance, trade and shipping of western Europe.[51] Thirdly, while the overland caravan trade had survived in Anatolia, the Mediterranean had become a highway to two new destinations.

The first of these was the Black Sea. Long closed to European merchants and shipping by its Ottoman gatekeepers, the Straits had first been prised open (by Russia) in the late eighteenth century. Later agreements admitted more European states, but delays and searches imposed by the Turkish authorities were a constant irritation.[52] The 1841 Straits Convention swept these away and extended the privilege to all mercantile shipping. It was the colonization of 'New Russia' (modern Ukraine) that made this important. From the 1780s southern Russia became a great grain producer, especially of wheat. Odessa, founded in 1794, became its port city. Hundreds of ships now passed through the Straits to buy wheat for southern and western Europe – a market that grew rapidly when the end of the Corn Laws in 1846 allowed foreign wheat freely into Britain. Odessa's wheat exports doubled between 1817 and 1846 and had almost doubled again by 1853.[53] Russia's commercial economy now pivoted south and Odessa's population rose swiftly from a modest 8,000 in 1803 to reach 100,000 by the 1850s. The second destination was India. As we will see later in more detail, long before the Suez Canal, mail and passenger traffic had come to prefer the transit through Egypt and the Red Sea to the far longer way round by the Cape. As the Raj expanded, this isthmian traffic grew heavier and heavier. The Dutch and French empires added their share. In a few short decades, the Mediterranean had become the hypersensitive corridor between the European powers and their eastern possessions.

In the eighteenth century, French shipping had been dominant in Mediterranean trade. The Napoleonic Wars were its downfall. Its place was taken by Greek-owned ships, at first mainly from islands still ruled by the Ottomans or from the Ionian Islands, ruled by the British until ceded to Greece in 1864. Greek ships now converted increasingly from the lateen-sail rigging of the *polacca* to that of the square-rigged two-masted brig of northern Europe.[54] Greek ships, and firms like Rallis and Argenti, quickly moved into the Black Sea and its wheat trade. By the 1850s, some 80 per cent of the deep-sea sailing ships in the eastern Mediterranean and Black Sea were flying the Greek flag.[55] Steamships came early to the Mediterranean, where distances were modest, coal was easily brought from Britain, and the frequency of calms or sudden changes of wind made them especially appealing. Steam packets were commonplace by the 1830s. Austrian Lloyd, based at Habsburg-ruled Trieste, offered a regular steam service to Constantinople and other ports from 1837; Messageries Impériales (later called Messageries Maritimes) from Marseilles (still much the Mediterranean's largest port) and Peninsular & Oriental (P&O) from Britain offered a similar schedule. The turning point may have come with the Crimean War of 1853–6. With a fleet of steamers that had been hired out as troopships, Liverpool ship-owners quickly took over much of the long-distance trade to northern Europe.[56] Steam had come to stay.

It may seem ironic that so much of the groundwork for a global economy in the nineteenth century was laid by the sailing ship. Yet across much of the world they remained the great carriers of bulk goods (whose convergence in price was the acid test of a globalized economy) into the 1880s. Bringing wheat from California, wheat and wool from Australia, rice from South East Asia, tea from China, they easily competed with costlier steamships. The demand for British coal (for railways and the growing number of coaling stations) helped to make their out-voyages profitable, avoiding the need to carry mere ballast. In Britain, the steamship pioneer, the registered sailing ship tonnage was ten times that of steam in 1860, and still four times in 1870. Indeed, sailing ships had become much more efficient as the century progressed. By the 1870s, 2,000-ton iron sailing ships were being built, ten times the size of the typical transatlantic ship of the late eighteenth century. With labour-saving (steam) machinery on board, crews were reduced by 50 per cent. Steam tugs made entering and leaving ports much quicker. For ships heading into the Black Sea through the Dardanelles, they saved the delays caused by the prevailing northerlies.[57] Much more accurate wind and current charts (especially those produced by Matthew Maury) helped captains to cut voyage times – in the case of the run to Australia by up to a quarter.[58] It also seems likely that the great fall in freight rates, on which trade growth depended, began well before steamships became cargo carriers, and reflected the large increase in the number of sailing ships built between the 1830s and 1860s.[59] In its first half-century steam globalization was driven as much by the partnership of sail and steam at sea as by the triumph of steam on land.

THE STEAMSHIP GLOBE

The age of the ocean-going steamship really began in the 1860s and 1870s. The turning point came with the gradual adoption of the compound engine after 1854. By using two cylinders, much higher pressure could be raised, increasing the power of the engine while halving the consumption of coal. By 1866, P&O had ten compound engine steamers, and Mauritius could be reached without re-coaling – a voyage of 8,500 miles.[60] With more space available for passengers and high-paying freight, it now became profitable to send steamers as far as China. The use of the screw propeller instead of the paddle-wheel improved performance still further. In the 1880s came the triple-expansion engine, much more powerful and much more economical than previous marine engines. Except on a few surviving routes and in certain bulk trades where time mattered less (like wool and grain from Australia), steamers had become supreme for passengers, mail and freight.

Once the steamship age was fully set, coal became king. Any port worth the name had to sell coal for bunkering, since only a few ships could steam (certainly not profitably) more than 3,000 miles without refuelling. Although deposits of coal were quite widely scattered across the world, in relatively few places was it available in quantity at coastal locations. Here Britain enjoyed an enormous advantage. With major coalfields in South Wales and North-East England (and many others elsewhere), coal could be brought easily and cheaply to its principal ports, including London. As other countries industrialized and built railways, coal became a huge British export, second only to cotton textiles by 1913. Much British shipping was employed carrying coal across the world, including to India and South America; and a good deal of this coal was destined for bunkering.

Bunkering was a complex business. Coal varied widely in quality. It could also deteriorate if not kept carefully. The crucial index of its value was its carbon content: this determined how much heat (and therefore steam energy) a given ton would generate. If space in the ship's hold was at a premium, and maintaining high speed was essential (as it was on mail carriers with specified voyage times in their contract), good-quality coal was essential. Top of the range was Welsh steam coal, exported from Cardiff, the leading coal port of the later nineteenth century.[61] By the 1880s it was available at coaling stations all over the world: in Nagasaki, Shanghai, Singapore, Colombo, Bombay, Aden, Suez, Port Said, Rio de Janeiro, Buenos Aires, Valparaiso, Malta and Gibraltar – to name but a few. Coaling agencies sprang up to arrange the delivery of the different coals on sale, and to organize the messy operation of refuelling. The largest of these was Richard Cory and Son of Cardiff (later Cory Brothers), who owned a fleet of colliers as well as mines of their own. By 1908 they had 118 agencies around the world and some seventy-eight coal depots.[62] For shipowners – and navies – knowing what coals were available at different ports, and at what price, was key information. It was also important to know how refuelling was organized – especially if time was of the essence.[63] In many ports, if not most, coal was brought out to the ship in lighters and dragged aboard in great baskets – a slow, laborious and filthy process. A coaling wharf from which coal could be discharged directly into a ship's bunkers was a costly but hugely time-saving improvement. For large shipping lines, the stockpiling of high-quality coal at their main ports of call was a strategic necessity. When Matthew Perry sailed east from Hampton Roads in Virginia on his famous mission to Japan in 1853, taking three steamers with him, he found the coal supply at Singapore was controlled by P&O, and had to bargain with them to refuel.[64] Coaling demanded intense physical labour. Coal had to be shovelled, barrowed or carried in baskets from depot to wharf, or stowed in lighters, sometimes by night. A large force of – usually casual – coal-heavers had to be recruited (often including women). In the hierarchy of port occupations it was by far the most humble: dirty, unhealthy, physically dangerous, irregular and poorly paid, with minimal protection against exploitation and brutality by employers and overseers.[65]

Coaling was not the only way in which the steamship transformed the nature of maritime labour. In a sailing ship, much of the crew was employed in setting the sails, a strenuous task carried out in all weathers often at dizzying heights.[66] A steamship also needed 'deck-hands' – not least because sails continued to be used as a 'backup' for steam until late in the century. But much of its crew worked below decks, tending and feeding its engines. While engineers looked after the boilers, pipework and drive shafts, 'firemen' and 'trimmers' (sometimes 'stokers') fed the furnaces that heated the boilers. Even in temperate climates this was savagely hot work, at temperatures up to 50 degrees centigrade. Firemen used huge shovels to distribute the coal and pull out 'clinker'. Trimmers broke up the coal in the bunkers using sledgehammers, and brought it in barrows to the furnace. Since coal often exhaled gas, no lights could be used, for fear of explosion, and the ship's motion threw trimmers and their barrows about in the narrow metal gangways between bunker and furnace. The boilers themselves had to be cleaned, usually by boys (Kipling's 'boiler-whelps' in his poem 'M'Andrew's Hymn') who climbed inside. These were gruelling, debilitating tasks, for trimmers especially. It was little wonder that firemen and trimmers were four times more likely to commit suicide than other seamen.[67]

East of Suez, the rise of the steamship increased the demand for local seamen or 'Lascars' – a term that came to embrace not only Indians (the original usage) but Arabs, Somalis, Malays and Chinese as well. Lascar seamen had long been employed on sailing ships in eastern seas, often in preference to undisciplined Europeans, and invariably at far lower pay. The ferocious regime of the stokehold and the voracious demand of the steamship for cheap, unskilled labour brought a huge expansion in Lascar crews, especially on lines like P&O and British-India. By 1914 they made up a quarter of the crews serving on British-owned ships.[68]

Certainly, the demand for firemen and trimmers grew and grew. The fifty years from 1860 to 1910 saw an enormous increase in ocean-going shipping: from some 10.6 million to over 28 million tons.[69] Sailing-ship tonnage peaked in 1880 at 13 million tons: even in 1890 steamship tonnage at 8.6 million was below the sailing-ship total. But thereafter steam tonnage accelerated rapidly to reach more than 22 million by 1910. By that date nearly half the world's mercantile fleet was British-owned or flew the British flag, a tribute to Britain's endowment in coal and iron and its early lead in industrialization, as well as the scale of its overseas trade. At the same time both the size and the capacity of merchant ships also increased significantly, partly because building in iron rather than wood made it possible, partly because larger ships were more economical to run. In the British merchant fleet of some 4,000 ocean-going steamers, the average among cargo carriers was close to 2,000 tons – which meant a capacity of 4,000–5,000 tons of cargo. In the case of 'liners' average size was higher, and getting much higher. By 1910 vessels of 45,000–50,000 tons were being built for the North Atlantic crossing. One result was an 'arms race' between rival ports to provide the equipment that allowed larger ships to load, unload and refuel as quickly as possible – since a ship only earned when at sea. This meant investing in docks, cranes, railways and storage to move passengers and goods in and out of the port, as well as managing an ever-growing workforce of dockers, coal-handlers, clerks and officials. Above all, it meant the constant widening and deepening of the harbour approaches. As we will see later on, fierce conflicts could arise over the costs and benefits of such port improvements.

The rise of the 'liner' was a striking feature of the second half of the century. Except for the packets, sailing ships had usually been owned singly or in twos and threes by individuals or small partnerships. The economics of ocean-going steamships dictated a different pattern. They were for long only viable when offering a subsidized mail service. That meant a regular schedule employing a fleet of ships under single management, operating as a 'line'. P&O (1837), the Royal Mail Steam Packet Company (1839) and Cunard (1840) were among the earliest of these,[70] but after 1850 more and more lines appeared, to serve Europe's connections with different parts of the world. By the end of the nineteenth century there were at least twenty to twenty-five British passenger lines, including the Allan Line (to Canada), later merged with Canadian Pacific, Bibby's (to India and Burma), British-India (India, Burma, the Persian Gulf and Australia), Clan Line (South and East Africa and the Indian Ocean), Elder Dempster (West Africa and the Caribbean), 'Blue Funnel' (Indian

Ocean and China), the Royal Mail Steam Packet Company (Caribbean and South America), Shaw Savill (New Zealand) and Union-Castle (South Africa), as well as Cunard and P&O. They competed with the large foreign lines, including Hamburg-Amerika (with 160 steamers), Norddeutscher Lloyd (also in the North Atlantic), Austrian Lloyd, Messageries Maritimes, Red Star (the Belgian line), Royal Netherlands and the Japanese NYK among others.

Liners offered a huge convenience: a fast, regular connection for passengers, mail and higher-value freight, especially for goods whose market was time-sensitive. But this came at a price. The operating and overhead costs of liners were very high – far higher than those of a fast sailing ship. Keeping to schedule placed a premium on speed. That meant burning large quantities of coal. In a slow 'tramp' ship, coal might make up a quarter of its running costs: in a liner, the figure could be twice as high. A liner had to buy the most expensive coal and its large bunkers restricted the space for revenue-earning cargo. It would need a large crew to serve its passengers, and a very large liner like Cunard's *Aquitania* needed nearly 270 firemen and trimmers. East of Suez, where the size of steamers was limited by the width of the Suez Canal, opened in 1869, the costs and risks were particularly high. 'Without a subsidy,' Sir Thomas Sutherland, chairman of P&O, told a Select Committee in 1901, 'no steamers like we employ for mail services would ever be built for the eastern trade.'[71] A fast mail steamer that could do eighteen knots cost three times as much to build as a slow cargo steamer. Its passenger traffic could be highly seasonal: except for two months of the year it might sail with most of its cabins unfilled. Return cargoes might be exiguous. As Sutherland's presence at the committee suggested, when subsidy was crucial, the role of a line's management was as much political as commercial. It was vital to maintain a network of connections in the City, but also with the navy (since troopship contracts were valuable), Whitehall and Parliament. In 1867 P&O had been threatened with the loss of its Indian mail contract to the French line Messageries Impériales. A parliamentary intervention, playing the patriotic card, was needed to quash what would have been a catastrophe for the company.[72] The Atlantic mail contracts were also the subject of fierce competition and lobbying.[73]

Influence and subsidy could not obviate all of the risks. In many parts of the world competition between liners became intense, nowhere more so than in the North Atlantic. There the main source of profit for the leading lines, including Cunard and Hamburg-Amerika, was the vast emigrant traffic to New York, carried in 'steerage' (typically a large communal space in the stern of the ship) – often in squalid and uncomfortable conditions.[74] This was not a trade open to lines sailing between Europe and the eastern world – although 'deck passengers' (who sat, slept and ate on deck) might be carried from India and China to South East Asia as part of the stream of migrant labour to its plantations and mines. There, as elsewhere, there was constant pressure to improve voyage times, which meant buying new, faster and more expensive ships. Every few years, as in the case of P&O, its mail contract had to be renewed, usually on more stringent terms: its loss could be commercially fatal. Freight rates declined steadily in the late nineteenth century and hit rock bottom in the early twentieth. But they were also subject to wild fluctuations. A commercial slump, wars or rumours of wars, crop failure or a disease epidemic of plague or cholera, could shut down trade in a number of ports, creating a crisis of overcapacity, with too many ships chasing too few freights. Equally, news of high freight rates in any particular region could suck in shipping from all over the world – and then lead to a sharp fall. For a shipping line, falling revenues (passenger and freight rates usually moved together) quickly drove down the 'book value' of its fleet and damaged its share price, making it hard to raise fresh capital. Survival required that owners and managers find ways of reducing the multiple uncertainties that afflicted their business.

One obvious recourse was to buy out or merge with competing shipping lines, often after a brutal rate-cutting war. Indeed, mergers became commonplace in the British shipping industry: the most spectacular was that between P&O and British-India in 1914. The alternative to engaging in ruinous freight-rate wars was to form a cartel. This was the so-called 'conference' system. Conferences began on the Calcutta run in 1875 and quickly spread elsewhere: to China (1879), Australia (1884), South Africa (1886), West Africa (1895), Brazil and Argentina (1895–6), and, eventually, after 1900 to the

North Atlantic as well.[75] Conferences comprised two key elements. The business of a particular route was shared between conference members; and inducements – 'rebates' – were paid to the leading import-export houses to confine their shipments to a member line. In this way a group of shipping lines could monopolize higher-value cargoes, drive out non-members and, over time, force up freight rates. Conferences were far from perfect. They were little use where the bulk of exports were 'rough cargo' – rice, grain, linseeds – more suitable for tramp ships. On some routes, conference rules only applied in one direction, depending on the volume and value of trade. And sometimes the attempt to impose freight rates was fiercely resisted by local merchants, especially where they feared that high rates would damage a port's entrepôt function as a regional hub – a particular fear in Singapore. As an infringement of 'free trade', conferences were bound to attract scrutiny – the reason for the Royal Commission on 'Shipping Rings' appointed in 1906. On that occasion the shipowners won the day, perhaps because they were able to argue that prohibition would destroy their commercial viability. 'We consider,' concluded the Majority Report, 'that, where a regular and organised service is required, the Conference system, fortified by some tie upon the shipper, is as a general rule necessary.'[76] The great British shipping lines had become 'too big to fail'. But perhaps it was also because disrupting the vast web of global connections that liners provided had become almost unthinkable.

By contrast with liners, tramps were the maids-of-all-work among steamships. They made up two-thirds of the British merchant fleet – and perhaps of all ocean-going steamships. By the end of the century, the vast proportion of bulk goods that travelled by sea would have crossed the ocean in tramps. Liners ran to a schedule with fixed ports of call. Tramps went wherever they could find a freight contract. A large proportion of British-owned tramps plied in the 'cross-trades', returning but rarely to Britain. Their freights were usually 'rough cargo' of the kind avoided by liners: coal, rails, grain, rice, metal ores. They had to accept the great fluctuations in freight rates as the price of sailing with a holdful of cargo.

The voyage of the *Bengal* in 1880–81 was not untypical. It sailed from Cardiff in September 1880 for Port Suez at the head of the Red

Sea with a holdful of coal. From there it went on to Jeddah (the captain having wisely obtained a chart of the Red Sea), carrying pilgrims for Mecca. There it took on returning *hajis* bound for Penang and Singapore, where it stopped to refuel. By February 1881 the *Bengal* was at Yokohama and then Kobe in Japan for a cargo of tea to New York. Rather than sail home round Cape Horn, the captain looked for additional 'freight', calling first at Shanghai and then at the emigrant ports of Amoy and Hong Kong. There he found a 'cargo' of 'deck-passengers' heading for Singapore, the great migrant destination in South East Asia. By late March the *Bengal* was at Aden, whence it sailed for Gibraltar via the Suez Canal, and from there to Halifax and New York to deliver its tea. It finally reached London, loaded with American grain, in June 1881.[77]

Tramp-ship owners like the Burrells and Runcimans could make a fortune from shipping. But success depended upon minute attention to detail and extraordinary vigilance to commercial conditions. A tramp-ship owner had to keep a watchful eye on every aspect of his ships' operations: the costs and efficiencies of innumerable ports; the loading and unloading times of different kinds of cargo; the likely movement of freight rates in different parts of the world – because *positioning* his ships was the real test of skill. His profit would also depend on close attention to the seasonality of crops and other commodities that might make up a freight; the price of coal at different depots and coaling stations; and the weather to be expected at different times of the year. He had to decide on the best time to buy ships – or to sell them. He had to make a good choice of the distant agents on whom he relied to find paying cargoes and strike a good contract. Juggling these variables was a stressful business, especially when freight rates sank lower and lower. Tramps had to be ready to take any cargo that offered – to switch from rails or grain to live cattle – and to fit up their hold to suit its new contents. But perhaps the biggest ingredient in most tramp ships' success was coal.

Coal was the staple of a tramp's outbound voyage from Britain. It was profitable to carry coal to almost any part of the world except the United States. Typically, a cargo of coal made up between a quarter and a third of a tramp ship's earnings. But even with coal, and the shrewdest of managers, tramps faced a hard decade after 1902, perhaps because of acute overcapacity in the world's shipping fleets. Long-term contracts for coaling, chartering a tramp to a line or winning a government contract could help. Yet tramps were also threatened by the trend for liners to carry more and more cargo, and by the rise of 'cargo-liners' running to schedule and capturing at least some of their trade. Above all, the decline of British coal exports was an existential danger. 'The more we reduce our exports of coal,' remarked a contemporary expert, 'the more we shall reduce employment for British tramp ships.'[78] But silver linings come in many guises. It may have been the outbreak of war in 1914 that saved many trampship owners from ruin.[79]

A MARITIME REVOLUTION

A maritime revolution, as much geopolitical as commercial or technological, lay at the heart of nineteenth-century globalization. Until the 1870s it was primarily a sailing-ship revolution, in which steam played at best an ancillary role in what had become a hybrid technology. It was then that much of the globe was drawn more fully into a global economy that was centred on the West. China, Japan, Siam, the Ottoman Empire and Egypt were 'opened' to free trade by force or 'persuasion'. South America and the Pacific were sucked into the sphere of Euro-American commerce. Old restrictions on waterways were swept aside: by the Straits Convention of 1841 and the abolition of tolls in the Sound between Denmark and Sweden and in the Scheldt (both by agreements in 1863). Beyond Europe, the River Plate estuary (1853), the Yangzi (1862) and the Amazon (1863) were declared open to 'free navigation'. Frequent, swift, scheduled voyages, initially by sailing packet, became commonplace in the Mediterranean, the North Atlantic and to South America, and were extended to India and China via the overland portage through Egypt. Sailing times were cut by the improvement of charts and the use of steam tugs. And a large increase in sailing-ship fleets brought a sharp reduction in freight rates – and a stimulus to trade. This was the sailing-ship legacy to the steamship era.

After 1870 steam moved steadily from being an auxiliary to sail to assume the prime role in oceanic commerce. The effect was to reshape globalization in transformative ways. The most obvious of these was the huge added capacity that steamships brought to overseas trade. The volume of world trade increased by approximately three times between 1870 and 1913.[80] In that same period *effective* ocean-going tonnage grew by between four and five times. A steamship's tonnage (much the largest proportion by 1913) was worth three to four times that of a sailing ship because it could make frequent voyages.[81] This offered a great gain in efficiency as long as ports were equipped to load, unload and refuel steamships without undue delay. In fact, it seems likely that improvements in cargo-handling at the quayside contributed substantially to the fall in the costs of seaborne trade.[82] The 'modern' (pre-container) port with its forest of cranes, its dense web of railway lines, its enclosed basins and docks, its coaling wharves and coal depots, its warehouses and terminals for grain or ore, its army of stevedores, and its grandly housed 'port authority' to manage the whole complex, was really the product of the steamship era after 1880. The West's commercial hegemony was entrenched by the rapid industrialization of seaborne movement (and virtually all the world's ocean-going steamships were owned by a handful of Western countries). Shipping by the end of the century was an industry like any other, with a proletarian workforce, a managerial class and directors and shareholders controlling vast capital assets.

No less remarkable was the colossal expansion of regular steamship services connecting Europe to other parts of the world. At the height of the steamship era, some eighty or ninety steamship lines offered a scheduled service for cargo or passengers to ports in the North and South Atlantic, and at least seventy to ports in the Indian Ocean as far east as Japan. A traveller embarking in London or Liverpool could reach New York in six days, Calcutta in nineteen, Cape Town in twenty, Singapore in twenty-three, Sydney in thirty-four and Shanghai in thirty-eight. Regularity and certainty in the transit times of people, goods and mail had become almost universal – in itself a revolution in history. It also made possible the new phenomenon of the 'serial migrant' who crossed and recrossed the Atlantic on several occasions: in the sailing-ship era, few migrants had returned.[83] Serial migration seems to have made up a significant portion of the emigrant traffic, deepening the social and cultural exchange between the Americas and Europe. In the Indian Ocean and beyond, the greater ease and speed of movement were largely the product of that other great progeny of the steamship era: the Suez Canal.

The Suez Canal had first been conceived before the long-distance steamship was more than a dream. The hazards of Red Sea navigation and the need to tow a sailing ship the 100-mile length of the Canal would certainly have limited its commercial utility in the age of sail. In fact, its opening in 1869 coincided with the technical improvements that made ocean-going steamships east of Suez a far more profitable venture. The combination soon had dramatic results. The Canal drastically shortened the distance between European ports and those of India, South East Asia and China: London to Bombay by 40 per cent; London to Calcutta by 32 per cent; London to Singapore by 29 per cent; London to Hong Kong by 26 per cent.[84] The result was a huge saving in time – and coal. At last the steamship could not just compete as a freight carrier, but (except in 'slow' trades) push the sailing ship out. By 1877 the steamer had driven even the fastest tea clippers out of the China trade.[85] After 1883 more shipping tonnage was using the Canal than sailing round the Cape.[86] The short route to Asia, long a convenience for passengers and mail, had become a great highway for trade.

In fact, the volume of shipping that passed through the Canal rose at a spectacular rate: from 3 million tons in 1880 to nearly 10 million in 1900, and over 19 million in 1914.[87] Northbound freight soon predominated, partly because India's exports were now increasingly directed towards Europe (and much less towards China). Indian wheat, jute, cotton and tea, and Burmese rice, found new markets in Europe. The value of India's exports rose fourfold between the opening of the Canal and the end of the century.[88] The subcontinent became the pivot of British trade and shipping in Asia, if only because an outbound cargo of coal could always be sold there. Indeed, India, Burma, Ceylon (Sri Lanka) and (a little later) Malaya became the chief source of northbound freight through the Canal, far more than China or elsewhere in Asia.[89] A substantial part of this trade in cotton and rice was destined for southern Europe, and one effect of the Canal was to make the Mediterranean a great market for India.

It mattered of course that the opening of the Canal had coincided not only with the arrival of more efficient steamships but with the eastward expansion of the cable and telegraph, linking India, China and Australia to Europe. 'The piercing of the Isthmus of Suez, like the breaking of a dam,' wrote Joseph Conrad in 1902, 'had let in upon the East a flood of new ships, new men, new methods of trade.'[90] Commercial intelligence speeded up, prices and contracts were adjusted, new consumers appeared. The Indian Ocean became a vast extension of the Atlantic economy. The circulation of people (now including tourists, women and many more pilgrims), information and ideas grew in volume and speed: the number of passengers passing through the Canal rose almost tenfold between 1870 and 1910.[91] Asian, and especially Indian, ports came under pressure to accommodate the new fleets of steamers and become more like the 'industrial' ports of the West. Culturally, the Canal may have had the effect of pulling the expatriate communities in Asia's port cities away from their hinterlands and closer to 'home'.[92] Strategically, the Canal intensified the geopolitical sensitivity of the eastern Mediterranean and of Egypt in particular. In both the cultural and strategic imagination, the Canal had become the gateway to the East, one of the 'keys that locked up the world'.

The Suez Canal was to highlight the fourth great tendency of the steamship age: the emergence of large maritime 'hubs' where traffic was concentrated. In the sailing-ship era, shipping was usually dispersed over wide tracts of sea in the search for the wind. Most sailing-ship voyages were made direct from the port of departure to a final destination – because stopping en route risked being stuck in a harbour because of contrary winds.[93] Steamships could follow the shortest passage, so that certain sea lanes became crowded with shipping and required 'rules of the road'. Without fear of delay, steamships could serve a whole series of ports on a fixed schedule, offering forward connections like a railway or bus service. It was those ports that could offer the best harbour facilities, the quickest onward connections (by rail or local shipping), the most modern bunkering equipment and the most accessible hinterland that became the 'hub' ports of the steamship age. A new pattern was riveted on to the globe: a series of 'trunk routes' from hub to hub, extending round the world

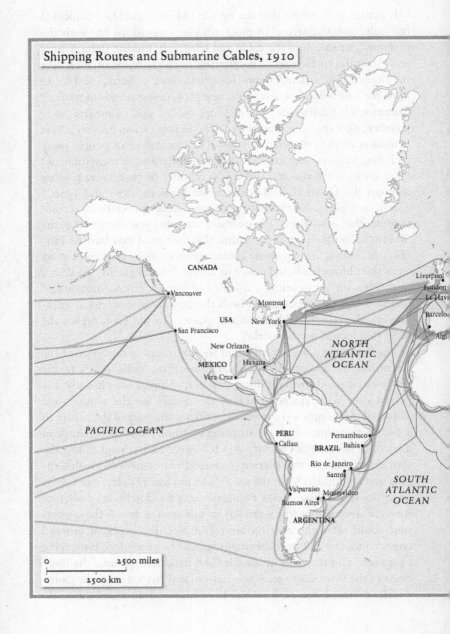

Shipping Routes and Submarine Cables, 1910

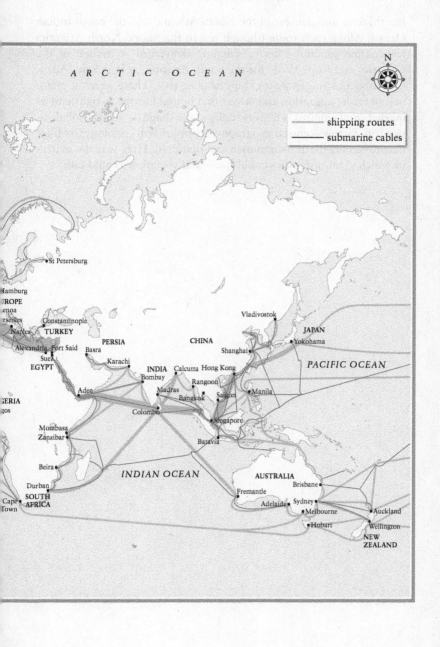

but thickest and densest in the North Atlantic and the north Indian Ocean. Along each route (though not in the 'short' North Atlantic) lay coaling junctions where shipping converged to refuel: in the Canaries and Cape Verde for the South Atlantic; at Port Said, Aden, Colombo and Singapore for ships heading east. These were the channels of trade, migration and power that bound Europe so tightly to its markets and empires. They crystallized the shape of 'steam globalization': its Europe-centred geography; its peculiar technology; its huge maritime bias (both imaginative and material). Here was the matrix in which great port cities could rise – and sometimes could fall.

PART TWO

The Dominion of Steam

5

American Gateways

A TALE OF THREE CITIES

In the second quarter of the nineteenth century, as the era of steam power got under way, there were three main gateways into the North American continent. In the north was Montreal, as far up the St Lawrence River as ships could then sail. In the far south lay New Orleans, at almost the lowest habitable site on the Mississippi, one hundred miles from its mouth. Between them lay New York, the 'Empire City', with its superlative harbour and (since 1825) its waterborne highway into the heart of the Midwest. The fortunes of all three came to depend on steam. All three hoped to exploit the fast-growing traffic across the Atlantic, as immigrants came west for America's bounty and American products flowed east to Europe's cities and industries. All three were caught up in the astonishing growth of the 'Atlantic economy' – the first great zone of 'steam globalization'. Their competition for wealth was an unequal one. Almost from the beginning, for reasons we shall see, New York overshadowed its rivals, and became more and more dominant as the century went on. Yet their three histories may tell us how far (if at all) these port cities were able to reshape their hinterlands, and on what terms they were able to 'globalize' the vast interiors behind them. And they may help us to see that this first modern globalization was much more than a matter of integrating market economies. Politics, geopolitics, ideology, technology and the sudden emergence of steam-powered 'big business' shaped North America's entry into the new world economy. As later chapters may show, in the fate of its port cities and that of its hinterlands, North America's globalization was to be highly unusual.

NEW ORLEANS: QUEEN OF THE SOUTH

A seaborne traveller to New Orleans, having crossed the Gulf of Mexico, entered the Mississippi by one of its mouths or 'passes', usually the South-West Pass. There sailing ships (from the early nineteenth century) would await a pilot or the arrival of a steam tug to pull them up the 100-mile journey to the city. The tug would lash a ship on each side and, if powerful enough, would tow a convoy of smaller vessels behind it. This was the way in which thousands of travellers – merchants, immigrants and slaves – caught their first sight of the 'Crescent City', stretching around the great bend in the river, with its skyline dominated by St Louis Cathedral in Jackson Square.

The river itself formed an extended harbour, crammed by the 1830s and 1840s, with shipping of all kinds. 'Opposite the upper portion of the town,' wrote a visitor in 1847:

> the river is chiefly occupied by the barges and keelboats which ascend and descend the river for short distances . . . and which are exclusively used for the loading and unloading the vessels in the harbour. A little below you discern a multitude of square-rigged vessels of almost every variety of tonnage, lying moored abreast of each other . . . Below them again are scores of steamers, built in the most fantastic manner, and painted of the most gaudy colours, most of them river boats, but some plying between New Orleans and Texas. There are also tugboats and ferry boats . . . Still further down and near the lower end of the harbour are brigs, schooners, and sloops designed for and used chiefly in the coasting trade of the Gulf . . . Mid-stream is crowded as well as the quays, some vessels dropping down with the current, others being tugged up against it – some steamers arriving from above and some from below, and others departing upwards and downwards.[1]

New Orleans in the 1830s and 1840s was a prodigy, a meteoric boom town and a sudden concentration of wealth. The value of its trade grew from some $10 million in 1821, to $44 million by 1840, $72 million by 1855 and $129 million on the eve of the American Civil War.[2] Its population also grew rapidly from some 8,000 (of whom half were slaves or free people of colour) in 1803, to 50,000 in

1830, over 100,000 in 1840 and over 170,000 by 1860. Between 1834 and 1842 its export trade was larger than that of any other American port, including New York.[3] Behind the boom lay one omnipotent fact. New Orleans commanded a vast inland empire of riverine commerce that stretched up the Mississippi, the Missouri, the Ohio and its tributaries (almost to Pittsburgh), as well as the Tennessee, Arkansas, Yazoo and Red rivers. It drew the produce and supplied the imports of a hinterland that comprised at its height the states of Ohio, Indiana, Illinois, Missouri, Kentucky, Tennessee, Arkansas, Mississippi and the northern parts of Alabama and Louisiana. As the Indian nations were driven out by successive wars and removals, white settlers and their slaves moved in, so that by 1830 more than one-third of the American population lived west and south of the Appalachian mountains. To many observers it seemed that this immense central basin – simply called 'the Valley' by contemporaries – would soon form the heartland of the American Republic. A favourite analogy likened the Mississippi to the Nile. 'It is no exaggeration to say,' declared the Cincinnati sage Daniel Drake in 1833, 'that . . . this valley is superior to any other on the globe.'[4] The rise of New Orleans as its metropolis would become unstoppable. 'New Orleans is destined to be the greatest city in the Western hemisphere,' declared a local newspaper in 1838.[5]

In a longer perspective, New Orleans's spectacular rise was almost as unpredictable as its subsequent fall. It was founded in 1718 by a French adventurer, Sieur de Bienville, to complete France's grip on the waterborne route from Quebec to the Gulf of Mexico, and thus bar the British colonies on the Atlantic seaboard from westward expansion. Along the river above the town a chain of plantations sprang up to form a small sugar colony, a mainland appendage to St Domingue (modern Haiti), the Caribbean jewel in France's colonial crown. Defeat in the Seven Years War ended the French dream of a North American empire: in 1763 everything east of the Mississippi passed to Britain (although not for long). But perhaps to pre-empt any British advance beyond the river, France transferred its huge Trans-Mississippian realm (a notional not an actual possession) – so-called Louisiana – to Spain. New Orleans, perched on the east bank of the river, was thrown into the bargain. Thus, when in 1783 the infant United States inherited Britain's claim to the lands lying east of the Mississippi (except for 'The Floridas' – the modern state of Florida, together with parts of today's Louisiana and Alabama – which were returned to Spain), it found New Orleans ruled by an unfriendly Spanish regime seemingly intent on choking off the new western states from their outlet to the sea. It took two further twists of geopolitical fortune before New Orleans was reunited with its trans-Appalachian interior. In 1800 Napoleon forced Spain to restore Louisiana to France as part of his plan for a new western empire. An army was sent to recapture St Domingue, lost in the great slave revolt of 1791. The expedition was a disaster, as much the victim of disease as of military failure. Napoleon gave up his project in disgust. 'I already consider this colony [Louisiana] entirely lost,' he said.[6] France's defeat was America's opportunity. To Thomas Jefferson it had been clear since the 1780s that 'the navigation of the Mississippi we must have'. The rest of Louisiana, some 900,000 square miles stretching away to the modern border of Canada, was a colossal bonus, doubling the size of the infant republic.[7] For Napoleon, sale to the United States was the best guarantee against American friendship with Britain: 'I have just given England a maritime rival that sooner or later will lay low her pride,' he declared.[8] The price was agreed at $15 million or £3 million. Ironically, the sale was completed by a loan raised in London.

Geopolitics explains much but not all of New Orleans's prosperity. It had acquired a hinterland carved out by imperial conquest, wars of colonization (still more were to come), and jurisdictional transfers over which the indigenous population had no say at all. However, the Louisiana Purchase also coincided with a series of technological changes of which New Orleans was to be an enormous beneficiary. The first and most general was the rapid mechanization of textile manufacture in Britain, creating Lancashire's seemingly insatiable appetite for cotton lint, the raw material from which the yarn was spun. In the American South cotton-growing was initially limited to the coasts of South Carolina and Georgia and to 'long-staple' (i.e. long-fibre) cotton – the only variety from which the lint could be easily plucked by hand. The second was Eli Whitney's famous cotton gin ('gin' was short for engine), invented in 1793. It supplied a device to

The Louisiana Purchase, 1803

N

Ceded by US 1818

Ceded by
Great Britain
1818

Washington
1853/1889

to US under
Oregon Treaty 1846

Montana
1864/1889

North Dakota
1861/1889

Oregon
1848/1859

Idaho
1863/1890

Wyoming
1868/1980

South Dakota
1861/1889

Nevada
1861/1864

Utah
1850/1896

Colorado
1861/1876

Nebraska
1859/1867

California
1850

U N I T E D

Kansas
1854/1861

Claimed by Spain and then Mexico

Arizona
1863/1912

New Mexico
1850/1912

Oklahoma
1890/1907

PACIFIC OCEAN

Texas
1845

MEXICO

Louisiana Purchase

1850 admission to US as
territory/state

0   500 miles

0   500 km

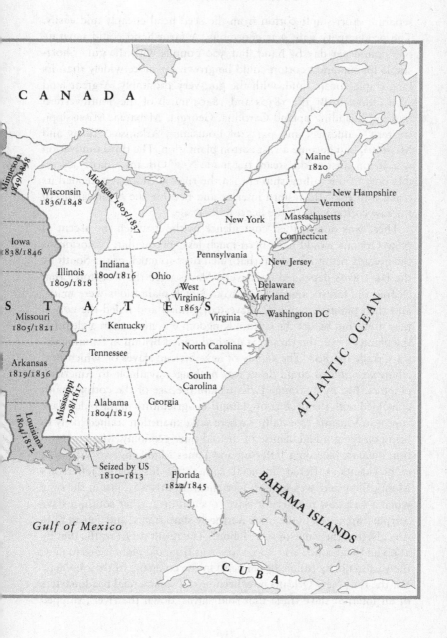

CANADA

Minnesota
1849/1858

Wisconsin
1836/1848

Michigan 1805/1837

Iowa
1838/1846

Illinois
1809/1818

Indiana
1800/1816

Ohio

Maine
1820

New Hampshire
Vermont

New York

Massachusetts

Connecticut

Pennsylvania

New Jersey

West
Virginia
1863

Delaware
Maryland

Washington DC

S T A T E S

Missouri
1805/1821

Kentucky

Virginia

Arkansas
1819/1836

Tennessee

North Carolina

South
Carolina

Mississippi
1798/1817

Alabama
1804/1819

Georgia

Louisiana
1804/1812

Seized by US
1810–1813

Florida
1822/1845

ATLANTIC OCEAN

BAHAMA ISLANDS

Gulf of Mexico

CUBA

separate short-staple cotton from the seed head cheaply and easily. The productivity gain was enormous. A farm hand could separate one pound per day by hand, but 300 pounds with the gin.[9] Short-staple (or 'upland') cotton could be grown far more widely than its long-staple cousin, and, with the gin, very profitably. A great land rush followed. By the 1830s and 1840s much of the Southwestern interior, including upland Carolina, Georgia, Alabama, Mississippi, western Tennessee, and parts of Louisiana, Arkansas, Texas and Missouri, had become a vast cotton plantation. The third innovation was steam. Just as the steam tug made New Orleans a more accessible port in the sailing-ship era, so the river steamboat extended its reach into the Midwestern interior and became the great carrier of the raw cotton bales at the heart of its trade.

There was one further 'coincidence' without which the ascent of New Orleans would have been much less spectacular. Notoriously, the great 'Cotton Kingdom' that ruled over so much of the South by the late 1830s depended on slavery. Slaves were the workforce that cleared the forests and swamps from which plantations were made, and then planted, weeded, harvested, ginned and baled the cotton they grew. But before the Cotton Kingdom was more than a gleam in the planter's eye, the United States had joined Britain in banning the slave trade in 1808. The supply of new African slaves on which Brazilian *fazendeiros* could draw was no longer available to American planters. But by a strange twist of fate the rise of the cotton South coincided with the decline of plantation agriculture in the older slave zone – in Virginia especially – where soil exhaustion seemed likely to bring on the gradual demise of the old slave economy. Many plantation owners, including Jefferson and James Madison, two Virginian ex-presidents, suffered financial ruin: after his death, Jefferson's Monticello estate was sold off piecemeal. In this way, just at the time when a vast new market for slaves opened up further south, a slave 'surplus' appeared in the more northerly slave states, and a grim fillip was given to the value of slave labour. The result was a traffic that by 1860 had sent south over 800,000 slaves from old plantations to new, the vast majority (some 84 per cent) in the company of their owners. For the rest, New Orleans now became the commercial headquarters of an internal slave trade that sold slaves 'down the river', shipped

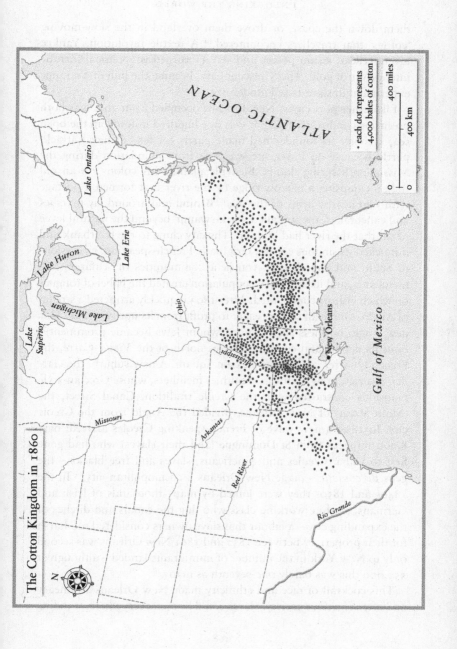

The Cotton Kingdom in 1860

• each dot represents
  4,000 bales of cotton

ATLANTIC OCEAN

Lake Ontario

Lake Erie

Lake Huron

Lake Michigan

Lake Superior

Ohio

Mississippi

Missouri

Arkansas

Red River

Rio Grande

New Orleans

Gulf of Mexico

0   400 miles

0   400 km

N

them down the coast, or drove them overland in the slow-moving 'coffles' that travellers encountered.[10] A textile revolution, Yankee inventiveness, steam power and slavery turned geopolitical fortune into a river of gold. The 'Crescent City' became the hub of a strange experiment in slave-based modernity.

Like other port cities, New Orleans occupied a site that was both precarious and restrictive.[11] It was one hundred miles from the open sea, a choice its founder had made partly for fear of naval attack, partly because no lower site was safe from inundation during the Mississippi's spring floods. Bienville planted his colony on an old Indian campsite: a narrow ridge by the river that formed a portage with two nearby arms of the sea.[12] Behind and around lay marshes and canebrakes, the so-called 'back-swamp' beyond the natural levee of silt that the river had built up. The city clung to the riverbank and mimicked its sinuous course. Originally French-speaking, its cessions to Spain and America, its transient communities of seafarers and merchants, and its large slave population created the babel of tongues on which visitors commented. After 1803 it quickly attracted a stream of Anglo-American settlers eager to profit from its upriver trade. This new Anglo business class (among whom Jews became prominent)[13] built its depots and counting houses north of the *Vieux-Carré*, the French Quarter centred on Jackson Square. A new suburb, the Garden District, grew up for its wealthier members, whose Grecian-style mansions contrasted with the Creole tradition. Canal Street, the 'Main Street' of New Orleans, divided the Anglo from the Creole city. In 1809 a new wave of French-speaking Creoles arrived: over 8,000 refugees from St Domingue (and their slaves) who had gone first to Cuba. Creoles and Americans, slaves and free blacks – the *gens de couleur* – made New Orleans a cosmopolitan city.[14] In the 1840s and 1850s they were joined by many thousands of Irish and Germans, a white working class who dug the canals and ditches of the expanding city – a labour that slave owners considered too harsh for their property.[15] Between 1837 and 1861 New Orleans was second only to New York in the number of immigrants landed – although at 550,000 this was barely one-seventh as many.[16]

This cocktail of race and ethnicity made New Orleans an uneasy and often fractious society. Slaves could be seen everywhere, standing

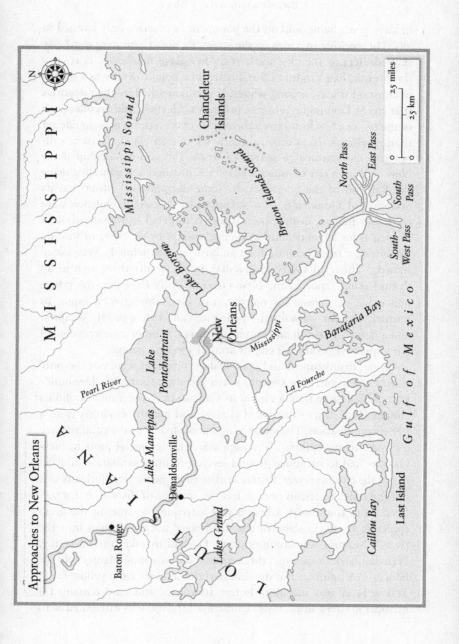

in slave pens, being sold on the pavement (a practice only banned in 1852) or working in gangs on the street. In 1842 there were some 185 slave dealers in the city and twenty-five slave markets.[17] Fear of a slave revolt, like Virginia's Nat Turner rebellion in 1831, was a source of constant unease among whites. It was nourished by the memories that the St Domingue refugees brought with them and recollections of the rising a few miles from the city in 1811. A more present danger than rebellious slaves was disorderly white men. The crowds of sailors and flatboatmen in search of drink and companionship made New Orleans a city of innumerable bars, brothels and gambling dens: the Babylon of the South, or, to some disapproving observers, its Sodom and Gomorrah. Not surprisingly, crimes of violence were common. Indeed, in the South it was considered legitimate (though not legal) for a 'gentleman' to avenge a slight by shooting or knifing the offender from behind, in an ambush or even while he was asleep in bed.[18] The results were spectacular. In the twenty-three months up to mid-1860, reported the New Orleans *Daily Crescent*, the police had made 62 arrests for murder, 146 for stabbing with intent to murder, 232 for swindling, 734 for assault with a deadly weapon, and 47,403 for assault and battery, threats and other transgressions.[19] An impressive total for a city of around 170,000 people.

Crime, drunkenness and fear of slave rebellion were not the only causes of tension. New Orleans was a subtropical city. Its older buildings carried more than a hint of its Caribbean connections. So did its climate. Indeed its subtropical climate and marshy environs were a lethal combination. The swamps and pools fed by heavy rainfall were a haven for mosquitoes. The high water table (burial plots in New Orleans had to be above ground level), primitive sanitation and the use of the river as sewer, fostered other contagions. New Orleans was not the only American port to feel the scourge of disease, but it suffered more than most. Cholera was a frequent visitor: in the great epidemic of 1832, some of the dead were simply thrown into the river.[20] Malaria was commonplace. He had to take 'the bark' (i.e. Peruvian bark or quinine) three times a day, a young planter told his fiancée in Virginia.[21] But the deadliest threat came from yellow fever. Yellow fever was mosquito-borne. Its causes and cure remained a medical mystery until 1905. Contemporary opinion attributed it to the 'pestilential exhalations' from partly drained marshlands.[22] Its carriers could arrive in a ship's water barrels and move into the barrels and cisterns of households in the city. The death of its victims was rapid and deeply distressing to see.[23] What made it more terrifying was its apparently random assault: taking some victims in a household but sparing others, and showing little regard for wealth or status. Worse still, the scale of mortality grew with time. After 1810 there were major outbreaks every three years, killing dozens if not hundreds at a time: the four epidemics of 1833, 1837, 1839 and 1841 averaged over 1,200 victims. Indeed, the larger the city's population, the more hosts it offered to the *Aedes aegypti*, the yellow-fever mosquito. The great influx of European immigrants after 1848 was a mosquito bonanza. The epidemic in 1853, presaged by a huge cloud of mosquitoes, brought the city to a standstill. The death toll in August alone was over 1,600, three hundred on one day. When it finally petered out, some 10,000 people had been carried off, around 10 per cent of the resident population.[24] All who could afford to do so had fled the city. Indeed, it had long been usual for merchants and other well-off inhabitants to abandon the city in summer to avoid the heat and the ever-present threat of disease. 'I do not like the idea of New Orleans much in the summer time,' wrote one Northern cotton buyer.[25] Business largely ground to a halt. By some estimates the city's population shrank by a third in the torrid months.

Despite hazards like these, New Orleans was a mecca for commercial ambition. Its hinterland was vast and in the three decades before 1860 it was developing at breakneck speed. Immediately above the city, for a hundred miles, the Mississippi was lined by about 1,300 sugar plantations, some dating back to the mid-eighteenth century. With the discovery of the granulation process in the 1790s, the introduction of steam mills and a ready supply of slaves, output rose rapidly, and sugar planters, a mixture of Creoles and Anglo-Americans, formed one of the richest groups in the South.[26] The scale of their wealth was visible in their grand neoclassical mansions, some of which have survived the transformation of the Louisiana landscape. A little further north, at the southern edge of the state of Mississippi, lay the Natchez District, first settled in the 1770s. This was a zone of legendary fertility, the reason for this early land-rush.[27]

Here, too, there were planters of exceptional wealth – one was reputed to own 2,000 slaves – and half the millionaires in the United States were said to live in the area.[28] The rest of Mississippi was only gradually wrested from the Choctaw and Chickasaw peoples in a series of treaties and purchases imposed by settler military power and the legal coercion of Andrew Jackson's Indian Removal Act of 1830.[29] Until the 1830s, the Indian nations had held more than half of the state. But by 1836 the whole state had been thrown open to settlers and land speculators and the cotton frenzy began. Less than twenty years later, Mississippi was producing more than a quarter of the raw cotton grown in the United States and more than any other state in the South.[30] Its slave labour force had grown in proportion. In 1830, before the 'opening' of its centre and north, Mississippi held some 65,000 slaves. Thirty years later that number had grown sevenfold to over 436,000.[31]

More cotton came down to New Orleans from Arkansas and Missouri, and from western Tennessee and northern Alabama by the Tennessee River which joined the Ohio just above its junction with the Mississippi at Cairo. From the Ohio Valley came a different stream of produce: wheat, maize, oats, beans, pork, lumber, hemp and tobacco, originally brought downriver in simply built flatboats with a crude deckhouse to protect cargo and crew. In just such a flatboat a youthful Abe Lincoln had set out from the landing at Rockport, 250 miles up the Ohio, in 1828 on the 1,300-mile voyage to New Orleans.[32] Some of this produce was sold en route to riverside plantations, but most in New Orleans for resale or export.[33] Flatboats and keelboats were cheap to build but flatboats could not return upriver against the current and in keelboats the trip was slow and laborious. Flatboats continued to bring Midwestern farm produce to market: nearly 3,000 tied up in New Orleans in 1846–7.[34] But by the 1830s steamboats connected almost every part of New Orleans's vast riverine hinterland.[35] In 1830 around 150 were in service; by 1840, there were 500; by 1860 more than 800.[36] Most were built on the upper Ohio. In 1860 there were more than 3,500 steamboat arrivals at the New Orleans Levee.[37]

The steamboat was the workhorse of the whole Mississippi system. Wide, shallow and flat-bottomed, it was designed to ride over shoals and sandbars, and to nudge onto the bank to load and unload from its bow. It needed almost nothing by way of wharves or quays – a crucial advantage at a time when the plantation economy was growing so fast. It helped to drive down the cost of river-borne freight by some 60 per cent by 1850.[38] Its fuel was provided from the plentiful woodlands that fringed the river. Passenger accommodation was rough and ready – often a squalid dormitory for men – and timetables were famously erratic. Piled high with cotton bales (sometimes up to 5,000 at a time), its decks might be almost awash, and fatal accidents were far from uncommon. The Mississippi had no lights or buoys to signal its hazards. It was prone to floods and droughts that shifted its navigable channels in unpredictable ways. In flood, it was 'a slimy monster hideous to behold', exclaimed an awed Charles Dickens.[39] A constant danger was hitting a 'snag', an uprooted tree hidden just below the surface: driven into at speed it could pierce the thin wooden hull with deadly results. Sparks from the funnels could set the bales alight: carrying oil and liquor as well could create an inferno. A steamboat fire burned down a large part of St Louis in 1849. Sudden eddies or currents could capsize a steamboat; collisions were easy where sandbars and shoals made the main channel narrow. But the most fearsome risk came from its boilers. Steamboats needed high-pressure boilers to drive them upstream against the current or through the mud and sand that slowed their passage. Speed and economy made them doubly attractive to steamboat owners.[40] But raising pressure too high or too quickly, using muddy water in the boiler, metal fatigue or too sharp a list, could produce an explosion, killing or scalding passengers and crew. (In his *Life on the Mississippi* (1883), Mark Twain gives a graphic description of the steamboat explosion in which his younger brother was killed.) Steamboat accidents killed over a thousand people between the mid-1820s and late 1840s. Dangerous as they were, steamboats were still safer than riding the trains of ante-bellum America. Moreover, safety improved: by the late 1850s steamboats had become as safe as car travel in 1970s America.[41] However, their life was short: few lasted more than four or five years before falling foul of a snag or some other disaster.

'No city in the world occupies a more important commercial position', boasted *Gardner's New Orleans Directory* in 1860. The city was home to nearly two thousand shops selling every variety of imported goods, some of it destined for wealthy planters inland. It had seven daily newspapers, four substantial banks, dozens of commission merchants, brokers (for cotton, tobacco, sugar and real estate), agents for shipping and steamboats, as well as slave dealers, numerous lawyers and nearly eighty physicians (the latter much in demand). The Levee was crowded with stevedores, boatmen, draymen and 'screwmen', screwing the cotton bales tight for shipment. There were clerks to grade and record the downriver cargoes of cotton or sugar. At the apex of this mercantile pyramid stood the hundred or so cotton factors, the pivot of New Orleans's commercial economy.

Like the business elite of many nineteenth-century port cities, the factors were rarely local-born: typically they were migrants from New York or New England.[42] The most influential factors, the Lizardi brothers, were refugees from Mexico.[43] The factors received raw cotton from planters and sold it (on commission or as the planter's agent) to (eventual) buyers in Europe's main cotton ports, Liverpool and Le Havre. Cotton was a speculative and volatile trade. Any number of shocks could disturb the market. A drought or infestation could damage the crop, driving up prices but reducing the volume of sales. A glut in Liverpool or a slowdown in Lancashire could drive the price down. A financial crash, drying up credit, as happened in 1837, could wreck the market for years, halving the cotton price. In setting how much he would pay, and accept on the sale, the factor paid attention to every snippet of news from Europe and the main cotton zones, including those in other parts of the world. He cocked his ear to every rumour of war, bankruptcy or outbreak of disease, upriver or overseas. 'The news from China in relation to the conclusion of war with England has upset all my calculations,' wrote one cotton buyer ruefully in 1842.[44]

Much of the factor's time was spent in correspondence with his clients, the up-country planters. He needed to keep in close touch with them to gain the earliest news of the crop and the plantation's affairs, not least the size and health of its slave labour force, the most critical factor in the plantation's fortunes. For the factor was not just a buyer. He advanced credit to the planter against the bales he produced, acted as his agent, arranged his purchases of dry goods, foodstuffs and even slaves, and entertained him when in town. The wealthy Natchez planter William Newton Mercer was informed by his factor that his order of pork and salt was coming on the steamboat 'Ellen Douglas'.[45] If the planter went to the North, or to Europe on vacation, the factor would arrange credit for his travels with his own correspondents in New York or Liverpool. Factoring was a furiously competitive and risk-laden business. A factor might buy dear but be forced to sell cheap. He might be let down by untrustworthy agents, incompetent planters, the loss of a ship or improvident debtors.[46] But the steady rise in demand, the phenomenal growth of the Cotton Kingdom's extent, and the great boom of the 1850s kept most above water and made some fabulously rich, with wealth to invest in plantations of their own. This was a wealthy and self-confident elite.

There seemed solid reasons for confidence. As a cotton port, New Orleans had far outdistanced its main Southern rivals: Charleston was in decline;[47] Savannah served only Georgia; the sandbar at Mobile (the port for southern Alabama) kept shipping twenty miles downstream. None could match New Orleans for hinterland. The city boiled with plans for southward expansion, first into Texas,[48] then to Central America, and above all to Cuba. The annexation of Cuba as another slave state (perhaps even two) would strengthen the South and ward off the threat of abolitionist pressure from Britain.[49] New Orleans politicians were behind the several abortive attempts to overthrow Spanish rule by a filibuster invasion, and had eagerly supported the two abortive attempts to buy Cuba from Spain in 1854 and 1859.[50] Some even dreamed of another slave empire in Brazil's Amazonia, to be colonized by Americans: the Amazon would be a 'continuation of the Mississippi Valley', claimed the oceanographer Matthew Maury.[51] Yet even before the great rupture of secession and war, to the critical eye there were many grounds for uncertainty about New Orleans's future prospects – and even more reason to doubt that the great Southern metropolis was in real command of its hinterland, politically, culturally or even commercially.

In part, this was because, for all its advantages, New Orleans suffered from a number of growing deficiencies as an expanding port city. It was expensive by comparison with other ports in America.[52]

Shipowners complained at the costs and delays of the steam-haul upstream. By 1850 ships of more than 1,000 tons found it difficult to enter the river over its sandbars and could face delays of up to two months.[53] Imports and exports lay on the Levee exposed to the weather and theft, and the Levee was often a muddy morass precariously navigated on duckboards. As a port New Orleans had rarely been able to balance its imports and exports, so that ships often arrived in ballast to collect a cargo of cotton or sugar – a significant cost factor. Worse still, by the 1850s the city was losing its place as the commercial outlet for much of the Upper Mississippi and Ohio valleys – its original hinterland. Canal-building had begun to suck some of their trade eastwards towards New York in the 1840s. But the real damage was done by the great burst of railway construction in the 1850s that linked the Midwest to New York. The Midwest's bare handful of lines in 1850 had turned into a relatively dense network by the end of the decade.[54] New Orleans's grain trade that had grown enormously by the mid-1840s now began to contract. Rail transport cost growers more, but it avoided the delays and deterioration (from heat) of the long river trip. By 1860 New York exported more than ten times as much wheat as New Orleans and vastly more maize.[55] New Orleans grew ever more dependent on its cotton staple. But even here it played a curiously subordinate role. The financing of the vast cotton crop largely depended on credit supplied from or through New York. 'The reimbursement for shipments from the South is frequently made in an indirect manner through New York,' wrote a contemporary expert in 1840.[56] By 1860 New Orleans had long surrendered financial primacy to the Empire City, and it was commonplace for merchants in the South to arrange their purchases of imported goods through the Northern not the Southern metropolis. And for all the loud talk about Southern expansion into the Caribbean and beyond, there was little that New Orleans could achieve without the active support of the Federal government in Washington. Without a merchant navy of its own (most merchant shipping was owned in the North), the scope for informal 'sub-imperialism' by New Orleans merchants was drastically limited – an explanation perhaps for the futile reliance on filibusters and exiles.

Many Southerners railed against what they saw as dependence on the shipping and finance of the North and against the 'tribute' (in interest, insurance and shipping charges) paid to New York in particular. But it would be a mistake to see the South as a backward, stagnant or 'pre-capitalist' zone mired in its doomed slave-labour system. When the South's slave states broke away to form the Confederacy in 1861, they made up together the world's fourth most prosperous economy with per capita incomes (even including the slave population) that were higher than those of Belgium, France, the Netherlands and Germany, and were only exceeded by those of the Australian colonies, the Northern United States and Britain. Indeed, large parts of the Northern states outside the very wealthy north-east had a lower income per head than the South.[57] Slave-state cotton provided half America's exports, and its volume and value seemed to be growing exponentially. Cotton production doubled between 1840 and 1850, and doubled again by the end of the decade with much of the increase coming between 1857 and 1860. It was reason enough for the South Carolina planter James Henry Hammond to declare in the Senate 'Cotton is king.' There seemed no limit to the surging demand from factories in Europe and the American North. Slave cultivation had weathered the long depression after 1837; cotton acreage had expanded, and seemed set to expand further.

Not surprisingly, capitalist attitudes were deeply ingrained in the planter mentality. Profits from cotton were turned into capital in the form of more slaves, because 'slaves made the crop'. Whites without slaves aspired to acquire them as the means to economic and social mobility; and, since slaves were capital, it was a curious fact that the possession of capital was more equally spread (among white men) in the South than in the North.[58] Planters were keenly alert to the commercial environment through the wide circulation of 'prices current', paid attention to issues of soil management and fertilizer, and experimented constantly with new cotton strains to improve their yield.[59] They extracted a huge increase in the productivity of their slaves (perhaps by almost 400 per cent between 1800 and 1860), partly by using new varieties of cotton that were easier to pick, and by adopting the 'gang-system' in which slave work was supervised throughout the day rather than broken up in individual 'tasks' after which the slaves' time was free. How widespread the use of brutal 'incentives' and the whip to raise picking rates was is unclear.[60] Indeed, many Southerners acknowledged that slavery was inhuman, but insisted upon its economic and social necessity.

That they did so is a reminder that globalization could produce many different forms of modernity. It was the global trade in cotton that made the Slave South economically and socially viable. It made Southern whites (and by compulsion their slaves) astonishingly mobile.[61] Most planters did not live in porticoed mansions but in quickly built log houses. The slovenly landscape on which visitors frequently commented was largely the product of the rawness and newness of the Cotton Kingdom, scarcely three decades old by 1860, and the nomad-like habits of the planter class, constantly moving to richer soils further on. In Arkansas a planter class was still in the making in the 1850s.[62] If aristocracy is really 'ancient riches', there were very few aristocrats in the Cotton Kingdom. Planters lived 'in the midst of the competitive, revolutionizing, destructive and chaotic swirl of frontier capitalism'.[63] Slavery was also compatible with a powerful ethic of egalitarianism between whites. Indeed, many loud voices insisted that slavery was the best means of preserving the Jeffersonian tradition of republican equality and avoiding descent into class division and oligarchy.[64] 'Slave-based modernity' was capitalist, seemingly egalitarian between white men (in reality poor whites were increasingly marginalized by the slave economy)[65] and intensely mobile: its spatial dynamism made rootedness an aberration.[66] Status derived chiefly from wealth and conspicuous consumption.[67] Slavery's champions claimed that it was not only historically 'normal' but the only means whereby vast areas of the subtropical globe could be developed commercially. Notoriously, they deployed the racial justification that blacks were incapable of purposeful labour (what the Victorians called 'progress') without white control. They denounced abolitionism as the road to regression and chaos: 'civilization itself', declared *De Bow's Review*, the leading commentator on Southern commerce and politics, 'may almost be said to depend upon the continual servitude of blacks in America'.[68] Far from assuming that history was against them, they thought that globalization would vindicate slavery. Nor was the racial ideology on which slavery rested too widely divergent from the racist assumptions that were current in the North.[69] Illinois, Abraham Lincoln's home state, made slavery unlawful in 1848, but two years later prohibited the entry of African Americans: violators would be sold into slavery outside the state.[70] Northerners and 'liberal' Southerners alike regarded the return of freed slaves to Africa (the original aim behind the founding of Liberia) as the best solution to the problem of slavery – a programme propagated by 'colonization societies' active in both the North and South. New Orleans's wealthiest citizen, the slave owner John McDonogh, was an ardent supporter.

All this casts a curious light on the role of New Orleans as a great Atlantic port city. We might expect a port city to 'command' its hinterland economically and, in an era of globalization, to act as its prime intermediary with the rest of the world, including its principal markets. As the commercial metropolis, we might assume it exerted a significant political influence on the interior region, shaping its laws and ideology to conform more closely to those of economically more powerful partners – Britain and France in this case. Culturally, too, we might imagine that port-city values and attitudes would be disseminated among its interior clients and customers, partly as a consequence of its commercial prestige or because it served as the source of new fashions, prestige consumer goods and, not least, foreign news. But, as we have seen, in almost all these respects, New Orleans fell short. A large part of its hinterland was being hacked away by the 1850s and diverted to New York or Baltimore by the construction of railways. In its core 'Cotton Kingdom' a substantial part of its exports went coastwise to New York and from there to Europe in shipping that was owned in the North. The financial machinery on which cotton production depended was managed mainly from New York. In political terms New Orleans was, and remained, a cosmopolitan outlier, suspected by Anglo-Americans of 'un-American' opinions, not least towards free blacks. It was stripped of its status as Louisiana's state capital in 1849. To many white Southerners, its creole traditions and the 'Yankee' provenance of its merchant elite, made it doubly alien. The laws and ideology that shaped New Orleans's hinterland did not derive from the city or its

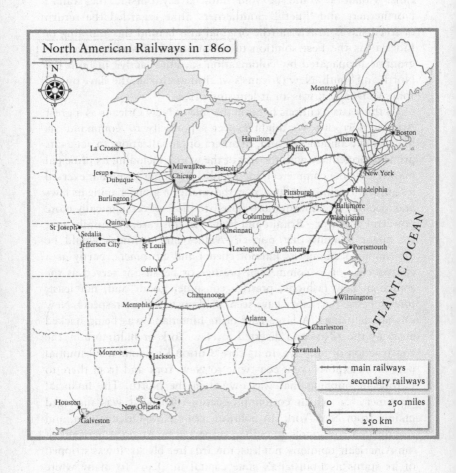

North American Railways in 1860

N

Montreal
Boston
Hamilton
Albany
La Crosse
Buffalo
Jesup
Milwaukee
Detroit
New York
Dubuque
Chicago
Philadelphia
Burlington
Pittsburgh
Baltimore
Quincy
Indianapolis
Columbus
Washington
St Joseph
Sedalia
Cincinnati
Jefferson City
St Louis
Lexington
Lynchburg
Portsmouth
Cairo
Chattanooga
Wilmington
Memphis
Atlanta
Charleston
Monroe
Savannah
Jackson
Houston
New Orleans
Galveston

ATLANTIC OCEAN

main railways
secondary railways

0   250 miles
0   250 km

external connections. They were brought from the old 'Upper South', from Virginia and South Carolina, whose planters and poorer whites had colonized Alabama, Mississippi, northern Louisiana, eastern Texas, Arkansas, Missouri and western Tennessee. This region had been conquered physically by white settlers in Andrew Jackson's wars before it was attached commercially to New Orleans. Its political elite was largely composed of those who had moved from the Upper to the Lower South, and proclaimed its values in an intensified version. Culturally, New Orleans represented an agreeable haunt for pleasure-seeking whites, not a beacon of taste or a literary magnet. The South had no 'great city', complained William Gilmore Simms, the South Carolinian doyen of Southern literature.[71] Even the news that arrived there usually came first from New York via its Atlantic packets, and it was from New York not New Orleans that Southern newspapers typically drew their commercial information.[72] The peculiar modernity that globalization had brought to the South thus owed little to New Orleans. Indeed, far from being the master of its hinterland, New Orleans was really a dependant of it.

The costs of this were graphically illustrated in the secession crisis of 1861. New Orleans's leaders were opposed to leaving the Union and hoped for a settlement along the lines of the previous great compromises between the slave and free states. But as the movement for separation spread, they fell in line with the rest of the South, not least because their own fortunes depended as much upon slavery as those of their planter clients. Indeed, many were themselves slave and plantation owners.[73] Perhaps some in the city believed that secession would turn New Orleans into the New York of the South.[74] The South's self-imposed embargo on the export of cotton (intended to force British and French recognition of the Confederacy and perhaps intervention on its behalf) froze New Orleans's trade. Its defence was a low priority to Confederate leaders and the city was captured by the Union's navy in 1862. Notoriously, the Confederate surrender in April 1865, and the enforced end of slavery, wrecked much of the South's economy, if only temporarily,[75] and that of New Orleans with it. The confiscation of slave 'capital', the impoverishment of planters, and the adoption of share-cropping across the cotton South, destroyed the commercial relationship between factor and planter, based as it was upon the planter's credit as the possessor of slaves. The advances to cotton farmers were now decentralized to country-store owners better able to monitor a mass of small growers.[76]

New Orleans itself sank into picturesque decline and became increasingly shabby. In the last quarter of the nineteenth century its wharves were ramshackle, the value of trade through the port in the 1890s was lower than it had been in 1859–60, and the city was plagued by yellow fever (which killed over 4,000 people in 1878), typhoid, smallpox and diphtheria. New Orleans sank from being America's sixth largest city in 1860 to its twelfth by 1900.[77] In 1860 it had shipped some 32 per cent of American exports; by 1901 the figure was just 7 per cent.[78] 'In 1913, commercially, the Mississippi was dead', was the crisp assessment of a British economist.[79] 'No first-rank American city's fortunes have ever collapsed as quickly as did those of New Orleans after 1860', concludes a recent historian.[80] The 'greatest city in the Western hemisphere' had fallen on very hard times.

By the early twentieth century the old French Quarter (the tourist mecca of the city today) had become almost a slum, only saved from destruction by a wealthy philanthropist. Much of New Orleans's cotton business moved north to St Louis or west to Galveston in nearby east Texas. New Orleans survived as a port, and the river slowly recovered as a commercial highway. Later the section through Louisiana became a 'chemical corridor' of refineries and chemical plants. But by the 1920s, perhaps, New Orleans was best known as the seedy Bohemia of jazz musicians and literary hopefuls. For one of those hopefuls, the poet Robert Penn Warren, it was most of all a town to get drunk in:

> Down Royal Street – Sunday and the street
> blank as my bank account
> with two checks bounced – we –
> C. and M. and I, every
> man-jack skunk-drunk –
> came.[81]

QUEEN OF THE NORTH: MONTREAL

Like New Orleans, Montreal looked out over a vast riverine hinter-land. It stretched north and west towards Hudson Bay and the prairies and forests beyond Lake Superior, south and west to the Great Lakes, and the Ohio and Mississippi valleys. Like New Orleans, it was a French foundation on an old Native American site, and was to play its part in the grand design for New France in North America. Like New Orleans, it was made largely by steam. Like New Orleans, its commercial fortunes would ride a rollercoaster of geopolitical change and be strained by the competition of New York City. But unlike the Southern city, its great days would come not in the first half of the steam century but late in its second half.

The site of Montreal, then the Indian town of Hochelaga, was visited by the French explorer Jacques Cartier in 1535. When the French returned in 1642, it was to establish an upriver outstation for their main base at Quebec, founded in 1608 and the kernel of 'New France'.[82] Montreal was at first a mission station, reflecting the large role that Jesuits and other Catholic orders were meant to play in winning the friendship of the Indian nations of the Cana-dian interior. But it quickly became the main inland depot for the trade in furs, the staple export of New France and the mainstay of its commercial economy. The settlement lay on the east side of an island, dominated by 'Mount Royal', the mountain that gave it its name. Its importance derived from its location at the head of navi-gation of the St Lawrence River. A few miles upstream a set of rapids which the French christened hopefully Lachine ('China') barred the way to the upper St Lawrence and the Great Lakes, and the northerly river route up the Ottawa river into the fur-rich north-west. These two great passages into the North American interior converged there. A third river route lay to the south, through Lake Champlain and on to the Hudson River (and New York). Thus Montreal was a riverine 'crossroads', and also a 'portage';[83] goods had to be carried round the rapids at Lachine and re-embarked there in the riverboats and canoes that would take them up the St Lawrence or the Ottawa. Quebec long remained the main port for

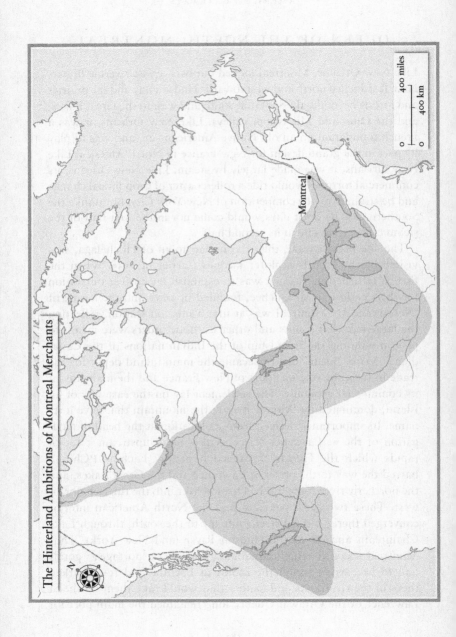

The Hinterland Ambitions of Montreal Merchants

Montreal

0   400 miles

0   400 km

New France and British Canada, but Montreal was the key to continental ambition.

When France was evicted from the North American mainland in 1763, Montreal became British. A crowd of merchants rushed in from the British colonies to the south. They hoped to exploit Montreal's connections with what would become the American Midwest and take over its fur trade.[84] Indeed, the new British province of Quebec was extended deep into the trans-Appalachian interior behind the 'American' colonies further south, partly to prevent its colonization by white settlers and preserve easy relations with the Indian nations. These hopes were quickly extinguished by the outcome of the American revolution: in 1783 the whole wide zone below the Great Lakes was ceded to the new republic, but Montreal and Canada remained British. By 1814, surviving British (and Montreal) influence among the Indian nations south of the Great Lakes had been crushed in a series of frontier wars, and what became known as the 'Old Northwest' was forced open to American settlers. For Montreal and its traders it was on the *Canadian* north-west and its fur trade that their commercial future now depended. A skein of canoe routes and innumerable portages (via the Ottawa River, Lake Superior and a gruelling trek to the Red River and Lake Winnipeg)[85] linked Montreal to the 'wintering partners' who bartered for furs from indigenous hunters in the *pays d'en haut*. But here too the Montrealers faced a struggle. As the fur frontier receded, it became harder and harder to compete with the Hudson's Bay Company, the English chartered company whose forts on the Bay gave it far closer access to the sources of fur.[86] By 1821, when the Montreal fur interests accepted defeat and merged with the Company, a new basis was needed for the city's economy.

The omens were mixed. Much of the interior stretching away to the north and west formed the Canadian 'shield': the thin, rocky soil and long hard winters repelled would-be farmers and made it at best the resort of the lumberjack. The southern parts of 'Upper Canada' (modern Ontario) were more promising, but the river route there was checked by rapids, by those at Lachine most of all. As an Atlantic port, Montreal suffered from three major handicaps. The St Lawrence was ice-bound for five months of the year from, November to

April; its fierce current made the upriver passage slow and difficult for sailing ships; and the approaches to Montreal through Lac St-Pierre were anyway too shallow for larger vessels. To make matters worse, from the Montreal merchants' perspective, in 1791 the imperial government in London had divided what remained of the old Quebec province into two separate colonies, 'Upper' and 'Lower' Canada: the first predominantly anglophone, Protestant and 'British'; the second mainly francophone, Catholic and 'French'. The Montreal merchant elite, increasingly reinforced by other migrants from Britain, found themselves locked into a province whose local politicians resented their influence, their ill-disguised contempt for the 'backward' *habitants*, and their apparent intention to make Montreal a 'British' metropolis for both the Canadas. This mutual ill-feeling helped to fuel the French-Canadian rebellion of 1837–8, which was largely centred in Montreal's rural surroundings.[87]

These demanding conditions jerked the old fur-trading factors out of the 'fatal inertia' that local critics had condemned in the cotton princes of New Orleans. They grasped straight away that Montreal's prosperity would depend on mobilizing political support to improve its waterway links. In Montreal, business was politics and politics was business: persuading local lawmakers to fund improvements in transport was the price of commercial survival. Thus the Lachine Canal was completed in 1825 at public expense, to be followed by further improvements on the upper St Lawrence to make an easier passage from Lake Ontario to Montreal. From an early date (1830) – far earlier than in Liverpool or London – Montreal's port facilities were brought under the control of a harbour commission. Montreal businessmen were also quick to grasp the opportunities of its riverhead location to diversify into local manufacture and processing: initially in brewing and flour-milling, but soon enough into shoes, clothes and metal goods. It was a brewer, John Molson, who financed the first steamboat service to link Montreal and Quebec, still Canada's real port city. They were helped by the willingness of the imperial government to contribute to the heavy costs of canal-building for strategic reasons: the threat of an American invasion and the need to ferry British troops to the frontier was not put to rest until the 1870s. Nevertheless, the danger that the huge debts the canals brought with them would not be offset by the revenues they earned, and wreck the public finances of both Canadian provinces, was a constant menace to political stability. Indeed, unifying the two Canadas in 1840 seemed to make little difference. It was a reminder of the fragile foundations of Montreal's – and Canada's – participation in the international economy.[88]

The real crisis came in the late 1840s. By then Montreal enjoyed communication by sail or steamboat all the way to the northern end of Lake Huron.[89] A substantial part of this traffic derived from the peculiar rule that allowed American-grown produce shipped through Canada to profit from tariff-free access to Britain at a time when the Corn Laws imposed a stiff duty on foreign wheat. But after 1846 the London government swiftly dismantled the apparatus of colonial protection: colonies like Canada now had to compete on equal terms with foreign producers and the profitable fiction of America's 'Canadian' wheat was swept away. In Montreal, the threat of commercial calamity loomed large. It was the tariff alone that had made it competitive with American ports to the south, New York especially. Economic depression and inter-ethnic strife made the city a tinderbox. In 1849 riots and disorder culminated in the burning of the Parliament building (the two Canadas had been united in 1840 with Montreal as the capital of the united provinces). A large part of the business community signed the notorious 'Annexation Manifesto', demanding that Canada be allowed to join the United States – an astonishing repudiation of the patriotic devotion to Britain so loudly proclaimed a few years before. 'We have no voice in the affairs of the Empire,' the Manifesto declared.[90] For Montreal, early globalization, in the form of free trade, had come as a seismic shock.

The consequences were less grim than the merchants had feared. Free trade in non-manufactured goods with the United States, negotiated by London in 1854, offered some hope that Montreal and the Canadian canal system would continue to draw American grain exports towards the St Lawrence, at least during summer when they could be shipped to Europe more quickly than by the American ports. In reality, there was little evidence of this.[91] Without better links with the American Midwest, it was still twice as dear to ship a barrel of flour via Montreal to Liverpool as to send it via New York,

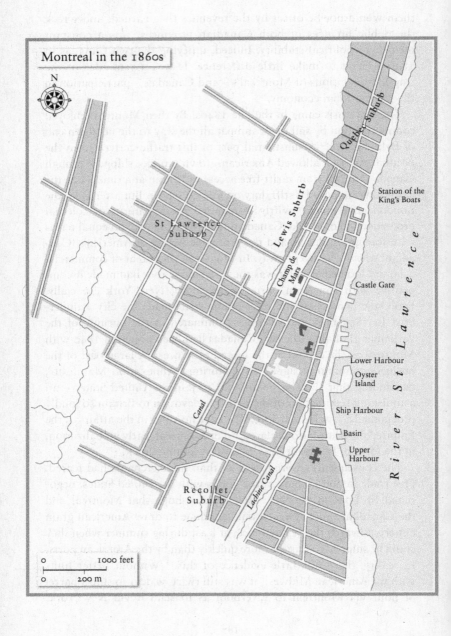

Montreal in the 1860s

N

St Lawrence
Suburb

Lewis Suburb

Quebec Suburb

Champ de
Mars

Canal

Récollet
Suburb

Lachine Canal

Station of the
King's Boats

Castle Gate

Lower Harbour

Oyster
Island

Ship Harbour

Basin

Upper
Harbour

River St Lawrence

0   1000 feet
0   200 m

complained a Montreal shipowner in 1855.[92] Much more important was the expansion of the Atlantic economy in the prosperous 1850s, widening the market for Canadian grain and expanding the farmlands of Upper Canada, the market for much of Montreal's goods and services.[93] The downriver channel was deepened, allowing the first ocean steamer to reach the city in 1853. Three years later Hugh Allan's Ocean Steamship Company established a subsidized packet service with Liverpool.[94] The city itself grew swiftly in size (from some 57,000 in 1851 to 90,000 ten years later), to the profit of its local agrarian hinterland, the fertile Montreal plain. 'I was scarcely prepared to find the "island city" so noble, prosperous and thoroughly British,' wrote an (English) visitor in 1864.[95] But it was the coming of the railways – an *all-season* transport system to end the commercial prison of winter – that sealed Montreal's status as Canada's leading port, finally supplanting Quebec.

Railway fever spread through North America in the 1850s. For Montreal and the commercial interests of the St Lawrence Valley, the danger was that the grain exports of the Great Lakes region, including those of Upper Canada, would be diverted along the American railroads to New York, Boston or Baltimore. Already in the late 1840s a group of Montreal businessmen had formed a partnership with merchants in Portland, Maine, to build the St Lawrence and Atlantic Railway and give Montreal the vital sea route for the ice-bound months from November to April. In 1853 a much more ambitious project was launched for a 'Grand Trunk Railway' to run the whole width of the Canadas from the St Lawrence estuary to the American boundary at Detroit. Montreal, with its connection to Portland, would be the hub.[96] In 1856, when much of the system was opened, a celebratory report, *Montreal in 1856*, proclaimed that now Montreal merchants would be able to offer Western consumers (both Canadian and American) the goods they wanted as quickly as New York or Boston. 'All that Canadian commerce has to gain from railways has yet to come,' it enthused. 'Judge for yourselves of [Montreal's] prospects, and say whether we, her citizens, have not reason to look forward to a brilliant future.'[97] When the Victoria Bridge was opened in 1860, bringing the railway line across the river and directly into the city, that brilliant future seemed assured.

Yet, as so often in Montreal's history, the reality was less promising. By 1860 the Grand Trunk Railway was bankrupt and its politics were a scandal. Across much of the world, railway-building depended (often controversially and as often corruptly) upon public subsidies, loan guarantees and promises of monopoly. In Canada, this dependence was intensified by the inherent fragility of its east–west communications in the railway age against the magnetic pull of north to south: the commercial power of America's railroads and its ice-free ports, New York above all. To make matters worse, the increasingly bitter inter-sectional politics between Protestant 'British' Upper Canada and Catholic 'French' Lower Canada, in their precarious union, left little room for a concerted programme of economic development. Indeed, agrarian Upper Canada viewed Montreal, and its bankers, merchants and railway promoters, with intense suspicion: American railways could carry its crops to market more cheaply and quickly than Canadian lines. Montreal would survive as a port and a regional manufacturing centre (half its occupied population was engaged in manufacture by 1871).[98] It was Canada's largest city, its main banking centre and the main seat of commerce. It had a stock exchange, a corn exchange and a multitude of commodity brokers and agents.[99] It was considerably larger than its nearest rival Toronto, whose merchants remained dependent on Montreal suppliers.[100] It had become the closest thing to a Canadian metropolis: but the ambition to serve as the great port city for the whole northern half of the continent – 'the brilliant future' its leading merchants had imagined – would require something more than the railways and steamships that had at last made Montreal, a thousand miles from the ocean, a major Atlantic seaport.

That change was to come, but in roundabout ways and more than thirty years later. In the mid-1860s the separate provinces of 'British North America' were strung out in a wafer-thin line some 3,000 miles long, from Newfoundland (an impoverished fishing colony), Nova Scotia, New Brunswick and tiny Prince Edward Island in the east, through the 'United Provinces' of the Canadas to the fledgling gold-rush colony of British Columbia on the Pacific. Its population was barely a tenth of the leviathan's to the south. Most of the land surface of modern Canada was the territory of Rupertsland, administered under its charter by the Hudson's Bay Company: a domain of tundra, vast coniferous forest and treeless prairie, meagrely populated by indigenous Indians and the mixed-race *metis* of the Red River settlement (near modern Winnipeg) who combined buffalo-hunting and farming.[101] That this straggle of colonies had eluded the northern march of American 'manifest destiny' was partly due to the Slave South's distaste for more 'free states', partly to the naval power of Great Britain: the threat of the blockade and bombardment of American ports.[102] But as the American Civil War drew to a close in 1865, tension between Britain and the victorious North, aggravated by what was seen in Washington as British complicity in Confederate commerce-raiding, revived the threat of annexation. Commercial relations broke down with American refusal to renew the free trade in 'natural' produce. It was in this highly charged atmosphere that a remarkable coalition of politicians from the Canadas, Nova Scotia and New Brunswick, led by John A. Macdonald, a consummate politician (some contemporaries described him differently),[103] fashioned Confederation between 1864 and 1867.[104] Federal union was meant to ward off the danger of American imperialism and strengthen the colonies' claim on British protection. Its promoters hoped for other benefits as well. Nova Scotia and New Brunswick hoped that a railway connection with Montreal would bring Canadian produce to their ports. In Lower Canada, now called Quebec, it relieved the French-Canadian majority from domination by more populous Upper Canada, now the separate province of Ontario. In 'British' Ontario much of the allure of Confederation lay in the expectation that the new dominion would acquire Rupertsland, and open a vast new frontier of agrarian settlement on the prairies, a second Ontario. Among the Anglo-Protestants of Montreal feelings were mixed. 'The great and varied interests of commerce, trade, banking, manufactures and material progress generally, which are supposed to centre in the city of Montreal,' declared John Rose, the well-connected lawyer and Montreal MP, 'have considered the scheme . . . and have deliberately come to the conclusion that it is calculated to promote the best interests and greatly enhance the prosperity of this country.'[105] But half the 'English' papers in Montreal were opposed, fearing isolation in an overwhelmingly French-Canadian province.[106]

The new dominion duly obtained the transfer of Rupertsland at a knock-down price, a huge endowment of space as significant for Canada's future as the Louisiana Purchase had been for the United States. It also persuaded faraway British Columbia to enter the Confederation with the promise of a transcontinental railway from the Atlantic to the Pacific. Here was a prospect to whet the appetite of Montreal business. The steamship owner Hugh Allan rushed forward with a scheme for a Pacific railway. It ended in scandal: Allan's financial ties with Prime Minister Macdonald and the Conservative Party and the revelation that much of the capital for his plan was American destroyed its credibility.[107] The dream of a great western settlement, and of a through-line to the Pacific and far-eastern trade, dissolved in the depression that settled over Canada in the 1870s. Tens of thousands of Canadians moved south of the border, perhaps more than a million by the end of the century. The 'national policy' of tariff protection, adopted in 1878, was a desperate defence against the freezing winds of the global economy. It sheltered Montreal, which grew rapidly, almost doubling its population to some 290,000 between 1871 and 1891. But this was Montreal as an increasingly industrial city, serving a partly closed and far from dynamic economy and what remained a frustratingly limited hinterland.

Yet it was still a Confederation commitment to build a transcontinental railway, and Macdonald's Conservative government, returned in 1878, was more anxious than ever to do so. A new scheme was hatched in Montreal's St James Street, the city's banking quarter. It brought together three of Montreal's most powerful financiers: Donald Smith of the Hudson's Bay Company (which had retained valuable pockets of land in the former Rupertsland); his nephew George Stephen, who combined large manufacturing interests, a large share in the railway from Minneapolis-St Paul to Manitoba, and presidency of the Bank of Montreal, Montreal and Canada's largest bank; and R. B. Angus, until recently the Bank's general manager and a major financier in his own right.[108] In 1880 they extracted a generous contract from Macdonald promising a large start-up grant, huge tracts of land along the line of rail and a twenty-year monopoly against any competitor line. Even so, the Canadian Pacific Railway (CPR) teetered on the brink of collapse before its completion in 1885 and had to be bailed out by the government, as well as by Smith and Stephen personally. The reason was simple. With vast overheads to cover on a line that ran through unsettled forest and prairie, commercial success was at best highly speculative.[109] By the mid-1890s even George Stephen, its principal architect, began to lose faith. With grain prices at rock bottom, the prairies as the great new Canadian wheat-land looked the wildest of dreams. But Canada's circumstances, and those of Montreal, were about to change with startling abruptness.

The first indication was the rise in the price of wheat after 1896 from its lowest point in some forty years. Combined with the filling up of the American West, and the use of hardier strains of wheat, the effect was to transform the promise of the Canadian prairies. As immigrants poured in, many from south of the border, wheat production there expanded rapidly. Exports of wheat to Britain increased fifteen-fold to over $100 million between 1901 and 1914.[110] Wheat was supplemented by the rise of a new export commodity, wood pulp for newsprint, and by the new base minerals of the Ontario north, copper, nickel, zinc and cobalt, as well as gold. After 1900 the pace of growth accelerated sharply. Immigration, which stood at some 40,000 a year in 1900, reached the staggering figure of over 400,000 in 1914. Most dramatic of all (and most important to Montreal) was Canada's newfound attractiveness to foreign, especially British, investors. Gone were the days when Canadian financiers had to wheedle and plead in the City of London. Canada's immigrant and export boom promised a generous return on investment in its railways, utilities, mines, farmlands and urban real estate. British investment soared from a scant $10 million sent in 1900 to nearly $400 million raised in 1913.[111] In little more than a decade the Canadian economy was globalized. Its external trade, increasing threefold in value, more than matched the doubling of world trade between 1900 and 1913. Far more than previously, the stability of the Canadian economy came to depend upon an ever-growing stream of exports and an ever-rising volume of imported capital to pay for the huge overheads of railway construction and build the infrastructure on which growth relied. 'Canada,' remarked the influential London banker Robert Brand in 1913, 'has as much interest in maintaining the flow of capital from England as a city has in preventing its water supply from being cut off.'[112] Indeed, by 1911–12 imported capital composed half the new capital raised in Canada.[113]

Montreal lay at the centre of this new commercial and financial regime. The Canadian Pacific Railway, headquartered there, paid a 10 per cent dividend; its steamship line turned it into a global brand. Montreal was the prime outlet for the cascade of wheat exports delivered to its docks by the CPR. The West's surging expansion expanded the market for Montreal's growing industries and for the manufactured imports that passed through its harbour.[114] Most of all, Montreal's wealth reflected its role as Canada's financial centre. Much of the new stream of capital passed through its banks, finance houses and financiers. The Bank of Montreal, already Canada's largest bank, managed around half of Canadian borrowing in London through its office there.[115] London-based moneymen (like Robert Brand of Lazards) on the lookout for profitable ventures, needed its commercial intelligence. As a transport hub for railways and shipping, and an industrial, commercial and financial city, Montreal was becoming a global metropolis. Then just as the pre-war boom seemed to be petering out, the outbreak of war in 1914 added a further huge stimulus. Canada became not just a vital supplier of wheat, but increasingly a producer of munitions and (ironically) a source of borrowing to aid the over-strained British economy and its dwindling reserves of foreign exchange. By the end of the war, Canada had become a significant force in world trade. Its share of world exports (in 1922) at 4.4 per cent was larger than that of India, Italy or Japan, and much larger than Australia's or Argentina's.[116] And as Canada became both a more integrated as well as more globalized economy, Montreal's importance – it seemed – could only grow and grow.

Montreal's pre-eminence could be traced to several distinctive features in its urban development. Of course, its command of rail and river routes into the Canadian interior was a vital endowment. Both had had to be improved continuously, and funded by the ruthless exertion of political influence and financial craft. The business elite was not as monolithically Scots as is sometimes suggested: it included English, Americans and French Canadians as well.[117] But at its core lay a close-knit, often intermarried, community of Scots, regularly reinforced by new recruits from the homeland.[118] The most powerful figures in the city's business world – John Young, George Stephen, Donald Smith, Sir George Drummond, Hugh Allan and Sir John Rose – were all Scots-born.[119] Crucially, this business elite quickly diversified from the commodity trades into manufacturing and transport, investing in railways, steamships, sugar-refining, textiles, ironworks, shoes and clothing (the contrast with New Orleans is startling). Men like Hugh Allan built a business empire that extended across shipping, railways, the Montreal Telegraph Company, banking, insurance, textiles, tobacco and coalmining.[120] It was this early emergence of a cluster of railway, industrial, commercial and financial capital that enabled Montreal to ride out the years of stagnation and exploit the new world that opened at the turn of the century. It was the private fortunes of Donald Smith of the Hudson's Bay Company (long based in Montreal), and his nephew George Stephen of the Bank of Montreal, that saved the Canadian Pacific Railway from financial collapse before its line was completed.[121] It was the close links forged between the Bank of Montreal and the City of London that speeded the flow of British capital before 1913. By one calculation, in 1900 Montreal's business elite controlled some 70 per cent of the Canadian economy.[122]

Strikingly, that business elite were not free traders: quite the reverse. Their instincts were mercantilist, protectionist and monopolist. They needed political help and political guile if they were not to be overwhelmed by the leviathan of New York, and were ready to pay for it: backhanders and side deals were the stuff of Montreal politics. Their programme of tariffs and state-aided development had been laid out by Alexander Galt (a Montrealer by interests and outlook) in the late 1850s.[123] Under Sir John A. Macdonald it became the 'national policy' successfully defended against 'reciprocity' (free trade with the United States) in 1911.[124] Yet with characteristic pragmatism, Montreal businessmen still hoped to draw the trade of the American Midwest down the St Lawrence. They were keenly aware how much Montreal's financial success depended on the mood of the City of London, just as the price of wheat was settled in Liverpool and came through the 'Liverpool cables'.[125] They recruited the first two general managers of the CPR (William Van Horne and Thomas Shaughnessy) from American railwaymen, and much of its early capital from

New York. Montreal and other Canadian banks also routinely kept their reserves on call in New York as well as in London.[126] Montreal could apply a powerful subterranean influence on the federal capital at Ottawa, a short train journey away. It could play New York to Ottawa's Washington. But, viewed in the round, Montreal's command of its vast transcontinental hinterland was very far from complete.

Its 'Anglo-Protestant' elite regarded Montreal as a 'British' city. It had had its own Nelson's Column since 1809. To a French observer in 1904, it seemed that 'visitors may pass whole weeks there, frequenting hotels, banks, shops, railway stations without ever imagining for a moment that the town is French by a great majority of its inhabitants. English society . . . seem to regard Montreal as their property.'[127] In the late nineteenth century the assertion of a 'British' identity grew stronger and stronger, fuelled by the tightening of commercial and financial connections, and the sense of dependence on British markets and capital. It reached fever pitch during the First World War, in which many British Montrealers served (the low volunteer rate among French Canadians was a rankling grievance). In Montreal, hospitals, schools and charitable institutions were all denominational – and ethnic. There was a 'Protestant House of Industry and Refuge', and a 'Protestant Bureau for Homeless Men'. Montreal's leading university, McGill, was an Anglo-Protestant bastion. Its elite private school, Lower Canada College, sought its teachers in England. But Montreal had no claim to be the cultural metropolis of British Canada. Most British immigrants had bypassed the city, going direct to Ontario or the Prairie West. And unlike Toronto, the 'Belfast of Canada', Montreal had never been a predominantly Protestant city. Its English-speaking community was divided between Protestants and Catholic Irish, who formed an anglophone working class. By the late nineteenth century, Catholics made up more than three-quarters of the urban population, reinforced by Italian and Polish immigration.[128] More to the point, from the mid-nineteenth century there had been a French-Canadian majority as Montreal's industries sucked in growing numbers of rural *habitants*. St Lawrence Boulevard, running through the centre of the city, separated the anglophone west from the francophone east. The two communities coexisted without mixing as 'two solitudes'[129] – although the business elite included some French Canadians and tycoons like Allan carefully cultivated French-Canadian allies. The Montreal British became acutely aware that they lived in a social and political enclave, one reason for the aggressive 'Britishness' of their leading newspaper, the *Montreal Star*. Moreover, by the turn of the century Montreal was becoming the hearth of a vehement French-Canadian *nationalisme*, given voice by Henri Bourassa and his newspaper, *Le Devoir*, founded in 1910.[130] French-Canadian intellectuals, led by the priest-historian Lionel Groulx, denounced the myth of Anglo-French cooperation (the so-called *bonne entente*), insisting that French Canadians were a conquered, oppressed and exploited people in search of liberation.[131] Groulx and his followers became deeply anxious at the impact of urban and industrial life on the French-Canadian family and its religious allegiance. Montreal was thus home to a business elite who favoured a carefully limited form of globalization; and to a majority population whose leaders were increasingly hostile to its social and ethical implications.

The end of the war in 1918 brought a violent check to Canadian prosperity.[132] But the later 1920s were years of expansion. In 1928 Canada produced some 53 per cent of the world's wheat exports, much of it shipped through Montreal.[133] The collapse of world trade in 1930–31 with the Great Depression was a brutal shock. The price of Canada's leading export commodities fell by half – a savage reminder that major exposure to the global economy carried huge risks. The effect on Montreal was traumatic. By early 1934 some 240,000 people, 28 per cent of the population, were on government relief.[134] The impact was worsened by the scale of existing poverty in Montreal, partly the consequence of low-skilled work in processing plants, partly because much work (in transport or at the docks) was seasonal. At the turn of the century mortality in Montreal had been higher than in industrialized England, and its infant mortality rate far higher.[135]

The problem ran deeper. In the 1920s there were already signs that the Canadian economy was becoming gradually more regionalized and less focused on Montreal. Since the 1890s Toronto had been challenging Montreal's commercial and financial hegemony in the Prairie West. It was linked by rail to the Prairie provinces by 1890 and could sell its own manufactures there. Its newspapers, periodicals and publishing houses were making Toronto the cultural capital of anglophone Canada – some two-thirds of the population.[136] In the financial realm, long Montreal's strongest claim to primacy, the 1930s were something of a watershed. By the middle of the decade, buoyed by its mining industry (especially the rising price of gold), Toronto's stock exchange grew larger and livelier than Montreal's, a status it maintained from then on.[137] Montreal's strongest suit had been its long-standing British connection: Liverpool, Glasgow and London were its main shipping partners. In the 1930s British capital stopped coming, and with the onset of agricultural protection in Britain, until then much the largest market for Canadian grain, wheat was no longer king. As new commodity exports replaced it – minerals, wood pulp, gas, oil and hydro-electric power – the Canadian economy pivoted more and more towards its great southern neighbour: indeed, in the 1920s American investment in Canada overtook that of the British. The Second World War, which emphasized Canada's strategic dependence on the United States, and impoverished Britain, accelerated the change. Toronto was the beneficiary of this new orientation, but not all at once. As late as 1939 it could be dismissed as 'an outpost, a species of suburb of New York', which controlled its mining and wood-pulp companies. Montreal was still the 'metropolis'.[138] In the post-war years the two cities were neck and neck in size and importance. By the 1970s, however, by which time American investment in Canada was eight times that of Britain, Toronto's supremacy in manufacturing, commerce and finance was firmly established. The commercial nexus that had bound Montreal to London and Liverpool had faded away. New York had triumphed after all.

THE EMPIRE CITY

'New-York is the London of the Western Continent, where all the great operations of exchange concentrate, receiving constant tribute from the industry of the world.'[139] For all the actual differences from London (in its role as an imperial capital, a centre of aristocratic consumption and a European entrepôt), the boast of the *New York Daily Times* (later to be the *New York Times*) in 1852 was not without substance. It was a remarkable feature of North America's Atlantic coast that it was so quickly to be dominated commercially by one great port city – New York – whose metropolitan claims were asserted steadily over the whole continental interior.

As we will see, much of the explanation lay in the distinctive pattern of the city's urban growth, its entrepreneurial traditions and its favoured geographical setting. But New York was also the beneficiary (like so many port cities) of geopolitical events that historians of its rise seldom if ever acknowledge. Its future command of the interior was only made possible by the imperial war that evicted France from mainland North America in 1763; by Napoleon's abandonment of his New World ambitions in 1803; and by the settler imperialism that drove the American frontier west and south in innumerable wars of colonization and conquest. Equally, failure to crush the Confederacy by force of arms in 1865 would have stymied New York's prospects of becoming the financial capital of the United States, just as a different outcome to the First World War (or its failure to happen) would have delayed or aborted its succession to London as the financial capital of the Western world. The central role played by New York in the global economy since 1945 owed much to the course of its previous career but also to events far beyond its control: the sudden emergence of the United States as a 'superpower' at the end of the Second World War and the supremacy in parallel of the American dollar.

New York was founded as an outpost of the Dutch West India Company in 1623. Like Montreal, it was an island site that enjoyed riverine access to a fur-bearing interior: as late as 1750 furs made up some 16 per cent of its export trade.[140] A British possession from 1664, it enjoyed a central position amid the Thirteen Colonies. Chosen for geographical convenience, it became the terminus for London's packet service to the American colonies in 1755, and the administrative headquarters of the British army in America. The army was big business in colonial New York, and its merchants became by default the contractors serving the needs of some forty garrisons spread across the colonies – foreshadowing the city's later ambitions.[141] Yet in 1790, in the first decade of the new Republic, New York was well behind Philadelphia and Boston in commercial importance and (in the case of Philadelphia) population as well. Philadelphia was the gateway to the South and the new settler world of the Ohio Valley, and the new nation's first capital; Boston, with its deep sheltered harbour and old maritime links to the Caribbean and Europe, was America's leading port with a commercial horizon that already extended to the Pacific and China. It seemed likely that, deprived of British favour, badly damaged in the War for Independence (most of its leading merchants were Loyalists and left the city at the end of the war), and lacking (as yet) an extensive hinterland, New York would trail behind its rivals for an indefinite time.

That this inferior rank was reversed so quickly remains something of a puzzle. But by 1796–7 New York had a larger import and export trade than Philadelphia and (by 1810) a larger population. By the early 1820s nearly 40 per cent of America's imports passed through its harbour. Here, too, geopolitics may have played a role, for the Great War in Europe was a bonanza for neutral (American) trade.[142] The larger size of merchant shipping at the turn of the century favoured New York over the shallower approaches to Philadelphia, which lay up the Delaware River. Indeed, it was the exceptional qualities of New York's harbour that made the city's commercial fortune. It was deep, sheltered and (usually) ice-free, with much room for manoeuvre – a valuable asset once larger steamships began to cross the Atlantic. It lay at the convergence of four sea lanes: towards Europe; towards the Caribbean and South America; via Long Island Sound to New England; and coastwise to the south. The shores of Manhattan along the East River offered a long line of wharves: here was South Street, the city's commercial hub. Wall Street, where a daily auction of stocks began in 1792, and Pearl Street, the centre of the dry-goods trade, lay close by. New York's central location promoted its entrepôt role for a mass of coastal shipping bringing goods for export and carrying home imports. This was soon reinforced by the early development of steam on the Hudson, the rapid colonization of upstate New York, and then, in the 1820s, by the building of the Erie Canal.[143] After 1825, New York had cheap waterborne access to a large swathe of the newly settled

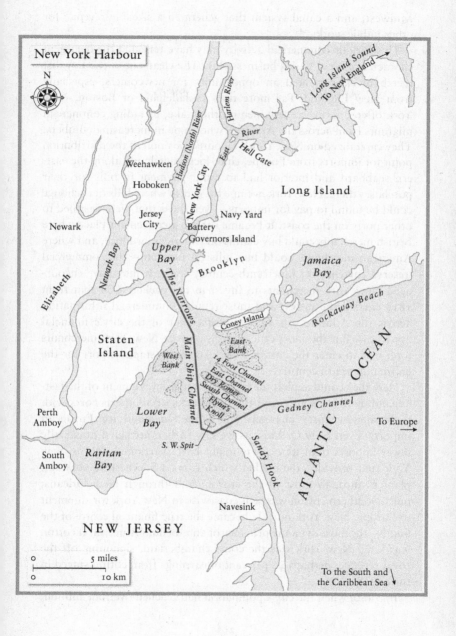

New York Harbour

N

Long Island Sound
To New England

Weehawken

Hoboken

Long Island

Hudson (North) River

East River

Harlem River

Hell Gate

River

New York City

Navy Yard

Jersey City

Battery

Governors Island

Newark

Newark Bay

Upper Bay

Brooklyn

Jamaica Bay

Elizabeth

The Narrows

Staten Island

Coney Island

Rockaway Beach

West Bank

Main Ship Channel

East Bank

14 Foot Channel

East Channel

Dry Romer

Swash Channel

Flynn's Knoll

Perth Amboy

Lower Bay

ATLANTIC OCEAN

Gedney Channel

To Europe

S. W. Spit

South Amboy

Raritan Bay

Sandy Hook

Navesink

NEW JERSEY

0   5 miles
0   10 km

To the South and
the Caribbean Sea

Midwest, and a canal system that generated a sizeable revenue for other public works.[144]

This furious commercial activity may have reflected the insurgent character of New York's business elite. The clear-out of the Loyalist merchant class created an opportunity for newcomers, especially from New England. Far more than Philadelphia or Boston, New York offered scope to new men on the make, including commercial migrants from across the Atlantics who came in increasing numbers. They capitalized on New York's favoured position as the distribution point for imports from Europe, since local merchants along the eastern seaboard and interior had to remit payment in bills for their purchases there. New York became the centre where bills of exchange could be found to pay for imports – even those that were destined to other ports on the coast. It became the most convenient place where British merchants could buy claims on American produce, and where American merchants could buy bills on London – the commercial 'reserve currency' of nineteenth-century trade. It may have encouraged New York merchants to invest in the packet ships that from 1818 carried the fastest and most regular commercial information across the Atlantic – a vital reinforcement of the city's financial apparatus. But the most crucial decision that New York merchants took was to enter the cotton trade, America's staple export for the entire nineteenth century.

Here they could exploit the financial underdevelopment of the fast-expanding Slave South, and the drawbacks of Southern ports with their shallow entry channels and limited demand for European imports. Even New Orleans, as we saw earlier, attracted drastically fewer imports than its exports might have warranted. It was New York that provided the credits which carried Southern factors and planters through most of the season; and through New Orleans, much Southern cotton was sent coastwise to New York for shipment to Europe. New York quickly became the true financial centre of the South – the most dynamic province of ante-bellum America. If cotton was king, New York was the court chamberlain, siphoning off the royal revenue: perhaps 40 per cent of earnings from cotton stayed in the city.[145]

By 1860, when the city's population had reached over one million, almost twice the size of Philadelphia, its nearest rival (and nearly twenty times that of Montreal), New York's commercial status seemed to have reached the metropolitan stage that the *New York Daily Times* had proclaimed. Cotton exports had doubled in the course of the 1850s. In 1860 New York port handled some two-thirds of America's imports and one-third of its exports.[146] Amid the frenzy of railway-building, New York was becoming the favoured port for the greater part of the Upper Mississippi Valley. From 1852 it had a direct rail connection with Chicago, already the great produce market of the upper Midwest, reducing the journey time there from three weeks to two days.[147] New York bank notes and bills commanded the widest circulation in the continental interior.[148] 'New York Exchange' meant notes that could circulate anywhere.[149] With more than one hundred newspapers, including five large dailies, as well as numerous periodicals, telegraph links with much of the continent, and its fast regular mail service to European ports, New York supplied the freshest and most reliable news and commercial information. Its large printing and publishing industry was also the main producer of books in the country.[150] New York was the shop window for European fashion, whether literary or material. Altogether, its astonishing ascent seemed to confirm the *New York Daily Times*'s claim that 'each nation has its one metropolitan port' – a claim intended to persuade Philadelphia 'to confess the primacy of her rival'.[151]

But a huge crisis was imminent. Throughout the 1850s New York merchants had been desperate to appease the South's discontents and avoid any threat to the Union – and their cotton trade. 'What would New York be without slavery?' jeered James De Bow, the New Orleans journalist. 'The ships would rot at her docks; grass would grow in Wall Street and Broadway.'[152] With secession in 1861, they faced the repudiation of the South's large debts.[153] The war choked off the inward investment from Europe on which Wall Street already depended. In fact, the Civil War and its outcome proved not so much a setback as an extraordinary boost to the city's fortunes. New York was already the main manufacturing centre in North America – in clothing, sugar-refining, machine-making, shipbuilding and much else. The war brought a huge new demand. The closure of the Mississippi (and of New Orleans) by blockade funnelled the mass of Western trade towards the east coast, and to New York in particular. The impact on the city's financial machinery was just as dramatic. With its huge war expenditure and limited revenues, the Union government had little choice but to raise loans at home – a task that Wall Street now undertook, creating what became the New York bond market. The National Bank Act of 1863, Washington's reward, limited the circulation of bank notes to so-called 'national' banks, many of them in New York, so that New York became the de facto capital of American finance, its reserve bank in all but name.[154] With the end of the war, the great stream of investment the struggle had mobilized poured into the West, now entering its golden period as the producer of wheat, flour and meat for export. Cotton production recovered swiftly and by 1873 New York was exporting twice as much as in 1861.[155] Together with foodstuffs and other raw products, cotton made up more than 60 per cent of American exports in 1880.[156]

In reality, much of that New York capital went into railway construction. America's railway mileage doubled from 35,000 to 70,000 miles between 1865 and 1873. By 1890 it had doubled again to some 140,000 miles, on its way to an astonishing peak of over 250,000 miles in 1920. There was much that was dysfunctional in this colossal expansion: the duplication of lines; the reckless competition; the exaggerated expectations; the losses through speculation, corruption and theft by financial miscreants. Nevertheless, railways were America's first big business, demanding new methods of management to control their costs and handle their traffic, and needing capital on a vaster scale than any previous enterprise in peacetime.[157] Funding the railways was far and away the main business of the New York Stock Exchange and the bankers of Wall Street. Indeed, the sums invested in railways between 1850 and 1900 were greater than those placed in all other industries put together.[158] For those managing the major rail companies, access to capital and to the financial and legal expertise required to negotiate mergers and rate agreements, or fend off political interference, became the highest priority. Increasingly, they relocated their headquarters to New York, where investment bankers and corporate lawyers proliferated. With the completion of America's vast infrastructure of railways and telegraphs came a new generation of manufacturing enterprises that relied on mass marketing and mass distribution. Large-scale firms producing oil, tobacco or steel had similar needs to railway companies for financial and managerial expertise, needs that brought them to New York as well. In fact, by the late nineteenth century the city's business elite was preoccupied much less with overseas trade than the management and finance of domestic manufacturing. Between 1870 and 1930, 'New York was transformed ... from a great port to the center of America's new manufacturing corporations'.[159]

Of course, New York was still a hugely important port. Between 1860 and 1900 the volume of traffic through its harbour grew by five times.[160] In the last thirty years of the century, half of America's foreign trade came through the city: some two-thirds of its imports, over 40 per cent of its exports.[161] Its shores were festooned with innumerable jetties and piers. Great efforts were made to overcome the congestion of its wharves and the inconvenient fact that no railway line crossed the Hudson below Albany, 150 miles to the north. Indeed, New York was long hampered by its island site and the cost of bridging its waterways. In 1916 five of the world's longest bridges were in New York City and much of the freight passing through it was laboriously ferried to the Jersey shore across the Hudson.[162] New York was the terminus for the new fleets of large liners that reduced the Atlantic to a five-day voyage in previously unimaginable comfort. It was the main destination for the 20 million immigrants who came to America after 1865, many of whom stayed in the city to join its growing industrial labour force – and live in its slums. Yet, like most port cities, New York was vulnerable to a whole range of risks. Its surging proletariat and gross inequalities threatened social unrest and political upheaval – one reason for the 'boss' systems that ran city politics with an arsenal of patronage, corruption and intimidation. Its commodity exports were notoriously prone to boom and bust. A bumper harvest in Europe, or a fall in demand for cotton, could trigger a crisis in the traffic of payments across the Atlantic. Anxious farmers and dealers in the South or Midwest might demand the deposits they had left in New York and start a run on the banks. A crash of the kind that had occurred repeatedly – in 1837, 1857, 1873, 1883, 1893 and 1907 – might set off a prolonged depression, as happened in the 1840s, 1870s and the first half of the 1890s. When that happened, enraged producers, facing a drastic fall in their income, denounced the deflationary strictures of the gold standard (the ark of the covenant to the bankers of New York) and pressed for the return to cheaper silver or paper money – the populist cry in the 1890s. To many Americans, New York was an alien city, where over 40 per cent of the population was foreign-born in 1900, and a den of speculation and fraud. Perhaps it was only in the 1920s that its image began to be refashioned as quintessentially American.[163]

Ironically, by then New York had largely escaped the pressure for cultural conformism that afflicted much of the country. Its ethnic communities were residentially segregated (not, of course, by law) but were large enough to sustain distinct thriving cultures. New York City politics acknowledged the need for mixed ethnic 'tickets' if elections were to be won. New York writers and intellectuals, nourished by its huge printing industry, remained far more open to 'foreign' ideas – not least those from the left in Europe – than was true elsewhere in America and the city was an intellectual bastion of Franklin D. Roosevelt's 'New Deal' after 1933.[164] New York had already become the model of urban modernity in the Western world, in its skyscraper architecture, constant rebuilding, omnipresent advertising, popular entertainment and rapacious commercialism. It was a world of incessant mobility, famously captured in John Dos Passos's novel *Manhattan Transfer* (1925), a collage of brief cinematic episodes. Its newspapers and magazines (like *Vanity Fair*, the *New Yorker* and *Esquire*) devised a stylish new formula of celebrity, consumption, elegance and wit, and attracted best-selling authors like Ring Lardner, Dorothy Parker, James M. Cain and John O'Hara.[165] Together with theatre production (though not film) and popular music, New York had become the cultural capital of North America, and vied with London as the cultural centre of the anglophone globe.

New York's distinctive trajectory as a port city-turned-metropolis casts an interesting light on the American experience of steam globalization. Long before independence in 1783, the American colonies had been closely integrated into the Atlantic economy, trading with Europe and the Caribbean. The marriage of slave-grown cotton and the Lancashire textile industry hugely deepened this transatlantic connection, requited by flows of manufactures, investment and migrants from Britain and Europe. In the later nineteenth century wheat and meat reinforced the heavy dependence upon commodity exports while the flow of migration turned into a torrent. Nevertheless, New York's transformation into a manufacturing city and a vast financial and managerial hub is a reminder that America's global exposure was highly selective. Between 1830 and 1900 America exported only around 6 per cent of its gross national product, and at most 6 per cent of its industrial output between 1879 and 1914.[166] The British figure in the Edwardian period was around 25 per cent.[167] Despite significant foreign investment, notably in railways, imported capital supplied on average only 5 per cent of America's capital needs[168] (in the case of Australia it was nearer 50 per cent). America was easily the world's largest economy by 1913 but its foreign investments were trivial, around one-sixth of the British figure when the American economy was three times the size. Whereas most countries in Europe imposed levels of tariff protection of between 5 and 8 per cent at the turn of the century, America's tariffs were at least four times as high,[169] while on some products like steel rails they reached 100 per cent.[170] And whereas foreign-owned or managed enterprises exerted considerable influence in much of the world beyond Europe, they cut a very small figure beside the huge corporations that came to dominate the American industrial scene.

In its role as America's metropolis, the headquarters of the 'core zone' that stretched west to Chicago,[171] New York had played a large role in fashioning this distinctive mixture of an open and partly closed economy. It was America's gateway to the world, but also the capital of its heavily defended industrial economy. Ironically, it was precisely because the financing of American industry, transport and commodity exports was so highly centralized in New York that the external shocks which came with the endemic volatility of commodity prices were so quickly transmitted to the rest of the economy.[172] But if some of its bankers looked east, many others looked west to the internal economy with its colossal home market. Indeed, despite the vast influx of European migrants, most American opinion remained resolutely continental rather than global in outlook – not least from mistrust of New York's cosmopolitan interests. After 1918, of course, the scale of American investment abroad underwent a massive expansion and foreign markets came to matter much more to its great corporations. American manufactures – motor vehicles especially – entertainment, music, literature and lifestyles began to exert the global appeal they have enjoyed ever since. But it was only with the final collapse of the old global economy centred on London (a consequence of Britain's geopolitical catastrophe in 1940–42) that America and New York began to construct the new architecture of global trade and finance with which we have lived for the last seventy years. Perhaps it was then that New York really transcended its metropolitan status to become – for some purposes – the centre of the world.

The 'Atlantic world' of Canada, the United States and north-western Europe is usually seen as the classic arena of nineteenth-century globalization, the core zone from which it spread across the rest of the world. Here the flow of migrants and capital in one direction and of commodities in the other grew to become a source if not of mutual dependence, then of massive mutual self-interest to both shores of the ocean. The decline in transport costs and the acceleration of transit over water, along rails or (for information) through wires, brought a gradual convergence of prices and (more modestly) of living standards. The vast human traffic between continents (perhaps one-third of migrants returned home in the steamship era) created a network of social and commercial connections, at its closest between Britain and Canada and between London and New York. There was less convergence (though some) of ideas and ideologies until late in the era of steam and even that was subject to a catastrophic reversal after 1930.

That North America was endowed with natural resources on a staggering scale, and could absorb the great Atlantic migrations with such ease, explains much of this process. But, as the history of its three leading port cities suggests, the pattern of globalization on the North American continent was not merely the ineluctable consequence of a free-market economy. All three began as 'gateway cities' on the edge of a vast interior, much of it barely reconnoitred by 1800. All three were indebted to steam power on water or over land for their commercial prosperity. But steam globalization was not just a matter of commercial opportunity. New Orleans was 'made' by the geopolitical calculations of faraway rulers, who won, lost, fought over or abandoned the city and its hinterland. It enjoyed a brief reign of glory when it promised to be the grand metropolis of the whole Western hemisphere. This sudden ascent owed much to the brutal efficiency with which white settler armies expelled the indigenous peoples of the trans-Appalachian interior. It owed even more to the forced migration of black slaves from the Upper to the Lower South to provide an instant labour force: the rejuvenation of slavery in the American South was the perverse corollary of its globalization. It was this that allowed the astonishing rise of the cotton economy over little more than three decades. But slavery, and the 'irrepressible conflict' to which it gave rise, also sealed New Orleans's fate as an ex-future metropolis. With minimal influence over its hinterland politics, and fatally addicted to the easy profits of King Cotton, it became the hapless dependant of a slave-based economy whose overconfident masters drove it onto the rocks.

Montreal was also the beneficiary of a geopolitical dividend, but one that lasted much longer. Once the early hopes of a far-reaching commerce south of the Great Lakes were dashed, and its northwestern fur trade petered out, it was left with a modest commercial imperium, much of it unsettled wilderness. The gradual filling up of what is now southern Ontario, and the energetic improvement of its riverine access, made Montreal the hub of a colonial economy of some three or four million people – but left it constantly threatened by the voracious reach of its big southern neighbour. Its remarkable growth by the end of the century was really a tribute to three political facts. The first was the achievement of Canadian Confederation in 1867. The second was Canada's acquisition of the vast inland empire west of the Great Lakes from the Hudson's Bay Company. The third was Canada's ability as a self-governing colony (whose autonomy was guaranteed by British sea power) to protect its industry and costly railway system behind the tariff wall of its 'national policy'. Globalization, in Canada's case, was filtered through a net of economic defences and imperial connections. Together they sheltered Montreal's industrial base, helped finance its railways and gave St James's Street a privileged link to the City of London.

New York was the most favoured geographically of all the gateways into North America. Once settler power had conquered the

Midwest, and the Erie Canal gave New York a waterborne highway to the Ohio Valley and beyond, the rise of New York port became unstoppable. Yet it was New York's (at first sight) unlikely role as the financial pivot of the cotton trade – America's leading export for the whole of the century – that first made its fortune, and cemented its claim to be a financial as well as a commercial metropolis. The colossal expansion of America's railway network, drawing on the capital and expertise that Wall Street could mobilize, confirmed New York's extraordinary dominance in the second half of the century. It became the headquarters of the great corporations into which American industry was increasingly organized.

New York thus played a double role. It was America's front door onto the rest of the world. Its huge transatlantic traffic made it the world's busiest port by 1910. It was the point of entry for the millions of immigrants who passed through Ellis Island in its harbour. Its large Italian, German, Jewish, African American and Caribbean communities made it famously cosmopolitan. But as a major industrial centre in its own right, and the capital of 'corporate America', it was also deeply committed to tariff protection, the great wall that surrounded America's industrial economy. Eager to penetrate other people's markets, determined to protect its own, New York remained faithful to this 'semi-globalization' until the Second World War conferred on the city an unexpected industrial and financial supremacy. It was then that the appeal of a truly open global economy became irresistible.

6

The Maritime *Raj*

India's response to steam globalization was bound to be very different from North America's. Until the 1870s and the opening of the Suez Canal, India still lay up to six months from Europe for bulk cargoes by sea (mail and passengers had travelled via Egypt and the Red Sea from the early years of the century). India's railway age arrived some twenty years after North America's, and, once built, its rail network was neither as dense nor as extensive. In 1900 rail mileage in the United States was around eight times the length of India's. The scope for wrenching India's agrarian economy in new commercial directions – the central feature of North America's 'economic miracle' – was much more restricted. The indigenous population remained in occupation of the land, except for a handful of British planters preparing indigo and (later) growing tea. There was no slave labour force to create the 'instant' commodity-producing economy that sprang up in the American Deep South. Nor could India hope to industrialize on the North American model behind the barrier of protective tariffs. London dared not insist on free trade in Britain's settlement colonies where local self-government was the rule by mid-century. It could hardly do so in the case of the American Republic. But it had no such qualms in India, which became Lancashire's largest market for textiles. Nor was India as attractive a field for foreign investment as North America: indeed, the capital that flowed there (much of it to build railways) usually only did so under a generous guarantee from its colonial regime, the Government of India, to be paid for if needed by its tax-paying peasants. In fact, it was largely to India's colonial government, rather than private enterprise, that outsiders looked to 'open up' the economy to the new global trades.

Behind these differences lay a deeper contrast in the history of

India. For perhaps five centuries up to 1800, India had been the workshop of the world. Its high-quality textiles had been much in demand by Europeans and Africans as well as Asians, and very widely traded. Like China's, India's economic fortunes had suffered from the 'great divergence'[1] triggered by industrialization in the West, which replicated Asia's textiles and ceramics but at a tenth of the cost. In India's case the effects had been sharpened by the political revolution that overtook the subcontinent. By the late 1750s the British East India Company had turned itself into a military power. For a century after 1757 its 'Company Raj' was a conquest state. By systematically dismantling the major Indian states and their princely courts, it cut down the local demand for India's high-value textiles, while Lancashire moved into India's old foreign markets. Meanwhile the Company's 'revenue offensive', driving up taxes to pay for its armies and wars, bore down on the incomes of the rural elite. The result was a prolonged depression from the 1820s to the 1840s, and a 'deurbanization' effect on weavers and artisans who were pushed back into agriculture.[2] The explosion set off by the Company's remorseless expansion – the Great Rebellion of 1857 – was to destroy the Company and impose a more cautious imperium. But it also coincided with the gradual integration of India into the new global economy (on very different terms from the past) and a huge absolute increase in the volume of its trade: exports were twenty-five times and imports more than thirty times larger in 1913 than in 1834.[3]

Not surprisingly, the impact of colonial rule on India has dominated the way in which its history has been written. Inevitably, this has imparted a powerful landward bias towards histories of the conquest, consolidation and unravelling of the colonial regime and the effects of foreign rule on an overwhelmingly agrarian society. Where an alternative history of India's external and seaborne connections survived, it was largely confined to the pre-colonial era before 1750. Yet India was as much a maritime as a land-based *raj*. Unlike the subcontinent's previous conquerors, the British arrived by sea. Their bridgeheads were ports and coastal trading towns. Madras (Chennai), Calcutta (Kolkata) and Bombay (Mumbai) were the bases from which they extended their rule; it was on Madras, Calcutta and Bombay that they planned to fall back in the desperate days of 1946 when

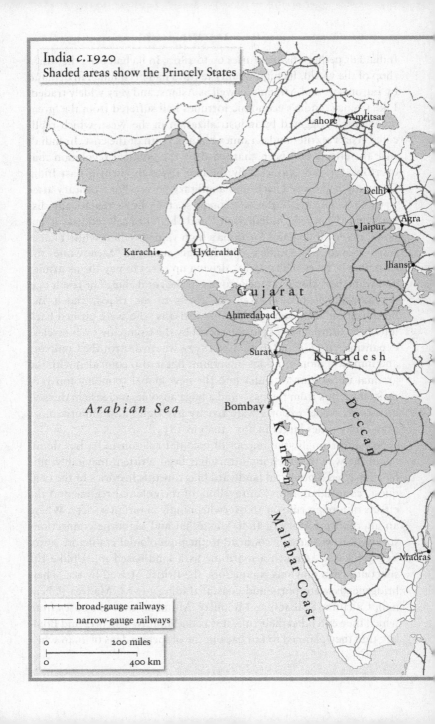

India c.1920
Shaded areas show the Princely States

Lahore
Amritsar
Delhi
Agra
Jaipur
Jhansi
Karachi
Hyderabad
Gujarat
Ahmedabad
Khandesh
Surat
Bombay
Konkan
Deccan
Malabar Coast
Madras

Arabian Sea

┼┼┼┼ broad-gauge railways
───── narrow-gauge railways

0   200 miles
0   400 km

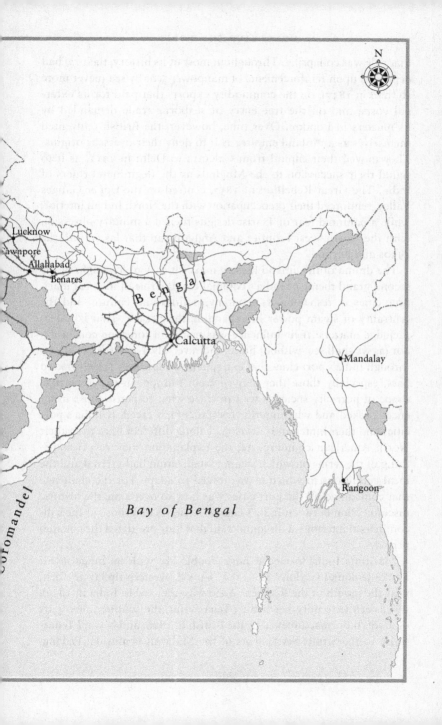

that rule was collapsing. Throughout most of its history, their *raj* had depended upon reinforcements of manpower sent by sea (never more so than in 1857); on the commodity exports that paid for its external costs; and on the free entry of seaborne trade demanded by its masters in London. Over time, however, the British reinvented themselves as an inland empire, as if to deny their overseas origins. They moved their capital from Calcutta to Delhi in 1911, as if to signal their succession to the Mughals as the (legitimate) rulers of India. The Great Rebellion of 1857, centred on the Upper Ganges Valley, reinforced their preoccupation with the North Indian interior, while a paranoid fear of Tsarist designs fuelled a military obsession with the North-West Frontier and Afghanistan that lasted into the 1930s and beyond.

The drama of this inland history makes it easy to lose sight of the second grand theme of India's colonial era: the role of its great maritime cities in reshaping its economy, politics and culture, and the centrality of steam power in expanding their reach. That is not to prejudge matters: their influence was neither a foregone conclusion nor (as we shall see) without limits and reversals. Nevertheless, it was through India's port cities that external influences very largely had to pass, especially those that derived from Europe. In the distinctive shape of port-city societies we can trace what response those influences evoked and what interior resistance they faced. If India's port cities and their hinterlands developed along different lines from their North American counterparts, the explanation may reveal something of the terms on which steam globalization had arrived and the local conditions to which it was forced to adapt. For the challenge that confronted all the port cities was how to overcome the historic disconnection between India's coastal societies and those of the subcontinental interior – a disconnection that long pre-dated the colonial period.[4]

Maritime India formed a huge double arc with its hinge at Sri Lanka (colonial Ceylon). Since the 1830s its western tip lay at Aden, near the mouth of the Red Sea (Aden was annexed to India in 1839). Its eastern extremity reached to Tenasserim, the southernmost part of modern Burma, annexed by the British in 1826, and beyond Tenasserim to the Straits Settlements of the Malayan peninsula: Penang,

Singapore, Malacca and Province Wellesley, governed from Calcutta until 1867. Indians had traded across the Arabian Sea and the Bay of Bengal for centuries past. But the British *pax* in the Indian Ocean and their acquisitions, annexations and spheres of interference around its shores opened a new phase in this Indian connection. As British subjects, Indian merchants travelled and traded more freely in Oman, in the Persian Gulf and on the East African coast. Chettiars from Madras followed the British armies into Burma in the 1820s, 1850s and 1880s, and helped finance the conversion of the vast Irrawaddy delta into a rice bowl.[5] In Sri Lanka, Malaya, Fiji, Mauritius, Natal, Trinidad and British Guiana, Indian indentured labour and other labour migrants provided the workforce for plantation economies in coffee, tea, sugar and rubber, as well as 'coolies' to build the East African railways. The result was a huge sphere in which Indian influence was not just diplomatic and military (the field of operations of Britain's Indian Army), but commercial, cultural and demographic as well. In the western Indian Ocean, where Indian merchants had long been active, British sea power and cheap manufactures afforded better protection and more commercial advantage. Indian mercantile enterprise was all but supreme.[6] 'Along some 6,000 miles of sea-coast in Africa and its islands, and nearly the same extent in Asia,' remarked Sir Bartle Frere (a former governor of Bombay) in 1873:

> the Indian trader is, if not the monopolist, the most influential, permanent and all-pervading element of the commercial community. I doubt whether along the whole coast from Delagoa Bay to Kurrachee [Karachi] there are half a dozen ports . . . at which Indian traders are not, as a body, better able to buy or sell a cargo than any other class, and at most of the great ports a cargo can only be sold or collected through them . . .[7]

By the mid-nineteenth century the two great arms of the Indian Ocean were only lightly policed by British sea power. The Indian navy was wound up in 1863, having long been reduced to the government's mail carrier. In 1869–70 the Royal Navy's East Indies station (separated from the China station in 1864) was patrolled by a mere eight or nine ships, two of which the Admiralty grudgingly committed to the Persian Gulf.[8] But commercially, the whole ocean was becoming increasingly a British possession. The cutting of the Suez Canal heralded the age of the steamship as the carrier of cargo in the eastern seas. The shipping tonnages handled in Bombay, Calcutta and Madras grew sixty-fold from 100,000 tons in 1798 to over six million by 1914,[9] most of it British, most of it steam. The dhow trade survived by virtue of cost and convenience, but not the large sailing ships from Oman once regularly seen in Bombay. Colombo on Sri Lanka became the great coal bunker of Asia, and one of the world's busiest ports. Eastbound or westbound, steamships that served China, South East Asia, Australia and the Bay of Bengal came there to refuel. Round India's coastline from Moulmein in Burma to Karachi in Sind, to the Persian Gulf, East Africa, Australia, South East Asia and China stretched the tentacles of the British India Steam Navigation Company (familiarly, 'BISN' or simply 'British-India') founded in 1862, and heavily subsidized by the Indian government. By 1873 it had more than thirty ships; twenty years later almost ninety.[10] Once the Suez Canal had been opened, it began a 'Home' service to Britain as well. For British shipping at large, and especially the vast tramp fleet, India was the pivot of its whole eastern trade – because on the outward leg British coal could be sold at a profit on India's west coast.[11] Nevertheless, much of the traffic in India's ports was only indirectly connected with Britain and Europe: ivory and dates from East Africa and the Gulf; rice and timber from Burma; opium from India to South East Asia and China. India was the junction where Asia's trade with Europe connected with an older intra-Asian trade that was growing just as rapidly.

India's port cities thus looked out over a wide maritime hinterland as well as into the agrarian world behind them. Their seaborne connections drew them towards East Asia and Africa as well as towards Europe. But they were also the beneficiaries – perhaps even the products – of an imperial regime which, uniquely in the history of South Asia, commanded both its seaward approaches and its subcontinental interior. What they made of this prospect we explore in what follows.

BOMBAY: THE WESTERN GATEWAY

In the early steam age the journey (for passengers) from London to Bombay, far quicker than the old four- or five-month voyage around the Cape, was still, by modern standards, arduous and slow. In the mid-1840s the traveller would leave London by train for Southampton. There he (most passengers were men) would board a Peninsular and Oriental (familiarly 'P&O') line steamer bound for Lisbon and Malta, a two-week trip if the weather was bad. At Malta he would transfer to another P&O steamer for a further six-day voyage to Alexandria, already booming with Egypt's cotton exports. The next stage was a boat ride up the Mahmoudieh Canal and on to the Nile. By using a steamboat, Cairo could be reached in twenty-four hours: by sail it might take several days. From Cairo to Suez ('a peculiarly filthy little town,' wrote one disgruntled visitor) at the southern end of the Isthmus, travellers shared a horse-drawn 'van' for the eighty-five-mile journey, passing camels carrying coal to the port. There they boarded a mail and passenger steamer, a 'floating fragment of India': British officers and engineers; an Arab pilot; Portuguese-speaking stewards from Goa; Muslim or low-caste Hindus as firemen and African 'coal-trimmers' (stokers) working in 130 degrees heat. Nine or ten days to Aden and ten more to Bombay would complete the journey – if the traveller were very lucky in just over a month, nearer two months if not.[12]

Bombay in the 1830s and 1840s was a thriving port city whose population had grown from some 200,000 in 1833 to over 500,000 by 1849.[13] It had not always been so. Despite being endowed with much the best harbour on India's west coast, it had held little appeal for the Portuguese who reached India in the late fifteenth century, or the English who followed them a hundred years later. Then it was Surat in the Gulf of Cambay, some one hundred and fifty miles further north, that was the magnet for Asian and European traders buying the textiles of Gujarat and Kathiawar. Bombay Island, cut off from the interior by the steep-sided Western Ghats in places 3,000 high, was merely an outpost of the small Portuguese station at Bassein. In 1661, for obscure reasons, it was given to Charles II as part

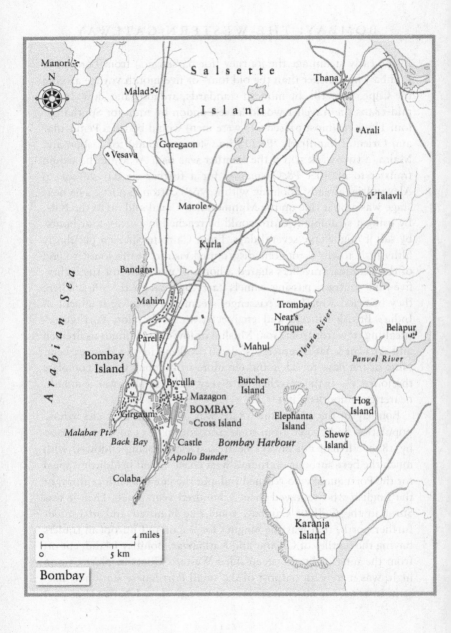

Bombay

of the dowry of his Portuguese bride. With little use for this gift, he passed it to the East India Company in 1668 on a feudal tenure and for a peppercorn rent. For the Company, too, Bombay had little to offer, except as a stronghold in case of attack by European rivals or their Indian 'hosts'. Even so, its value was limited. The town was sacked by the 'Sidi' – the Mughals' freewheeling naval commander – in 1689, and constantly threatened by the Angria, a maritime clan who were hereditary 'grand admirals' to the Maratha Confederacy, the rising power of the Deccan interior. With the Angria's final defeat in 1756, Bombay was safer from naval attack. But it remained a precarious outpost of the Company, whose commercial interests and military ambitions were now heavily concentrated on the east coast and Bengal. As the costs of its conquests and wars rose steeply in the 1780s and 1790s, the burden of Bombay, heavily subsidized from Bengal, and with little by way of exports to Britain, weighed more and more heavily on the Company's finances. To a testy new governor-general in Calcutta, the best solution was to cut down the top-heavy apparatus of governor and castle and reduce Bombay to a lesser 'factory' with a Company resident.[14]

Bombay was saved from this fate by a curious twist in its fortunes. In the 1790s renewed war with France, and fear of French intrigue with Mysore and the Marathas, the strongest Indian military powers, raised the strategic importance of the western Indian Ocean and with it Bombay. At the same time the Company was coming to depend for its profits on its tea trade with China, for which Indian goods, especially raw cotton and opium, supplied the vital exchange. As some of these might come from Bombay, London insisted that the Company's base there should be kept at full strength. The Company's struggle with the Maratha Confederacy gave a further incentive. Bombay merchants helped to finance the attack on the Maratha fiefdoms in the fertile province of Gujarat north-east of the city. Bombay's reward was to be granted the revenues of some of its richest districts. At a stroke it acquired a hinterland and the means to enlarge it. In fact, by 1818, Bombay Island ruled over much of Gujarat, Kathiawar, the coastal plain to its south (the Konkan) and the great inland plateau of the Deccan. Bombay was a port city, but now also the capital of a substantial land empire, with an army to boot.

Yet it was not until after 1800 that Bombay replaced Surat as the leading commercial and financial centre on India's west coast.[15] Behind Bombay's new status lay the Company's naval and diplomatic power as much as its commercial prowess. Its Bombay Marine (some twenty armed cruisers) enforced the Company's monopoly as the supplier of 'passes' for ships on the coast at a time when several local maritime powers – predictably denounced as 'pirates' by the Company – tried to impose their own passes and tolls on merchant shipping. In Surat itself, a city of 500,000 people in the late eighteenth century, the Company was the beneficiary of imperial decline – that of the Mughals. Surati merchants increasingly looked to the Company for protection against interference by the Maratha states or more local disorder. Bombay, too, had become the port of delivery for silver to pay for exports from western India. The Company's growing power on the coast, its formal annexation of Surat in 1800, and its acquisition of revenue-bearing districts in Gujarat in 1803, enhanced the appeal of the island city for Parsis, Muslim Bohras and Khojas and Hindu banias, reversing its old role as the commercial satellite of Surat.

As this suggests, while Bombay had a British governor and a handful of European merchants, and while it had become the capital of an extensive 'presidency', it was an Indian city, not just an outpost of Europe. The number of European merchants rose after 1813, when the Company's monopoly on trade between Britain and India was abolished (intra-Asian or 'country' trade had always been open). But much of the city's foreign trade was in the hands of Indian merchants from Gujarat, pre-eminently the Parsis. It was they who handled the traffic in raw cotton from Gujarat's alluvial plain, brought to Bombay by sea. It was Indian traders, too, who took a large share in Bombay's second major export business: the traffic in opium from Malwa, far away to the north-east in central India.

Malwa opium was the East India Company's bugbear. Already in the 1770s the Company had established a monopoly over the production and sale of opium from Bengal and maintained its own factories in Patna and Benares (Varanasi). The opium was destined for China to provide the exchange for the Company's tea purchases in Canton. To avoid the Chinese ban on its import, the opium was sold on at auction in Calcutta to private traders (Jardine Matheson was the best known) who arranged its distribution in China. But Malwa opium was beyond the Company's control. It reached the west coast by a number of routes but Bombay soon became the chief export centre. After abortive attempts at a ban, the Company had reluctantly settled for an export tax by 1831.[16] The result was a highly lucrative trade (Malwa opium could undercut Bengal's) in which Parsi firms like that of Jamsetjee Jejeebhoy (who supplied half of Jardine Matheson's opium by the 1840s) and Cama and Company took the lead. In the late 1830s the export of raw cotton and opium to China dominated Bombay's export trade, worth more than twice as much as goods sent to Britain – at 32 million rupees in 1836–7, compared with 13 million for goods sent to Britain.[17] It was the profits from these that allowed Bombay's Indian merchants to accumulate the wealth that secured their social and commercial status against the overweening superiority of British merchants and officialdom.

Bombay's trade (with China, Britain and the Persian Gulf) and its population were both growing rapidly. Its commodity trade grew by four times between the 1830s and 1850s.[18] Bombay was the entrepôt for India's west coast from Kutch and Kathiawar to Malabar in the south. But it still had only limited access to the interior behind it. In the late 1820s a road was cut though the Bhor Ghat to provide an easier route on to the Deccan plateau, and Poona became the government's hot-weather capital from 1835. However, the inland districts, only recently brought under Company rule, were often unsettled, and few Europeans went into the *mofussil* unless on official business. Bombay merchants had their eyes on Khandesh, a district that later became a key cotton zone. But Khandesh had been devastated by Maratha armies and famine, many of its villages had been abandoned and (said a contemporary report) there was 'hardly a town worth the name'.[19] Worse still, the road to Khandesh ran through the tangled forests and hills held by the Bhils, one of the 'wild tribes' who resisted British authority, and even employed Arab mercenaries to help them to do so.[20] Merchants complained bitterly that produce from the interior spent weeks on the journey on pack bullocks or slow-moving bullock carts, exposed to wind, weather and local predation, and doubling its price in transit,[21] and they denounced the

Company's failure to invest in better roads. Legally and administra-tively, too, Bombay City was kept strictly separate. It enjoyed a very limited measure of local self-government (through its justices of the peace) and (more important) access to a High Court where English judicial procedure was followed, English-trained judges presided and (by the 1820s) English barristers were active. In the Presidency's in-terior, however, as successive governors insisted, the High Court had no jurisdiction. There versions of 'customary law', interpreted by British officials and the local scribal elite of Chitpavan Brahmins, held sway. Bombay governors, like their later counterparts in British West Africa, dreaded the impact of the 'Law of England' on the complex caste, tenurial and family relations of interior communities which – as part of their compact with the local elite – they had sworn to safeguard.[22]

If Bombay had become the premier port city for western India, much of its commercial promise, in the eyes of its merchants, remained unfulfilled. Despite its unrivalled position and far larger population, its export trade was much smaller than that of New Orleans, the great cotton port of the Atlantic Ocean – at around 60 per cent of the New Orleans figure.[23] Its own shipping and shipbuilding were in decline in the face of British competition, even before the advent of steam.[24] In sending cargo (rather than passengers) to Europe, Bom-bay enjoyed no advantage over Calcutta: in the era of sail, when wind and current ruled shipping, sailing times from Europe were the same for both ports. The Company Raj, deprived since 1833 of its trading monopolies, was unsympathetic to commercial demands, and dan-gerously fixated – in Bombay merchant opinion – on futile and costly wars of conquest. 'Affghan mania' had wasted a million pounds, and the cost of conquering Sind – 'a sickly province' – had fallen on Bom-bay, complained the *Bombay Times*, the merchants' organ of news.[25] The Bombay Chamber of Commerce, founded in 1836 with both Indian and European members, railed against the Company's export duties and other shortcomings. It is easy to see why steam communi-cation with Europe became a Bombay obsession. A 'Bombay Steam Committee' was formed to lobby the Select Committee in London on 'Steam Navigation to India', whose report had appeared in 1834. But although the steam link to Suez and from Alexandria to Britain had transformed the speed and frequency of mail and travel, even in the 1840s it was far from clear what wider benefits steam could offer Bombay. Steamships for cargo were as yet not viable by the long Cape of Good Hope route, and freight could hardly be hauled overland through Egypt. India was not immune from the 'railway mania' that swept across Britain and North America. In the early 1840s plans began to be hatched in London and Manchester for railways in India. To local opinion, however, such schemes were at best highly speculative. Railways in India, declared the *Bombay Times*, would be 'a gigantic commercial speculation',[26] not least because of the formidable barrier of the coastal mountains.

It was in the 1850s, in fact, that Bombay began its ascent to become by the end of the century a great Victorian metropolis, Europe's 'Gateway of India'. An early sign was the redirection of its raw cotton exports more towards Europe than China, symptomatic perhaps of the chaos that had been brought by the Taiping Rebellion of 1850–64, and Lancashire's growing appetite. On average, for much of the 1850s, more than three times as much raw cotton was sent to Britain as to China.[27] Ships bound for Liverpool began to fill Bombay's harbour.[28] Then in 1853 the first miles of railway track were laid from Bombay to the mainland town of Thana by the magnificently titled Great Indian Peninsula Railway (GIPR). It took another eight years for the GIPR to crawl over the formidable barrier of the Western Ghats and reach Poona on the Deccan plateau. The slow rate of progress was due partly to the engineering challenge of the Bhor Ghat pass, and partly to the inexperience of British contractors with Indian conditions, whether in geology, building materials or the local labour supply.[29] However, by the mid-1860s, the railway had reached Khandesh with its promise of a rich freight in cotton. At exactly that moment, Bombay was plunged into a huge cotton boom as the unexpected beneficiary of a faraway struggle. When the Confederate states imposed their own stoppage on raw cotton exports (to coerce Britain and France into diplomatic recognition), soon to be followed by the Union blockade, cotton prices soared upward. Bombay's cotton exports quadrupled in value, cash poured in and a speculative frenzy began. The bust that came with the collapse of the Confederacy and the expected revival of the South's cotton economy was just as extreme. It brought down Bombay's leading bank amid a torrent of scandal.[30] But this brief burst of exuberance left a more positive legacy. The sudden explosion in commercial wealth and government revenue encouraged an ambitious refashioning of the city's public face. 'Bombay at the present day, in its buildings, its docks, and its land reclamations', remarked the *Imperial Gazetteer of India* in 1881, 'stands as a monument of the grand schemes of public utility which were started in these four years of unhealthy excitement.'[31] Bombay began to take on the outward appearance of a European city.

Indeed, for the rest of the century its commercial expansion was almost continuous. Exports of grain and oil seeds supplemented its old reliance on cotton and opium as Bombay's railways extended their reach into the Ganges Valley and the Punjab – which became India's great wheat field. In turn, Bombay imported ever-growing amounts of Lancashire's cotton piece goods. In part, this traffic was a consequence of the change of regime in India itself. The Great Rebellion of 1857 had fatally wounded the old Company Raj, to be replaced by a system in which London's control was asserted more forcefully. One result was India's adoption of almost complete free trade by 1882. Another was the constant pressure from business lobbies in Britain to build more railways (and distribute more British goods). But more than anything else, it was the maritime revolution set off by the opening of the Suez Canal in 1869 that transformed Bombay's prospects.

Bombay's British population had long been obsessed with the city's communications with Europe. Apart from the movement of passengers, it was the timely arrival of mail, both commercial and personal, that touched the Europeans' nerves. Since 1855 the carriage of mail had been taken over by the P&O line for an annual subsidy from London. The contract was renewable, and each renewal saw a fierce campaign by Bombay's leading merchants for a faster time than the company offered. An angry meeting in July 1874 agreed to petition the House of Commons and rally other chambers of commerce in Britain and Asia against a contract allowing P&O twenty-one days from London to Bombay.[32] Four years later a meeting of British and Indian merchants demanded the throwing open of the mail contract to competition, and delivery in sixteen days.[33] The opening of the

Suez Canal offered the hope of a major improvement in the transit of mail and passengers, but also a huge boost to trade. Bombay was now much closer to northern Europe than its great rival Calcutta: the Canal had cut the sea journey to London by 40 per cent. Moreover, the Canal would open new markets for Indian produce in Mediterranean countries, and cotton could be sent directly to textile manufacturers in France, Italy and, via Odessa in the Black Sea, Russia. Within a few years the western Indian Ocean, hitherto the preserve of the dhows and baggalas of the Gulf, Hadhramaut and Zanzibar, had become the main trunk route between Europe and the ports of Asia, Australia and the Pacific. While British mercantile houses scoured its shores for new trades and customers, Indian banias moved in as its new business class. More than ever before, Bombay became the hub of this wide maritime region.

The secret was steam. It was the Suez Canal that made steam navigation viable in the eastern world and no longer dependent on the subsidized transport of mail. Within a few years the iron-built steamship had made huge inroads into the sailing-ship business, which was forced back, as we saw earlier, into the rougher, slower, bulk cargoes. Bombay's Indian shipowners, who (despite British competition) had enjoyed a profitable trade with South East Asia and China, could not compete with the ubiquitous steamer, built of British iron and burning British coal. Indeed, while 'native craft' survived in huge numbers to serve very localized needs,[34] India's foreign trade with Europe and Asia, its passenger services east and west, and even its coastal traffic in mail and freight, became almost entirely concentrated in British-owned firms. By the 1880s the grand conglomerate, the British-India, the favoured carrier of the Indian government, offered a regular service to no fewer than ninety-seven ports around the Bay of Bengal and the western Indian Ocean, and was spreading its net to Australia as well. For Bombay, the great prize was to be Europe's main entry port to India. After 1871 the traveller arriving in Bombay could now, if he wished, cross India by train to Calcutta. 'Bombay,' trumpeted the *Times of India* in 1872, was 'becoming the centre of the eastern postal system',[35] the first port of call for European news and newspapers. The harbour was brought under the control of the Port Trust in 1873. The new 'Prince's Dock' opened in 1880, and the grand 'high Gothic' Victoria Terminus of the GIPR, completed in 1887, symbolized Bombay's enthusiastic embrace of 'steam modernity'.

The Suez Canal might have brought a maritime revolution to Bombay, but together with the telegraph (at first slow and expensive) that linked the city to Europe after 1864, and the railway, it brought a commercial revolution as well. Old firms, remarked the *Times of India*, were now 'as redundant as muzzle-loaders'.[36] 'The electric telegraph, the increase in locomotion, the opening of the Suez Canal, and general improvement in water carriage, have revolutionised trade, diminished profits, brought the markets of the world into closer contact, and they centre in the United Kingdom. Prices there regulate prices here . . .'[37] As Bombay's cotton business swung westwards, voyage times shortened and communications speeded up, the old methods of trade fell into disuse. It was no longer so common for merchants in Bombay to buy local cotton and 'consign' it to Liverpool, or sell it there on commission. Increasingly, buyers in Europe placed their orders directly with a Bombay merchant who supplied the requisite quantity. A 'Liverpool standard' on grades of raw cotton now had to be met.[38] The railway companies insisted that cotton be pressed into tightly packed bales to save space before it was shipped. All these changes favoured the European firms in Bombay, with whom buyers 'at home' preferred to deal, and who had the means to pay for steam presses at the railheads. Increasingly, Indian firms, many of whom had been wiped out in the 'bust' of 1866–7, confined their business to China or turned instead to making cotton yarn or cloth for the domestic market in India.[39] In the 1870s cotton mills sprang up around Bombay, managed or owned largely by Indian firms, including the Tatas, soon to be one of India's great merchant dynasties. Like other port cities elsewhere, Bombay began to make the transition from a city reliant on trade towards an industrial city looking to a domestic market, and recruiting a workforce from far and near.

In the second half of the century port-city society began to change as well. Bombay had long been the magnet for many different communities. In 1900, as earlier, three-quarters of its population had been born elsewhere. The 'European' community (in India all whites, including the British, were termed 'Europeans'), at just under 11,000 in 1901, was one of the smallest. It included the cadre of officials who manned the Secretariat and a handful of professionals – doctors, lawyers, teachers and journalists. There was a small army garrison whose officers were much sought after in European society. The two railway companies employed European managers and engineers, and Europeans could be found on the staff of P&O and British-India as well as in the shipping agencies and the expanding docks. Probably the wealthiest were those in the leading 'agency houses' who managed the cotton trade and the array of other businesses that grew up to service a large urban complex. There were also the transients: sailors, discharged soldiers from British regiments, or travelling entertainers. Some of them washed up as vagrants in the European Workhouse: its inmates in 1874 included a musician and a circus clown.[40] The European merchant elite dominated, but did not monopolize, the Chamber of Commerce. In Bombay there was no formal residential segregation and many Europeans found themselves living in Parsi-owned properties.

Europeans, however, were 'birds of passage'. They were constantly coming and going on leave, or forced home by ill-health. Few expected to stay beyond the term of their career or contract. For some indeed, contrary to the delusions of nostalgia, 'the best view of India was over the stern of a ship'. When a European merchant retired, he would sell out his partnership and retreat to Cheltenham, Tunbridge Wells or Bedford, or other favoured haunts of 'Old India Hands'. Notoriously, few European children were allowed to grow up in India lest they be stricken by the climate or acquire undesirable accents, and the European population was predominantly male. On both counts they differed from the Parsis. Like Europeans, Parsis were a small minority, less than 50,000 in 1901 in a population approaching one million. As Zoroastrians, they had migrated from Iran to Gujarat in medieval times. Originally artisans, they had moved into trade and shipping to become the favoured agents of the East India Company. They were early settlers in Bombay as merchants and shipbuilders. Bombay City became their homeland. They were soon indispensable to British trade and governance and leading Parsi businessmen were treated with deference and rewarded with honours. The first Indian to be knighted was a Parsi, Jamsetjee Jejeebhoy.[41] Governors went out of their way to lavish praise on their achievements. 'You Parsees . . . have the bluest blood in Asia,' declaimed one,[42] and Parsis responded with affirmations of loyalty to the 'British connection'. Parsi dignitaries were given a special place at the coronation of Edward VII in 1902.[43]

Yet it should not be thought that they were uncritical servants of their imperial masters. Disrespect for their rites could prompt a fierce reaction.[44] Like other Asian communities who dealt with Europeans, Parsis adopted a mixed mode of dress that preserved a distinctive appearance. Their mercantile wealth was heavily spent on education and philanthropy designed to reinforce the religious solidarity of the Parsi population. In 1909, in the case of *Petit v Jijibhai*, they obtained a ruling (from the Bombay High Court) that no one could convert to become a Parsi, now *de jure* an *ethnic* identity.[45] Far from seeing themselves solely as Indians, they looked back to Iran, eagerly welcomed the Iranian consul and persuaded the Shah, for a price, to lift the restrictions placed on their religious brothers 'at home'.[46] The 'Persian Zoroastrian Amelioration Society' was founded to educate Parsis in Iran and repair their places of worship.[47] As was often the case in Afro-Asia's port cities, their outlook was complex. Wealthy and well-educated *shetias* (merchant princes) in Bombay resented the racial exclusions at the heart of the Raj. The 'father of Indian nationalism', Dadabhai Naoroji, was a Parsi. A British official might sneer that Parsis were 'quite as much alien to the people of India as the English can possibly be. They are indeed less sympathetic to the native than are the English.'[48] But it was Parsis who were among those who took the lead in forming the Indian National Congress in 1885.

Bombay was also home to a small community of Jews (some 5,000 in 1901), of whom the Sassoons were the best known, and an even smaller one of Armenians. But Hindus and Muslims formed the vast majority. Muslims made up some 20 per cent of the city's population, and Bombay was, among other things, a great Muslim centre. Muslims divided themselves into many different sections, who practised different versions of Islam, lived in separate *mohallas* or quarters, prayed at different mosques, and adopted different styles of dress and hairstyle.[49] Among the most prominent were Hadhrami Arabs, active as merchants in western India for centuries; Bohras, some of whom claimed Egyptian or Yemeni descent, and who practised the Shia faith; Memons, a trading class found all round the Indian Ocean, and reputed to be major property owners in Bombay; and Khojas (or Ismailis), originally refugees from Iran, whose partly European-style dress and close-cut hair made them hard to distinguish from Parsis. Khojas owed allegiance (and tithes) to a hereditary chief, the Aga Khan, who had moved from Iran to India in 1840 and to Bombay in 1848 and occupied a grand palace. There were also Sidis, the African Indian descendants of slaves and sailors from Ethiopia and the East African coast, who supplied much of the workforce on Bombay's ever-growing fleet of steamers. A special dockyard shrine was created for them.

For wealthy Muslim businessmen, as for Parsis, the key to social prestige lay in a philanthropic commitment to the 'uplift' of their religious fellows, through the building of shrines and the support of *madrasas* or religious schools. Religious ties with Iran, the Persian Gulf and along the East African coast reinforced the westward pull of Bombay's oceanic hinterland. Many thousands of pilgrims on their way to Mecca passed through Bombay – in increasing numbers as steamers reduced the cost of the passage to Jeddah. Bombay's printing industry, which published some fifty newspapers in Indian languages, produced large numbers of books in Arabic, Urdu and Persian, and Islamic texts in Urdu, Gujarati, Tamil, Malay and Swahili.[50] For Muslims in the western Indian Ocean and beyond, Bombay was an Islamic metropolis.

Yet Bombay was overwhelmingly a Hindu city if numbers are counted, Hindus making up some two-thirds of the population at the end of the nineteenth century. Banias from Gujarat were part of its merchant elite, and Gujarati was widely spoken by Hindus, Muslims and Parsis. Much of the hard labour in the city and its growing mill industry was performed by migrants from the Konkan, the impoverished coastal plain south of Bombay. Once Bombay was connected by rail to the Deccan it attracted Maratha migrants in large numbers, fleeing the plateau's rural poverty and frequent famines. Literate Marathas, less restricted by religious prohibitions, took more readily than Muslims to Western-style schooling and the degrees offered by Bombay University, established in 1857. They were more likely to be employed in the public services or as teachers and journalists. But Bombay Marathas were far less likely than Parsis or Muslims to regard the city as their cultural home. Chitpavan Brahmins, the scribal elite who commanded the deference of other Marathas, looked back to Poona, the former capital of the Maratha Confederacy. 'Poona,' remarked the *Times of India* in 1886, 'is the heart and brain of the political and intellectual life of the Presidency . . . it is one of the few places in India where the spirit of nationality survives.'[51] By the late nineteenth century, Poona had become the cultural, religious and political hub of the Maratha awakening, and the battleground between those who favoured close cooperation with the British in widening (very gradually) the share of Indians in government (the British called them 'moderates'), and their opponents ('extremists'), like Bal Gangadhar Tilak, who urged the mobilization of the rural masses by an appeal to religious revivalism.[52]

By the turn of the century, Bombay was established as one of the great ports of the world. It drew more steamship traffic than Calcutta and handled more imports (Calcutta retained the lead in exports). For many Western visitors Bombay was not just the gateway to India but the gateway to Asia – since India was often the first stop for those going on to South East Asia or China. Passengers for Europe had the choice of more than half a dozen lines offering a regular service, including P&O, Austrian Lloyd, the Italian line Rubattino, the Clan Line to Marseilles, the Anchor Line, the Ball Line and British-India. There was a constant traffic in pilgrims to and from Mecca, Europeans coming and going on furlough (whose movements were meticulously recorded in the *Times of India*), as well as the troopships bringing the regular contingents of British soldiers to keep up the garrison of 70,000 men maintained since the 1857 Rebellion in India (a proportion of one British to two Indian soldiers, or 'sepoys', of the locally raised and British-officered 'Indian Army' was rigorously upheld). Bombay was served by its two great railway companies, the GIPR and the Bombay, Baroda and Central India, linking it to most of India's principal cities. As a financial centre, it was still second to Calcutta; as an industrial city it took pride of place as the largest cotton textile manufacturer in Asia with a near monopoly of the China market.[53]

As with so many port cities, there was a darker side. Bombay's rapid growth meant that much of its population were recent arrivals. Living conditions for the poor were appalling, and, far from rising, living standards fell steeply towards the end of the century as wages (already very low) stagnated while living costs rose.[54] Some 80 per cent of the population occupied single-room tenements, and in 1901 a case was recorded of fifty-four persons in a single room. Bombay's swampy, waterlogged ecology and heavy rainfall made conditions much worse. Huge cesspools were common. Much of the city was without drains, so that waste matter flowed through the streets. Most of these problems were already apparent in the mid-1860s.[55] In the industrial areas in the north of the city much of the population was housed in the infamous chawls, in which a three-foot-wide passage (in practice an open drain) gave access to dark and windowless cubicles filled to capacity.[56] In 1925, it was noted, 'Bombay possesses the inglorious distinction of having probably the highest infant death-rate in the world: 667 per thousand.'[57] In fact, death rates rose steeply after 1896 when Bombay was visited repeatedly by bubonic plague, whose toll was far higher than in other Asian cities, including Calcutta.[58] Much of the population fled the city, and the forcible entry of homes by the British authorities to remove plague cases to camps outside the city, fumigate chawls, and (in some cases) raze dwellings, led to fierce resistance. Bombay itself looked out over a rural interior swept by famines that reduced the province's overall population growth close to zero in the later part of the century. And while the city was home to many different ethnic and religious communities, it was, as we have seen, no melting pot. Indeed, communal tensions seemed on the rise with friction between Parsis and Muslims and, by the 1890s, violent outbreaks between Hindus and Muslims. In 1893 three days of communal rioting killed eighty-one people and injured more than 700.[59]

Bombay's distinctive encounter (for many a deadly embrace) with steam modernity was bound to limit its interior influence. Its railways and telegraphs linked it to distant parts of India. Indian business opinion in the city was keenly interested in questions of protection and taxation decided by British India's central government (in Calcutta until 1911). Tata's had founded an iron and steel factory at

Jamshedpur in eastern India. But in many respects, Bombay remained a social, cultural and political enclave with a limited commercial impact on its own regional hinterland. Around 60 per cent of the freight carried on the GIPR derived from outside the province.[60] Despite the spread of cotton cultivation on the Deccan, investment in rural improvement was modest and the structure of rural society changed little.[61] This was partly because the colonial authorities, fearful of social unrest, had closely restricted the sale of land outside the existing cultivating castes. But large areas were too far from the nearest railway to benefit from a fall in transport costs, and inland towns without railways faced commercial decline.[62] Socially and culturally, Bombay City was the homeland to Parsis and Muslims in an overwhelmingly Hindu province, but Hindus (as we saw) looked back to the Deccan or to Gujarat as theirs. Even in the city, the embrace of Western-style culture was equivocal and selective, used more to reinforce local religious and cultural identities than to adopt the alien attitudes of the tiny European community.[63]

Politically, the Indian business elite in Bombay was deeply attracted to British ideas of representative government and to the ethos of Gladstonian liberalism – if with reservations about free trade. They denounced the 'unBritishness of British rule': its reliance on authoritarian methods; the racial exclusiveness of the governing 'caste', the Indian Civil Service; the studied refusal to grant Indian representative bodies any real control over taxation or the executive. They demanded 'responsible' (i.e. parliamentary) government at the Indian centre, but before the widening of the franchise to the masses. The merchant princes of Bombay might have aspired to be the leading lights of a new Indian nation, but political arithmetic was against them. Bombay City politics, where no single community was dominant, required an intricate coalition of interests and the careful avoidance of sectional or religious appeals.[64] But beyond the city, this kind of politics had little purchase in rural societies, where religious allegiance, caste identity, land taxation and agrarian conflict preoccupied peasant opinion. It was not the *shetias* of Bombay who inspired the mobilization of the Indian masses and the radical transformation of the subcontinent's politics, but the expatriate Gujarati, Mahatma Gandhi, who returned to India in 1915 to preach a doctrine of moral renewal to peasant communities.[65] Once India entered the age of mass politics after 1918, the Bombay Presidency became a storm centre. Yet it was not Bombay City but rural Gujarat that made the political weather.[66] For it was there that Gandhi found his closest allies, and applied the techniques of non-violent protest to subvert the legitimacy (and the morale) of the colonial regime. Gandhian tactics of demonstrations, marches, sit-downs and *hartals* (a general shutdown) soon spread to Bombay.[67] It was Gujaratis who took control of the provincial branch of the Indian National Congress. *Shetia* leaders fell back on abortive schemes for a 'moderates' party and resisted Gandhi's programme of civil disobedience.[68] But they were careful to pay deference to Gandhi's moral authority. Indeed, when faced by strikes and unrest among Bombay's factory workers, they turned to Gandhi as the indispensable peacemaker.

The First World War was a watershed in India, as across much of the world. While Bombay continued to grow, India's trade stagnated in real terms after the war and then dropped sharply from 1930. In many respects India had turned inward. Its rural heartlands, not its port cities, became the focus of its politics, as the Indian National Congress set out to rouse the countryside against the Raj. Constitutional reform and the containment of unrest dominated the agenda of government. The mobilization of religious identity became more intense and communal conflict more severe. Local efforts in Bombay to promote a political party that would reconcile European and Indian interests came to nothing. As their grip on India itself weakened, the British moved to reduce Indian influence along its maritime frontiers: Aden and Burma were separated from India: the paramountcy of African interests was proclaimed in British East Africa. Partly to meet India's heavy wartime expenditure, London conceded 'fiscal autonomy' in 1919: in effect the right to impose tariffs on British goods. Import duties quickly became the largest item of government revenue. With tariffs on manufactured imports at 15 per cent by 1925, India became a protectionist economy.[69] The old staple trade in Lancashire cotton piece goods collapsed under the strain of Japanese competition and the onset of the Depression in 1930, with obvious consequences for the British merchants in Bombay who had made it *their* business. Bombay's raw cotton exports were sent increasingly to

Japan. For much of the interwar period the Bombay government was under siege from the Gandhian mass movement that was at its strongest in Gujarat. As a bridgehead of British power and influence, a powerhouse of the West's steam modernity, Bombay by the interwar years looked near the end of its tether.

CALCUTTA: THE 'METROPOLIS OF BRITISH INDIA'[70]

'Of all European nations who have planted distant settlements,' remarked a scientific observer in the 1840s, 'the English have invariably shown the least regard to the proper selection of localities for their colonial cities.'[71] He was referring to Calcutta's notoriously unhealthy site. It lay (not unlike New Orleans) a hundred miles from the open sea, up a winding and shoal-ridden channel, and stood on the natural levee of the River Hooghly that sloped inward towards marshy ground and the Saltwater Lake, three miles to the east. Drainage was difficult with inevitable consequences before modern sanitation, malaria was endemic and mortality crushing. What became Calcutta had been three riverside villages purchased from their zamindar landlords in 1690. The East India Company had chosen the site for its commercial advantages. It was the lowest habitable point on the Hooghly before it entered the flooded wilderness of the Sundarbans. The curve of the river offered a deep-water anchorage for the Company's ships. And the Hooghly was then the great highway into the most productive part of Bengal: the source of the valuable muslins and other costly cottons that the Company sold at great profit in Europe.[72]

Notoriously, the Company's affairs in 1756 were plunged into crisis when it fell out with the Nawab of Bengal, who ruled from his capital upriver at Murshidabad. Most of the English fled the city, except for those (the number is disputed) locked up in the infamous 'Black Hole'. But when Robert Clive returned with a naval squadron and a contingent of the Company's army from Madras (then the Company's main base in India), he routed the Nawab at Plassey in June 1757, having won over much of the enemy's army to the

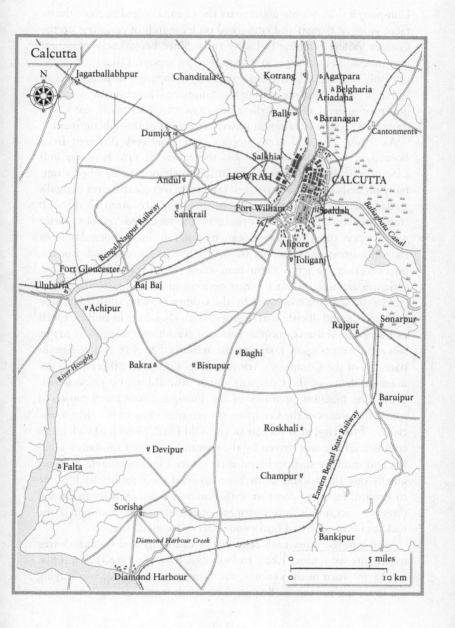

Calcutta

N

Jagatballabhpur
Chanditala
Kotrang
Agarpara
Belgharia
Ariadaha
Bally
Baranagar
Cantonments
Dumjor
Salkhia
HOWRAH
CALCUTTA
Andul
Fort William
Sealdah
Sankrail
Baliaghatta Canal
Alipore
Toliganj
Fort Gloucester
Baj Baj
Ulubaria
Achipur
Sonarpur
Rajpur
Bengal Nagpur Railway
River Hooghly
Baghi
Bakra
Bistupur
Baruipur
Roskhali
Eastern Bengal State Railway
Devipur
Champur
Bankipur
Sorisha
Diamond Harbour Creek
0   5 miles
0   10 km
Diamond Harbour

Company's side. Within eight years the Company had become the de facto ruler of Bengal and embarked on its march of conquest up the Ganges Valley, reaching Delhi by 1803. Since Bengal was its richest province and could support a vast army of sepoys, Calcutta became not only its capital but, from 1773, the Company's headquarters in India. It was from there that the 'Supreme Government' and the governor-general directed the campaigns that had made the Company by 1820 the paramount power over most of the subcontinent.

As a port city Calcutta's origins were thus very different from Bombay's. From the 1760s it was the centre of British power and enterprise in India. It was where in the freebooting era, when Company officials exercised privileged (and coercive) control over Bengal's trade, huge fortunes were made as much by predation as through trade and were remitted to Britain by the so-called 'nabobs'. After 1800, when the Company began to separate its commercial from its administrative functions, the worst abuses were tamed. But the buccaneering era left a permanent mark. From the very beginning, Calcutta attracted a much larger contingent of European 'free merchants' (those, not employed by the Company, who traded lawfully within Asia and illicitly with Europe) than elsewhere in India, as well as European artisans, shopkeepers and even house servants ready to serve the extravagant tastes of the nabobs.[73] It was also the main barracks of the Company's army, with its European officers, and the main residence of the Company's high officialdom, on princely salaries. The business premises of the European merchants clustered round the offices of the Company government close to the river in the centre of the city, near the site of the 'Old Fort'.[74] Much of Calcutta's commercial life was driven by the eagerness of the Company's civilian and military staff to invest their salaries in a profitable venture, ideally one that would allow them to send their profits back home to Britain. In sharp contrast with Bombay, it was European capital (however acquired) and European merchants that dominated the Calcutta economy and European officials its social life.

Well into the nineteenth century the Company and Calcutta's free merchants were more likely to look east than west for their profits. For by the turn of the century, the Company's mainstay was buying tea in China for sale in Britain. The result was a strange triangular trade. To pay for the tea, the Company had discovered a much more acceptable product than British textiles or metal goods, and one much easier to provide than silver bullion, the old standby. This was opium, manufactured from the 1770s in the Company's factories along the Ganges. Since the Company dared not sell opium openly in Canton, each January, when the winter monsoon brought the first ships back from China, it auctioned the chests of opium balls in its salerooms in Calcutta to the 'country traders', the private merchants who took the risk and much of the profit.[75] Even more than in Bombay, opium was the jewel in the crown of Calcutta's commerce, the source of the wealth that made it 'the city of palaces'. Calcutta's exports of opium increased more than tenfold between 1830–31 and 1862–3.[76] But, unlike Bombay, it was European merchants who dominated this trade. Calcutta's second main staple was indigo, a deep-blue vegetable dye derived from the juice of the plant and dried into cakes for export. Indigo, too, was a 'European' trade. It was typically grown by peasant cultivators, but European 'planters' near Cawnpore (Kanpur) and Allahabad controlled the processing and sent the indigo cakes in chests to Calcutta.[77] Indigo's main market lay in Europe, and indigo, like opium, made mercantile fortunes in the city.

Calcutta in the 1820s and 1830s was the scene of feverish speculation in these two 'wonder crops', spurred on by the fact that most European merchants aimed to make their fortune as quickly as possible and retreat to Britain before malaria, cholera, dysentery, smallpox or typhus could claim them. The result was often a reckless overexposure by the 'agency houses' – the merchant partnerships that ruled the Calcutta market – who took deposits and lent heavily to local clients and planters against uncertain earnings abroad. In 1830 the leading agency house, John Palmer and Co., collapsed on the fall of indigo prices, and within three years every other agency house went bankrupt, inflicting large losses on those (usually Europeans) who had deposited their savings in them.[78] New agency houses appeared, and a further wipe-out occurred in the late 1840s before more stable conditions (and perhaps wiser management) prevailed. But these two disasters had an enduring legacy. Before the 1830s, agency houses had looked increasingly to wealthy Indians to enlarge their capital, and some Bengali merchants had entered into partnerships. One firm,

Carr Tagore, was a joint venture between a European merchant and Dwarkanath Tagore, from the leading Bengali family in the city. Two commercial catastrophes were enough to dissuade Calcutta's Bengali elite from again trusting their wealth to European merchants, a disillusionment with important social consequences.

Calcutta's hopes of becoming a great commercial metropolis, the New Orleans of the Ganges Valley, depended on its access to Upper India and its produce via the Hooghly and Bhagirathi rivers that connected with the Ganges. But unlike New Orleans, its riverine network was far from reliable. For much of the year, when the water was low, it was impracticable to bring boats downriver from Patna, Allahabad, Cawnpore or Mirzapore, 'the great mart of Upper India', except by a huge diversion to the east of Calcutta and thence through the Sundarbans, more than doubling the distance. It took up to three months to send a cargo by boat from Mirzapore to Calcutta,[79] and cargo space was often unavailable. Nor could steamboats be of much help since the rivers were often too shallow for them to cruise safely. The result was that the costs (including insurance), delays and losses of river-borne freight greatly reduced the competitiveness of Indian sugar and cotton, and restricted the market for goods imported through Calcutta. Overland transport was even costlier and slower, and losses to weather damage still greater. (One complaint was that the pack bullocks would eat the raw cotton they carried on their backs.)

From the early 1840s there was a strenuous campaign for the building of railways. In 1849 it won the support of the governor-general, Lord Dalhousie, and the East India Company (nervous of the costs) gave way. An 'experimental railway' of some 150 miles was permitted, and opened in 1855. It linked Calcutta to the coalfields round Burdwan, but it was far short of reaching the Ganges. Under the shock of the Great Rebellion of 1857, a new urgency appeared, and by 1865 the East India Railway had reached Delhi, a thousand miles from Calcutta, opening Upper India to its trade.[80] Railways reshaped Calcutta's commercial connections. Opium (like indigo) remained very important,[81] but Calcutta merchants were now more likely to face west towards Europe rather than east towards China. Then, from the 1860s, it was jute, the raw material for the ubiquitous 'gunny-bag' in which raw products were shipped, and tea for the British consumer (gradually weaned from the Chinese variety),[82] that became staple exports along with cotton and indigo. By 1900–1901 raw and manufactured jute together with tea made up over 25 per cent of Indian exports by value.[83] But to a remarkable extent these new trades like the old remained in the hands of British firms in the city.

Much of the explanation could be found in the so-called 'managing agency' system.[84] The old 'agency houses' had acted as traders and factors for the indigo planters, as well as taking deposits from local (mainly European) savers. Managing agencies also engaged in export and import, took local savings and acted as factors. But their typical function was to provide the management for a multitude of mainly European-owned enterprises in jute processing, tea growing and coalmining in the districts north and east of Calcutta, as well as for the mass of ancillary firms that serviced Calcutta's internal trade and its shipping, transport and insurance. The great managing agencies with their offices in Clive Street were masters of the (Calcutta) universe. Their partners were personages that even the lordly officials of the Bengal government dared not ignore. They dominated the Chamber of Commerce (unlike the Bombay chamber, the member firms were all European) and the Calcutta Trades Association – the main business lobbies. One leading agency, Mackinnon Mackenzie, supplied the management for British-India, the shipping line founded by William Mackinnon, and its influence was felt all round the Indian Ocean.[85] What lent managing agencies their commercial power was, above all, their ability to draw capital from Britain to invest in India – an ability based upon the careful stewardship of their reputations in London. They were the crucial intermediaries between new business ventures in India and the nervous (and ill-informed) investor at home.[86] Alongside the guaranteed railway companies, they were the lynchpin of private British investment in India. They symbolized the strange bifurcation of business life on the subcontinent by the later nineteenth century in which Indian capital and enterprise concentrated on its domestic market while that of the British was almost entirely confined to the transport and export sectors, where management remained firmly in British hands. Indeed, on the eve of the First

World War it was estimated that some 60 per cent of British invest-ment in India was managed in or through Calcutta.[87]

What kind of city had Calcutta grown into by the second half of the century? It remained above all a city of the river. But the river below as well as above Calcutta was very capricious. The deep water channel to the sea was constantly shifting. Extending cultivation (and deforestation) upriver brought down ever larger amounts of silt, slowing the current and worsening the shoals. It was already the case, remarked an 1865 report, that larger vessels had to wait for high water before reaching Calcutta, imposing 'great delays'.[88] As ships grew larger, the problem grew worse, so that Calcutta's survival as a major port depended on dredging, the constant improvement of its channel to the sea, and the handling of cargo on its riverside quays.[89] A growing network of railways had spread out like a fan, bringing old cash crops (like cotton) and new (jute and tea) to the city: not only the great East India Railway, but the East Bengal Railway carrying mainly jute and coal (by the 1920s, jute made up over 40 per cent of its revenue),[90] the line to Assam and its tea plantations, as well as a skein of narrow-gauge railways. Yet Calcutta's riverine links remained vital: indeed, as its commerce was increasingly dominated by jute, rice and tea from eastern Bengal and Assam rather than the products of northern India, its waterborne access to the eastern side of the delta became a more vital priority. By the early twentieth century three times as much tea reached Calcutta by river steamer as by rail, and half of the jute delivered to the Hooghly came the same way.[91]

The growing concentration especially upon jute, which made up nearly 40 per cent of Calcutta's export trade by the turn of the cen-tury,[92] and the eastward shift in the city's regional interests had important social and political consequences. Far from slackening, as time went on, the grip of Calcutta's tiny European community on its commercial life grew ever tighter. The growth of manufacturing made little difference. In Bombay's cotton industry it was Indian mer-chants who took the lead. Calcutta's equivalent, the manufacture of jute fabric in the mill district north of the city, was firmly in Euro-pean hands. The nexus of jute, tea and coal with the river-steamer and railway companies, and the shipping interests, was a commercial complex of enormous power, to which the colonial regime was usually bound to defer. James Lyle Mackay, the effective head of the British-India line from 1893, sat on the Viceroy's Legislative Council, and became the home government's unofficial adviser on commercial relations with India for much of the Edwardian period.[93] Perhaps in an echo of their business lives, Calcutta's Europeans were famously introverted: the social (and racial) barriers to contact with Indians, or partnership with them, remained high, except among teachers, clergymen and journalists, whose professions encouraged less rigid seclusion.[94] This pattern was both ironic and tragic. For Calcutta was home to the largest community on the subcontinent of Indians famil- iar with Western culture, English literature and English law. Since the early part of the century schools and colleges had sprung up in the city to offer literate Bengalis an 'English' education. Calcutta's main industry, it was sometimes remarked, was really education. For many thousands of Bengali Hindus, Calcutta offered employment in government service, where English was required or useful, and in the ever-growing number of clerical jobs in the city's commerce. The key social group in Calcutta society was the *bhadralok*, the 'respectable people', literate and educated.[95] Many depended, if only in part, on rents drawn from (often quite modest) rural properties. It was from their ranks that sprang the vocal contingent of lawyers, teachers, journalists and literary men that helped to make Calcutta the most politically conscious of Indian cities by the later part of the century. Exclusion from both commerce and political power fuelled the sense of deepening injustice at the 'unBritishness of British rule': the conflict between the liberal values the British preached and the authoritarian racism they often displayed in practice.

This political grievance was part of a wider social and cultural phenomenon. European attitudes – the stress on individualism, physical exertion and 'manliness' (Europeans typically disparaged the supposed softness and 'effeminacy' of Bengali men) – as well as their modes of dress and leisure pursuits, exerted a powerful appeal. But they also evoked an anxious reaction, and sparked a moral debate.[96] How far were these new modes of behaviour either modest or honourable? Could they be reconciled with traditional notions of virtue, with obligations to kin, or to the life of the extended joint- family, the key social unit of Bengali society. These debates and dilemmas found expression in poems, pamphlets and plays, as well as in the new form of the novel. They encouraged the growth of a new and more flexible Bengali language, the vehicle for a new Bengali consciousness. Thus the self-confident British 'box-wallahs' of Dalhousie Square (the heart of the European business district) found an articulate Bengali nationalism growing up under their feet. Surendranath Banerjea (1848–1925), the 'uncrowned king of Bengal', assailed British injustice in his paper *The Bengalee*. To the Calcutta *bhadralok*, their city and province were under alien rule: in a juster world the political kingdom should be theirs. At first, this demand for a share (at least) of political power could be reconciled with acceptance of the 'British connection' and allegiance to the 'Queen-Empress' or King-Emperor. But when a hyperactive British Viceroy, Lord Curzon, proposed in 1905 to cut the province in half (separating eastern Bengal with its Muslim majority and Assam), in a blatant attempt to crush *bhadralok* aspirations – ('Bengal united is a power,' remarked one of his senior officials, 'Bengal divided will pull in different ways. That is one of the merits of the scheme')[97] – it triggered a furious reaction: a *Swadeshi* campaign to boycott British goods and a growing trend towards political violence. Political frustration turned Bengal into the land of the bomb. Reversing the partition in 1911 (when the capital was moved to Delhi) came too late: a deep sense of alienation now separated the British more than ever from those who had once seen themselves as the 'providential' beneficiaries of the British Raj. But, as so often happened in colonial politics, the claim of the *bhadralok* to speak for the whole of Bengal, or even all of Calcutta, was to prove dangerously fragile.

At the turn of the century Calcutta continued to grow at astonishing speed. Its European population (some 6,000 in 1856) had only grown modestly. But the city at large had more than doubled in size to over 800,000 by 1901, the vast majority born outside the city. Much of its labour force came from Bihar and the United Provinces (now Uttar Pradesh) and spoke not Bengali but 'Hindustani' (a composite of modern Urdu and Hindi), the lingua franca of Upper India. The frantic pace of demographic growth (the population had grown by 30 per cent in the last decade of the century) had a predictable consequence. Overcrowding was desperate and living conditions in the *bustees*, the huts and shacks in which the poor had to live, were unimaginably squalid and dangerous, sanitation non-existent. In the 'city of dreadful night'[98] thousands slept on the street. Plague killed over 8,000 people in 1903, and water-borne diseases (the poor drank water from the grossly polluted Hooghly or the public cisterns) constantly swept many others away. Urban improvements, like sewage systems, paved roads, lighting and trams, served mainly the European quarters and the wealthier suburbs to the south, like Ballygunge, to which Indian professionals began to move.[99] For most of the population, the benefits of Calcutta's long boom up to 1914, if they existed at all, were spread very thin indeed: real wages were falling. But for the 'second city of the Empire' a great change was coming.

After the first shock of the war in 1914 when its shipping seized up (German commerce-raiders briefly ran riot in the Bay of Bengal) and jute prices slumped, Calcutta and jute enjoyed a wartime boom on the back of the ubiquitous trench sandbag.[100] After a brief post-war slump, the 1920s were also prosperous years. At some 1.4 million, Calcutta's population in 1931 was larger than Bombay's and three times that of Delhi or Hyderabad, India's largest inland cities. Calcutta retained its lead over Bombay in the shipment of exports. But commercially and politically the shape of the port city began to look very different. Bengal and Calcutta were drawn into the great Gandhian campaign for 'Swaraj (self-rule) in one year' – the 'non-cooperation' campaign of 1920–22. A new constitution brought electoral politics to the province and the promise of *bhadralok* rule. Calcutta city corporation was reformed in 1923 to give Indian representatives real executive power.[101] Commercially, Marwari merchants, originally from Rajasthan in northern India, moved into the jute trade and jute manufacture, and Indian capital became increasingly important in the industry.[102] The European managing agencies, anxious to keep the Indian-owned firms inside the cartel that set raw-jute prices, had to come to terms.[103] The wiser among the Europeans, like Edward Benthall, head of the great firm of Bird's, saw that their commercial survival depended on accommodation with Indian businessmen, like G. D. Birla, a devotee of Gandhi, and the Indian politicians who ruled the city and, increasingly, the province. With the onset of depression in 1930, which brought a huge crash in jute prices and a savage contraction in trade, solidarity between Indian and European firms, and cultivating political goodwill to ward off labour unrest or unwelcome regulation, became more important than ever. Yet European business interests were still strong enough to secure special representation when provincial self-government arrived in 1937. Holding the balance of power inside the provincial assembly, they exerted their influence over ministers whose own private fortunes were tied up in jute and whose political careers required discreet subsidy.[104] 'What a powerful position we have with this government,' remarked Benthall, the leader of the non-official Europeans in the city. 'I believe they would adopt any policy we liked to press on them.'[105] The respite was temporary.

Notoriously, Calcutta's transition towards an Indian-ruled city had a tragic denouement. Calcutta's Hindu *bhadralok*, a governing class in waiting, had expected to inherit a united Bengal (Curzon's division had been reversed in 1911). But by the 1920s the fate of the city and the province was being decided far away. Gandhi's non-cooperation movement had depended very heavily on the mobilization of Muslims and their grievance against the British demolition of the Ottoman caliphate in 1920. Once aroused, Muslim political consciousness proved hard to assuage: and Bengal was a province in which Muslims formed the majority – mainly among the impoverished cultivators in the eastern part of the province. Gandhi's insistence that the Congress must represent both Hindus and Muslims, and the British insistence that the path to self-government meant widening the franchise, destroyed *bhadralok* power: the 'Communal Award' of 1932 acknowledged Bengal as a Muslim-majority province and the *bhadralok* Congressmen dared not resist.[106] Muslim politicians took over the province in 1937. But already communal conflict was on the rise: there had been savage communal riots in Calcutta in 1926 in which over one hundred were killed and nearly a thousand injured. With the outbreak of war in 1939 there opened the tragic last phase of colonial Calcutta: the terrible Bengal famine of 1943 which cost three million lives; the mass killings in the city in 1946 as British rule collapsed; and the traumatic partition of 1947 that cut Bengal in half and sent hundreds of thousands of refugees fleeing east and west.

STEAMING INTO INDIA: PORT CITIES AND 'PROGRESS'

Bombay and Calcutta dominated India's seaborne connections and its maritime trade: Madras and Karachi trailed far behind. For much of the period between 1860 and 1940 they were also India's largest and wealthiest cities. They symbolized what, at first sight, seemed the chief impact of the British in India: the reversal of the long-standing hegemony of its inland states and empires in favour of the coast and its maritime commerce. Bombay and Calcutta were Europe's bridgeheads on the subcontinent: through them its multiple influences – political, commercial, cultural, religious and technological – might have been expected to flow into the Indian interior and, as (British) contemporaries imagined, inject energy and dynamism into a stagnant society. But, as we have seen, the pattern of change was far less clear-cut.

Both Bombay and Calcutta had thrived on steam. The steamship and railway had transformed them from ports facing east towards China and turned them instead into the West's gateways to India. They became India's main hubs for both shipping and railways, with two railway systems that stretched deep into the subcontinent. In fact, the history of those railways reveals much about the strength and the weakness of India's port cities. At some 42,000 miles by 1930, the rail network was skeletal for a subcontinent with a population of over 300 million. A report at the turn of the century had shown that while there was a mile of railway line for every 383 people in the United States, and even for every 3,556 in 'backward' Russia, the figure in India was a mile of railway line for every 12,231 people.[107] The figure was still as high as 8,400 in 1930. This exiguous scale reflected in part the limits of local demand (railways in North America were often promoted by local initiative) but chiefly the absence of all but a thin trickle of capital with which to construct them. Notoriously, railway-building in India required a financial guarantee from the government: the system of land grants on the North American model could not be deployed in a densely settled interior. A parsimonious colonial regime deeply averse to financial risk and often preoccupied by internal security or frontier defence was India's frail substitute for the capitalists of the Pennsylvania Railroad or New York Central. Indeed, far from being 'privatized', India's main railways had moved back under full state control by the mid-1920s. The capital employed in India's railways and the scale of the management its system required were trivial compared with the North American model. Here lies one reason why neither Bombay nor Calcutta would resemble New York: the huge concentration of railway finance and management that helped make New York had no parallel there.

There was another great contrast. Despite their pretensions and sometimes ill-tempered rivalry, neither Bombay nor Calcutta could claim outright primacy as India's chief port: the spoils of commerce were divided between them. Perhaps more to the point, neither could find a great export trade that remotely rivalled in scale the colossal traffic in cotton that made New York's fortune. For much of the steam century after 1830, India's commercial significance was as the chief market for Lancashire's output of cotton piece goods – and thus indirectly for American cotton. Much of the activity in its port cities turned on the need to widen that market and find the commodities that would pay for the import of textiles. Later the manufacture of cotton cloth (in Bombay) and jute fabric (in Calcutta) turned them into industrial centres as well. But the finance and management of both those enterprises revealed a key characteristic of India's port-city economies.

Bombay cotton cloth was chiefly marketed in India; Calcutta's jute fabric was exported to 'bag' the world's trade in grain, rice, sugar and coffee. Bombay's cotton mills were mainly owned and managed by Indian merchants drawing on Indian-owned capital; Calcutta's jute mills by British expatriates. This division was no accident. With few exceptions, expatriate merchants and capital confined themselves to external trade and export commodities and left the internal market to Indians – reflecting a judgement of where lay their strategic advantage in market intelligence and access to credit and political influence. Thus although banks and other institutions spread inland from the ports, especially along the line of rail, the commercial integration of the interior economy with the major port cities and their global connections remained at best patchy and partial. Far from 'colonizing' the subcontinent with their technology and capital, the expatriate merchants, those agents of the global economy, preferred to carve out a series of profitable 'niches', defended, like jute, against rival producers. By the 1920s they resembled commercial garrisons, guarded by privilege and (as British capital dried up) faced with decline.

Behind this evolution lay another great fact: the seemingly ineradicable poverty of Indian rural society except where, as in the Punjab, 'new' land had been opened by irrigation canals. Rural poverty drove the migration to Bombay and Calcutta (and new kinds of poverty) and towards the plantations in tropical colonies from Trinidad to Fiji. Harsh landscapes (like the Deccan) were partly to blame but ecological instability was another huge factor. The annual monsoon on which the grain harvest depended was notoriously fickle: failure could mean famine. Earthquake, storm and flood were regular visitors. In Bengal the eastward drift of the Ganges denied western Bengal the fertilizing power of its silt and the annual 'cleansing' of its creeks and pools. Increasingly, western districts became quilted with malarial swamps: their cultivators migrated and agriculture declined. In one anxious forecast Calcutta's own survival was threatened. 'It is the steady decline of active deltaic conditions in the region which will in all probability bring about the ruin of Calcutta as a port,' wrote one gloomy expert. 'The port of Calcutta will one day be remembered only with ancient Tamluk or Satgaon on the tablets of history.'[108] Environmental uncertainty reduced the appeal of agricultural improvement, reinforced the preference for subsistence crops over cash crops, and may have encouraged the persistence of collective forms of landholding as insurance against ecological misfortune. Certainly there was never remotely enough capital to transform peasant agriculture and the colonial regime was proverbially fearful of imposing any change on agrarian society. This alone was enough to blunt the interior impact of India's port cities. The mercantile profits of European firms in Bombay and Calcutta were remitted sooner or later back home to Britain.

India thus had a highly distinctive experience of steam globalization. Indian agriculture, from which over 80 per cent of the population drew a living, became more commercialized and rights of proprietorship were greatly extended – in part because of the way that land was taxed by the colonial regime. More land was bought and sold, or was used to raise mortgages. Cash crops like cotton, wheat and jute became quite widely grown. In theory, this should have transformed the efficiency and productivity of the agrarian economy. In practice, the results were very uneven, and success depended upon proximity to a railway, access to irrigation, and the variations of climate between 'wet' and 'dry' regions. The real wages of labour (i.e. in terms of food prices) remained stagnant, partly because of the rising cost of food grains, and (as we saw) actually fell in port cities. In the first five decades after 1860, increases in agricultural output were largely achieved by the extension of cultivable land: when 'new' land ran out agricultural growth dried up, crop yields began to fall and living standards fell back – a retreat accelerated by the huge fall in crop prices after 1930. Technological inertia and the lack of investment were the culprits – another huge contrast with the North American pattern. While that prevailed, vast swathes of the agrarian interior remained locked in poverty.[109] India's foreign trade, far smaller in the interwar years than Canada's (which had barely one-thirtieth of India's population), hardly touched the lives of most of its people.[110]

Yet the histories of Bombay and Calcutta reveal more about steam globalization than the limited extent of its commercial or technological penetration. They show that the 'opening' of India to industrial Europe required the catalyst of the triangular trade with China and depended heavily upon opium deep into the nineteenth century. The contrasting character of their merchant elites suggests that even in a colonial port city there was no guarantee of European predominance. Both cities were more than just entries and exits for manufactures and commodities: they developed an industrial base which the European jute merchants in Calcutta were determined to protect against interference from 'Home'. Politically and culturally the effects of globalization were deeply ambiguous. Western legal and constitutional forms were absorbed, and Western education made welcome. But they triggered moral debate, not ready acceptance, and prompted distinctive versions of ethno-religious mobilization among the different communities drawn into the cities. Nor, as it turned out, did the commercial performance and civic stability of India's port cities depend chiefly on local endeavour or their overseas links. After 1914 their future was tied to political change in the northern Indian interior where the fate of the Raj was decided: in an ironic reversal of their metropolitan claims, at this crucial stage their influence was minimal. Calcutta's prosperity required a united Bengal and ready access to the resources of its eastern districts: but these were cut away in the traumatic partition of 1947.[111] Bombay (like Madras) might have preferred to be a separate 'city-state' province in independent India and preserve its cosmopolitan society: neither prevailed against the demands of inland politicians. Both needed to trade freely with the world beyond India: but the Congress 'licence *raj*' after 1947 imposed restrictions and quotas in the interests of independent India's 'planned development' that persisted until deregulation in 1990. 'Calcutta de-globalized and de-industrialized after 1947.'[112] In India, as elsewhere, globalization might have arrived on the back of trade and technology, but its erratic course, its advances and retreats, were driven by the winds of geopolitical change.

7

From the Nanyang to the Yangzi: The Port-City World in the China Seas

'Nanyang' – a term still current – was the Chinese word for the 'Southern Ocean', the maritime world that stretched south from China into the vast Indonesian archipelago. By extension, it has come to include the coastlands of Indo-China (modern Vietnam and Cambodia), Siam (Thailand since 1939), the Malay peninsula and even Burma's far south. Since the sixteenth century the Nanyang had been the highway for European efforts to engage with China by trade and diplomacy. With the opening of Shanghai as a 'treaty port' in 1842, and of Yokohama in 1858, it became the great sea lane by which Europeans aimed to reach the Yangzi Valley, China's commercial heartland, and on to Japan. By the 1870s, when steam came into its own east of Suez, globalization seemed to be remaking the commercial, cultural and political landscape of this whole huge region at dramatic speed, if with uncertain results.

Yet the Nanyang was a setting that was strikingly different from British-ruled India, let alone settler-occupied North America: and its nineteenth-century globalization followed a quite different path. Indeed, the Nanyang had long been part of a global economy. Its spices and exotics had been traded as far as the Americas since the sixteenth century. It had been the market for Indian and Chinese manufactures for even longer. Indian, Arab, Dutch, Portuguese and even English merchants had competed for its produce. But the most constant commercial presence had been Chinese, sometimes in partnership with the Dutch. The Nanyang might almost be thought of as China's 'informal empire', where Chinese merchants practised a

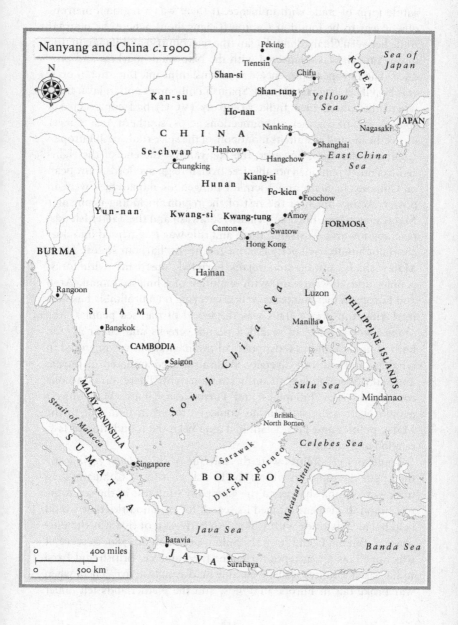

Nanyang and China *c.* 1900

N

Sea of Japan

Peking
Tientsin
Chifu
KOREA

Shan-si
Shan-tung
Yellow Sea

Kan-su

Ho-nan
JAPAN
Nagasaki

C H I N A
Nanking

Se-chwan
Hankow
Shanghai
East China Sea

Chungking
Hangchow

Hunan
Kiang-si

Yun-nan
Fo-kien
Foochow

Kwang-si
Kwang-tung
Amoy

Canton
Swatow
FORMOSA

BURMA
Hong Kong

Rangoon
Hainan

Luzon

S I A M
PHILIPPINE ISLANDS

Bangkok
Manilla

CAMBODIA

Saigon

South China Sea
Sulu Sea

Mindanao

MALAY PENINSULA

British
North Borneo
Celebes Sea

Strait of Malacca

S U M A T R A
Singapore
Sarawak
B O R N E O
Dutch Borneo

Macassar Strait

Java Sea

Batavia
Banda Sea

J A V A
Surabaya

0   400 miles
0   500 km

subtle form of trade with influence. If there was a regional metropolis, it was to be found at Canton (Guangzhou), where the internal trade between Guangdong, Fujian (the tea country) and Jiangnan (the lower Yangzi) was connected with the Nanyang's markets and produce. The European presence was not insignificant. But after 1600 it was heavily concentrated in the Spanish Philippines and in Java, from where the Dutch East India Company (VOC) had constructed a spider's web of commercial connections across southern Asia to meet its overheads and sustain its monopoly of the spice trade with Europe.[1]

On a wider view, however, the Nanyang at the end of the eighteenth century remained notably free from foreign overlords, European or Chinese. In Siam and Vietnam indigenous monarchies were in power. Across much of the rest of the region, including peninsular Malaya, Sumatra, Borneo, Celebes (Sulawesi) and the 'Outer Islands' reaching towards Australia, trade and rule was fragmented into dozens if not hundreds of petty riverine polities or 'harbour states'. There Malay chiefs, sultans and rajahs bartered 'upstream' with forest peoples and 'downstream' with a motley of Chinese, Indian, Arab and European merchants, as well as carrying on a profitable business in slaving and piracy. This was the world of the 'sea peoples' (the *orang-laut*), a maze of secluded islands, creeks and channels. On both mainland and islands, political fragmentation was mirrored in religious and cultural diversity. Buddhism predominated in Burma and Siam. Vietnam was a Confucian monarchy. There were Catholic converts in the Philippines and Portuguese Timor. Many forest peoples were animists. Hindus could be found in Bali. But in the Malay polities and Java, Islam had long been the foundation of law, religion and culture.

Trade and geopolitics were the solvents of this *ancien régime*. By the 1780s the rapid growth of the British East India Company's tea trade with China sharpened the Company's interest in the sea route to Canton. It also encouraged its search for commodities that would help balance its trade with China. An early sign of this was the purchase of Penang Island from the Sultan of Kedah in 1786, to serve, it was hoped, as an entrepôt for regional commerce. British and Parsi India-based 'country traders' became increasingly active. Then, when war broke out in Europe in 1790s, and the Netherlands fell under

French domination, the British began to roll up Dutch possessions in Asia, taking the Cape of Good Hope (formally a dependency of Java), Ceylon (Sri Lanka) and Malacca in 1795. The Company government in Calcutta cast an envious eye on Java, the jewel in the Dutch crown, and sent an army to seize it in 1811. A vast extension of the Company's territories was in prospect. But at the peace in 1814–15 the urgency of restoring the Netherlands (sustained by its colonial wealth and enlarged to include what later became Belgium) as a strategic barrier to French expansion scotched the plans of Stamford Raffles, the Company's man on the spot, for a new East Indian empire. From the wreck of these schemes, Raffles snatched the consolation prize of Singapore Island, bought in 1819 from the ruler of Johore on the mainland nearby. After a period of jostling, the Anglo-Dutch Treaty of 1824 drew a partition line just south of Singapore. The British abandoned their posts on Sumatra in return for Malacca, now part of what became a small fringe of port towns round the Malayan peninsula, the so-called 'Straits Settlements'. But their ambition remained to command the trade of the whole Indonesian archipelago, and secure the seaway between Calcutta and Canton through the Malacca Strait and the South China Sea.

At the time of Singapore's founding, Raffles had outlined a far grander project. 'Our eventual object,' he told a friend at Court, 'is of course to secure the independence of Bornean, Sumatran and other States with which we have been in alliance for the last seventy years . . .' Their trade had to be rescued from the 'withering grasp of the Hollander'. Singapore was 'within a week's sail of China; still closer to Siam, Cochin China &c, in the very heart of the Archipelago . . . Our object is not territory but Trade; a great commercial emporium and a *fulcrum* whence we may extend our influence politically as circumstances may hereafter require.'[2] Free trade was to be the means of the 'advancement and improvement of the native states . . . by upholding their independence, and strengthening their power and importance'.[3] The Dutch would be left with Java and the Moluccas, but the rest of the region would look to the British for trade and enlightenment. Indeed, Raffles planned that his 'Singapore Institution' (later to be named after him) would serve as a great training college for the region's 'higher classes', to encourage the eradication of slavery, debt bondage and man-hunting, offer a modern education to Chinese, and teach Arabic and Malay to the Company's officials.[4]

In the fifty years after Singapore's founding the sphere it was meant to command was transformed in ways that Raffles could not have imagined. In 1819 China was still 'closed' to Westerners and their trade except at Canton. The First Opium War, followed by the Treaty of Nanjing in 1842, opened five 'treaty ports', including Shanghai, to Western merchants. The British acquired the island of Hong Kong, henceforth to be their main China base and a safe haven for the opium traffic. It, like Singapore, became a 'free port', without tariffs or charges. In 1855 the British concluded the 'Bowring Treaty' with the king of Siam, abolishing the royal monopoly over trade and opening the country to British (and soon other Western) merchants. The treaty, which permitted the free import of opium, was swiftly concluded, in Bowring's own account, when he threatened to bring the cruiser *Rattler* upriver to the royal palace in Bangkok.[5] But the great zone of free trade that Raffles had envisaged was slow to appear. The Dutch colonial regime in Java proved far from moribund. Having crushed local opposition in the five-year Java War (1825–30), it imposed the notorious *kultuurstelsel* (cultivation system) under which Javanese cultivators were compelled to produce sugar and coffee for the colonial state. A state monopoly, the Nederlandse Handel Maatschappij or NHM, sold the produce in Europe. Meanwhile, to the growing alarm of British merchants in Singapore, the Dutch steadily imposed their control over the native polities along the east coast of Sumatra and around the coast of Borneo, restricting their freedom of trade. In the late 1850s a new rival appeared. Between 1858 and 1864 the French imposed colonial rule on Cochin-China, the southernmost part of Vietnam and the 'rice basket' of the region.

From a commercial point of view, the maritime world between Shanghai in the north and Singapore in the west remained for most of this period a vast zone of uncertainty. Far from being a sphere of open, legitimate trade, much of its business was conducted by smugglers, since the import of opium into China was still prohibited. Indeed, opium was the lubricant of commercial exchange almost everywhere. Trade was constantly disrupted by wars: the Java War, the two 'Opium Wars' of 1839–42 and 1856–60, and the civil war waged by the Taipings that engulfed much of China between 1850 and 1864. Piracy thrived along the China coast[6] and across the Indonesian archipelago. Between December and January each year, reported a Singapore newspaper in April 1847, a pirate fleet of 200 prahus sailed down the Macassar Strait before splitting into raiding parties to capture shipping and slaves.[7] Private traders sought influence with Malay rajahs and sultans, the most famous being James Brooke, who acquired Sarawak as a private empire on Borneo in 1841. On the China coast the first British consuls to arrive in the treaty ports struggled to impose their authority against local resistance or harassment, a task made much harder by the violent or disorderly behaviour of European ship crews – a constant source of friction – and the recurrent wars and rebellions of the period.[8] Much of the Indonesian archipelago was a 'middle ground' where political power was shared and disputed between the colonial regimes, European 'freelancers', Malay rajahs, and Chinese *kongsis* or brotherhoods, like those panning for gold on the west coast of Borneo. Travel around the archipelago, as the naturalist Alfred Russel Wallace discovered, could be a rough and ready business, entailing nerve-wracking voyages in small open boats as well as the hazards of disease or predation.[9]

This was the world, still familiar to Joseph Conrad in the 1880s, when steam globalization had already begun to remake it.

SINGAPORE: THE ENTREPÔT CITY

'Few places are more interesting to a traveller from Europe than the town and island of Singapore,' wrote Alfred Russel Wallace, a regular visitor between 1854 and 1862:

> The government, the garrison, and the chief merchants are English; but the great mass of the population is Chinese ... The native Malays are usually fishermen and boatmen ... The Portuguese of Malacca supply a large number of the clerks and smaller merchants. The Klings of Western India are a numerous body of Mahometans, and, with

many Arabs, are petty merchants and shopkeepers. The grooms and washermen are all Bengalees, and there is a small but highly respectable class of Parsee merchants. Besides these, there are numbers of Javanese sailors and domestic servants, as well as traders from Celebes, Bali, and many other islands of the Archipelago. The harbour is crowded with men-of-war and trading vessels of many European nations, and hundreds of Malay praus and Chinese junks ... and the town comprises handsome public buildings and churches, Mahometan mosques, Hindoo temples, Chinese joss-houses, good European houses, massive warehouses, queer old Kling and China bazaars, and long suburbs of Chinese and Malay cottages.[10]

But the overriding impression was of a Chinese town. In the interior of the island, much of it still heavily forested, Chinese merchants had carved out plantations to grow pepper and gambier (a plant used for tanning), worked by coolies brought from China.

The commercial heart of the town was the Singapore River, quickly lined with godowns (warehouses), rice mills and tanneries. Larger ships loaded and unloaded in the outer harbour and their freight was brought into the river on lighters. But, as Wallace had seen, much of the traffic had been in smaller craft, in junks and praus (or prahus). The 'junk season' was from January to March, when the North-East Monsoon brought junks from China carrying earthenware, vermicelli, joss-sticks, nankeens (Chinese cottons), silks, camphor and tea. There were also passengers: merchants and labourers looking for work. From June to November was the 'Bugis season', when Bugis merchants from Celebes brought 'Straits produce' to Singapore, much of it for Chinese consumers: ivory, tortoiseshell, seaweed, gambier, gold dust, rattans, birds' nests, sea cucumber, beeswax, tin and sandalwood. Malay traders from Sumatra brought sago (a foodstuff extracted from the sago palm); 'Arab' ships from Java brought coffee and sugar. Then there were junks from Siam and Cochin-China bringing sugar, rice, coconut oil and raw silk. European-owned ships brought opium from India and manufactures from Britain.[11]

Singapore was a marketplace that produced almost nothing itself. The rapid growth of its trade was a tribute above all to its favoured location. It lay at a maritime crossroads between Sumatra, Borneo,

Singapore in 1910

N

Malacca Strait

Pulai

Johor Bharu
• Pelentong
• Johor Dama

Pomo
Bokokangi •
SINGAPORE
Tinah
• Berbukit
Pasir Serkat
Cape Romania

C. Bulus
Pasir Panjung • Singapore

Singapore Strait

Little Karimon
Nongsa
• Sabang
Seriboe •
Great Karimon
Batam
RIO

Boelang
Archipelago
• Baleh
Pahat

15 miles
20 km

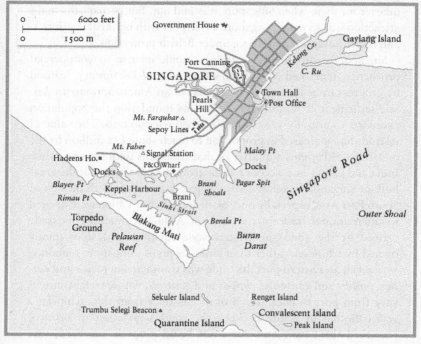

0   6000 feet
0   1500 m

Government House ⚓

SINGAPORE

Fort Canning

Kelang Cr.
C. Ru

Gaylang Island

Town Hall •
• Post Office
Pearls
Hill
Mt. Farquhar △
Sepoy Lines

Mt. Faber
△ Signal Station
Hadeens Ho. ■
P&O Wharf
Malay Pt
Docks
Docks
Blayer Pt
Singapore Road
Keppel Harbour
Brani
Shoals
Pagar Spit
Rimau Pt
Brani
Sinki Strait
Outer Shoal
Torpedo
Ground
Blakang Mati
Berala Pt
Pelawan
Reef
Buran
Darat

Sekuler Island
Renget Island
Trumbu Selegi Beacon ▲
Convalescent Island
Quarantine Island
⌒ Peak Island

the Malay peninsula and Java, and within easy reach of Celebes, Bali, the Moluccas, Timor and the Philippines. In the age of sail it was also the crossroads where the sea lane from Europe to South East Asia and China, which used the Sunda Strait between Sumatra and Java, met the sea lane from India through the Malacca Strait. Singapore lay only fifty miles (perhaps half a day's sail) to the west of the main sea route from Europe to China.[12] Raffles may have spotted its potential but the southern tip of the Malay peninsula had long been a place of exchange for the peoples of the region. 'Singapura' itself had been a settlement as far back as the fourteenth century; the Riau archipelago a few miles to the south had served as an entrepôt until destroyed by the Dutch.[13] Like the Dutch before him, Raffles had grasped that the key to commercial success lay in attracting Chinese merchants, and inserting Singapore into the Chinese-run network of commerce that linked the ports and trade of the Indonesian archipelago, mainland South East Asia and China. He had reserved a quarter for them when Singapore was laid out. But perhaps the main attraction was to make Singapore a free port with no tariffs or duties, and a safe haven for commerce under British protection.

Singapore's growth was certainly rapid. Its rise to commercial prosperity, remarked M'Culloch's *Commercial Dictionary*, 'caused its progress to be likened rather to that of an American than an Asiatic settlement'.[14] Within five years of its foundation the population exceeded 10,000. By 1865 it had reached over 90,000. The value of its trade had increased in proportion to reach some £12 million by the mid-1860s.[15] Perhaps a quarter of that trade was with Europe, while India and China each accounted for around 15 per cent. But the great bulk of Singapore's commerce (over 40 per cent) was with the rest of South East Asia, especially once Siam and Cochin-China were opened to international trade in the 1850s.[16] Although much of its trade arrived by the 1860s in Western-style square-rigged ships (many owned by Chinese), rather than junks or praus, Singapore remained very much an Eastern port. Its trade was transacted in *piculs* and *catties*, *parahs* and *gantangs*, *chopas* and *gantons*, whose weights might vary from port to port. Much of the produce from the archipelago was collected in penny packets: the south-west coast of Borneo, remarked the *China Directory*, not being properly surveyed, was 'only visited by small vessels, mostly armed and commanded by Chinamen and Malays'.[17] The number of Europeans in the city was tiny: a mere 360 in the census of 1860,[18] and the European merchants were few enough to conduct their business with each other in person.

On the eve of the steamship era after 1870, Singapore was an unusual and highly distinctive port city. Its trade was substantial but not overwhelming: about the same as Sydney, much less than gold-swollen Melbourne, less than half that of Bombay.[19] Unlike Bombay or Calcutta, there was no inland interior to be exploited by railways: only much later was Singapore linked by rail to the Malayan penin-sula. Nor at this stage could Singapore rely upon a handful of great staples like the cotton and opium that poured out of Bombay, the wool from Sydney, tea from Shanghai, coffee from Rio de Janeiro, or slave-cotton from New Orleans. Its commercial links with the West were correspondingly narrower, and the scope for Western merchants more restricted. Just as striking, perhaps, was Singapore's singular lack of a territorial annexe. The Straits Settlements, of which it had been the capital since 1832, were mere pocket handkerchiefs. To the European merchants the reluctance of Calcutta (from where they were ruled until 1867) or London to add more territory in the island's vicinity was a standing offence. Without a land revenue to meet its administrative costs, or the tariffs and duties that might destroy its trade, Singapore was forced back on a peculiar expedient. The import of opium from India had long been a key item of trade, and local demand with a fast-growing population was exceptionally buoyant. It seemed an obvious course (since the British insisted that opium was a commodity like any other)[20] to farm out the retail sale of government-imported opium to a syndicate of Chinese merchants. Indeed, the revenue from the opium farm became the critical element of Singa-pore's public finances for the rest of the century.

In the second half of the century Singapore's prospects were trans-formed by the combined effects of three great changes. The first was the cutting of the Suez Canal, eventually opened in November 1869. The Canal gave a huge boost to direct communication by steam between Europe and Asia, and Singapore became a great steamship city: already by 1877 steamship tonnage at Singapore vastly out-weighed that of sailing ships.[21] Secondly, the economic exploitation of the Malay peninsula, Singapore's backyard, was now accelerated by the progressive extension of British control over the rulers of the Malay states. Singapore acquired what it had conspicuously lacked, a territorial hinterland for whose staple exports of tin and (later) rubber it became the principal outlet. Thirdly, after 1869, and stimulated by the 'opening up' of the peninsula, the flow of migrants from China increased to massive proportions, turning Singapore into a great immigrant port and (even more than before) an overwhelmingly Chinese city.

The Suez Canal both shortened the voyage from Singapore to Europe by almost a third (from some 12,000 miles to 8,300) and speeded the transit over the distance that remained. Indeed, passengers from Britain soon took to boarding their ship not in London or Southampton but at Marseilles or Brindisi, saving the time spent in the Bay of Biscay and rounding Gibraltar. Singapore now lay some forty days steaming from Europe, and by 1913 could be reached from London in twenty-three days by using a combination of express train and liner. The reaction in Singapore to the Canal's opening was ecstatic. 'The Canal must give an impetus to Commerce that will eventually be felt all over the world', crowed the merchants' mouthpiece, the *Straits Times*. 'The traffic between Europe and China will eventually be diverted from the Straits of Sunda to the Straits of Singapore; sailing vessels will be replaced by steamers, which must make Singapore their coaling station and halting place.'[22] In reality, of course, this vision depended upon the ability of larger, heavier steamships to use the Canal, and compete with sailing ships unburdened by its tolls and the costs of their fuel. Indeed, early calculations suggested at best a very marginal gain.[23] But the optimists were right. Between 1870 and 1885 the tonnage of shipping in Singapore's harbour grew quickly from 1.3 million tons to five million.[24] But, perhaps surprisingly, the Canal did not turn Singapore into a commercial outpost of Europe. For, although its trade grew by six times between 1870 and the end of the century, Europe's share of that trade grew only marginally.[25] Instead, for Singapore's merchants, what still mattered most was to command the regional trade of South East Asia and ward off the threat that other ports in the archipelago and on the mainland would open direct trade with China and Europe. If that were to happen,

Singapore would be reduced to 'little more than a coaling station and docking port'.[26] As we shall see, fears of this kind were frequently voiced over the next forty years.

By the 1880s the new steamer trunk route from Europe to Asia extended across the Bay of Bengal via Colombo to the Straits of Malacca and Singapore. Shipping lines, British, French and Italian, competed to offer a regular service, and called there en route to China and Japan. The arrival of the telegraph from Europe by 1870 meant that news and commercial (especially price) information (for which the telegraph was chiefly used) reached Singapore first, just as the liners brought early delivery of mail and newspapers from Europe, India and China. The telegraph could also be used to manage the movement of shipping, allowing shipping agents and brokers to respond more quickly to the demand for cargo space and the rise and fall of freight prices – a vital consideration especially for tramps. As steamers replaced sailing ships in South East Asia's regional trades (a process under way even before the Canal) – 'little steam vessels are now everywhere plying about in every creek like a swarm of wasps', reported the *Straits Times* in 1872[27] – and Singapore was connected by telegraph with other ports in the Nanyang, it became the hub for a mass of forward connections. It provided the new infrastructure that steam navigation required: coal and water for the ships' boilers (fear of a water shortage was a periodic concern); docking facilities for the swift turn-around that liners required; a reservoir of seamen to fill up the crews; the promise of cargo for the tramp ships that called. The reward was spectacular. While the world's ocean-going tonnage grew by between three and four times from 1870 to 1913, the tonnage using Singapore's harbour (not all of it ocean-going) multiplied tenfold.[28]

While its entrepôt trade profited from the advent of steam and the Suez Canal, and the rapid growth of rice exports from Siam and French Indo-China (for which Singapore served as the prime market and distribution centre in South East Asia), Singapore gradually became after 1870 a great staple port as well. Much of this was due to the 'co-colonization' of peninsular Malaya by the Chinese and British. Chinese miners had long been active in panning for tin on the peninsula's west coast. The surging demand for tin in the later nineteenth century to make rust-free tin-plate (much of it used in the canning industry) brought a 'tin rush', induced in part by the ease with which 'stream tin' ore could be mined. The unhappy result was an increasingly chaotic frontier where miners fought over claims or with Malay rulers ill-equipped to control them. In 1873, raged the *Straits Times*, Perak and Selangor (the main tin producers) were 'a terror to traders and a bugbear to capitalists'. As so often in the past, the London government was denounced for its failure to act or annex: it was 'a meddling, apathetic policy without definite aim . . .' In Selangor the weakness of the Sultan's government had discouraged the investment of capital.[29] The pressure of local opinion forced the colonial authorities' hand. 'We should possess the whole Western coast of the Malay Peninsula,' urged the *Straits Times Overland Journal* in 1876. 'Chinese immigration would fill both countries [Perak and Selangor] with the labour they . . . need . . . English and Chinese capital would render the riches of the soil fully available . . .'[30] Over the next twenty years the peninsular states were reduced to protectorates under a form of indirect rule that retained their Malay rulers. But they were effectively thrown open to Chinese labour and a combination of British and Chinese capital. Tin production soared, growing sixfold between 1874/77 and 1896/99, equal to half the world's output.[31] Then at the turn of the century rubber seedlings from the Amazon, brought first to Ceylon (Sri Lanka) in 1876, began to be planted in Malaya. The demand for rubber was a product of steam power. 'Every steam vessel afloat, every train and every factory . . . employing steam power, must of necessity use India-rubber,' declared the explorer-geographer Clements Markham.[32] After 1900 the older demand for steam tubing and gaskets was first matched and then exceeded by the demand for rubber tyres, as the automobile revolution took off. In 1900 a mere 2,000 acres were planted with rubber in Malaya; by 1913 this number had grown to one million.[33] Singapore became the leading exporter of milled rubber, much of it sent not to Europe but the United States, which already consumed some 37 per cent of the world's rubber production by 1907, and more than three-quarters a decade later.[34]

As its hinterland opened up, Singapore became not just a staple port, but an immigrant port on a massive scale. Tamils from India's east coast crossed the Bay of Bengal, usually as indentured 'coolie' labour. But it was migrants from China who formed the vast majority, arriving in Singapore before being sent on to plantations and mines in the region beyond. Immigration from China, already some 10,000 a year in 1877, ran at over 100,000 ten years later, to reach an average of 250,000 in the years 1911–13.[35] Almost all came from impoverished districts in southern China, from Fujian (the Hokkien and Teochew dialect communities) and Guangdong ('Cantonese' speakers). Amoy (modern Xiamen), Swatow (modern Shantou) and Hong Kong (for Cantonese) were the main emigrant ports. Alongside Siam, the Straits Settlements and the Malay peninsula were the main destinations. Emigration was big business for shipping companies and brokers, and the numerous lodging houses that accommodated intending migrants during the main emigrant season in April and May: ships sailing to South East Asia took six to eight days and typically carried 1,000 migrants at a time.[36] In Singapore the uninterrupted flow of migration (almost entirely male and typically between the ages of seventeen and thirty-five) was regarded not just as desirable but essential by European merchants as much as Chinese. 'Chinese immigration is the mainstay of the Colony and the Federated Malay States,' remarked the *Straits Times* in 1904. 'It may be said emphatically that the more there is of imported Chinese labour the merrier and better it is for trade, industry and business generally . . .'[37] In more philosophic mood the paper observed: 'On the whole . . . the conditions in the world are fairly equal. There are vast areas which Asiatics will have to themselves, and we have steadily urged that one of these areas is the great northern or . . . tropical area of Australia, where white men may live but will never prosper . . .'[38] Not a view that would have been well received in 'White Australia'.

Immigration linked Singapore's fortunes symbiotically to China's. When the First World War and its aftermath drastically cut the inflow of migrants, and the rising value of silver made money plentiful in China, Singapore businessmen fell into despair. 'Nothing short of a terrible slump in silver, or a couple of lean crop years in succession, with assisted immigration, abundant shipping facilities, and an organisation . . . to count and despatch the coolies . . . will help us out of our difficulties.' It was 'incredible' that industry in Singapore could carry on at all.[39] The link with southern China was not just a matter of labour and commerce. It also brought a reshaping of the culture and politics of Singapore's port-city society.

From its beginnings Singapore had been a strikingly multi-ethnic settlement. It had attracted Indian merchants from Bombay, and Chettiar moneymen from Madras, as well as Tamils who came as indentured labour; Arab traders and shipowners from the Hadhramaut, reputed to own much of Singapore's real estate (Singapore still has an 'Arab Street'); Jews and Armenians (who had their own church by the 1830s); Javanese and Bugis as well as local Malays; Europeans and Eurasians. But from the beginning the Chinese had predominated, to make up half the population by the 1860s and more than three-quarters by late in the century. Yet the term 'Chinese' was far from conveying a single identity. It was the 'Straits Chinese' who enjoyed most prestige. As the name implied, they were Chinese long settled in the colony. 'Straits' or 'Malacca' Chinese had typically intermarried with local Malays to form a *baba* community. They adopted a distinctive 'creole' culture, mixing Chinese customs and dress with local variations. Thus *baba* men retained the queue or *towchang* which mainland Chinese were required to display, and the robe characteristic of Chinese dress. But they smoked and drank alcohol and used the European-style handshake as a mode of greeting. They used 'bazaar Malay' at home and as a lingua franca, but retained Chinese for more formal occasions. Some became Christians. Long familiar with European business methods and languages, the Malacca Chinese were perfectly placed to be the commercial intermediaries on whom (as Stamford Raffles had seen) Singapore's prospects depended. They soon moved to the new settlement. The British quickly turned to them not just as the agents for regional trade, but as the 'farmers' of tax revenues, opium above all. Combining the 'cash flow' of monopolies and taxes with commercial activity, leading Straits Chinese merchants formed a powerful elite. They were the patrons of temples around which the main Chinese dialect groups (Hokkien, Teochew, Hakka and Cantonese) cohered. The British (very few of whom spoke Chinese) looked to them to keep order in a population they found socially and culturally impenetrable.[40]

That task was complicated by the stream of migration, even before this turned into a flood. The Chinese migrants who came had little in common with the Straits Chinese. Separated from their lineages (the key social unit in rural China), they found social solidarity in their dialect group and in the secret societies which filled the void. Hostility between dialect groups over access to space and employment or ritual concerns (and perhaps the overwhelming proportion of young males) fuelled outbreaks of violence: 400 were killed in the riot of 1854 between different Chinese factions.[41] The British were uncertain whether the secret societies were a threat to law and order or an element of stability, but eventually banned them. In the 1870s they abandoned the informal reliance on Straits Chinese notables to set up a 'Chinese Protectorate' and later a Chinese Advisory Board. Meanwhile the growing scale of migration from China (the Qing ban on emigration was lifted unofficially in 1860 and formally in 1893), and of the regional trade across South East Asia in which Chinese merchants were predominant, was shifting the balance among Singapore's Chinese communities. Local-born Chinese might affirm their British allegiance, but retained a keen sense of their Chinese identity – symbolized by keeping the queue. In 1898 the retired first 'Protector of Chinese', William Pickering, argued that Straits Chinese loyalty was only skin-deep. 'Whatever these people, born under our rule, educated in our schools and made wealthy by our protection, may say or write,' he complained, 'in their hearts they consider themselves Chinese, despise all other races as being inferior foreigners, and only plead British nationality to enforce a claim or when they are in trouble.'[42]

For both Straits Chinese and the more recent arrivals, the issues were not so simple. The deepening crisis in China after 1890 was bound to arouse strong political emotions. Wealthy Singapore Chinese were sympathetic to reform movements aimed at 'self-strengthening' China, and also loyal to the embattled Qing monarchy. Many retained their links with their mainland home towns, and aspired to scholar-gentry status – a status secured by conspicuous philanthropy and careful cultivation of the local bureaucracy. Like the Bombay Parsis, these 'mandarin capitalists' hoped to exploit their 'British connection', and the protection it offered, to revitalize their homeland.[43] Hong Kong University, intended as a beacon of modernity in southern

China, owed its survival in part to Singapore money (and students).[44] Indeed, the outward flow of migration from China was complemented by the inward flow of remittances home, much of it channelled through Hong Kong. For Straits Chinese in particular the conflict of loyalties could become acute. Lim Boon Keng was a Straits-born Chinese, a Christian who trained as a doctor in Britain. In 1895 he was appointed an 'unofficial' member of the Straits Settlement legislative council, the colony's (nominated not elected) law-making body. Like other Straits Chinese, he was disturbed by the growing influence of the China-born in the city. The Straits Chinese British Association was founded in 1900 to reassert their primary loyalty to British institutions: 'We Straits Chinese are free men,' said Lim in 1900, implicitly contrasting the regime of the Qing.[45] But Lim also favoured the deliberate promotion of Chinese (not English) education in Singapore, urged the revival of Confucian culture and ended his career as a university leader in Republican China.[46]

Like the port cities of British India on which it was modelled, Singapore was laid out with separate zones for its different ethnic communities. The 'European town' occupied the prime site north of the river. South of the river was allocated to the 'Chinese campong' and the 'Chulia campong' (for Indians). North of the river, beyond the European town, was an area for Arabs, and beyond that a campong for Bugis and Malays. By the 1840s the European town had acquired some grand villa residences like those occupied by wealthy Europeans in Madras or Calcutta, as well as a range of public buildings in the classical style popular in British India. In the Hokkien quarter around Amoy Street, the Teochew along Boat Quay or the Hakka further out at Tanjong Pagar, elaborate temples were being built by the 1830s. The Chulia Mosque (1830–35) and Sri Maraiamman temple (1827–43) reflected the presence (and wealth) of Hindus and Muslims from India. Along South Bridge Street and its numerous side streets, so-called 'shophouses' proliferated, extending back from the business premises on the street to a warren of dark and often insanitary cubicles. By the end of the century Singapore had grand hotels, monumental banks (the Hongkong and Shanghai Bank, the Chartered Bank), and a Western-style central business district: the boom years after 1900 saw an explosion of large office buildings and stores. Wealthy Europeans and Chinese built suburban mansions: the grandest suburb was Tanglin.[47] But much of the city, like port cities elsewhere, was a mosaic 'of specialized trade areas, bazaars, densely packed tenement housing, and concentrations of eating houses, theatres, and brothels'.[48] Overcrowding (the price of mass immigration) was commonplace and sanitation primitive. The result was a mortality rate even higher than in Indian cities or Hong Kong: the infant mortality rate for 1900–1929 reached the appalling figure of 305 per 1,000 for Chinese and nearly 344 per 1,000 for Malays.[49] Tuberculosis, malaria and cholera were the main killers. In a city so reliant on the huge inflow of people, and so relentlessly dedicated to commerce, neither the means nor the will to force through improvements were easy to mobilize.

If the constant and almost unregulated movement of people imposed a huge cost in health, it also encouraged another side of Singapore that its colonial masters found just as hard to control. The traffic of people was also a traffic of information, ideas and allegiances that were alien to empire and colonial rule or subversive of it. As a shipping hub in the midst of Islamic South East Asia, Singapore was the natural port of embarkation for Muslims going to Mecca or returning from it.[50] In the late nineteenth century Islamic reformism and the appeal of a 'pan-Islamic' allegiance spread out along the world's steamship routes, carried by pilgrim deck-passengers. Once nationalism won a popular following in China, it too could follow the migrants' watery trail. As a part of what one historian has called the 'global waterfront', Singapore was host to the floating communities of sailors, dockworkers and other port labourers and the radical, anarchist or socialist ideas that rippled through them in the late nineteenth century.[51] As an 'open city' Singapore, like other ports, had its 'anti-city',[52] a space beyond the control of its rulers. Openness, too, brought printing shops and presses, and encouraged the publication of newspapers, pamphlets, newsletters and books directed to subject populations all around the Indian Ocean – a potent means of reinforcing the messages of travellers and pilgrims. If Singapore's booming central business district was the public face of globalizing modernity in South East Asia, its mobile waterfront labour, its long-distance connections with radical or non-Western movements and its backstreet printers and scribblers serving faraway readers, were its subversive companions.

The impact of this was perhaps felt only lightly before 1915 and the short-lived (but to Europeans in Singapore terrifying) mutiny by Indian soldiers in that year. Up to 1914 and beyond, Singapore's business was shipping: gathering the produce of the South China Sea and the Malayan peninsula; redistributing the rice from Siam and Vietnam to regional consumers (Singapore was the great rice market of South East Asia); selling on the manufactures (cotton piece goods above all) that arrived from the West. As a great maritime hub, Singapore was part of the network of the world's major sea lanes. But its place in that network was very different from that of the maritime metropoles like London or Liverpool, Hamburg or Marseilles.

This was partly a matter of the tenacious survival of 'traditional' shipping: Chinese junks and the 'Bugis boats . . . strange little schooners' were still to be seen in Singapore harbour in 1902, along with Chinese-owned tramps with their 'patched wooden hulls, scarce fit to carry their engines', but transporting 'a great percentage of local trade'.[53] Apart from long-distance trade between the 'Far East' (East Asia) and Europe and Australia, noted the *Straits Times* in 1903, the proportion of Chinese shipping 'is very large indeed'.[54] But, for both Chinese merchants and the leading European agency houses, like Boustead's or Guthrie's, that dominated trade with the West, there were other reminders of Singapore's peripheral status in seaborne commerce. Shipping, like gold and silver, flowed to where demand (and freight prices) were highest and fled from a glut. During the South African War of 1899–1902 shipping was sucked into the huge supply chain the British army required. At the Straits, shipping was short, prices shot up and trade was delayed, with consequent loss. In 1903 the prospect of a war between Russia and Japan led to a doubling of insurance rates in the region.[55] As steamships became larger, and turnaround times speeded up, Singapore, like other port cities, was forced to compete. When the Tanjong Pagar Dock Company, the main owners of wharfage, coaling and ship-repair facilities at Singapore, resisted further expansion, so great was commercial anxiety that the Colony government took the highly controversial step of expropriating the company in 1905, most of whose capital was held in London, and taking it into public ownership – a step reluctantly sanctioned by the Colonial Office. Even more controversial was the decision by the leading British and European steamship lines that served Singapore to form a 'conference' – in effect a cartel – to pool cargo between them and tie in the leading shippers by so-called 'rebates'. To smaller merchants, especially, the inevitable rise in freight prices seemed likely to damage Singapore's position as the main entrepôt of the Indonesian archipelago on the altar of profits in London and Liverpool. 'This ring of home shippers is crushing the prosperity out of this town,' declaimed the *Straits Times* in 1902.[56] And much as they trumpeted Singapore's unique commercial advantages, Singapore merchants lived in fear of competition from neighbouring ports, of French protectionism in Indo-China, of German incursion in Singapore's vital trade with Bangkok, or of the loss of the free-port status that was universally seen as the foundation of prosperity.

In practice, as we saw, Singapore's commercial future was assured by its rapid development as a staple port, providing finance and management as well as processing, marketing and export facilities to tin mines and then rubber production in the Malayan peninsula and the Dutch possessions nearby. If the First World War was an awkward hiatus, the 1920s saw a boom. It was then that Singapore acquired its third great staple as the main export centre for the oilfields of the region in Sumatra and Borneo. By the mid-1920s Singapore's trade was larger than that of either Calcutta or Bombay.[57] But the age of steam globalization, undergirded by British imperial power, was approaching its climax. If the moment of crisis came later to Singapore than elsewhere in the world, its impact was to be, if anything, more devastating.

SINGAPORE AND GLOBALIZATION

At first sight, Singapore appears a classic case of a port city that served as an outpost of Europe, transmitting its globalizing influences into the maritime world of the South China Sea. Certainly, it is not hard to explain its commercial success. Location was primary, but not only because Singapore sat at the crossroads of the two main sea lanes (and the two main 'choke points') through which shipping had to pass between the Indian Ocean and the South China Sea. As we have seen, that locational advantage was hugely magnified once the Suez Canal made steam competitive in long-distance trade between Europe and eastern Asia, because steamships preferred the Malacca Strait at Singapore's backdoor to the Sunda Strait further south. By 1914 around five times as much shipping took the Malacca rather than the Sunda passage.[58] The need for steamships to refuel frequently made Singapore the obvious coaling station east of Colombo. As well as being a necessary port of call for 'through traffic', Singapore enjoyed a central location within the island and peninsular world of South East Asia. And since it proved easy to attract indigenous shipping, Singapore could gather the produce of an extensive region without building the costly and time-consuming infrastructure of roads or railways that access to hinterlands demanded elsewhere (a good fortune it shared with ante-bellum New Orleans). By the late nineteenth century it had combined the functions of a regional entrepôt with those of a staple port. Indeed, Singapore was astonishingly lucky with its staples: the demand for tin, then rubber and finally petroleum accelerated dramatically as manufacturing technology evolved in the West. Yet, as with most successful port cities, politics and geopolitics also played a key role. The British had realized from the first that commercial survival in South East Asia required an 'alliance' with Chinese merchants and shipping: there was no question of Singapore becoming an exclusively European settlement. But it was also the presence of a small but vociferous British mercantile community, well connected in London, that preserved the crucial concession of free-port status, and secured (in 1867) the limited autonomy of a 'Crown Colony' constitution, answerable to faraway London, not overbearing Calcutta. It helped that very few of its tiny European minority regarded Singapore as a permanent home. Thus, beneath the carapace of authoritarian rule and European privilege, Singapore's government enjoyed remarkable freedom to 'manage' relations with its Chinese and other communities, and, more remarkably still, to maintain a complete open door to migration from China (and India) – until the change of political mood in the fraught 1930s. It was only then, perhaps, that the true extent of Singapore's dependence on a benign geopolitical regime under-written by British imperial power became frighteningly obvious.

Singapore's exceptional openness to the movement of goods, money, people and information, its worldwide shipping connections, and the presence of trading diasporas – Chinese, Indian, Malay, Arab, Jew-ish, Armenian and European – made it the global city par excellence. But how much influence did it exert on the regions around it, eco-nomically, politically and culturally? Was it the centre from which 'globalizing' influences radiated outwards to remake the Nanyang? Of course, had Singapore not existed other port cities might have filled its shoes: Batavia, Surabaya, Bangkok, Saigon and Manila were all competitors to a greater or lesser degree. Commercially, Singa-pore's critical role was to bring together British mercantile credit and the Chinese business networks that expanded so rapidly from the mid-nineteenth century. The security it offered both, together with its locational advantages, speeded the Nanyang's integration into the new global economy of the Victorian era, and the *regional* integra-tion of the Nanyang itself. Singapore became the export point for the produce (especially the sugar) of the Netherlands East Indies, and the 'rice entrepôt' distributing rice from Siam and Vietnam to consumers in Malaya, Java, Sumatra, Borneo and elsewhere. It thrived hugely on the profits of tin, rubber and oil. But its part in supplying investment and management to the production of staples (the vital functions of a staple port) was largely confined to neighbouring British Malaya.[59]

Politically, its influence was much more ambiguous. Raffles's hopes for a British imperium across the Indonesian archipelago and beyond, directed from Singapore, were never fulfilled. South East Asia was partitioned, and, leaving aside Burma, which faced the Bay of Bengal, the British share was comparatively modest. The Dutch proved more vigorous imperialists than expected and by the end of the century had consolidated their grip on the vast sphere allotted under the 1824 treaty. The Philippines passed in 1898 into the hands of the United States, a colonial power richer and stronger than Spain. Indo-China fell to the French, and while London and Paris bickered over inde-pendent Siam, neither was dominant. Singapore was also a haven for those who dreamed of the *end* of colonialism, but, before 1940, this was only a dream. Much more real was the link between the Over-seas Chinese of Singapore and mainland China.

Both the Straits Chinese elite and more recent arrivals wanted to join forces with 'modernizers' in Hong Kong and China's coastal cities to reshape the Qing Empire and find a stable accommodation with the Western powers. Perhaps what they hoped was that a wealthy mercantile class, used to dealing (and dealing firmly) with the West, would replace the scholar-gentry with its Confucian ethos. A Chinese nation would be built from above: the West conciliated but kept at bay. But if that was the aim, nothing went to plan. China's revolution when it came in 1911 owed little to its merchants. With the West in turmoil after 1914, Japan became the dominant external power, sym-bolized in the 'Twenty-One Demands' of 1915 – in effect a bid for informal dominion over China. When, in 1919, Japan seemed set on retaining Germany's claims and concessions in northern China, the promise of self-determination mooted in the Peace Conference at Paris appeared to dissolve, and popular nationalism in China became (understandably) increasingly xenophobic. When police in the Shanghai International (but British-administered) Settlement fired on demonstrators in May 1925, strikes and boycotts, orches-trated in Canton, swiftly crippled Hong Kong.

For Overseas Chinese in Singapore, this was a moment of truth. They continued to support the Guomindang, the great vehicle of Chinese nationalism, financially. A branch was set up in Singapore and survived the British ban. But the Singapore Chinese elite declined to support the anti-colonial movement on the Chinese mainland with direct action, or even to join in the anti-Japanese boycott. They used their social power to prevent the strikes and boycotts that brought Hong Kong to its knees.[60] With the rise of communism in mainland China in uneasy alliance with the Guomindang, the divergence of interests between Singapore as a great trading city and a mass nation-alist movement intent on expelling foreign influence from China became acute. As China descended into civil war and Japan's ambi-tions became more overt, stability at home in the face of economic depression, not influence abroad, became the priority. Singapore set-tled into its role as the undisputed metropolis of British Malaya.

If that was the case commercially, it was much less obvious in culture and politics. As we have seen, in Singapore, like Bombay or Calcutta, adaptation to Western modernity had been highly selective. Political authority in Singapore remained vested in a racially exclusive colonial bureaucracy. Chinese, Indian and Malay elites were preoccupied with maintaining their influence over their own (divided) ethnic communities. Although there was no formal segregation, Singapore showed few signs of becoming a cosmopolitan 'melting pot'. Quite the contrary. One of the most powerful effects of 'global modernity' was to combine the much greater mingling of peoples with the means and the motive for mobilizing allegiance by ethnic or religious identity. Politics and culture were yoked together. On the Malayan peninsula, Singapore's commercial, political and cultural hinterland, the effect was to be critical. There the British had carefully preserved (and enhanced) the 'traditional' authority of the Malay sultans amid the mass inward movement of Chinese colonists. The sense of a distinct Malay identity as the true 'sons of the soil' was reinforced by a shared religious allegiance. Singapore, with its small Malay minority, was an alien, Chinese city, whose influence over Chinese living in the Malay sultanates was a source of unease. Even after the devastation of war, the Malay rulers would flatly reject in 1946 the idea of a 'Malayan Union' with its capital at Singapore, and the inclusion of Singapore in the independent Malaysian Federation in 1963 lasted barely two years. For all its commercial success, Singapore was fated to remain what it had grown up to be in the era of steam globalization, a great trading entrepôt with a distinct political culture, dependent for its safety on geopolitical regimes over which it had little control.

CONNECTING THE 'COAST': THE RISE OF MARITIME CHINA

Singapore was originally designed as the advanced British base to capture the trade with China at the time when only Canton was open to foreigners. The First Opium War and the seizure of Hong Kong made that role redundant. Hong Kong was the northern pole of the South China Sea. It lay close to the Taiwan Strait, beyond which lay the East China Sea and the mouth of the Yangzi. Still further north was the Yellow Sea and Tianjin, the port for Beijing, the 'Hermit Kingdom' Korea, the Tsushima Strait and the Sea of Japan, rarely visited by Western shipping before the 1840s. When the Nanjing Treaty of 1842 threw open five 'treaty ports' to Western merchants – Shanghai was the most northerly – it signalled the beginning of the West's forced entry into China. But it also set off a momentous shift in Chinese society, tilting the balance of wealth and power away from the agrarian interior and towards the coast. It was no coincidence that the nationalist project to first reform and then overthrow the monarchy and renew Chinese culture began in the treaty ports. Like Asian nationalisms elsewhere, it was simultaneously attracted to and repelled by the West and, in the search for self-strengthening, eventually turned to the masses with dramatic results.

Notoriously, the taking of Hong Kong in 1841 was regarded in London as a lamentable blunder by a headstrong man on the spot. A 'barren rock' with no Chinese merchants, what trade could it offer? Indeed, even six years later, a Select Committee of the British Parliament dismissed its commercial potential with contempt. Worse still, perhaps, the opening of the treaty ports at Canton, near the tea districts of Fujian, and at Shanghai, with its vast riverine hinterland, suggested that Hong Kong's commercial future was likely to be limited at best.[61] But, like other port cities, Hong Kong was rescued by good fortune as much as by the promise held by its magnificent harbour for seaborne intruders: for the Chinese, with Canton and its interior connections, Hong Kong had been merely a part of its outer defences, the site of a fishing village and the small walled city of Kowloon. Hong Kong's first saviour, and for long the bedrock of its prosperity, was opium. Even after the Nanjing Treaty, it remained illegal to import opium into China. Hong Kong, as British territory, was a safe haven where Indian opium could be unloaded and then smuggled into China. The opium importers, with Jardine Matheson in the lead, quickly invested in godowns and offices along Hong Kong's foreshore and Hong Kong acquired a small but wealthy European population, as well as its garrison and colonial officials.[62] As it took a decade or more for commercial conditions in the five treaty ports to settle, Hong Kong as 'first mover' retained its advantage.

Hong Kong long remained the centre where imported opium was processed, repackaged and forwarded to customers in China. The second piece of good fortune was much more dramatic. In 1848 gold was discovered in California. The following year the Australian gold rush began, with smaller rushes in the North and South Islands of New Zealand. The demand for labour and the prospect of wealth exerted a magnetic effect on impoverished communities in southern China, and a migrant 'rush' began to successive 'Gold Mountains'. Hong Kong quickly became the main port of departure for these transpacific migrations, with regular sailings to and from San Francisco. Since Chinese in California and Australia preserved links with home, often chose to return after a few years and wished in the meantime to remit their earnings, Hong Kong quickly developed the range of services that this human traffic required: brokers to advance the costs of a passage; lodging houses to accommodate intending passengers; banks and agencies to handle remittances; newspapers to keep in touch with those overseas. And since Chinese migrants (like most others) preferred to consume what was familiar to them (including opium), Hong Kong also became the key supplier of this new overseas market.[63]

The effect of all this was, by the 1850s, to make Hong Kong the maritime hub of the China coast, combining its Pacific connections with its existing links to the Nanyang, India and Europe. Already in 1845 it had become the terminus of the P&O service via Suez to Europe, and Europe's mailbox in East Asia. Not surprisingly, shipbuilding and ship repair became a major activity, and Hong Kong became the main base of the Royal Navy's new China Station. Ships' chandlers multiplied, and it was here too that ships' crews, from China and elsewhere, could be recruited for eastern voyages. The British came to rely on the local Tanka people – traditionally an oppressed 'floating community' of boatmen and fishermen. With the spread of steamers along the China coast, and, after 1869, arriving from Europe, Hong Kong became a huge coaling station – another big business – importing over 800,000 tons of coal by the 1890s. But perhaps it was the third piece of good fortune that really 'made' Hong Kong, an ill wind that turned in its favour. From the 1850s, for more than a decade, South and Central China was convulsed by the

Taiping Rebellion against the Qing – a movement in which economic, religious, social and ethnic discontents were fused. From the chaos it brought, many wealthy Chinese in Canton and other parts of South China sought refuge in Hong Kong. The city's Chinese population now grew rapidly, driving up the value of property, and drawing in a new merchant elite with inland connections. In this way Hong Kong came to resemble Singapore: its colonial rulers and narrow European mercantile class, with the benefit of free-port status and imperial protection, could now rely upon a growing Chinese business network to expand its trade. It was with good reason that the Hong Kong government, like that of Singapore, maintained a completely open door to the movement of Chinese in and out of the city. By the 1890s a shrewd colonial minister in London could note that Hong Kong was really a Chinese, not a European, community.[64]

None of this made Hong Kong an easy or restful place to pursue a career. Nearby Canton was long regarded as fiercely anti-foreign and anti-British – an antipathy which British actions in the two Opium Wars of 1839–42 and 1856–60 did nothing to dispel. Europeans in Hong Kong were constantly fearful of murderous plots against them. Periodic rumours of a great poisoning conspiracy swept through the city. In the early decades large-scale piracy on the South China coast disrupted shipping, drove up insurance and posed almost insoluble problems about how to police local shipping.[65] Hong Kong was also notoriously unhealthy, afflicted by malaria and the waterborne diseases that came with poor sanitation. The large inflows of people, together with dreadful housing conditions, helped to make plague endemic in the city until the 1920s. Yet Hong Kong proved a magnet for a fast-growing population of both Chinese and non-Chinese. Baghdadi Jews, Armenians and Parsis, as well as Europeans, came in search of a commercial fortune, often with opium as the vehicle. Formal segregation was avoided, but, as if by mutual consent, Europeans and Chinese met for business, not for pleasure: Hong Kong's Jockey Club was for Europeans only. By the later part of the century Hong Kong was established as the leading port on the China coast, where up to 40 per cent or more of China's imports and exports arrived for trans-shipment.[66] Hong Kong, remarked a contemporary observer, was 'a sort of cosmopolitan Clapham Junction, where passengers change and goods are transhipped for everywhere'.[67] A more enduring achievement, built on Hong Kong's role as an entrepôt, opium seller (bringing in plentiful silver), migrant port and receiver of remittances, was to become the chief financial market in China, China's 'City'. It was here that financial information on investment opportunities, currency movements (especially complex in China), commodity prices and freight rates, as well as the state of markets in other parts of the world, was most readily available. A large proportion of non-Chinese in the city were employed in managing money, and what quickly became China's most powerful bank, the Hongkong and Shanghai Bank, was founded there in 1864. Crucially, too, Hong Kong was where two 'social networks of capital' – European and Chinese – engaged with each other, and mobilizing local Chinese capital was vital to most commercial ventures in the region.[68]

By 1914 an unpredictable combination of global and local conditions had made Hong Kong into one of China's two great maritime gateways. Canton, commanding the Pearl River delta, was still a great commercial city, and Tianjin (then called Tientsin, a treaty port from 1860), which had developed rapidly as the outport of Beijing, was another.[69] But Hong Kong's great rival was of course Shanghai. Even by the standard of other Asian port cities, Shanghai's rise was meteoric. Before 1842 it was a substantial commercial town: the centre of a large cotton-growing and manufacturing district in the reclaimed lands of the Yangzi delta, with a considerable coastwise trade.[70] Indeed, it was Shanghai's large junk trade that had attracted British attention[71] and made it one of the five treaty ports to which they demanded access. Shanghai enjoyed what soon came to seem an incomparable location. It lay a short distance up the Huangpu River, a navigable tributary close to the mouth of the Yangzi, and (like New Orleans or Calcutta) commanded a far-reaching riverine hinterland, that included Jiangnan, China's richest and most commercially developed region. Shanghai was also China's most northerly ice-free port. If the early signs were uncertain (Canton kept its grip on China's foreign trade for the best part of a decade) during the 1850s Shanghai pulled clear of its competitors. The volume of its shipping rose tenfold; the value of its imports increased by a factor of three; and its population doubled to 500,000.

Much of this had to do with Shanghai's peculiar history as a treaty port. Treaty ports were open to foreign trade subject only to a strictly limited tariff, set at 5 per cent by value. Foreign merchants there were exempt from Chinese taxation and China's legal regime and answerable only to their consuls: the vital privileges of extra-territoriality. The consul was thus a magistrate, an administrator and a coroner, as well as the diplomatic intermediary with the Chinese authorities. It was usual in treaty ports for foreign merchants to be allocated a separate part of the town for their godowns and residences. Where this was a 'concession', it was reserved for foreigners; where a 'settlement', Chinese residents were also allowed. In Shanghai the British acquired a large riverside settlement to the north of the Chinese city, later merged with the American zone to form the notorious 'International Settlement', nine square miles on the banks of the Huangpu. By the mid-1850s its European residents had gained a large measure of local self-government as the 'Shanghai Municipal Council', with its own volunteer defence force and police. It became to all intents a European colony, with colonial attitudes and – in its own eyes – almost the status of a settler republic.[72] The Shanghai Settlement quickly became the favoured location for almost all the larger foreign enterprises that sought business in China. In the 1880s its riverbank was filled in to form the famous 'Bund', lined with the great names of the China trade: Jardine Matheson, Butterfield and Swire, Dent and Co., Russell and Co., the P&O and British-India offices, the Hongkong and Shanghai Bank, the Customs House and the British consulate on its seven-acre site.[73] As at Hong Kong, Singapore, Bombay and Calcutta, that trade relied heavily on opium, for long its most valuable import. Because importing opium was technically illegal it was stored in hulks moored in the river to evade overzealous inspection, but the silver it earned supplied the exchange to buy the tea and silks on which foreign trade thrived.

However, Shanghai's commercial success was not simply the result of Western mercantile energy. Everywhere in China, Westerners needed Chinese intermediaries for their business transactions. These were the 'compradors'.[74] Language was a barrier since few Westerners acquired more than a smattering of 'port-pidgin'. China's weights and measures were notoriously complicated, and varied from region

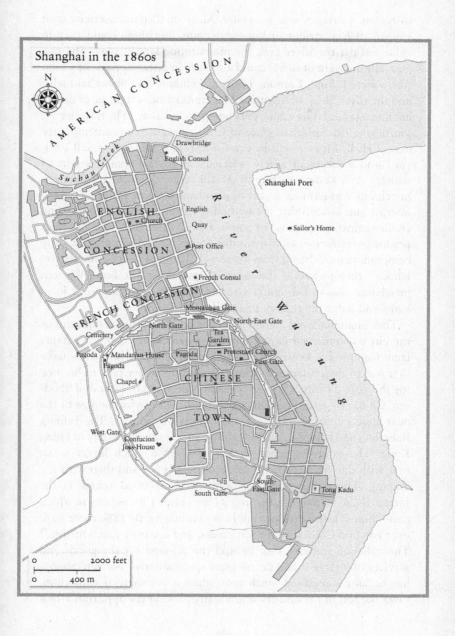

Shanghai in the 1860s

N

AMERICAN CONCESSION

Suchau Creek

Drawbridge

English Consul

Shanghai Port

ENGLISH

Church

English

Quay

CONCESSION

Sailor's Home

Post Office

French Consul

FRENCH CONCESSION

Montauban Gate

North Gate   North-East Gate

Cemetery   Tea
Garden

Pagoda   Mandarin House   Pagoda   Protestant Church

Pagoda   East Gate

Chapel   CHINESE

TOWN

West Gate

Confucion
Joss-House

South-
East-Gate

South Gate   East-Gate   Tong Kadu

River Wusung

0   2000 feet

0   400 m

to region. Currency was no easier. Most smaller transactions used copper 'cash' – strings of low-value coins. But these could vary in value against the silver tael, the measure for larger sums. The tael (actually a weight of silver) could also vary in different parts of China (there were Peking, Canton, Tientsin, Hankow and Shanghai taels), and the silver 'shoe' or ingot used for transactions might be of different fineness (and thus value), depending on location. 'The traveller . . . journeying from place to place in China,' warned the contemporary expert H. B. Morse, 'will be careful to take with him a small steel-yard and a string of a few selected "cash", the exact weight of which . . . is known to him.'[75] A still larger problem for Western merchants was gaining access to merchant networks in the Chinese interior and establishing the mutual trust required when advancing credit against the promise of goods. For all these functions the comprador or *maiban* was indispensable. It was no accident that the early compradors were drawn from owners of Shanghai's numerous 'native' banks:[76] they possessed the means to put down the bond Western merchants demanded, could convert Western advances into local loans and judge the risks of financial transactions.

Thus Shanghai's old merchant elite was an essential component of the city's commercial expansion. It was soon joined by merchants from Canton and nearby Ningbo. But it was a political earthquake that was to raise Shanghai from a prosperous treaty port to become (by the 1930s) China's largest city, the cosmopolitan capital of 'modern' China. By 1940 Shanghai's population was twice the size of the next largest cities, Beijing or Tianjin, and of Calcutta.[77] The Taiping Rebellion had helped to push wealthy Chinese into the safety of Hong Kong. The same happened in Shanghai on a much larger scale, first with the 'Small Swords' rebellion of 1853–5 and then with the Taiping. There Chinese gentry and merchants took refuge in the International Settlement, turning it into a large Chinese city in which non-Chinese formed a tiny (but ruling) minority. By 1880 there were over 100,000 Chinese in the settlement, and just over 1,000 British.[78] The value of property shot up and the demand for the goods and services of a large urban centre grew spectacularly. 'Foreign' Shanghai became something much more than a commercial emporium. Over the rest of the century it gradually took on the appearance of a great modern city with wide thoroughfares, hotels and department stores, and elegant suburbs as well as the grand edifices lining the Bund. There were theatres, modern hospitals, schools and colleges, libraries and museums, as well as a racecourse (a very early arrival). There were newspapers, European and Chinese, including the *North China Herald*, a weekly founded in 1850, with up to ninety pages densely packed with news from all parts of the world, and its counterpart daily, the *North China Daily News*. There were also the innumerable bars, brothels and opium dens that catered for both Chinese and foreigners, and the shophouses behind which (as in Singapore or Hong Kong) much of the Chinese population – shopkeepers, craftsmen, mill-workers, labourers, porters, hawkers, rickshaw-pullers, prostitutes and servants – had to live: these were the 'shed people'. Shanghai, wrote a twentieth-century observer, was 'a city of forty-eight storey skyscrapers built upon twenty-four layers of hell'.[79] Nor was its foreign population solely a wealthy elite of *taipans* – rich merchants. Steamship companies, banks and insurance companies, utilities, dockyards and the Municipal Council itself all employed European staffs, many on quite modest pay. Europeans worked as teachers, nurses, policemen, stenographers, clerks, innkeepers, pilots, printers, tax collectors and undertakers – and also as prostitutes.[80] By 1925 the largest category of European employment was 'mill, filature and factory staff'.[81] For many of these the prospect of going 'home', to restricted opportunities and a much lower living standard, was deeply unattractive. 'For all but a few lucky ones', remarked the *North China Herald* in 1919, Shanghai was their permanent place of abode.[82] This was a settler world. Even to other Europeans in China, Shanghailanders could seem insular, ignorant and deeply complacent.[83]

Towards the end of the nineteenth century, as China's foreign trade grew rapidly and the great powers competed for railway concessions, the commercial progress of Shanghai seemed unstoppable. By then its port, improved and expanded, was handling half China's trade. There, and at China's other main ports, a new organization from the 1860s had taken over the management of customs, and the provision of navigational aids like lighthouses and buoys. This was the Imperial Maritime Customs Administration, formally answerable to the Qing government, but staffed by (mainly British) Westerners, under

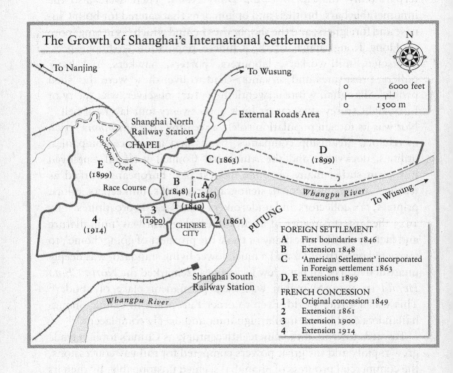

The Growth of Shanghai's International Settlements

To Nanjing

To Wusung

External Roads Area

Shanghai North Railway Station

CHAPEI

Soochow Creek

E (1899)

Race Course

B (1848)

A (1846)

C (1863)

D (1899)

Whangpu River

To Wusung

1 (1849)

3 (1900)

4 (1914)

2 (1861)

CHINESE CITY

PUTUNG

Shanghai South Railway Station

Whangpu River

FOREIGN SETTLEMENT
A First boundaries 1846
B Extension 1848
C 'American Settlement' incorporated in Foreign settlement 1863
D, E Extensions 1899

FRENCH CONCESSION
1 Original concession 1849
2 Extension 1861
3 Extension 1900
4 Extension 1914

N

0   6000 feet
0   1500 m

its formidable inspector-general, the Ulsterman Robert Hart (1835–1911). 'I want to make China strong,' said Hart, 'and I want her to make England her best friend.'[84] The Customs Service was a powerful agency in the modernization of China's ports, as well as supplying its increasingly beleaguered government with a growing revenue stream.[85] Together with extraterritorial privilege, the low-tariff regime imposed by the West, the mass of treaty ports and other 'open places' on the coast and far up the Yangzi, guards and garrisons, as well as some dozens of gunboats (eventually British, French, Italian, Japanese and American) to 'police' China's waterways and protect the dispersed Western communities ('the foreign gunboat remains an essential factor in the protection of coast and river shipping', declared the *North China Herald* in 1929),[86] the Customs Service formed part of the 'steel frame' that shaped – and constricted – China's foreign relations.

Steam and the Yangzi as much as anything else had been the making of the Westerners' Shanghai. Until 1860, Westerners had been restricted from entering inland China beyond the few treaty ports. The end of that ban brought a rush of Western-owned steamboats into the river to capture its trade. Steamboats could make the journey to Hankou, the great inland tea market, in a matter of days against the Yangzi's fierce current: the junks that carried much of the trade on China's inland waterways took weeks. The main British and American merchant houses in Shanghai, including Jardine Matheson and Russell and Co., invested in fleets of steamboats and by the 1890s an English visitor, the intrepid Isabella Bird, found eighteen steamboats at Shanghai providing a regular service to Hankou. Shanghai became the hub where this riverboat traffic met the growing numbers of coastal steamers as well as the ocean-going shipping from Europe and North America. At the end of the century the remaining restrictions on inland steam navigation had been lifted, partly as a result of Japan's victory over China in their 'Korean' war of 1895 (until the 1890s steamboats, whether Chinese- or foreign-owned, could only stop at treaty ports – one reason for the pressure to open new ones upriver). By 1913 the inland waterways in the Yangzi basin and beyond were being ploughed by more than a thousand steam vessels.[87]

In Shanghai and at Hong Kong a 'coastal' society was evolving in which a wealthy Chinese elite was attracted to Western notions of political and personal freedom, administration and law, education and leisure (dancing especially), comportment and dress. By the 1920s and 1930s Shanghai abounded in cafes, dance halls and cinemas.[88] Some of the atmosphere is delightfully captured in Qian Zhongshu's satirical novel *Fortress Besieged*, first published (in Chinese) in 1947. Like the Overseas Chinese in Singapore and elsewhere, coastal society looked forward to the 'modernization' of China as the means of resisting the assertion of Western control. A plethora of clubs and associations sprang up to debate these ideas, among them the 'China Revival Society' of 1894, forerunner of the Guomindang or National-ist Party: its leader Sun Yat-sen spent much time in Hong Kong – and much time on steamships. When the Qing monarchy collapsed in 1911 in a revolt of the provinces, China embarked on a constitutional experiment with an elected national assembly and a republican gov-ernment. But Japanese intervention after 1915, the struggle between a 'monarchical' president and the elected assembly, and the emergence of provincial 'warlords' who held power on the ground, created political chaos. Then in 1919 Japan's refusal to give up the German concession in Shandong it had seized in the war ignited a mass nation-alist movement in which social and economic discontent was fused with resentment at foreign influence and control, Japanese and West-ern. Trades unions were formed and strikes and boycotts became commonplace in treaty ports and settlements. Between January and March 1922 a seamen's strike paralysed Hong Kong shipping. Three years later, in May 1925, an industrial dispute in Shanghai led to the killing of twelve Chinese by the International Settlement police: this was the notorious 'Thirtieth May Incident'. As widespread anti-British demonstrations erupted across southern China, British and French troops shot dead fifty-two Chinese in a confrontation at the Shamian concession in Canton on 23 June. The explosion of popular anger brought a sixteen-month-long general strike in Hong Kong. As the protection of its citizens and extraterritorial rights in China became increasingly fraught, the government in London prepared to abandon the 'unequal treaties' as the price of preserving Britain's economic interests, still the largest of any foreign power in China.[89]

Perhaps surprisingly, the struggle between the north and the south (the Guomindang was first based in Canton) which engulfed much of China seems to have had little effect on Shanghai's prosperity, perhaps because much of its foreign-owned business (including now textiles and other manufactures) served Shanghai itself or its neighbouring region: this was in part an enclave economy. Competing factions in China solicited loans from the wealthy Chinese capitalist class of bankers, shipowners and industrialists that had come to the fore in the 1920s,[90] and eyed Shanghai's huge customs revenue, applied in the past as security for Beijing's foreign loans. The year 1928 was a turning point, for this was when the Guomindang army under Chiang Kai-shek restored a unified government in China, now with its capital in Nanjing, 'the southern capital', not Beijing, 'the northern capital'. The Guomindang, perhaps mindful of the need for Western sympathy against the threat from Japan, abandoned – if only temporarily – the demand to end extraterritorial status. But foreign business in China had to come to terms with a regime that imposed stiff protectionist tariffs, demanded new taxes, could subvert its labour or obstruct its trade. This change coincided with the appearance of new multinational corporations like British American Tobacco, Royal Dutch Shell, ICI, the Asiatic Petroleum Company and Unilever, which abandoned the old comprador system and used Chinese staff to reach markets beyond the treaty ports or Hong Kong. Pragmatic accommodation with the Nationalist government, not standing pat on their treaty rights, was the path they chose.[91] In the depths of the Great Depression, London persuaded the Guomindang government to encourage trade and lending by pegging its new currency to sterling, since British banks and business were still the largest foreign commercial presence in China. Cooperation with the Guomindang, not the defence of treaty-port privilege, became the priority. Its emissary, Sir Frederick Leith-Ross, was dismissive of treaty-port ways: British merchants, he said, had enjoyed a 'sheltered and artificial existence' with the help of gunboats and consuls. The 'Shanghai mind' was obsolete.[92] Where all this might have led is unknown. The escalating conflict between Nationalist China and Imperial Japan that opened with the Japanese occupation of Manchuria in 1932 and exploded into an all-out war in 1937 transformed the geopolitical setting in which globalizing influences from Europe had entrenched themselves in China. Indeed, across much of Asia, the economic relationship with Europe was already changing dramatically. In China (as in India) the market for British cotton goods crashed as tariff barriers went up and a powerful new trade rival appeared on the scene.[93] By the interwar years the number of Japanese in Shanghai was far larger than its European population, even including the White Russian refugees who poured into the city after 1920. By the mid-1930s in Asia the old order of globalization, forged on the anvil of Western imperialism, was crumbling away.

Hong Kong and Shanghai had been the great bridgeheads of steam globalization in China. Steam had helped make both of them. Much of Shanghai's hinterland was connected by river steamer, the key (as in New Orleans) to its rapid commercial expansion. Hong Kong was the hub for East Asian steam shipping, and great coaling station, offering shipbuilding and repair, marine engineering and boiler-making.[94] In the interwar years it remained a great port, seventh in the world by tonnage in 1935.[95] For one three-week period in early 1930 there were some four hundred advertised sailings by steamship to more than sixty destinations in Europe and Asia.[96] 'Hong Kong owes its very existence to shipping,' declared its Chamber of Commerce.[97] Its leading newspaper, the *China Mail*, was festooned with steamship advertisements. It devoted daily space to a 'shipping section', and frequent coverage to naval affairs. 'The [Singapore] Base,' it declaimed, 'is as essential to the safety of Hong Kong and of its trade routes as to those of New Zealand and Australia and even of India.'[98] In the interwar years Hong Kong also retained its place as a great banking centre, safe from depredation, and the receiver of remittances and investment from Chinese overseas. But its leaders well knew how much it depended on its China connection: over 40 per cent of its trade was with China, and the Hong Kong dollar carefully shadowed its counterpart in Shanghai.[99] For it had long ceded primacy to Shanghai in commercial importance. 'As a centre of British commercial activity on the Mainland [Shanghai] far outstripped Hong Kong in its importance to the U.K.,' concluded a survey in 1939.[100] Hong Kong, with its free port rules and entrepôt economy, acquired some local industry between the wars.[101] But Shanghai had begun to industrialize on a significant scale – a shift that was encouraged by the First World War and the diversion of European manufactures. Chinese capital began to be mobilized in much larger volume and a huge influx of labour had followed. It was Chinese industry, as much as Shanghai's external connections, that made Shanghai with its three million people China's largest city.

Steam globalization had left a legacy both cultural and political: indeed, the Guomindang government was its ambiguous legatee, not least in its ardent commitment to railway-building. But the results of China's ninety-year opening to the West were decidedly mixed. Between 1870 and 1913 the value of its exports had doubled; but still to less than half the value of India's. Per capita income continued to slip further and further behind that in the West.[102] Its standard of living was half that of India's, claimed a contemporary expert.[103] Perhaps 98 per cent of its economy remained 'pre-modern'.[104] Rural poverty, a largely inaccessible hinterland, the decay of the old hydraulic infrastructure and the very slow growth of overland transport (a mere 10,000 miles of railway by the 1930s) had created two Chinas: a port-city world and its coastal environs and a great interior. How far these coastal economies could have transformed their hinterlands (and when) remains an open question. In the interwar years huge political turbulence, civil wars and the encroachment of Japan destroyed any prospect of their closer integration. By the late 1930s most of coastal China was being brutally dragged into Japan's closed economic bloc, the 'Greater East Asia Co-Prosperity Sphere'. One of the century's greatest wars, the eight-year-long struggle between Japan and Nationalist China, was to follow. In China, perhaps more vividly than anywhere else in the world, we can see how acutely the fate of port cities, and their scope for reshaping the interior behind them, turned on the twists of geopolitical fortune.

8

The Crisis of the Metropoles

GLOBALIZATION UNCHAINED

By 1913 steam globalization had become a world-transforming force of seemingly unlimited power. Far from slowing down, its scale and pace continued to grow at extraordinary speed. The value of world trade, which had risen to some £3 billion by 1880, touched £4 billion in 1900, and then almost doubled to around £8 billion by 1913.[1] As we saw in an earlier chapter, the capacity of world shipping (in which most of this trade was carried) rose by between four and five times between 1870 and 1913, with spectacular growth towards the end of that period. What made these figures all the more significant was that they revealed a huge increase in the extent to which different parts of the world engaged in trade, and exposed their economies and societies (willingly or otherwise) to foreign manufactures or produce. Authoritative estimates suggest that the proportion of the world's gross domestic product (GDP) that was exported in the form of merchandise rose from 1 per cent in 1820 to nearly 8 per cent by 1913,[2] and that trade overall (imports and exports) was equivalent to 2 per cent of the world's GDP in 1820, but 22 per cent by 1913.[3] Of course, there was wide variation in the value of trade per head of population, high in settlement colonies like Australia and Canada, very low in countries like China and India. But even in India, whose trade had grown seven to eight times between 1834 and 1870, and nearly forty-fold by 1913,[4] and China, it was widely assumed that an ever-increasing share of economic activity would be turned to trade.

In much the same way, the stream of capital flowing round the world was turning into a flood. Estimates can only be rough. But at the beginning of the twentieth century the total of foreign capital invested around the world (including in Europe and the United States) was about £5 billion in current values. By the outbreak of war in 1914 that figure had risen to between £8 and £9 billion. Almost all came from Europe, a much smaller proportion (perhaps 8 per cent) from the United States.[5] Nearly half the world's foreign capital in 1913 derived from Britain or was remitted through London, Europe (and the world's) financial headquarters. France's share was just under 20 per cent, Germany's nearly 13 per cent. By one estimate, by 1913, half of Britain's annual savings were being placed abroad, and the size of her foreign property income had all but doubled since the start of the century. It was no coincidence that this great acceleration in the export of capital was matched by the tide of migration from Europe. More than 30 per cent of British foreign investment was placed in the United States and Canada; and a further 20 per cent in Argentina, Australia and Brazil.[6] It was to these countries that the vast bulk of European migrants travelled: nearly seven million between 1892 and 1900; over 11 million between 1901 and 1910; nearly eight million, despite the interruption of war, between 1911 and 1920.[7] This accelerating migration from Europe was mirrored (though on a smaller scale) by the movement of people from China and India. Migrant numbers from South China (mostly to South East Asia) rose from under 300,000 a year in 1901 to more than 400,000 by 1911.[8] The 20,000 Indians crossing the sea each year to the Malay peninsula at the end of the 1880s had risen to 100,000 by 1911.[9] The world was on the move and not just across the seas. Three and half million Russians settled in Siberia between 1906 and 1913, increasing its population by 50 per cent; some 10 million Chinese entered Manchuria between 1898 and 1908, more than doubling its population.[10] There was large-scale internal migration in Burma, the Dutch East Indies and French Vietnam to bring new lands under cultivation. The number of African migrant workers employed in the mines of the South African Rand shot up from under 80,000 in 1903–4 to over 214,000 in 1913.[11]

This explosive growth in trade, migration and the movement of capital accompanied what seemed to contemporaries to be the final stages of Europe's colonization of the rest of the world, the prelude to its more intensive exploitation under European auspices. Famously,

Frederick Jackson Turner had called attention in 1893 to the closing of America's frontier of settlement, the end of 'free' land. The Canadian prairies were occupied at frantic speed between 1900 and 1914. In Australia the rapid occupation of tropical Queensland and the 'mallee' lands of northern Victoria implied a similar advance to the limits of white settlement. In Argentina too, where the pampas lands were swiftly appropriated by large landowners, the frontier had closed by 1914.[12] This parcelling up of the temperate world ran in parallel with the partition of the tropical and subtropical world by the Western powers (including the United States by 1898) – though 'effective occupation' (supposedly the criterion of colonial legitimacy) was little more than an aspiration in much of sub-Saharan Africa. The final division of the Ottoman Empire (much reduced by 1913) and Persia (already divided into spheres of interference) had been postponed; that of China suspended to the mutual convenience of the 'treaty powers'. But this was a world that, to an extent unimaginable before 1870, lay open to the commerce and capital of Western states.

The furious pace of steam globalization is readily explained by the spread of steam technology and its revolutionary impact on transport and manufacture – above all of textiles. The mobilization of capital, the traffic of migrants and the readiness of the European powers, with Britain in the van, to force open markets by treaty or rule drove this new Europe-centred economy deep into Asia and the Americas. Less obvious, perhaps, are the reasons why steam globalization gained a 'second wind' after 1900, and why the pace of change, far from slowing down, appeared to grow faster and faster. Part of the answer must lie in the rapid march of industrialization across Europe from the 1890s, generating new wealth, more urbanization, and greater consumption of raw materials and foodstuffs. In many parts of Europe industrialization coincided with crises of rural overpopulation and impoverishment, creating huge new reservoirs of migration (both permanent and temporary) in Italy, Spain, eastern Europe and Russia. Cheap steamship fares enabled the transfer of this vast pool of labour to more productive employment in the Americas. Towards the end of the century, a second industrial revolution in electricity, chemicals and the internal combustion engine, all the stepchildren of steam technology, cheapened many processes, created new products and demanded new raw materials – like rubber and oil. But why were investors in Europe so willing to supply a stream of new capital, doubling their existing stake? Of course, much of what came from investors in France and Germany was intended for borrowers elsewhere in Europe: loans to the Russian government, France's great ally after 1892, absorbed much French lending. By contrast, most British investment flowed out of Europe, and much of it was funded from the profits of earlier transfers. Indeed, it was often these earlier pioneering investments that had created safer and more reliable conditions for the profitable use of new capital.[13] In Britain, at least, expert opinion had few doubts that prosperity at home required increasing investment abroad. 'England was always prosperous when she was making issues of new capital freely for colonial and foreign countries,' declared the leading statistician, George Paish, whose views were sought by the then finance minister, David Lloyd George.[14] The risks of foreign investment were falling, argued the young John Maynard Keynes, and any reduction in foreign investment would destroy a good part of Britain's export trade.[15]

By the early twentieth century what we might call a sophisticated globalizing system was in place: its commercial, monetary, ideological and geopolitical elements had created powerful incentives to accept its disciplines and pursue its trajectory. These were acknowledged most strongly in Europe, but their influence was felt – if to different degrees – all round the world. In Europe's industrial districts, a large and growing proportion of output, and of the workforce that produced it, depended on foreign markets. An elaborate mercantile apparatus, staffed by a large phalanx of 'white-collar' workers, existed to service the traffic of imports and exports, arrange their distribution, and provide insurance and credit. Processing industries, usually in ports, drew on the grain, rice, sugar and oil seeds from distant farms and plantations to feed and clean Europe's urban populations. Steamship and railway companies, as well as banks and finance houses, all had a vested interest in widening the channels of trade and resisting the pressure for protection and tariffs. Indeed, it was widely assumed that finding new markets in the world beyond Europe, and expanding world trade, was the best guarantee of economic growth. By contrast, increasing consumption at home by driving up wages or redistributing income by an interventionist state was regarded by all orthodox opinion as acts of economic illiteracy: dangerous, stupid and scientifically wrong. Few 'experts' in Britain endorsed the protectionist argument that a fully open economy inflicted poverty, insecurity and unemployment on working populations, creating the urban slums that blighted industrial cities. These 'metropolitan' orthodoxies were mirrored in the attitudes of commercial and landowning elites across much of the world beyond Europe. In countries where land was abundant, exporting commodities seemed the only way to turn property into income, pay for consumer goods, and finance the equipment like railways, harbours, urban transport and utilities that would modernize the economy and attract more migration. Even where new land was relatively scarce, as in China or India, economic progress seemed to depend on increasing exports to draw more money into inland districts, reduce rural poverty and pay for improvements. Where, as in India, a critique had emerged to denounce the 'drain' of wealth, it was directed at the siphoning off of India's export earnings to pay the 'Home Charges': the rent London levied for its garrison in India, the cost of expatriate pensions and the interest paid on India's borrowings in London. Few among the leaders of the Indian National Congress before 1914 would have favoured Gandhi's notion of India as an anarchist commonwealth of self-sufficient village republics.

Belief in the benefits of multilateral trade and a low tariff regime was not universal: powerful (industrial) interest groups in the United States and Russia resisted its logic. But in most countries it came to appear the natural corollary to social and economic stability. In 1870 few countries had adhered to the so-called 'gold standard' – the commitment to convert paper notes into gold on demand and (it followed) to link the circulation of currency to a 'reserve' of gold. By 1913 the vast majority of independent states had accepted this discipline, including Japan: it helped that (as we saw earlier) the supply of mined gold had grown enormously in the second half of the century. The gold standard conferred two significant benefits. Firstly, it stabilized exchange rates between trading partners and, by reducing this risk, encouraged more traffic. Secondly, it offered reassurance to foreign lenders and investors that the value of their capital would not be destroyed by a cascade of inconvertible paper. From the mid-1890s, when international trade revived vigorously, the appeal of the gold standard became stronger than ever. For all those states whose hopes of growing prosperity were pinned on increasing the value of their commodity exports and who faced fierce competition from other producers, rejecting the gold standard would reduce their appeal to buyers in Europe. It was likely to have an even more chilling effect on those from whom they hoped to attract the very investments they needed to increase production and smooth its path from farm to grain elevator, freezing works and harbour. In many states also, where direct taxation was politically or administratively difficult, much government activity relied upon borrowing, usually, since local capital was scarce, from lenders abroad. Here the necessity of reassuring the lender seemed even more urgent: the sudden restriction of their foreign cash flow was likely to plunge them into a political crisis or even regime change. Thus free trade and the gold standard acted together to lock many states into an ever deeper commitment to an integrated global economy. To give up free trade in favour of protection would reduce export income. Without export income the flow of inward investment would shrink or dry up. Worse still, it might set off a crisis, bankrupt the state and overthrow the regime.

These fears were felt most acutely in agrarian states reliant upon a few staple exports (the obvious examples were in South America). Among the European great powers the logic of globalization was viewed somewhat differently. For many contemporaries the last decade before the First World War was the crucial phase when the terms on which the world was globalized would be finally fixed and sealed in a series of bargains between five 'world states': Britain, France, Germany, Russia and the United States. Failure to act quickly to secure a zone of expansion might mean permanent exclusion from future sources of wealth, in a form of economic encirclement. In an age of partitions, occupations, spheres of influence and concessions, of new industrial powers and surging investment, it is easy to see why this expectation took root. 'Whether we like it or not,' wrote the influential British geographer Halford Mackinder in 1909, 'we have come to the time of great empires, and of commercial and industrial trusts [cartels].'[16] Others in Europe had earlier drawn the same conclusion. If her overseas interests were not brought 'to the fore-front', argued Admiral Tirpitz, the *éminence grise* of German naval policy, in 1895, 'Germany will swiftly sink from her position as a great Power in the coming century'.[17] 'The more inert countries [of Asia] will fall a prey to the powerful invaders,' the Russian minister Count Witte told the Tsar in 1903. 'The problem of each country concerned is to obtain as large a share as possible of the inheritance of the outlived oriental states, especially of the Chinese Colossus.'[18] The staking of claims, not only to territory but to commercial and financial influence, took on a new urgency. But as the world was being parcelled up, it was maritime access that was all important. 'A country is never small when it is bathed by the sea,' said the Belgian king, Leopold II, hopefully.[19] 'Our future lies on the water,' declared Kaiser Wilhelm II in robuster mood. Those states without sea power, commercial and naval, risked being excluded from the formal and informal empires into which the globalized world would soon be divided. The fate of Spain in 1898, stripped of (almost) all that remained of its empire by the United States, was hardly reassuring.

Yet, for all their rivalries, the European powers were agreed that their continent's place at the centre of the world was more certain than ever. The course of steam globalization had confirmed the commercial, financial, scientific and technological superiority of Europe and its western annexe in North America. Far from levelling up living standards and wealth, it had widened the gap between the West and the 'Rest'. The cruder index of military power and colonial rule pointed in the same direction, and encouraged the view that white Europeans enjoyed a 'genetic' advantage in energy, morals and intellect. Expert opinion suggested that Europe also enjoyed a demographic advantage over Asia and Africa, since its population seemed to be rising far faster than theirs. In a century's time, predicted the eminent statistician Sir Robert Giffen, Europe's population would exceed one billion and be 'enormously' greater than the present populations of India or China.[20] Experts also dismissed as a myth that Europeans were unsuited to colonize tropical regions. 'I now firmly believe,' wrote Sir Patrick Manson, the foremost expert in tropical medicine, in 1898, 'in the possibility of tropical colonization by the white races.'[21] The whole world was their oyster. Indeed, an influential strand of ethnographical inquiry argued that 'aboriginal' peoples in the Americas and Australasia (including the Maori) were 'dying races' whose disappearance was sad but inevitable. Nor were these claims of irresistible primacy merely the trumpeting of European blowhards. In those parts of Asia and Africa where European influence was felt most strongly, their force was acknowledged by local elites. Their task, as they saw it, was to adapt Europe's institutions, ideas and technologies to the goal of defending their religions and cultures, and whatever remained of their political freedom. In most cases the real issue at hand was the terms on which they would be admitted to partnership with the European powers, as allies (like Japan), or the chosen representatives of their colonial community. It was widely assumed that, except in a handful of cases, some form of indefinite tutelage was the eventual fate of non-European peoples. American influence in the Caribbean, and Central America (where the territory around the Panama Canal had been forcibly separated from Colombia), remarked the *Economist* in January 1914, would 'soon be almost as powerful and irresistible as that of the Government of Great Britain over . . . her colonial territories'.[22]

What was (as it turned out) the last great phase of steam globalization presented a strangely discordant spectacle. The exceptionally rapid growth in trade and investment promised a world in which the scale of economic interdependence would soothe away frictions and make the costs of war unthinkably high. A war between Britain and Germany, warned the *Economist*, 'would affect the commercial equilibrium of the world for all time'.[23] But in the world beyond Europe the pacific effects of more trade and capital were rather less obvious. For states that depended on commodity exports deeper engagement with the world economy also carried the risk that faraway events could thrust them into a crisis of social and political as well as commercial stability.[24] A financial default might bring foreign armed intervention: seizing the custom house (the custom house had been the main target of the American occupation of Vera Cruz in April 1914). Too flamboyant a presence of foreign-owned business could spark a rebellion of clerics or artisans, fearful of cultural or industrial competition. Worse still, the furious pursuit of a commodity whose value had suddenly risen could bring an incursion of predatory outsiders seizing land and labour with appalling violence as had happened in the Congo. More prosaically, as the case of India among others revealed, steam globalization was more likely than not to widen the gap in overall living standards between the West and the Afro-Asian 'Rest' than to narrow it.

This Janus face of globalization arose of course from the gross disparities in wealth and power that steam technology had helped to install. They licensed the rapid advance of European states into other parts of the world by occupation, annexation and coercion as much as by commercial penetration. This by its nature was a competitive process, and the competition warmed up – or so it seemed – in the 1890s, to reach a feverish level. Hence, the rising tide of trade and investment was accompanied not only by a fractious diplomacy to demarcate territories and spheres but by a huge increase in the naval spending of the main sea powers – Britain, France, Germany, Italy, Austria-Hungary, Japan and the United States – up by almost 70 per cent between 1906–7 and 1913–14. It seemed that steam globalization had given birth to 'high imperialism' in an increasingly militarized form. But, as in previous eras, globalization gave rise to contradictory trends. If it encouraged the outreach of powerful states it also promoted new forms of local resistance. Globalization assisted the cause, and increased the appeal, of *territorial* integration, so that states could take full advantage of the global economy, typically by investing in railways and the telegraph. This offered the promise of new 'national' states in ways inconceivable in earlier times: the railway was the father of the 'nation state'. In regions exposed to the full force of Europe's imperialism, new modes of connection (as we have seen) provided the means for cultural and ethnic mobilization, just as 'imperial globalization' became more intense. Indeed, this phenomenon could be seen at work within the dynastic empires of Europe and the Near East – in Imperial Germany, Russia, Austria-Hungary and the Ottoman Empire. Both imperialism and nationalism were globalization's progeny. That may help to explain, alongside the sense of rapid technological change, the febrile mixture of bravado and anxiety in the mood of the period.

Before 1914, despite the jeremiads of interested parties, the signs were ambiguous. The conflicting claims and ambitions of the European powers in the 'outer world' had largely been settled by sometimes ill-tempered diplomacy – if only because the prospect of a war *within* Europe over African desert and bush was ruled out as absurd. Where wars had occurred, as between Spain and America and Russia and Japan, they had been carefully localized, even if their consequences spread wider. In the Afro-Asian world nationalist or ethnic revolts against the Western powers had either been crushed – like those of Filipinos or Hereros – or contained by Machiavellian 'reform' – a British speciality. How far Republican China would escape the 'semi-colonialism' imposed on the Qing was very uncertain. Perhaps the real problem was that intense globalization was bound to produce frictions. Its impact was also grossly uneven. It was certain to ignite unpredictable consequences, both politically and economically. Yet the diplomatic machinery required to manage a world whose 'nervous system' had been recently unified at breakneck speed was half-developed at best. When the precipitate break-up of European Turkey threatened a confrontation not in the African bush but in a region deemed crucial to Europe's balance of power, all the deficiencies of dynastic diplomacy were laid bare.[25] And steam globalization came to a juddering halt.

MARITIME EUROPE

This was the setting in which Europe's maritime metropoles had reached the peak of their influence. Indeed, everything seemed to point towards the irresistible growth of their commercial importance. The huge rise in world trade had, after all, been accompanied by a still larger increase in the tonnage of ocean-going steamers. Even in the age of the railway, there were limits to the capacity of overland transport before traffic congestion set in. It was precisely this problem, concluded a leading geographer, that worked 'in favour of the growth of a comparatively small number of immense seaport cities like London and New York', from which goods would be distributed by sea to smaller coastal cities. 'The large seaport is a permanent and increasing necessity.'[26] Indeed, Europe's leading port cities – London, Liverpool, Antwerp, Rotterdam, Hamburg, Le Havre, Marseilles,

Trieste and Genoa – all seemed to be engaged in furious competition to enlarge their harbours and attract the ever-bigger merchant ships that shipowners wanted and shipyards were building.

Much of the pressure arose from the fact that European port cities had a double function. Collectively they served as the metropoles that connected Europe to the 'wider world' of the Americas, Afro-Asia and the South Pacific. Here they were agents of Europe's steam globalization. But they were also caught up in the enormous increase in the trade *within* Europe, amounting to some 60 per cent of the world total. But there were other features as well that set them apart from most of the great port cities of the extra-European world. Firstly, Europe's physical and political geography had conspired to encourage a remarkable concentration of large port cities. In the late nineteenth century no fewer than thirteen sovereign states were crowded into western and central Europe (Norway was separated from Sweden in 1905) with access to the indented coastline of this 'peninsula of peninsulas'. Each needed, or wanted, a grand port (and preferably several) to project its interests and expand its trade. Secondly, they served as the outlets for much the largest outflow of migrants anywhere in the world (a parallel can be found in Hong Kong), a flow that, as we have seen, showed no signs of abating, and imposed a large social burden. Thirdly, behind them lay almost all the most heavily industrialized regions in the world apart from those in the north-east of the United States. Hence, most European ports were 'importing' ports by weight and volume, receiving huge quantities of foodstuffs, raw materials and fuel that had to be transported inland to factories and consumers. Unlike many of the great 'exporting' ports of the world outside Europe, they drew upon a wide variety of producing regions north and south of the equator so that their trade was less seasonal than theirs – an important factor in meeting the costs of their harbour improvements and sustaining a large working population. Fourthly, unlike the port cities of the rest of the world, Europe's major port cities were home to the great shipping lines that (as we saw) were tightening their grip on seaborne trade and imposing their rules (through the 'conference system') on steamship traffic. It was in Europe's port-city boardrooms that the world's maritime corridors were meant to be managed.

One other feature set them apart. In most parts of the world port cities had had to compete with rivals hoping to capture their external connections, draw their shipping away and intrude on their hinterlands. By the early twentieth century the combination of railways and steamship 'trunk routes' and coaling stations had tipped the balance in favour of a handful of 'hubs', and pushed many once-favoured harbours (like Quebec City, Boston, Madras, Penang and Canton) into a secondary role. In Europe, however, a different pattern prevailed. Here 'hubbing' was restrained by political influence intended to safeguard a state's principal ports. It was also drastically complicated by the exceptional density of Europe's network of railways and waterways. Neither the great railway corridor that linked New York to Chicago nor the extraordinary iron 'fan' that spread out from Buenos Aires could be found in Europe. Instead (as we shall see) hinterlands overlapped, and different 'rules of distribution' applied to the multiple products that ports received and dispatched. This lent competition an edge and intensity that were, perhaps, greater than anywhere else. Europe's own globalization created both mutual dependence and extreme sensitivity to its political risks: a volatile cocktail of hope and fear.

Sizeable port cities could be found all along Europe's maritime fringe. The Baltic, once the seat of the Hanseatic League, had long been reduced to a secondary role in European commerce. Copenhagen (once an imperial capital, but long stripped of its empire) and Gothenburg, Sweden's main port, occupied strategic locations near the entrance to the sea. Copenhagen was an entrepôt where passengers could trans-ship for the remoter Baltic ports. It acquired a 'free port' in 1904, where goods could rest without paying duty. The Kiel Canal, cut by Germany across the neck of the Danish peninsula and opened in 1895, had reduced its trade. No single port commanded the inner Baltic. The German ports of Stettin and Danzig suffered from limited hinterlands, Danzig in part because its great waterway, the mighty Vistula, offered few landing places for traffic and its railway connection was poor.[27] Stettin had suffered from the competition of Hamburg. Riga, at the mouth of the Dvina, was Russia's third port after St Petersburg and Odessa. Its population had quadrupled since 1870 to reach nearly 500,000 in 1913. The value of its trade had risen eightfold and it had become one of Russia's main industrial districts. By the early twentieth century it was the scene of increasingly bitter conflict between its German-speaking elite, who controlled the city's government, and the Latvians and Russians drawn to its factories. As in many port cities beyond Europe, its three ethnic groups largely kept their own company.[28] Reval, modern Tallinn, was a cotton-importing port that served the mills of St Petersburg, although, from the mid-1880s, a canal through the shallow waters above Kronstadt (Russia's great naval base) had given larger ships direct access to St Petersburg. St Petersburg-Kronstadt had long been Russia's leading port, although its actual share of Russian exports had fallen sharply since the 1860s. But its population had grown massively between 1870 and 1914, from less than one million to well over two million, because the city had become a great industrial centre, whose workers were housed in overcrowded, squalid and dangerously unhealthy conditions: cholera was a constant menace.[29] But, like most Baltic ports, it was icebound in winter and its nearer hinterland was thinly populated.

Grain made up half of Russia's exports, much of it grown in the south of the country, and shipped from Black Sea ports like Odessa, Kherson and Taganrog, the birthplace of Chekhov. Odessa was the largest of these, with a population of some half a million after 1900. Less than 10 per cent of its population spoke Ukrainian, the language of the surrounding region; less than half spoke Russian. Odessa was a city of forty-nine languages and French, Italians, Greeks, Albanians, Bulgarians, Germans, Poles, Armenians, Georgians and Turks could all be found there. But it was Jews who really commanded the city. They formed a third of the population by 1914, and increasingly mastered its trade and industry. Intriguingly, Odessa was also surrounded by a ring of 'German colonies' – emigrants attracted to Russia by the promise of free land and municipal privilege: their subsequent fate – like that of most of Odessa's population by 1941 – was to be grim. Before 1914, Odessa itself faced an uncertain future. In an era of 'Russification', its cosmopolitan character attracted official hostility. Local self-government was drastically cut back. Large numbers of troops were quartered on the city. Odessa's own trade suffered from the competition of neighbouring ports. Wealthy merchants began

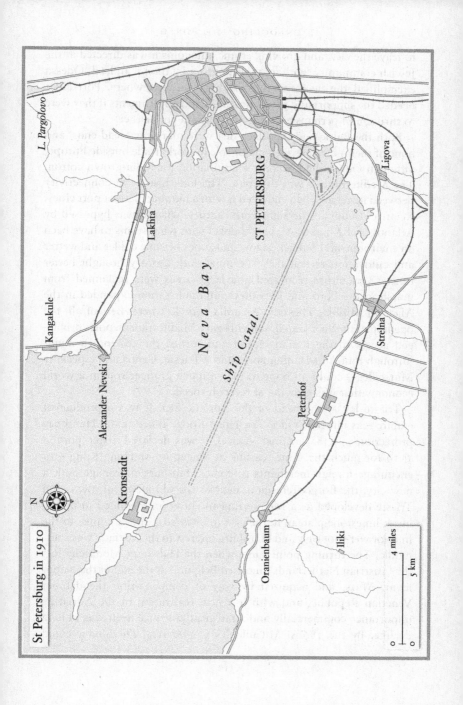

St Petersburg in 1910

N

Kronstadt

Alexander Nevski

Kangakule

Lakhta

L. Pargolovo

Neva Bay

Ship Canal

ST PETERSBURG

Ligova

Strelna

Peterhof

Oranienbaum

Iliki

0   4 miles
0   5 km

to leave the city, and growing ethnic antagonism was directed at the Jewish community, with a major pogrom in 1905.[30] Indeed, Odessa exemplified the necessity that we have seen elsewhere. Port cities needed the support and protection of inland governments if they were to thrive, and perhaps even survive. Odessa got neither.

Both the Baltic and the Black Sea were maritime 'dead ends' and none of their ports played a major role in world trade outside Europe, although Odessa had become a destination for India-grown cotton. The Mediterranean was different. The long history of connectivity between its regions had endowed it with a number of great port cities. Relative decline in the eighteenth century, when it was bypassed by Atlantic and Asian trade, was coupled with what seems to have been an environmental setback as lowland zones became colder and wetter and cultivation retreated.[31] The nineteenth century brought better times. Agriculture recovered and large areas were reclaimed from marsh in the Ebro and Po valleys, and cultivation expanded in the Algerian Mitidja, Thessaly, Anatolia and elsewhere. Best of all, the opening of the Suez Canal suddenly gave Mediterranean ports privileged access to the Indian Ocean and turned the sea into a major 'through route'. Its leading port cities – Trieste, Genoa and especially Marseilles – could all hope to play a much grander role in a world economy that was growing at feverish speed.

Trieste lay at the head of the Adriatic Sea. It was a product of empire – as much as Odessa or Hong Kong. Taken under Habsburg protection in 1382 (against Venice), it was declared a free port in 1719 for much the same reasons as Singapore or Hong Kong – to encourage foreign merchants to come. Habsburg patronage built a new city, the Borgo Teresiano, next to the old medieval town, and Trieste developed as a Mediterranean entrepôt. Hemmed in by the bleak limestone plateau to the east (the *Carso*), Trieste's links to the interior were not easy and Habsburg interest in the Adriatic was spasmodic. The turning point came when the Habsburg Monarchy lost the 'Austrian Netherlands' (modern Belgium) at the end of the Napoleonic Wars, and acquired by way of compensation the defunct Venetian Republic, and with it a new realization of the Adriatic's importance commercially and strategically. Venice itself was in long decline. By the 1860s, M'Culloch's *Commercial Dictionary* could describe its commerce as 'comparatively trifling'.[32] Meanwhile, merchants in Trieste had founded a steamship line, the 'Austrian Lloyd', in 1835, helped by the Rothschilds in Vienna, to exploit the growing trade in the eastern Mediterranean. Government backing brought the vital mail contract and subsidy.[33] In the 1850s the city was linked to Vienna by the Semmering Railway and later by the Südbahn, while the loss of Venice to Italy in 1866 made it the Empire's only major seaport. Then in 1869 the opening of the Suez Canal suddenly made Trieste the closest European port to the Indian Ocean: a steamer from Trieste was the first vessel to traverse the Canal. By the mid-1870s Austrian Lloyd was advertising regular sailings to Bombay in *The Times*.[34]

By the late nineteenth century, Trieste was established as one of Europe's leading ports, ranking eighth in tonnage by 1913.[35] Austrian Lloyd was a major shipping line with services to East Asia and the Americas as well as the Levant. Austria-Hungary's modern navy was built in Trieste's shipyards. It acquired a new harbour in the 1880s and an additional railway connection in 1909. As a Mediterranean port, Trieste itself was characteristically cosmopolitan. If Italians were the largest ethnic group, they were supplemented by Slovenes, Serbs and other Balkan peoples. A wealthy *haute bourgeoisie* of merchants, bankers and shipowners was a compound of Greeks, Armenians, Germans, Venetians and Jews. Trieste was a major coffee port – the firm of Illy survives as a reminder – and profited from the expansion of the Empire's industry and agriculture. Perhaps no one in 1913 could have predicted its fate. With the collapse of the Empire in 1918, much of Trieste's commercial importance vanished like a dream. Its brief golden age became a long diminuendo – even if the charm survived.[36] 'All that vast hinterland the produce and needs of which used necessarily to pass through this port has been carved up,' reported the *Economist* sadly in 1927. 'There is no longer any compelling reason why certain traffic should be handled on these quays . . .'[37]

Italy's long coastline was studded with port cities, most with a great future behind them. Naples, long the capital of southern Italy until unification in the 1860s, attracted a great deal of shipping, but mainly through its function as a major emigrant port for the millions of Italians who left to live or work in the Americas. A great cultural revival in the late nineteenth century still left it a huge, overcrowded and impoverished city, looking out over a desperately poor Mezzogiorno.[38] Genoa's history was different. In early modern times it had been the commercial and financial hub of the western Mediterranean, and had shared its relative decline. The later nineteenth century opened a new chapter. As part of Piedmont-Sardinia, the dominant element in the new kingdom of Italy after 1860, it was well placed to become Italy's leading port, especially once industrialization took off around Turin and Milan. Whereas four-fifths of Italy's trade was confined to Europe in the late 1880s, by 1913 it had greatly diversified: more than a third now went elsewhere.[39] At the same time, Genoa became a great migrant port: nearly 400,000 migrants departed from there in 1906, while an almost equal number returned.[40] Migration and trade were not unconnected since the large numbers of Italians settled permanently or temporarily in Argentina and the United States were a loyal market for Italian fabrics and foodstuffs. Genoa was also home to a major shipping line, the Rubattino, which, from the 1870s, offered 'the quickest, cheapest and most agreeable route to Bombay' via the Suez Canal.[41] As the traffic in its port expanded, so did the city's population, more than doubling to some 270,000 by 1911.[42]

Yet its role as a metropole was hobbled in a number of ways. The city sat on a shelf wedged between the mountains and the sea: safe and convenient for an early modern entrepôt, far less so for a port in the railway age. By reclaiming the foreshore, Genoa acquired a new harbour in the 1870s, but its inland communications remained very constricted. It was linked by railways to Turin and Milan, but steep gradients and narrow passes through the coastal mountains sharply reduced their capacity. To complicate railway traffic still further, Genoa had a huge imbalance of imports over exports, with large quantities of coal, raw cotton and grain coming in but little going out: only one ship in seven left with a full cargo. As a port, Genoa was expensive, and prone to strike action. Nor by the early twentieth century had it made much headway in acquiring a hinterland beyond northern Italy, despite the new railway links through the Alps: scarcely 5 per cent of its trade within Europe crossed national boundaries. High railway charges over the routes to Switzerland and southern Germany meant that it competed poorly with faraway Rotterdam or Antwerp.[43]

Genoa's difficulties were emblematic of a wider Italian problem in an age of competing great powers and the fear of 'encirclement'. Despite its glorious past, Genoa could not remotely play the role of London, Hamburg or Antwerp as a great entrepôt for industrial Europe. It could not even claim to be Italy's leading financial and commercial centre, though a third of Italy's seaborne trade passed through its port.[44] Genoa had to wait on the further advance of northern Italy's industrialization. It shared with much of Italy the problem of internal communications, the lack of which held back the economic integration that was the key to prosperity elsewhere in Europe. Southern Italy remained a world apart. It was little wonder, perhaps, that Italian leaders were acutely dissatisfied with the legacy of unification as a platform for great-power status and nourished irredentist claims and colonial ambitions. They knew that Italy was 'the least of the great powers'.[45] But the struggle to escape this demeaning status was to lead to disaster.

It was Marseilles that was the undisputed queen of the Mediterranean. A port since antiquity, Marseilles was endowed with a narrow but exceptionally sheltered harbour (today's Vieux Port) and guarded by defences still strikingly visible to the visitor arriving by sea. It became a grand base for the Mediterranean ambitions of the French monarchy who ruled the city from 1481. Under Louis XIV, whose designs were nothing less than imperial, it was declared a free port and a programme of massive expansion was decreed, tripling the size of the city.[46] In early modern times Marseilles was the only French port allowed direct trade with the Levant by the Ottomans, a privilege that made it both highly cosmopolitan and susceptible to the plague, which killed a third of the population in 1720.[47] In the eighteenth century, Marseilles expanded its reach to the Americas, West Africa, India and China, but its trade was devastated by the British blockade in the long wars between 1793 and 1815.[48]

Marseilles' fortunes were revived by steam and Algeria. The French conquest began in 1830 and the city became the main supply base for the French *armée d'Afrique*. A steam packet service linked Marseilles and Algiers from 1831, and in the 1880s Algiers could be reached in

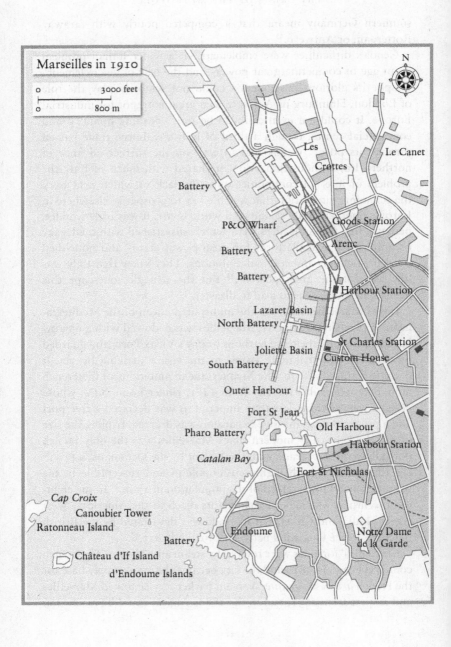

Marseilles in 1910

0   3000 feet
0   800 m

Les Crottes

Le Canet

Battery

P&O Wharf

Goods Station

Arenc

Battery

Battery

Harbour Station

Lazaret Basin

North Battery

St Charles Station

Joliette Basin

South Battery

Custom House

Outer Harbour

Fort St Jean

Old Harbour

Pharo Battery

Harbour Station

Catalan Bay

Fort St Nicholas

Cap Croix

Canoubier Tower

Ratonneau Island

Battery

Endoume

Notre Dame
de la Garde

Château d'If Island

d'Endoume Islands

just over twenty-four hours almost any day of the week. From the 1870s, Marseilles was connected by telegraph with the main North African cities and by steamship services and submarine cables to the rest of the Mediterranean.[49] Marseilles was the natural metropole for Algeria's colonial economy with its exports of wine and wheat, and its settler community of some 600,000 by the late nineteenth century, amid a much larger, but marginalized, native population.[50] Marseilles merchants were ardent supporters of French colonization of the Maghreb from Tunis to Morocco. They were also quick to see the need to adapt Marseilles to the age of steam, and make the Mediterranean a 'lac français' – a phrase already current by the 1830s. What became the great shipping line Messageries Maritimes was founded by a Marseilles merchant in 1851, and between 1844 and 1853 Marseilles acquired a new harbour at the foot of the Vieux Port. The opening of the Suez Canal, coinciding with French colonial expansion in Indo-China and the Pacific, vastly extended its sphere of commercial ambition. In 1857 the Paris-Lyon-Méditerranée railway (PLM) ended Marseilles' long physical separation from Lyons, France's second city, and the capital.

By the early twentieth century, Marseilles was France's leading port, the base of several great shipping lines, and an industrial centre refining sugar, processing grain from Russia, India and Argentina as well as Algeria, and manufacturing soap. But, *as a port*, remarked a contemporary assessment, its progress was disappointing. The Suez Canal had restored the Mediterranean as a great sea route, but the price had been to sharpen the competition between its ports at Marseilles' expense. Marseilles shared little of the entrepôt or transit trade so important to Antwerp or London. Its links with southern Germany were poor. Its immediate hinterland, the Midi, had little to offer by way of exports. Worse still, Marseilles lay too far from France's main industrial centres further north to serve as their main outlet. Much of the fault lay with the inadequacy of its rail connections, and the freight rates charged by the PLM. But Marseilles was also hampered by the limited capacity of its docks and (like Genoa) by the coastal mountains which made inland communication difficult.[51] Nor had it much help from government. The return to high tariffs in 1892 had damaged its trade while the 'log-rolling' practices of the Third Republic, 'notre mesquine politique électorale', meant that any assistance to French ports had had to be shared between multiple claimants each with its champion in parliament.[52]

The result had been Marseilles' growing dependence on France's highly protected colonial trade. The Mediterranean made it the obvious port for trade and travel to France's colonies there, in the Indian Ocean (Madagascar was conquered in the 1890s) and in South East Asia. 'Marseille colonial' was the slogan of its Chamber of Commerce.[53] France's first colonial exposition was held there, not in Paris. To its large population of Italian migrants were added Kabyles from Algeria – the 'Arabs' whose employment as stokers was one grievance behind the strikes that plagued Marseilles before 1914.[54] Indeed, of all Europe's leading port cities, Marseilles was by far the most focused on colonial trade and colonial expansion (perhaps Lisbon was similar but on a much smaller scale), and the most deeply committed to a single colony, Algeria. This may have reflected in part the relative poverty of Mediterranean economies, where incomes were well below those of north-western Europe and the gap was widening.[55] Indeed, the trade of Mediterranean countries was little more than a tenth of their northern counterparts. Expecting little from the rest of Europe, for Marseilles, 'our colonies are our hope and our future'.[56]

The vast bulk of Europe's seaborne trade was transacted within a shallow rectangle in north-western Europe some 600 miles long and 250 miles wide – a mere pinprick on the surface of the globe. Here were found its five leading ports: London, Liverpool, Antwerp, Rotterdam and Hamburg. There were two important outliers: Bremen, the home of the shipping line Norddeutscher Lloyd, and a major cotton market,[57] and Le Havre, where a tight-knit Protestant *haute bourgeoisie*, known locally as the 'Côte' from their cliff-top residences,[58] ruled over its trade in cotton and coffee.

London was still the grand metropole. Its importance derived not just from its port, the largest in the world in the value and volume of traffic. What made London unique was that it combined the functions of government, manufacture, commerce and finance with a scale of local consumption that reflected its huge concentrations of personal wealth. It was an imperial as well as a national capital. London was also the 'nerve centre' of a vast information network, where newspapers, periodicals, pamphlets, a mass of specialized journals as well as business houses and innumerable professional bodies (the Institution of Civil Engineers is one example) collected, digested and distributed news and expertise from all parts of the world. In the City of London, the 'Square Mile', were most of the world's leading commodity markets – for wool, sugar, tea, metals and timber among others – and the huge produce markets for local consumption like Billingsgate, Smithfield, Spitalfields and the Coal Exchange. Shipbrokers and shipping lines had their offices here and so did the numerous British-owned overseas railways, clustered in Finsbury Circus. Close by was Lloyds of London, the daily pulse of the sea lanes. The City was crowded with the 'accepting houses' that financed its overseas trade, more than forty British overseas banks, nearly thirty foreign-owned ones, and specialized merchants dealing in more unusual commodities, like ostrich feathers or gambier.[59] Through the London Stock Exchange flowed the stream of foreign investment (some four-fifths of its business) destined for overseas governments, railway companies ('American Rails' was a large section) and public utilities, and increasingly for mines, plantations and processing plants. Presiding over this anthill of finance was the Bank of England (still a private concern), grand regulator of the world's gold standard. In 1911 almost 100,000 people in the City were employed in 'commodities', and another 30,000 in firms providing credit or capital.[60]

Much of the foreign business attracted to London was drawn there by the ease with which goods could be bought and sold using the 'Bill on London', a paper promise to pay acceptable anywhere. In that sense London was in part a 'virtual port': goods were bought and sold there without their physical presence. For 'real' goods, too, it offered many advantages. Britain was a free trade economy, with minimal barriers to imported produce. London offered a wide range of specialized dealers in exotic or luxury items as well as its main commodity markets. The sheer volume of goods passing through the port made it easy to find a full cargo – an important consideration for a shipowner – while the high volume of shipping from all corners of the world promised the timely delivery of merchandise exports. Over 9,000 ships arrived in London in 1912, including 99 from Japan, 215 from Argentina, 1,100 from India, and over 1,300 from Australia and New Zealand.[61] Of course, these advantages were not born of

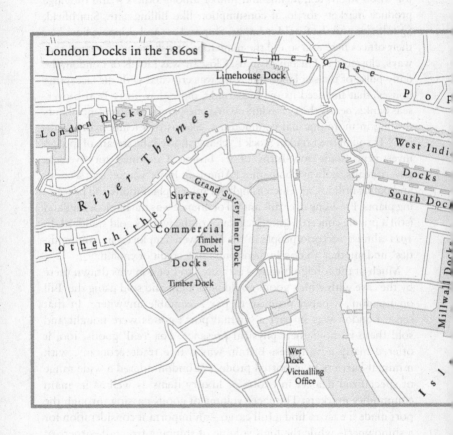

London Docks in the 1860s

Limehouse

Limehouse Dock

London Docks

River Thames

Po

West Indi

Docks

South Dock

Surrey

Grand Surrey Inner Dock

Rotherhithe

Commercial

Timber Dock

Docks

Timber Dock

Millwall Dock

Isl

Wet Dock Victualling Office

Isl

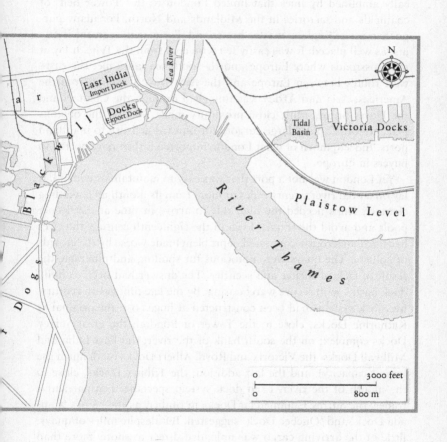

chance. London was uniquely favoured by site and location. It was the lowest point on the Thames where a large town could be built, and the lowest point where the river could be bridged.[62] Its inland communications via the Thames and its tributaries gave easy access to much of southern England: in the railway age these were drastically amplified by lines that linked London to the 'Power Belt' of coalfields and factories in the Midlands and North. For many purposes most of England was its hinterland. For maritime traffic it was just as well placed. It was easily fed with coal from the Tyne. It lay at the crossroads where Europe's north–south sea lanes met the east–west routes between Europe and the Americas. Shipping from the Americas, Asia and Africa was funnelled through the Channel and the Dover Strait, while close proximity made London the obvious place to 'break bulk' large cargoes for onward delivery to mainland ports. Indeed, much of what London imported it then re-exported to buyers in Europe.

Yet London was not a port that was easy to maintain or expand. It lay on a tidal river twenty miles or more from its mouth up a winding channel. Ships needed the high tide to arrive in time at the deeper pools and avoid the shoals. Even in the eighteenth century the river became dangerously congested, a problem made worse by the crowds of colliers. The quays were notorious for spoiling and pilferage, the result of lack of shelter and security. The answer had been to build dock basins with secure warehousing. By the late nineteenth century, five dock systems had been constructed at huge cost: the original St Katharine Docks, close to the Tower of London; the great Surrey Docks complex, on the south bank of the river; the East India and Millwall Docks; the Victoria and Royal Albert Docks (with much the largest capacity); and the last addition, the Tilbury Docks, close to the mouth of the river. Each dock system specialized in particular trades: the Surrey Commercial Docks in timber, as the names 'Canada Dock' and 'Quebec Dock' suggested. But despite miles of quays, little of the arriving cargo was unloaded direct to shore: more than 80 per cent went over the side into hundreds of lighters and was discharged upriver. Some 30,000 dockworkers, employed as was customary as 'casual' workers, provided the human muscle needed to carry, push, pull, shape and shove an immense variety of goods in bags, packets or loose like timber (a notoriously awkward cargo) into and out of the holds.[63] Steam helped to make the river easier to manage, but the ever-growing size of deep-sea ships was a huge challenge, demanding a costly programme of dredging. Nor was it easy to reconcile the innumerable private interests at work on the river. Even providing the railways needed to carry goods into and out of the docks was a struggle against the vested claims of long-settled residents. It was the urgent need to coordinate all the various elements of the port economy at a time when both the volume and size of shipping were increasing rapidly that led to the creation of the Port of London Authority in 1909.[64]

The exceptional range of its maritime connections made London the global port par excellence. Variety was its strength: no single market predominated. But like all other port cities, it feared competition and the loss of its entrepôt trade as its rivals expanded their 'direct' connections with ports elsewhere in the world. In Britain itself it had little to fear. Liverpool ran it close in the tonnage unloaded and was more important for exports. But in fact its role was more complementary than competitive, for it served a distinct industrial zone whose needs London was ill-placed to supply. London and Liverpool stood head and shoulders above other British ports, transacting between them over half of Britain's trade.

Liverpool[65] began modestly as the port for Ireland once Chester declined with the silting up of the Dee. But (like Bordeaux and Nantes) its fortune was made early by sugar and slaves. Liverpool was the apex of the 'triangular trade' which took cloth and metal goods to West Africa, slaves to the West Indies, and brought sugar back home. Some Liverpool merchants, like the Gladstones, acquired slave plantations as well. Liverpool's advantage lay in the wide estuary of the Mersey, and its convenient location for sailing ships seeking the fastest sea lanes to and from the Americas. This advantage came with a cost. The Mersey approaches lay through shifting sandbanks and shoals, and the tides in the river could reach thirty feet or more.[66] Well before London, Liverpool merchants were forced to build enclosed dock basins where ships could unload safely, and by the mid-1850s the city could boast five miles of docks along its foreshore.[67] By the early twentieth century this system had expanded to

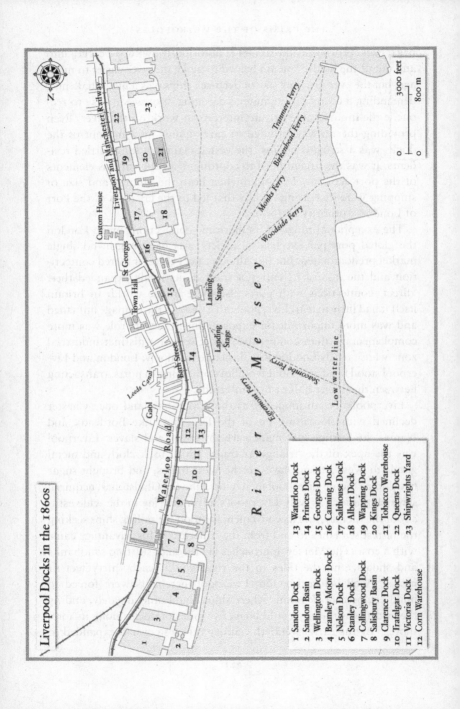

Liverpool Docks in the 1860s

N

River Mersey

Low water line

Tranmere Ferry
Birkenhead Ferry
Monks Ferry
Woodside Ferry
Seacombe Ferry
Egremont Ferry

Landing Stage
Landing Stage

Custom House
Liverpool and Manchester Railway
St Georges
Town Hall
Bath Street
Leeds Canal
Gaol
Waterloo Road

3000 feet
800 m

1 Sandom Dock
2 Sandom Basin
3 Wellington Dock
4 Bramley Moore Dock
5 Nelson Dock
6 Stanley Dock
7 Collingwood Dock
8 Salisbury Basin
9 Clarence Dock
10 Trafalgar Dock
11 Victoria Dock
12 Corn Warehouse

13 Waterloo Dock
14 Princes Dock
15 Georges Dock
16 Canning Dock
17 Salthouse Dock
18 Albert Dock
19 Wapping Dock
20 Kings Dock
21 Tobacco Warehouse
22 Queens Dock
23 Shipwrights Yard

include some thirty large docks extending for several miles north and south of the original 'pool', and served by railways running in parallel.[68] What made this vast expansion affordable had been the convergence of slave-grown cotton from the American South and the Industrial Revolution that turned south Lancashire into an enormous textile factory, the source of some 40 per cent of Britain's merchandise exports in 1913. Liverpool imported three-quarters of the raw cotton that came into Britain and exported most of the cotton fabric and yarn Lancashire sent out to the world. Its North American traffic made it the favoured port for Canadian and American grain, and, once its nefarious traffic in slaves was replaced by the trade in palm oil (and later cacao), Liverpool also asserted its claim to be the commercial capital of British West Africa. Nor were British consumers its only concern. Liverpool had a large re-export trade, not least in cotton, to Europe. As much the largest cotton market in the world, it set the price for continental consumers in 'spot' and 'futures'.[69] Liverpool was also much the largest of Britain's emigrant ports: some 90 per cent of the five million emigrants (many from elsewhere in Europe) to the United States between 1870 and 1900 left from its dockside,[70] a valuable traffic that contributed significantly to the profits of Liverpool's numerous steamship lines.[71] Most travellers from North America, whether going to Britain or the continent, came via the city.

This spectacular growth created a wealthy patrician class of shipowners, the 'steamship kings of Water Street' (some twenty-five lines were based in the city), cotton brokers and merchants. But, as in so many of the port cities of the steam age, it exacted a high social price. Liverpool's population doubled in the half-century to 1911, reaching some three-quarters of a million. It was a magnet for unskilled labour drawn by the prospect of work in and around the docks. The result was a huge pool of 'surplus' labour that entrenched the system of 'casual' employment, far larger in Liverpool than in industrial towns. Some 20 per cent of Liverpool workers were 'casuals' in 1920; the industrial average was 5 per cent.[72] Low wages were further depressed by irregular work, often for no more than three days a week.[73] Poverty and overcrowding, made worse by clearance to make way for railways,[74] blighted the working-class districts close to the docks, forcing many to live in slum-like conditions. Unstable employment exacerbated the sectarian animosity between Catholics and Protestants, and before 1914 Liverpool was already notorious for sectarian violence and labour unrest.[75] The pattern of ethnic animosities may have helped to fuel the racial violence against blacks in 1919: West Indians and West Africans drawn to the city by the labour shortage of wartime.[76] But before 1914 commercial confidence remained high. New docks were constructed; and in 1911 the waterfront acquired in the Royal Liver Building, with its twin clock towers, the grandest symbol of its maritime history.

Both London and Liverpool were closely connected with continental ports: ships from the Netherlands, Belgium and Germany were among the most numerous arrivals in London in 1912. But it was Antwerp that illustrated most vividly the overlapping hinterlands and interconnected economies of north-western Europe before 1914. By some calculations Antwerp was the busiest port on the European mainland, although Hamburg and Rotterdam made similar claims. This rise had been meteoric. In early modern times, Antwerp had indeed been the great marketplace of northern Europe. But the separation of the Netherlands and rule by first Spain and then Austria had drastically reduced its commercial power. The key to Antwerp's commercial pre-eminence then (as later) was its position deep inland at the head of the Scheldt estuary with easy communication by water with northern France, the Netherlands and the Rhine. But the Dutch had used control of the mouth of the Scheldt to cripple its trade to the advantage of Amsterdam and Rotterdam. By the early nineteenth century, Antwerp was less a port than a manufacturing centre, making its living as a textile town. Three great changes transformed its prospects. Firstly, Belgium became an independent state in 1830, and one that needed a port. Secondly, as part of the terms of Belgian independence, the Netherlands was compelled in 1839 to open the Scheldt, subject to the payment of certain dues.[77] Thirdly, this freeing of the Scheldt coincided with the rapid advance of industrialization in Belgium, northern France and the Ruhr – all within the compass of Antwerp's network of waterways and (soon) railways. Trade and shipping expanded rapidly: the tonnage of shipping by some twenty-five times between 1860 and 1911.[78] The result, as in so many

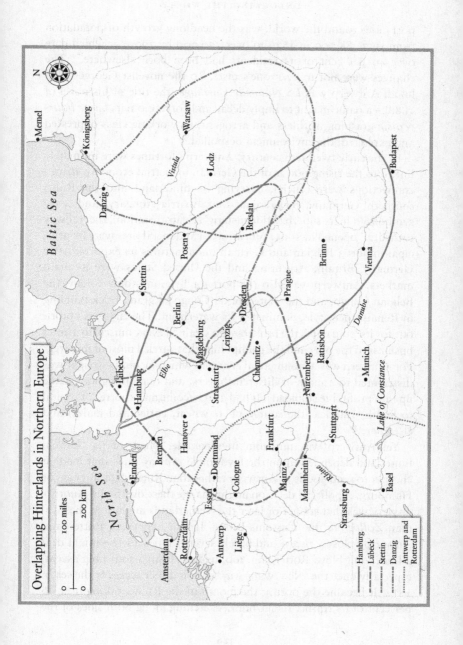

Overlapping Hinterlands in Northern Europe

	Hamburg
	Lübeck
	Stettin
	Danzig
	Antwerp and Rotterdam

port cities round the world, was the headlong growth of population from some 88,000 in 1846 to over 270,000 by 1900, at which date over 40 per cent of its residents had been born elsewhere.[79] The changes were not to everyone's taste. To the novelist Georges Eekhoud, Antwerp was *La Nouvelle Carthage* (the title of his novel of 1888) – a name meant to imply decay and corruption: its *haute bourgeoisie* grasping, ruthless and arrogant; its working class oppressed and exploited; the environment despoiled.[80]

By the early twentieth century, Antwerp's fortunes were intimately linked to the rising power of the German industrial economy. Its rail connections were crucial, carrying its hinterland into the Ruhr, southern Germany, Switzerland and Austria-Hungary, and aptly symbolized in its superb 'Middenstatie' (Central Station), the 'railway cathedral' opened in 1905. Wheat, wool and metal ores were its principal imports; Belgian and German manufactures its exports. After Germany, Britain, Argentina and the United States were its main markets. Antwerp was also the port for Belgium's only colony, the Belgian Congo, and the 'Entrepôt du Congo', a grand brick building in Renaissance style, dominated its waterfront. The city was notorious for its 'courtiers', the brokers who strained every muscle to attract business to the port and the tramp ships that carried most of its cargo. For Antwerp was a commercial centre in which incoming freight was distributed to a mass of different buyers, and outgoing goods made up into profitable shiploads. It had also become an exporter of capital to South America (the source of its wheat, coffee and maize) and elsewhere.[81]

Yet Antwerp was far from invulnerable. Much of its German hinterland depended upon the favourable railway rates that made it cheaper to send goods to Antwerp rather than Rotterdam, Bremen or Hamburg. A political decision might change these overnight. Another anxiety was that sooner or later the Netherlands might join the German *Zollverein*, the Customs Union. If that happened, Rotterdam, Antwerp's closest rival – and barely seventy miles away – might deal a knock-out blow. Rotterdam, too, had made an astonishing ascent, especially once the 'New Waterway' gave it direct access to the sea in 1872. It became the port at the mouth of the Rhine, taking over 90 per cent of its traffic. Its harbour, stretching along both sides of the

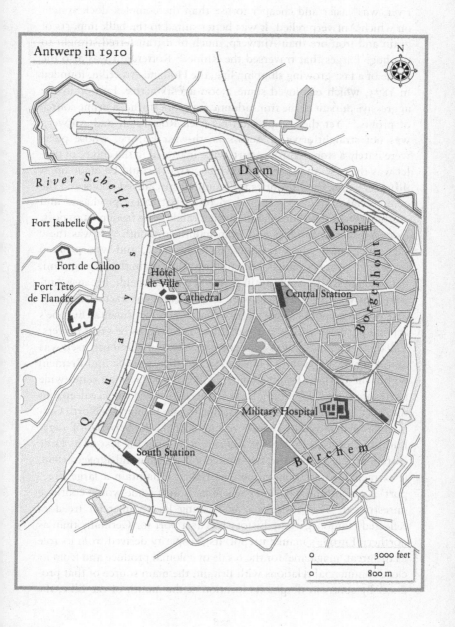

Antwerp in 1910

N

River Scheldt

Dam

Fort Isabelle

Fort de Calloo

Fort Tête
de Flandre

Q u a y s

Hôtel
de Ville

Cathedral

Hospital

Borgerhout

Central Station

Military Hospital

South Station

B e r c h e m

0   3000 feet

0   800 m

river, was easier and cheaper to use than the complex dock system on which Antwerp relied. It was better suited to the bulk imports of grain and iron ore than Antwerp, much of it transferred straight to the huge barges that traversed the Rhine.[82] Rotterdam was also the home of a fast-growing shipping line, the Holland-Amerika, founded in 1873, which employed some 2,000 agents across Europe in the aggressive pursuit of the transatlantic emigrant traffic, a prime source of profits.[83] Yet the competition between Rotterdam and Antwerp was not straightforward. Across north-west Europe, whose ports were barely a stone's throw apart, what mattered in the choice of outlet was the ease and speed with which cargoes could be made up at different ports, their facilities for handling specialized goods and the commercial apparatus required to bring particular producers and customers together: considerations that might vary from port to port, from product to product and from month to month.[84] It was these that determined where transactions were made, and who profited from them. Antwerp might have imported less grain than Rotterdam, but much of Rotterdam's grain was sold on the Scheldt, because Antwerp was where grain prices were set and grain contracts arranged.

It was a geopolitical peculiarity that two of continental Europe's leading ports lay within states that had no claim to be great powers. The third, Hamburg, was quite the opposite. But Hamburg itself was an oddity. It was a 'Free Hanseatic City' (like Lübeck and Bremen) within the German Empire, enjoying like all the German states wide local autonomy.[85] Hamburg had preserved its independence deep into the nineteenth century, before agreeing to join Bismarck's North German Confederation in 1866, forerunner of the *Kaiserreich* of 1871. But it had refused to join the *Zollverein*, fearing the loss of its large entrepôt trade behind a wall of protection. When it did agree in 1888, it extracted a huge concession: the right to maintain a large 'free-port' zone within its harbour where its transit trade would continue unrestricted. This insistence on keeping its commercial freedom reflected Hamburg's long history less as a port for Germany than as northern Europe's main entrepôt. Its prosperity derived from its role as the great 'magazine' for the resale of colonial produce and from its close commercial relations with Britain, the main source of that produce. By contrast, despite its location at the mouth of the Elbe, the

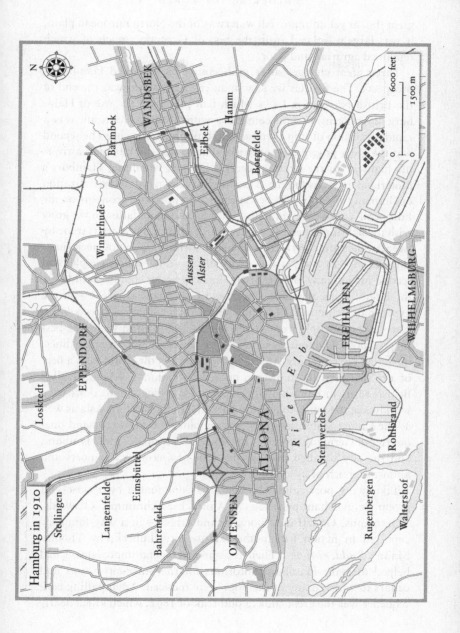

Hamburg in 1910

N

6000 feet
1500 m

Losktedt
Stellingen
Langenfelde
Bahrenfeld
Eimsbüttel
EPPENDORF
Winterhude
Barmbek
WANDSBEK
Eilbek
Hamm
Borgfelde
Aussen Alster
OTTENSEN
ALTONA
River Elbe
Steinwerder
FREIHAFEN
WILHELMSBURG
Rohbrand
Rugenbergen
Waltershof

great (but as yet unimproved) waterway of the North European plain, it was largely isolated from the rest of Germany, much of which remained agrarian and poor.

Three great changes after mid-century transformed Hamburg's prospects. The first (as we saw in an earlier chapter) was the end of the British Navigation Laws which had prevented the use of Hamburg shipping in its vital commerce with Britain. The result was a rapid expansion of ship-owning and -building in the city. The second was the great programme of works that turned the Elbe into a river-ine highway to the heart of central Europe, extending Hamburg's hinterland as far as Prague. The third was the rapid industrialization of Germany and its rise to become the most powerful economy on the European continent. Hamburg's trade and population now grew with the lightning speed characteristic of other port cities: its trade by twenty times after 1852; the tonnage in its harbour by fourteen times since 1860.[86] By 1913 it was a city of over one million people, and second in Germany only to Berlin. Its deep-water channel could take the largest ships afloat. Its docks had been vastly enlarged – at the expense of its poorest residents. When the new Freeport was built, some 24,000 people were driven out and left to find shelter as best they could.[87] Hamburg was home to several major shipping lines, including the Hamburg-Amerika, the largest in the world with a fleet of 175 steamers. Its shipyards, headed by Blohm and Voss, rivalled British yards in efficiency. Its trade and shipping connections were worldwide, to South America, the Pacific, India and East Asia as well as the United States, its main partner outside Europe. Around one-quarter of Germany's foreign investments were made from Hamburg, and the city handled over 40 per cent of Germany's imports and almost as much of its exports.[88]

Like many port cities, Hamburg was dominated by a close-knit group of merchant-patricians – Amsincks, Schramms, O'Swalds, Woermanns, Godeffroys, Slomans and others – in a way famously captured in fiction for another Hanse city, Lübeck, by Thomas Mann's *Buddenbrooks*. Their resistance to social improvement had helped to make Hamburg notorious for the inner-city slums and cellars to which many of the poor were reduced. An appalling con-sequence was the great cholera outbreak of 1892, which killed nearly

10,000 people, almost certainly brought to the city by its huge emigrant trade from eastern Europe, but triggered by Hamburg's dreadful sanitation (Bremen, nearby, with as large an emigrant trade, had only six deaths from cholera).[89] Hamburg's leaders were 'liberals' in politics, deeply attached to free trade, and acutely aware of how crucial to prosperity were their relations with Britain and the United States. Yet, by the early twentieth century they had also come to share the wider German view that they were engaged in a struggle for commercial survival in which the support of the state was vital. Albert Ballin (once an emigration agent) was the charismatic managing director of the Hamburg-Amerika who had master-minded its global expansion. Germany, he wrote in 1900, was 'a competitor in world markets', but 'in the brutal struggle of a nation for light and air, strength alone matters in the final analysis'.[90] Ballin, like other patricians in Hamburg, backed the building of a new battle fleet, aimed by Admiral Tirpitz against Britain, but drew back as Anglo-German relations became increasingly bitter. When the July crisis came, he convinced himself that Britain would stay out of the First World War and was devastated when it entered it. The catastrophic effect on Hamburg's trade and shipping would soon become clear.

It is easy to imagine that steam globalization was something exported from Europe to the rest of the world. Yet, of all the continents in 1914, Europe had been the most intensely globalized. This could be seen most vividly in the great outpouring of people and the growing practice of serial migration that cheap steamship fares encouraged, as well as the constant flow of travellers to and from distant parts of the globe. While many settlement countries in the temperate world (including the United States and Argentina) depended on European markets for their agricultural produce, Europe's richer economies had a much wider dependence on the rest of the world for raw materials and food, as buyers for their manufactures, and, increasingly, as destinations for their capital. Europe's port cities had the most extensive connections with every part of the world and relied on them for their port economies. European states had conquered and colonized in every continent or imposed their will under 'semi-colonial' conditions. The result was an intensive, if often one-sided, engagement with other peoples and cultures, and a vast compendium of ethnographic knowledge to reinforce, justify, romanticize or legitimate it. From the mid-century onwards, Europeans had become ever more conscious of their continent's 'central place' in the world (as their maps of the globe proclaimed), and its world-historical 'destiny' to improve and enlighten other civilizations and peoples – not least through Christianity. This global awareness was reaching an ever-wider audience by the turn of the century: the logic of world dominance became an imperative. It coincided with the realization that (as Albert Ballin put it) 'the whole world instead of continental Europe has become the arena of politics',[91] in which Europe's great powers had to compete to survive. The need to 'go global' had reached fever pitch.

Europe's port cities were the agents of its globalization, but also the scene of its disturbing effects. The torrent of incomers needing work and shelter; the squalor and horror of overcrowded 'rent-barracks' (the Hamburg term); the reliance on casual or seasonal labour; the ruthless power of ship-owning cartels; the resistance to social or sanitary improvement; the risks of epidemic disease; the vulnerability to boom and bust: all these could be seen in Europe as much as anywhere else – if mitigated slightly by a higher level of subsistence. They remind us that Europe's globalization, like globalizations elsewhere, was always a partial and uneven process that rewarded some but impoverished others, connected some places but 'disconnected' others, dismantled some prejudices but reinforced others. Globalization encouraged in Europe not only pride in its technological prowess but a growing conviction of cultural and even biological superiority, the elements of racism. Europe was the most urbanized of continents, but many regions remained overwhelmingly rural and an agrarian aristocracy, and its obsolete ethos, was embedded in the direction of its strongest military power. Europe was the most industrial of continents, but more than half its area was ruled by dynastic empires, not by governments answerable to representative assemblies. In the deepest irony of all, north-western Europe was the most intensely integrated region anywhere in the world both commercially and culturally. But it was the states in this region that were to fight the bloodiest war (thus far) in human history. That globalization would bring peace was indeed a 'great illusion' and, for all their wealth and patrician self-confidence, Europe's port-city elites had almost no influence in the great crisis that now overtook them.

THE GREAT DISLOCATION

The global order that plunged into war in 1914 was both newer and more fragile than the pomp and circumstance of its public face might suggest. 'Very few of us realise,' John Maynard Keynes was to remark in 1919, 'the intensely unusual, unstable, complicated, unreliable, temporary nature of the economic organisation by which Western Europe has lived for the last half century.'[92] The scale of commercial integration in north-western Europe, and the heavy dependence upon foreign trade for food and raw materials, were (except for Britain) comparatively recent developments. They depended upon open sea lanes, the ease of telegraphic communication and the passage of credits between buyers and sellers in all parts of the world. Much of the supply of overseas food came from regions only very recently settled: both the Canadian prairies and the Argentine pampas had been 'opened up' in the 1890s when rising prices made their grain production viable. South African gold production – one of the key resources for lubricating international finance – had only begun on the Rand in the late 1880s. The huge steamship fleets that carried the world's raw materials and foodstuffs to Europe, and manufactures back, had seen much of their growth in the last decade and a half before the outbreak of the First World War. Railway mileage had also gathered pace dramatically in the last decades of the nineteenth century: world railway mileage had increased from 130,361 in 1870 to 490,974 in 1900.[93] The banks and insurance companies that mobilized credit and capital had grown more assertive, and their physical presence more commanding – dominating the centre of so many port cities by the turn of the century.

In fact, it took some time to be clear that the war would lead (as the *Economist* had predicted) to a change in the world economy 'for all time'. In retrospect that moment came when the scale of the effort required to evict the Germans from the territory they had seized in the early months of the conflict first became apparent. Since neither Russia nor France had the industrial capacity to sustain the struggle (and had committed so much of their manpower to military service), it was necessary for London to support their purchases of vital war materials from the United States by advancing large credits on their behalf as well as its own. By mid-1917 this had created a vast ballooning of debts – to Britain and by Britain – with the United States as the ultimate creditor: a figure that eventually reached some $10 billion (roughly equivalent to around 40 per cent of all Britain's overseas assets in 1913). This was the invisible backdrop to the enormous physical damage of war: the loss of life, property, industry, infrastructure and crops; the diversion of production from exports to armaments (with the loss of markets and income); the destruction of shipping; the closure by blockade of Germany's overseas trade and of the zones it controlled. But if it was the need to recover from the terrible physical effects of the war that seemed most obvious, in fact – as it turned out – it was the 'invisible' problem of war debts that blocked the way to restoring the global economy of 1913.

The huge scale of indebtedness deranged the mechanisms of credit and capital that had sustained Europe's pre-war trade and its wider role in the global economy. Pre-war Britain, France and Germany had been creditor nations whose income from abroad helped pay for their imports and fund their investment in overseas infrastructure, mines and plantations. Critically, too, a healthy surplus in their balance of payments helped keep their currencies stable, and anchor them firmly to the global gold standard. The prospect of paying back huge sums in hard-to-earn dollars was certain to impose a drastic reduction in overseas income and destabilize currency values. What made things worse for France was the repudiation by the new Bolshevik regime in Russia of the large Tsarist debts to France, both in wartime and pre-war. It was this, and the cost of repairing the damage to French towns and villages, that made the scale of Germany's 'reparations' such an acrimonious issue in Paris, and between Paris, London and Washington. Neither Britain nor France wished to repay their debts to the United States without securing compensation from Germany. But the German economy itself was in extreme disarray, and in the political turbulence that followed the collapse of the

Kaiserreich, the governments of the new republic dared not agree to financial terms that would add impoverishment to defeat. The result was a pattern of impasse and crisis that lasted five years until the Dawes Agreement of 1924 paved the way for a comparatively modest reparations total, and – crucially – for the flow of American capital into Germany and eastern Europe.[94] Then the three debtor powers, Britain, France and Italy, reached a more or less amicable agreement with their American creditor.

The prospect for a return to economic 'normality' in Europe was the cue for the British attempt to restore London and sterling's old role in the world economy. Britain's return to gold in 1925 was a key part of London's plan to revive the pre-war patterns of trade and payments that had underpinned both Europe's own commercial integration and its advantageous relations with the rest of the world. It would encourage a return to the gold standard worldwide and resuscitate the outflow of European capital so beneficial to the growth of European exports. This hopeful scenario gained further encouragement from the promise of geopolitical stability. The Locarno Agreements of 1925 guaranteeing the new frontiers of western Europe marked – as it seemed – the reconciliation of Britain, France, Italy and Germany after a decade of conflict. Three years earlier, at the Washington Conference, all the leading powers, including Japan, had promised to respect China's integrity and not to seek any special sphere of influence there. At Lausanne in 1923 the Turks had accepted the loss of their Arab possessions to Britain and France as 'Mandatary Powers' under the League of Nations. As if in reaction to the threats and bluster of the 'old diplomacy' of pre-war times, the 1920s saw the blossoming of internationalist ideas, and a raft of institutions under the aegis of the League promoted the protection of minorities, better conditions for labour and the improvement of public health.

The late 1920s also saw a remarkable recovery in the level of world trade. The volume of seaborne trade rose by more than 50 per cent between 1920 and 1929.[95] Globalization resumed its course with the help of a huge infusion of American capital: US foreign investment rose to eight times its pre-war level at some $17 billion. Notoriously, it proved a false dawn. Unlike the pre-war decade, in the late 1920s commodity prices were falling, partly because the war had encouraged huge oversupply. The gush of American capital encouraged overlending in Europe. The New York Stock Exchange crash in 1929 was a major shock, but what turned it into an economic disaster was the lack of resilience in Germany's banking system – the unhappy product of the financial turbulence before 1925. There the fear that bank failure (the result of overlending) might trigger again the debacle of valueless paper experienced in 1923 led the Central Bank to impose a fierce deflation.[96] The effect was not to restore financial confidence but to open the door to capital flight and a run on the banks. As credit contracted, unemployment rose, incomes collapsed and markets imploded. Financial contagion spread round the world. Neither London nor New York could or would shore up the system. Britain's return to gold had damaged its export trade and weakened its balance of payments. Nor had London come near making good the immense overseas assets spent in the war, especially in dollars. Faced with its own financial Armageddon, the government in London abandoned the twin pillars of the restored global economy: it left the gold standard in September 1931 and threw out free trade. Across the Atlantic, where pockets were much deeper, the response was similar. Washington piled on protection against cheap foreign imports and took the dollar off gold. In a crisp diagnosis a Harvard professor remarked that there was no longer anywhere where a debtor country could be sure of selling its produce to escape depression. By 1932 most parts of the world reliant on the sale of raw materials and foodstuffs had seen their foreign earnings cut in half. The dynamic relationship between an industrial West and its suppliers and markets in the rest of the world on which the global economy – and much else – had been built collapsed in disorder.

In its place a new global regime emerged by default. It was strikingly different from the pre-1914 world in almost every respect. Instead of the gold standard, currencies were 'managed', deliberately devalued, allowed to 'float' or guarded by exchange controls. The widening sphere of free or free-ish trade gave way to protectionist blocs: Britain's sterling bloc of 'imperial preference'; the United States' dollar zone; the Japanese yen zone, soon to be expanded into the 'Greater East Asia Co-Prosperity Sphere'; Germany's 'barter' zone in central and eastern Europe; the almost closed economy of the Soviet

Union, now industrializing at a frantic pace. Countries outside these blocs also resorted to protective tariffs to encourage 'import substitution industrialisation'.[97] The great stream of migration of the pre-war decades (which had recovered significantly in the 1920s) was choked off: even Argentina, the most welcoming of economies, imposed severe restrictions in 1932.[98] In fact, desperate reverse migration back to Europe from depression-hit primary producers became the pattern. The export of capital from the West followed much the same course. In Britain, for long the wellspring of foreign investment, government borrowing absorbed much of home savings and what went overseas was largely restricted to sterling-bloc countries.[99] American foreign investment shrank precipitately after 1930.[100] Far from flowing 'out', capital abroad was as likely to be repatriated to earn more at home. Whereas the share of the world's output taken by trade had risen dramatically up to 1914, in the 1930s it contracted sharply. Indeed, expert opinion now assumed that, with the spread of industrialization around the world, this reduction would become a permanent feature. 'No one can yet tell whether the march towards world integration will be resumed,' sighed an American economist in 1939.[101]

Some of the most painful effects were felt in those regions beyond Europe which had concentrated heavily on producing for the world market. For grain farmers in Canada, coffee and sugar growers in the Caribbean and Brazil, rice farmers in Burma, pastoralists in Australia, the sudden collapse in prices, often by as much as 50 per cent, threatened not just a fall in income but loss of land, livelihood and status. An investigation in the British West Indies revealed a picture of grinding poverty worsened by the contraction of the sugar economy.[102] In colonial Tanganyika (today's mainland Tanzania), declining employment on the sisal plantations cut down demand for food grains and cattle: their prices fell too.[103] Depression helped fuel a huge new round of political unrest in India in 1930, and the 'Saya San' rebellion in Burma in 1931, where native Burman farmers were often deeply indebted to Indian lenders. Across the colonial world the implicit economic bargain that underlay acquiescence in alien rule came under intense strain where it was not broken already.[104]

This sudden fracturing of the global economy was quickly echoed in the geopolitical realm. The brief experiment in Anglo-American partnership collapsed in the wake of economic disaster. When Washington raised tariffs and devalued the dollar (by going off gold), London despaired of meeting its dollar debt and defaulted. The response of Congress was the Johnson Act of 1934, barring future loans to defaulting countries – a move plainly aimed against Britain. The League of Nations, as a 'coalition of the willing' against any aggressor, depended on the willingness of Britain and France to risk their own interests in the common cause. Over Manchuria (1931) and Ethiopia (1934–5), they preferred acquiescence to conflict. Before 1914 the huffing and puffing of the European great powers had disguised an acceptance (tragically lacking in July 1914) that the world system imposed a form of 'competitive coexistence', limiting the gains any power could expect. After 1930 the 'have-not' powers, Germany, Italy and Japan, rejected the existing world order in favour of revolutionary change – a rejection shared, in principle at least, by the Soviet Union. Since the American view of Europe's colonial empires was ambivalent at best, the defence of the status quo fell upon Britain and France, partners divided by mutual mistrust. If global trade was conducted before 1914 as if almost entirely oblivious of diplomatic squabbles and scuffles, in the 1930s the threat of trade wars and tariffs, quotas and boycotts, civil wars and occupations, created an increasingly fraught and fearful mood. In a revolutionary age the landmarks of geopolitical order were alarmingly fragile.

This was the setting to which the world's major port cities now had to adapt. All were vulnerable to the sudden loss of trade which brought mass unemployment and poverty. In Liverpool over 100,000 were put out of work; in Hamburg nearly twice as many.[105] The pattern was similar in port cities as far afield as Montreal and Adelaide.[106] A gradual recovery set in by 1936, but it masked a series of structural shifts that affected some port cities more than others. The most obvious was the drastic change in the terms of trade: foodstuffs and raw materials declined sharply in value against manufactures. Industrial countries could afford to import a much larger quantity of primary produce. In Britain that helped London – an 'importing' port – and worked against Liverpool. Some staple exports now lost their markets: Lancashire cottons were a prime example. Demand in

India, long their principal buyer, sank by three-quarters or more in the course of the decade. Liverpool had been their 'export' port. Britain's coal trade was another victim of change – in part because a growing share of world shipping was switching to fuel oil. More fundamental still, perhaps, was the increasing power of the state, and its intervention in questions of finance and trade that directly affected port-city interests.

The most important of these (as we have seen already) was the almost universal recourse to protective tariffs to shield local industry. In many cases, of course, manufacturing expanded around port cities themselves: in Liverpool, Bombay, Shanghai, Sydney, Melbourne and Port Elizabeth among many. Australia industrialized behind a tariff increase of 80 per cent.[107] The old preponderance of trade and shipping was diluted; a new industrial workforce sprang up. Where states controlled the money supply, credit and foreign exchange, much of the old freedom of port-city merchants and bankers was cut down. Tariffs and preferences came to dictate their choice of markets. Mergers, cartels and price agreements between shipowners became commonplace. Many shipping fleets (though not the British) received government subsidies.[108] A more subtle shift was under way. Almost everywhere (except in cash-strapped colonies like Nigeria or the Sudan) the size of governments grew. Their bureaucracies swelled. Where the capital lay inland, port-city influence declined. Where coastal cities housed central or (as in Australia) provincial governments, industry and bureaucracy now predominated. Across much of the world, the rise of 'inland' politics was also the rise of nationalism, in search of a distinctive identity and deeply suspicious of 'cosmopolitan' values or outsiders' interests. The classic function of the 'globalizing' port city – to receive 'foreign' influences and transmit them internally – was out of place in a world absorbed in the struggle for racial, ethnic or national solidarity, where doctrinal or cultural conformity was often strictly policed. Where port cities lacked external protection, as the case of Smyrna revealed, catastrophic consequences could follow.

These global trends concealed wide variation. Some port cities, like Hamburg, were subjected to draconian control: others far less so. Some grew prosperous on technological change: American demand for rubber tyres was good for Singapore. The rise in the gold price (when the gold standard collapsed) was an unexpected bonanza that brought a surge of new wealth (and imports) to South African ports. Depression brought revolution in both Argentina and Brazil. In Brazil conflict within the ruling oligarchies brought the overthrow of the 'Old Republic' and led to a new-style economy of exchange control, tariffs and industrialization.[109] But in Argentina, the landowning elite and its port-city allies imposed an authoritarian regime that clung to the old staple exports of grain and beef, and rejected industrialization in favour of what its critics saw as abject dependence on its principal market, Great Britain. The Roca–Runciman Pact in 1933 assured Argentinian beef a place in the (now-protected) British market in return for the promise that British investment income from the railways and utilities would not be imprisoned by exchange controls.[110] As the decade advanced, some port cities became trapped in a war zone: Barcelona in 1936, Shanghai by 1937. Others, like Hamburg and Liverpool, profited from programmes of rearmament. But what most had in common was to find themselves hostages to political or geopolitical fortune.

'THE OLD LADY GOES OFF TOMORROW'

This phrase was the coded warning that the Bank of England ('The Old Lady of Threadneedle Street') was about to abandon the gold standard. To John Maynard Keynes, it was an act of liberation by which London could lead the revival of world trade and escape the savage contraction imposed by the gold standard. He expected much of the world, including Germany and central Europe, to join the 'Sterling Group' of countries, so that sterling not gold would be the international unit of value.[111] It proved a vain hope. But to Moritz Bonn, an Anglophile German Jew, the influential academic scion of a Frankfurt banking family, leaving the gold standard was an act of gross abdication, 'the last day of the age of economic liberalism'.[112] Far from offering a route out of impoverishment, it presaged the rise of autarkic empires and states and would not end well. Thrown back upon their own natural resources, the less well-endowed among these – the 'have-nots' – could no longer improve their position through trade. Indeed, their ideological world view ruled out any concession to the discredited system of global free trade, seen by left and right alike as the confidence trick of cosmopolitan finance. The only escape from economic inequality would be to seize more resources by predation or war.[113] By the mid-1930s this was an outcome that seemed increasingly likely. It was symbolic, perhaps, that by then steam power was no longer the talisman of progress. Now it was the aeroplane, a child of the oil age. In the era of autarky, so it was feared, 'the bomber would always get through'.

Yet globalization had not come to a halt, except in the sense of commercial integration. With China and India in turmoil, its disruptive effects seemed more apparent than ever.[114] Meanwhile the apparatus of a Europe-centred world order was still much in evidence. European-owned shipping still dominated the sea lanes, except in East Asia. European trading companies still managed much of world trade. Above all, the colonial and semi-colonial regimes fashioned in the century before 1914 largely remained in place, and with them control over the commercial orientation of much of the world. New forms of global modernity were exerting their influence: radio, cinema and the increasing circulation of teachers and students between East and West. As liberalism wilted in the firestorm of the Great Depression, Marxism and Fascism, both European creeds, claimed new adherents in every part of the globe – and offered global visions of irresistible change. It could even be argued that the economic imperatives of globalization were becoming stronger than ever. Technological change and the dependence of manufactures upon an ever-larger number of raw material inputs, urged the American economist Eugene Staley, demanded a 'planetary' economy. In the 'Paleotechnic era' of coal and iron, steamship and railway, independence and self-sufficiency might have been possible. In the 'Neotechnic' age of electricity and alloys, radio and automobiles, diesel-electric locomotives and aeroplanes, 'isolation and national hostilities are forms of deliberate technological suicide'.[115] But at the end of the decade, it remained to be seen whether new wars of conquest could remake the globe that steam had created.

9

Lessons from Smyrna

GIAOUR IZMIR

No port city in the interwar years suffered a harsher fate than Smyrna (modern Izmir). Smyrna had been a port since Antiquity. In early modern times it flourished as the terminus of the caravan route bringing Persian silks across Anatolia for shipment to Europe. In the eighteenth century its main trading partner had been Marseilles and French merchants were prominent in its expatriate community.[1] But its great days were to come after 1830. With the Ottoman Empire in a crisis from which its recovery was uncertain, the European powers forced it to concede new freedoms to its Christian subjects and open up its economy to European merchants. Smyrna was the chief beneficiary of both these changes.

Much of its success was due to geography. With its large sheltered harbour and convenient location at the junction of the shipping lanes to the Black Sea, the Aegean and the eastern Mediterranean, and its wide Anatolian hinterland, Smyrna was perfectly placed to become the chief entrepot of the region just at the time when the Ottoman Empire's foreign trade began to grow rapidly. 'Smyrna . . . is the main point of commercial contact betwixt Europe and Asia,' remarked A. W. Kinglake, the traveller and historian.[2] Its exports rose by more than three times in value between 1839 and 1862. 'Smyrna is the great steam centre for the whole Levant,' reported M'Culloch's *Commercial Dictionary* in 1869, visited by the main shipping lines and by steamers from Liverpool.[3] During the 1850s and 1860s two railway lines were driven into the interior to carry the cotton and dry fruit that were Smyrna's main exports.[4] The city's commercial life was largely in the hands of Greek (i.e. adherents to the Greek Orthodox

Church), Armenian and Jewish merchants, with Greeks increasingly taking the leading role. Greek sailors and traders managed much of the traffic of the whole maritime zone from Odessa in the north to Alexandria in the south. 'The Greeks are the Yankees of the Levant,' wrote the American minister in Constantinople in 1857.[5] Indeed, with the creation of an independent Greek state in 1830, and the Ottoman sultans' commitment to reform and 'modernization', Greeks *within* the Ottoman Empire began to display more and more ethnic awareness, further encouraged by their contact with Europe. Smyrna itself acquired a degree of municipal self-government, and the typical attributes of a successful port city: an expanded harbour; a grand promenade; hotels and public buildings. It acquired the sobriquet the 'Paris of the Levant'.[6] Far more prosperous and cosmopolitan than Athens, it became the cultural metropolis of the whole Greek world. To the Turks it was 'Giaour Izmir' – 'Infidel Izmir'.

This precocious modernity and the relative freedom enjoyed by the port-city elite depended upon two vital defences. The first was the reluctance of the Ottoman government to risk the displeasure of the Western powers, especially Britain, its principal champion. The second was the curious legal protection provided by 'Capitulations' – the agreements by which the Ottomans had granted privileged status to resident Westerners since the mid-sixteenth century. Under Capitulations, Westerners were subject not to Ottoman jurisdiction but only to that of their own consuls – the obvious parallel was with treaty port China. They paid no taxes to the Ottoman government. But Capitulations were open to massive abuse. By late in the century, of a total population of some 200,000, between a fifth and a quarter claimed to be 'foreigners' – a status they obtained through the complaisance (or worse) of European consuls (one Italian consul complained that of the 6,400 'Italians' in the city, hardly any spoke the language).[7] Smyrna was thus a strange 'semi-colonial' city in which the Muslim population were second-class citizens, and whose cosmopolitan character rested on the willingness of the Western powers to protect its wealthy expatriate community and uphold the fictitious foreignness of its merchant elite.

Even before 1914 this had come into question. The Young Turk revolution of 1908 brought into power an army-based nationalist regime hardened by defending the Empire's vulnerable Balkan possessions (it was no coincidence that Mustapha Kemal, later Kemal Ataturk, was a Macedonian Muslim). To make matters worse, Russia's century-long advance in the Caucasus, and the creation of the Bulgarian state, pushed before them waves of Muslim refugees, many of whom were deposited in western Anatolia, a restless, resentful, impoverished population.[8] One million came from Bulgaria alone. By the turn of the century Smyrna's environs had become increasingly lawless, a situation made worse by the factional struggles of the revolutionary period.[9] The outbreak of war in October 1914 unleashed a whirlwind for Greeks and other minorities. For the Armenians of Anatolia it brought genocide. But for the Smyrna Greeks eventual victory by the Entente Powers promised something else: the prospect of union between much of Asia Minor ('Ionia') and mainland Greece, with Ottoman Turkey reduced to a rump in the Anatolian interior. This was the programme on which the victorious Allies agreed in the Treaty of Sèvres of August 1920: to destroy for ever Turkish command of the Straits and to create a sprawling new kingdom of Greece. There was one great flaw: the armed Turkish resistance led by Mustapha Kemal. Faced with yet another unwelcome commitment, and already at odds over their Near Eastern interests, Britain and France left Greece to defend its ill-gotten gains. The result was catastrophe. By 1922 the Greek armies in Anatolia had been broken and fell back on Smyrna. As they fled the city, it was torched by the Turks and non-Muslims were massacred. The surviving Greek population was expelled or resettled in Greece under the population exchange that followed the Treaty of Lausanne in 1923.[10] In the new Turkish Republic economic nationalism was the rule and Smyrna (now Izmir) dwindled from being the great Levantine entrepôt to a modest industrial centre sheltered by tariffs.

Smyrna's grim fate starkly reveals the uneasy foundations on which port-city fortunes and freedoms were built. However prosperous and privileged, the merchant elite in the city could not hope to control the turbulent politics of the wider region around them. To its Muslim majority they were strangers at best. Once great-power protection was lost, and Greece was no substitute, the city was desperately vulnerable in the inflamed conditions of the war and its aftermath. It became the plaything of nationalist ambition and geopolitical chance. But extreme as it was, Smyrna's harsh history allows us to see the conditions for success and survival of other port cities in the globalization century after 1830.

STEAM GLOBALIZATION AT WORK

Across that century between 1830 and 1930 two great systems were at work. The first was Free Trade – the opening by force or self-interest of the world beyond Europe to European influence, commercial and cultural. The second was Empire. For this was the century in which vast tracts of the world were occupied, ruled or informally dominated by Europeans or by Euro-Americans in Europe's western annexe. What bound these systems together was steam. It was steam that conferred on Europe and its daughter societies an extraordinary disparity in economic and physical power, reversing the long equilibrium between civilizations and continents. Steam power was the catalyst for a host of ancillary technologies in metallurgy, engineering, communications and chemicals. By arming Europeans with cheaply made textiles with which to exploit the new markets first opened up by alcohol, opium and guns, steam helped to create new kinds of exchange and new zones of commerce. Self-sufficient economies where imports had been few became 'primary producers', selling raw materials and foodstuffs for 'must-have' manufactures. Steam hugely increased the volume and frequency of movement and migration on rivers, along coasts, across oceans and then overland, supplying the labour required to exploit 'new' lands and resources. The relative ease and speed of connection by steam whetted the appetite of audiences in all parts of the world for information and knowledge – an appetite which steam printing, the telegraph and the subsidized steam mail-ship existed to satisfy. And by spreading the worldwide demand for coal, steam promoted a bulk export from Britain that cut shipping costs to and from ports as far distant as Buenos Aires and Bombay.

Of course, steam globalization had other dimensions not so

obviously benign. Steam power enabled the European states and their North American offspring to deliver armed force in locations that were either inaccessible in the sailing-ship era, or reachable only at far greater cost. It was steamships driving their way up the Yangzi that forced the Qing to agree to open their ports in 1842. It was steamships that allowed Britain to shuffle an army of less than 300,000 men (British and Indian) between global commitments tens of thousands of miles apart. Steam facilitated their conquest of Burma, as well as France's colonization of North Africa and Indo-China, and the Dutch 'pacification' of the Outer Islands of the Indonesian archipelago. Speed and penetration up hitherto inaccessible rivers, across seas and, when military railways were laid, over land transformed the striking power of colonial armies, as much, perhaps, as superior weaponry. The railway was deliberately used to entrench British rule on the Indian subcontinent: much of the network had a primarily military purpose. It was also the critical means whereby frontiers of white settlement were rapidly filled in with large numbers of newcomers.[11] Against such mechanized migrations, indigenous resistance had little chance of success. They faced an adversary whose supply lines and manpower must have seemed inexhaustible.

This aspect of globalization is a reminder that the commercial benefits that the word conjures up came at a cost. Free trade was meant to propagate peace. Yet the ninety years between 1830 and 1914 were scarcely a peaceful era. There were nearly three hundred wars (on a huge range of scales) across the globe in this period.[12] Even in Europe there were over 500,000 battle deaths, nearly 800,000 if we include the war between Russian and Turkey in 1877–8. Nearly 700,000 died in the American Civil War. No reliable count exists for the hundreds of wars in Asia, Africa, North and South America, Australia and New Zealand between local combatants, or between colonial and indigenous forces. Moreover, the effects of war and conquest reached far beyond the number of battle deaths. The displacement of peoples, the destruction of food supplies, the disruption of trade and (the usual accompaniment of colonial wars) the spread of disease carried off far larger numbers.[13] One careful estimate that excludes the Americas but includes famine deaths not directly attributable to conquest suggests a loss of indigenous life amounting to over 25 million people outside India, and a further 28 million in India itself, for the period from the mid-eighteenth century up to 1914.[14] The Taiping Rebellion in China against the Qing monarchy (1850–64) cost the lives of between 20 and 30 million people.[15] This was a world in which the extraordinary fertility of European peoples seemed in graphic contrast to the stagnation, decline or (as in North America and Australasia) the expected disappearance of non-European populations.

Port cities performed a wide range of roles. In Asia and Africa they were where non-Western peoples would encounter in full force the globalizing influences exerted from Europe. Port cities were also a 'bridgehead' where outsiders (in the nineteenth century this included Indians, Chinese and a scattering of other peoples as well as Europeans) sought to push their way into promising hinterlands to find commodities, land, converts, work or just loot. For commercial, military or administrative purposes they were the centres of 'command and control'. They collected local information and recruited local allies, while eagerly touting the prospects of gain to merchants, investors, migrants and missionaries 'at home'. They had to compete against one another for public attention and material support. They were also the funnels for thousands (even millions) of settlers, injected into the interior along waterways or railway lines, running in parallel like those from New York or like a vast metal fan in the case of Buenos Aires. In the temperate world, Quebec, Montreal, Boston, New York, Baltimore, New Orleans, San Francisco, Rio, Santos, Montevideo and Buenos Aires supplied the Americas; Melbourne, Sydney, Adelaide, Brisbane, Wellington, Auckland, Christchurch and Dunedin, Australasia; Cape Town, Port Elizabeth, East London and Durban (modestly), southern Africa; and Algiers and Oran, French possessions in North Africa. In the tropical world, Rangoon, Penang and Singapore, and smaller ports in the Caribbean and South Pacific, handled the flow of Chinese and Indians, some to settle, more to work for a term as migrant labour. And since port cities supplied many of the needs of their agrarian interiors – equipment, machinery, clothing, credit, capital, education, news and entertainment – as well as packing and processing their produce for export, they tended to grow at disproportionate speed and retain many of the migrants who arrived on their docks.

Port cities were the hinge between specific places and regions and the global transformations unleashed by the huge growth of trade, the rise of industrialized manufacture, the vast streams of migration and the partition of continents. They rode a roller coaster of fortune in which not all won prizes – or kept those won earlier. Over the past two millennia innumerable port cities have declined to the state of archaeological sites or mere shrunken remnants of lost urban splendour. Choked by silt in their harbours or (in the case of some inland port cities) swallowed by the desert, they could disappear from the map. For others their fate was prosaic: the melting away of the mercantile promise that had once drawn shipping, traders, professionals, artisans, labourers, slave-sellers and slaves. Kingston, Jamaica, had once been the base from which English merchants conducted a contraband trade with a 'closed' Spanish America. It was also the capital of Britain's richest colony in the eighteenth century, a great sugar-and-slave plantation. By the 1830s and 1840s both sources of wealth had all but dried up, and Kingston decayed. When sugar was king in the Brazilian economy, Recife and Salvador were the cities that mattered. First gold and then coffee sucked wealth away to the south, to Rio and São Paulo. Before 1820, Charleston had been the queen city of the Slave South. But agrarian decline in South Carolina, and perhaps the lack of inland railway connections, had created a sense of commercial decline even before the Civil War crisis. New Orleans took the crown – though not for long. Madras had been the pivot of British power in India before 1760. A hundred years later Calcutta and Bombay had made it a commercial backwater. Penang, for thirty years the main base of British commercial ambition in South East Asia, survived better, but soon languished by comparison with unstoppable Singapore – a shift explained partly at least by the Suez Canal and steam shipping. When they imposed the Nanjing Treaty on China in 1842, the British expected that Ningpo and Amoy would become key treaty ports: but Shanghai soon swept the board and reduced Canton – long China's front door to the world – to secondary status. Most of the treaty ports on China's coast or along its rivers soon lapsed into commercial stagnation.[16]

Success – or survival – required a mixture of blessings, not all in
the hands of port-city elites. When port cities were mainly entrepôts,
exchanging goods between distant ports rather than with their agrarian neighbours – a common enough pattern before 1800 – their own
naval power or that of a sovereign protector was a vital resource.
Where their chief business lay in finding and serving a profitable hinterland, and remaking its commerce to a port-centred design, other
needs became crucial. The first was a hinterland whose products
enjoyed universal demand, or were varied enough to survive soil
exhaustion, competition from elsewhere, devastating disease or the
indifference of consumers. Much might depend on the energy with
which port-city entrepreneurs reconnoitred fresh tracts for settlement
or rapid conversion into cash-crop cultivation. Thus merchants in
Wellington, New Zealand, took the lead in surveying and settling the
Manawatu, a marshy plain a hundred miles north of the city, in the
1880s.[17] But as Smyrna's history reminds us, a profitable hinterland
also required effective policing against internal predators or outside
invaders. A more familiar danger was the rise of an inland regime
hostile to the political influence and 'cosmopolitan' values of port-
city societies, or one driven by slump towards a closed economy.[18]
Most port cities had faced this challenge successfully before 1930, but
many were overwhelmed by it in the decades that followed. Indeed,
the challenge might come in a more insidious guise. An expanding
port city, where dock work and processing encouraged the beginnings of industrial enterprise, would draw in a new labour force
whose religious or political sympathies might be at odds with those
of the city's ruling elite, becoming natural allies of its inland opponents. Sometimes the power of inland society could be irresistible. In
New Orleans' case, external influence from 'Liberal Europe' was
blunted by the fact that its hinterland had been colonized physically
and culturally from the slave-holding Upper South. Far from being a
cosmopolitan 'bridgehead', New Orleans was captive to the values of
the slave-owning elite, and was forced to follow it over the cliff.

But the immediate priority of port-city politics was to defend the
port and its trade. Almost every port city suffered recurrent fears of
decline. The threat might come from the emergence of rivals: merchants in Bombay cast nervous glances at the rise of Karachi. New

railway connections might favour a parvenu port or a 'new' commodity (gold, diamonds, tin, rubber) could 'make' a new port, dragging trade and shipping away: hence the sudden emergence of San Francisco and Melbourne. Changes in sea lanes, like those that followed the general adoption of steam or, more dramatically, the opening of the Suez and Panama Canals, were good news for some ports, bad news for others. But perhaps the most constant anxiety arose from the pressure to improve the port and protect its approaches against shoals and sandbars, riverine silt or the other obstructions thrown up by a dynamic environment. When this was combined with the need to cater for mercantile shipping growing rapidly larger in volume and deeper in draught, it posed a problem not just of cost (for dredging and dock-building) but of reconciling the self-interest of a wide range of parties: shipping lines and their agents; import and export merchants; property owners and public authorities; railway companies and the suppliers of dock labour; inland producers. To overcome these divisions required an elaborate micro-politics of marriage alliance, club friendships, tacit business favours and hierarchical deference, as well as the institutional support of chambers of commerce and municipal bodies. The special demands of Liverpool's harbour lay behind its early adoption of a 'port authority' to provide overall management. In Singapore the shared sense of dependence on its entrepôt trade drove the colonial authorities to 'nationalize' its main port facilities. But political power could obstruct as well as advance port-city ambitions. The prospects of Norfolk, Virginia, as an outlet for the trans-Appalachian interior were blocked by the jealousy of commercial interests in towns on the Fall Line – the break of inland navigation – fearful of seeing their trade migrate to the coast. Virginia's failure to build a railway from Norfolk to the Ohio was to cost the state dear – to the profit of Baltimore, which made the connection.[19]

Yet for all the port cities whose histories we have followed, the local environment was only one part of a larger equation. Their safety and prosperity were also closely bound up with the wider geopolitical regime – the distribution of power and authority across the world. Between 1830 and 1914 that regime had been exceptionally favourable to their interests. The European great powers had localized their conflicts within Europe and generally avoided open combat between themselves beyond it. Ideologically, they shared a common allegiance to the sanctity of private property, the legitimacy of colonialism and the necessity of the 'civilizing mission'. They supported intervention in the extra-European world to protect foreign lives and property so long as it preserved the balance of interests between them. Of course, tensions persisted and great-power diplomacy lurched from crisis to crisis: jostling and sabre-rattling were endemic along the innumerable fault lines where their spheres of interference made contact. But as late as June 1914 no European state seemed willing to risk the continental balance of power for colonial gain.

Part of the reason could be found in the peculiar shape of the *global* power balance. Since Trafalgar in 1805, Britain had enjoyed an extraordinary maritime primacy. Thinly spread as it was, the Royal Navy was still strong enough to overawe any challenger. The world's sea lanes might suffer local disruption by pirates or the occasional blockade but seaborne commerce enjoyed overall a remarkable freedom from the wars and exclusions of the mercantilist era. Few of the local rebellions and wars that littered the century were allowed to intrude upon the main ocean highways. The huge growth of trade in the North and South Atlantic, the volume of shipping between Europe and Asia, or the migrant flows out of Europe, India and China, would not have been viable without this *pax maritima*. Britain's seaborne primacy was also a vital accessory to enforcing free trade against closed economies, and discouraging recourse to financial default or the expropriation of assets. In the Western Hemisphere, the shield of British sea power drastically lowered the costs of external defence for all American states. In Asia it was the ultimate guarantor of the British imperium in India, and of treaty-port safety in China. And, since free trade was the ruling ideology of Victorian Britain, there was a striking alignment between the outlook and interests of the prime global power and those of the port-city world. The First World War was a brutal test of resilience for this global regime. Despite revolutions in Russia and China, the late 1920s saw its brief Indian summer warmed by the friendship between London and Washington. But a hard winter soon followed. By the late 1930s the geopolitical scaffolding of steam's global economy had collapsed altogether.

A TALE OF TWO WORLDS

These were general conditions. Steam globalization connected a world many of whose interior regions were far from peaceful but whose coasts and sea lanes were remarkably safe. Its effects were uneven, incomplete and commercially volatile. Viewing its impact through the history of port cities reveals the huge variations in what is too easily imagined as a uniform process of economic, political and cultural integration – a world growing 'flat'.

Economically, two quite different patterns can be seen. Across the temperate word beyond Europe, in the Americas and Australasia, globalization brought a gradual *convergence* between the living standards and lifestyles of their settler populations and those of their homelands in western Europe. The settler zones were converted with astonishing rapidity into integral parts of the global economy, while the benefits of their high wages and cheap food slowly diffused across Europe from west to east as more emigrants came and tariff barriers fell. Their wealth of natural resources was part of the story. But just as important was the fact that the invading populations were free to impose a commercialized 'developmental' economy from the start, with private property rights, the apparatus of credit and capital and, not least, widespread access to steam technology. This freedom was bought dearly at others' expense: by the ruthless elimination of indigenous land claims (and often indigenous people); and the no less ruthless deployment of slave labour to achieve the 'instant' conversion to a cash-crop economy – in the Deep South and Brazil. The transfer in rough and ready form of western Europe's commercial institutions to the settler frontier opened the way for the extension of credit and infusions of capital to hasten the building of networks of transport and maintain the headlong pace of colonization and conquest. In the 1920s and 1930s a pioneer fringe of white colonization was still to be found in northern Canada, the American West, Brazil, Argentina, South-Central Africa, Australia and Soviet Siberia; and its Chinese counterpart in contested Manchuria.[20]

In the non-settler world the pattern was starkly different. Here the Western agents of steam globalization found willing allies among indigenous merchants, indeed relied upon them to reach consumers and cultivators. But far from being able to impose wholesale the laws and customs of Western-style commerce, they faced regimes of labour and property rights that were highly resistant to instant conversion and agrarian economies where 'free' land was usually absent or scarce. Even in India, where the colonial ruler was theoretically committed to an open economy, the forced imposition of Western-style capitalism was out of the question. Instead, the scope of commercial outsiders was strictly controlled lest they endanger the Raj's relations with the agrarian elite – the bedrock of its rule. Consequently, Western capital could only be enticed on the vast scale needed for railways by a government guarantee. India's railways were built to government plan and (by comparison with the United States or even Argentina) its network was miserly. In China almost no lines were laid before 1900. Port-city merchants could profit from the freedom to import British textiles and undercut local production. But they lacked the means to be more ambitious and preferred instead to rely on building a series of niche economies whose produce was favoured by their external connections. That left most of the burden of internal development to Indian merchants or government: neither had adequate funds for the task. The persistence of famine in India, China and Russia was eloquent testimony to the gross limitations of steam's global economy across vast swathes of the globe, and to its distorting effects on the local market for food. Thus, while the settler world converged with north-western Europe, most of Afro-Asia, despite limited gains, diverged ever further in incomes and living standards from the West – and continued to do so until the late twentieth century. Even in Europe, 'modern' port cities could be found a stone's throw away from regions of intense rural poverty – in Spain, Italy, the Balkans and Russia – a poverty little helped, sometimes deepened, by the global economy. Indeed, all round the rim of the 'globalized' world still lay a vast periphery of shifting cultivators, land-hungry peasants, impoverished reservoirs of migrant labour and the battered remains of displaced indigenous peoples.

The record of port cities as transmitters of European values, habits, lifestyles and beliefs was equally mixed. In the settler world, where transmission should have been easy, cultural deference was qualified by the comforting prejudice – common to settler communities – that the 'old world' was decadent, class-bound and stagnant. Where European attitudes conflicted with settler self-interest – as they did over slavery or the eviction of indigenes – repudiation was fierce. In the non-settler world, as we saw in India, South East Asia and China, local port-city elites were highly receptive to messages of economic and political freedom, but resolute in preserving the language, religion, family structures and lineages on which their status depended. They proved adept at applying imported techniques – the printing press, Western-style schooling, associations and lobbies – to speed the cultural mobilization of their own ethnic or religious communities. All over the world port cities were the cradle of creole societies in which a myriad of different ethnicities constructed 'modern' identities by the selective adaptation of the foreign and familiar. More often than not, their political sympathies had been progressively alienated by racial exclusion. By the mid-twentieth century many if not most had been lost to view under the mantle of nationalism. Singapore and embattled Hong Kong are among the survivors; conflict-wrecked Aden a reminder of the costs of absorption within a failed nation state.[21]

A less visible legacy can be found scattered along the sea lanes and railway lines that steam power created. Steamships and riverboats, harbour works and railway junctions, telegraph offices and hotels, and all the apparatus of steam-powered mobility required whole cadres of specialists – engineers and mechanics, engine-drivers and fitters, clerks and scribes, cooks and waiters – often unavailable in the immediate locality. As aliens and outsiders this new labour force was settled in enclaves, cantonments or 'railway colonies', under the shelter of European domination or colonial control. At Atbara in the Sudan, its main railway junction, the skilled artisans included Greeks, Maltese, Egyptian Copts, Poles, Albanians, Syrians and Indians.[22] The 'Abyssinian Quarter' was where the prostitutes lived.[23] Goans supplied ship stewards and waiters along the East African coast, and then moved inland to work for the railways, or as professionals and businessmen.[24] Mixed-race Anglo-Indians, settled in 'railway colonies', filled the skilled occupations on India's railways. Unofficial incomers followed the new lines of rail where opportunity beckoned, opening shops, offering credit, supplying the services, respectable or otherwise, wanted in the new urban settlements that steam propagated. These were petty migrations, the infinite fragments of a newly globalized workforce, for whom a return to their 'homeland' had ceased to be practicable. An uneasy adjustment to their alien surroundings was the usual response until the rise of new nations made them conspicuous. Obscuring their origins was sometimes enough; flight or expulsion often the outcome. These are 'hidden histories', many yet to be told.

There is, finally, a wider perspective that we ought to consider. Across most of the world outside Europe and North America, the realm of steam globalization remained essentially coastal – in what some geographers call the 'Rimlands'. It exerted long tentacles inland and drew some interior regions – like the wheat plains of Russia – into commodity production. But, behind the port cities, in parts of Latin America, in most of sub-Saharan Africa and in the vast agrarian interiors of China, India and even Russia, whose agricultural populations still made up some 80 per cent of the whole in 1930,[25] rural society had almost nothing in common with the forms of capitalism that flourished in port-city communities. Russia's farmers might have contributed heavily to its economic growth before 1914, but much of the countryside remained locked in communal tenure, and riven by the discontents that boiled over ferociously in 1917–18.[26] In India it was the Gandhian programme of village self-sufficiency, not a vision of commercialized agriculture, that mobilized the peasants against British rule after 1918. In China it was the revolt of the rural masses that eventually brought Mao to power. Viewed in this light, we might be tempted to say that, influential as port cities might have been, they left almost untouched the vast agrarian landscapes of the world whose (forced) conversion to socialism (in Russia and China) was to define so much of the twentieth century.

In today's globalization, so-called 'global cities' play the part of port cities in that earlier version described in this book. Some things look familiar: the increasing dependence upon remote sources of food, raw materials and manufactures; the huge proportion of world trade that is carried by sea; the ever-rising scale of human migration and the omnipresence of migrants in the professions and business as well as low-skilled occupations; the increasing ease and regularity of long-distance travel; the vast flows of capital criss-crossing the globe; the staggering growth in the volume and speed of information exchange; the assault on the landscape for agricultural or mineral production. We might be tempted to think that 'our' globalization is simply bigger and faster, and touches the parts that its steam-powered forerunner had no hope of reaching. But familiarity is deceptive: there is much that is different, and not just in scale. The geopolitical setting that favoured a Europe-centred world order has long disappeared, and with it the empires that turned steam technology to their particular ends. Europe's hegemonic successor has been in retreat and with China now set on a globe-spanning presence a new global order is in the making. New empires are being forged and new semi-colonial peripheries. This has followed in part from the great 'reversal of fortune' that turned Asian economies – China above all – into the workshops of the world and increasingly the centres of technological innovation.

A long-delayed 'great convergence', enabled by the ease of techno-logical transfer in the internet age, has overturned the 'divergence' that steam helped to widen. Because complex manufactures can now be controlled at long distance by information technology, much industrial capacity has been shifted to what were once poor primary producers.[27] Their newfound wealth has been poured into imports, or exported as capital. For now the tide of foreign investment is as likely to flow from East to West as the other way round. Once London directed the *outflow* of capital to the rest of the world. Now it earns much of its living from promoting the inflow. Although shipping still carries the vast bulk of world trade, the main shipping lanes have come to look very different. Now it is the trans-Pacific traffic from Asia to North America that dwarfs all the rest – carrying nearly double what is sent from Asia to northern Europe, and almost ten times what crosses from North America to Europe, once the busiest of seaborne highways. The world's ten largest ports (by volume) are all in Asia: Rotterdam, Europe's biggest, has less than one-third of the traffic of Asia's largest, Shanghai.[28] Meanwhile 'financialization' – the product of the free movement of money – has sliced and diced

ownership into unaccountable fragments, cloaked in shell companies or parked in tax havens – expedients rarely available to early
twentieth-century capitalism. Today's 'globalized' enterprises readily escape their obligations (whether social or fiscal) to their host
communities – a key source of their profits.[29] The main streams of
migration now run, not from the North into an 'emptier' South, but
in the opposite direction – albeit still fuelled by economic ambition,
fear of oppression or sheer desperation. The norms and values (if
not always the practice) of 'our' globalization are different again:
repudiating racial hierarchies and Europe's old civilizational claims;
embracing ideals of racial and gender equality (occasionally voiced in
the era of steam). There was no nineteenth-century precedent for the
monopoly power of vast data mills, their grip on the supply and diffusion of knowledge or the networking power of electronic media.
Nor (despite the efforts of early environmentalists like the American
George Perkins Marsh) for the widespread anxiety that environmental fragility has come to inspire. Consequently, we live in a world that
steam globalization helped to create, but which we have made almost
unrecognizably different. Nevertheless, we might be struck by a parallel. Just as the advance of steam globalization appeared irresistible,
driving Europe's commerce and culture deeper and deeper into the
non-Western world, it evoked a resistance that swiftly destroyed its
legitimacy. Armed with new doctrines of anti-imperialism, its enemies
lay in wait for the time of troubles to come. In 1913 the crash of a
world so recently made would have been inconceivable. But at what
stage are we in our own global cycle?

Notes

INTRODUCTION: THE KEYS AND THE LOCK

1. The concept was first framed in A. F. Burghardt, 'A Hypothesis about Gateway Cities', *Annals of the Association of American Geographers*, 61, 2 (1971), 269–85.
2. J. Scheele, 'Traders, Saints and Irrigation: Reflections on Saharan Connectivity', *Journal of African History*, 51, 3 (2010), 281–300.
3. For the case of Hamwic (Anglo-Saxon Southampton) in the kingdom of Wessex, see R. Hodges, *The Anglo-Saxon Achievement* (London, 1989), ch. 4.
4. G. Milne, *The Port of Medieval London* (Stroud, 2003), p. 73.
5. B. Martinetti, *Les Négociants de la Rochelle au XVIIIe siècle* (Rennes, 2013), pp. 17–18.
6. See M. B. Gleave, 'Port Activities and the Spatial Structure of Cities: The Case of Freetown, Sierra Leone', *Journal of Transport Geography*, 5, 4 (1997), 257–75.
7. For the classic description of such entrepôt cities, see Edward Whiting Fox, *History in Geographical Perspective: The Other France* (New York, 1971).
8. See J.-P. Pousson, *Bordeaux et le Sud-Ouest au XVIIIe siècle* (Paris, 1983), p. 241.
9. A. Rosenthal, 'The Arrival of the Electric Streetcar and the Conflict over Progress in Early Twentieth-Century Montevideo', *Journal of Latin American Studies*, 27, 2 (1995), 5.
10. J. W. Crowfoot, 'Some Red Sea Ports in the Anglo-Egyptian Sudan', *Geographical Journal*, 37, 5 (1911), 528.
11. See J. Booker, *Maritime Quarantine: The British Experience c.1650–1900* (Aldershot, 2007); P. Baldwin, *Contagion and the State in Europe 1830–1930* (Cambridge, 1999).

12. See G. J. Milne, 'Knowledge, Communications and the Information Order in Nineteenth-Century Liverpool', *International Journal of Maritime History*, 14, 1 (2002), 209–24.

13. See the phases set out by N. S. B. Gras, the pioneer business historian, in his *Introduction to Economic History* (New York, 1922), p. 244.

14. The case for this view was brilliantly set out in A. G. Hopkins (ed.), *Globalization in World History* (London, 2002).

15. T. Earle and C. Gamble with H. Poinar, 'Migration', in A. Shryock and D. L. Smail (eds.), *Deep History: The Architecture of Past and Present* (Berkeley, 2011), p. 214.

16. See P. V. Kirch, 'Peopling of the Pacific: A Holistic Anthropological Perspective', *Annual Review of Anthropology*, 39 (2010), 131–48, esp. 141.

17. See J. G. Manning, *The Open Sea: The Economic Life of the Ancient Mediterranean World from the Iron Age to the Rise of Rome* (Princeton, 2018), ch. 8; P. D. Curtin, *Cross-Cultural Trade in World History* (Cambridge, 1984), ch. 4.

18. The celebrated study is A. W. Crosby, *The Columbian Exchange: Biological and Cultural Consequences of 1492* (Westport, CT, 1972).

19. Quoted in L. Mumford, *Technics and Civilization* (New York, 1934), p. 121.

20. The phrase was coined by Lewis Mumford in *Technics and Civilization*.

21. See A. McCrae, 'The Irrawaddy Flotilla Company', *Business History*, 22, 1 (1980), 87–99. By the late 1920s, with more than 250 powered vessels and over 350 'flats' or barges, the company had become 'the greatest inland waterway enterprise the world has ever known' (p. 97).

22. See R. Hora, *The Landowners of the Argentine Pampas* (Oxford, 2001), ch. 2.

23. See the description in G. Freyre, *The Mansions and the Shanties* [1936] (Eng. trans., New York, 1963), pp. 293ff. For returning Indiamen, see C. R. Boxer, *The Portuguese Seaborne Empire* (Harmondsworth, 1969), p. 222; A. J. R. Russell-Wood, 'Ports of Colonial Brazil', in F. Knight and P. Liss (eds.), *Atlantic Port Cities: Economy, Culture and Society in the Atlantic World, 1650–1850* (Knoxville, 1991), pp. 201ff.

24. Freyre, *Mansions*, p. 223.

25. J. Needell, *A Tropical Belle Epoque: Elite Culture and Society in Turn-of-the-Century Rio de Janeiro* (Cambridge, 1987), p. 167.

26. Freyre, *Mansions*, p. 229. For the appeal of European 'taste', see G. Freyre, *Order and Progress: Brazil from Monarchy to Republic* [1957] (Eng. trans., New York, 1970), ch. 2.

27. See W. E. Rudolph, 'Strategic Roads of the World', *Geographical Review*, 33, 1 (1943), 110–31.
28. For a vivid illustration of the consequences in early twentieth-century China, see J. E. Baker, 'Transportation in China', *Annals of the American Academy of Political and Social Sciences*, 152, 1 (1930), 160–72.
29. W. Ashworth, *A Short History of the International Economy, 1850–1950* (London, 1952), p. 63.
30. E. Shann, *An Economic History of Australia* (Cambridge, 1930), p. 292.
31. R. Wenzlhuemer, *Connecting the Nineteenth-Century World: The Telegraph and Globalization* (Cambridge, 2013).

CHAPTER I: THE PORT CITY IN THE OLD WORLD

1. L. Paine, *The Sea and Civilization* (New York, 2015), p. 36.
2. D. Abulafia, *The Great Sea: A Human History of the Mediterranean* (London, 2011), p. 37.
3. Paine, *The Sea*, p. 80.
4. E. Alpers, *The Indian Ocean in World History* (Oxford, 2014), p. 25.
5. See M. Vink, 'Indian Ocean Studies and the "New Thalassology"', *Journal of Global History*, 2 (2007), 41–62.
6. B. Cunliffe, *By Steppe, Desert and Ocean: The Birth of Eurasia* (Oxford, 2015), p. 279; M. Fitzpatrick, 'Provincializing Rome: The Indian Ocean Trade Network and Roman Imperialism', *Journal of World History* 22, 1 (2011), 27–54.
7. See R. B. Marks, *China: Its Environment and History* (Lanham, MD, 2012), pp. 123–30.
8. É. de la Vaissiére, 'Trans-Asian Trade, or the Silk Road Deconstructed (Antiquity, Middle Ages)', in L. Neal and J. G. Williamson (eds.), *The Cambridge History of Capitalism*, vol. 1 (Cambridge, 2014), pp. 102–4.
9. See K. McPherson, *The Indian Ocean: A History of People and the Sea* (New Delhi, 1993), pp. 66–7.
10. Cunliffe, *Steppe, Desert and Ocean*, p. 293.
11. See W. M. Jongman, 'Re-constructing the Roman Economy', in Neal and Williamson (eds.), *The Cambridge History of Capitalism*, vol. 1, pp. 91–6.
12. See S. E. Sidebotham, *Berenike and the Ancient Maritime Spice Route* (Berkeley and London, 2011), pp. 279–81.
13. M. Elvin, *The Pattern of the Chinese Past* (London, 1973), Part Two.
14. Ibid., p. 113.

15. See L. Cooke Johnson, *Shanghai: From Market Town to Treaty Port 1074–1858* (Stanford, 1995); M. Elvin, *Another History: Essays on China from a European Perspective* (Sydney, 1996), p. 106.

16. See A. Wink, *Al-Hind: The Making of the Indo-Islamic World*, vol. 1: *Early Medieval India and the Expansion of Islam, 7th to 11th Centuries* (Leiden, 1990), pp. 296ff.; R. M. Eaton, *The Rise of Islam and the Bengal Frontier 1204–1760* (Berkeley, Los Angeles and London, 1993); V. Lieberman, *Strange Parallels: Southeast Asia in Global Context c.800–1830*, vol. 2: *Mainland Mirrors* (Cambridge, 2009), pp. 681ff.

17. Lieberman, *Strange Parallels*, vol. 2, ch. 6.

18. McPherson, *Indian Ocean*, p. 96.

19. Wink, *Al-Hind*, vol. 1, pp. 324–8.

20. For a persuasive statement of this, B. M. S. Campbell, *The Great Transition* (Cambridge, 2016).

21. For the recovery of aristocratic revenues after AD 800, and their importance for trade, see C. Wickham, *Framing the Early Middle Ages* (Oxford, 2005), pp. 818ff.

22. P. Spufford, *Power and Profit: The Merchant in Medieval Europe* (London, 2002), pp. 356–8.

23. The classic description is J. Abu-Lughod, *Before European Hegemony: The World System AD 1250–1350* (New York, 1989).

24. See Ṣ. Pamuk and M. Shatzmiller, 'Plagues, Wages, and Economic Change in the Islamic Middle East, 700–1500', *Journal of Economic History*, 74, 1 (2014), 196–229.

25. I have drawn much of this survey from Wink, *Al-Hind*, vol. 1, chs. 2 and 3.

26. See R. W. Bulliet, *Cotton, Climate and Camels in Early Islamic Iran* (New York, 2009).

27. B. V. Schmid et al., 'Climate-Driven Introduction of the Black Death and Successive Plague Reintroductions into Europe', *Proceedings of the National Academy of Sciences*, 112, 10 (2015), 3020–25.

28. See Pamuk and Shatzmiller, 'Plagues, Wages, and Economic Change'.

29. Lieberman, *Strange Parallels*, vol. 2, pp. 692ff.

30. Marks, *China*, p. 170.

31. T. Brook, *The Confusions of Pleasure: Commerce and Culture in Ming China* (Berkeley, Los Angeles and London, 1998), p. 18.

32. Lieberman, *Strange Parallels*, vol. 2, p. 558.

33. For a sumptuously illustrated introduction to Ming China, see C. Clunas and J. Harrison-Hall (eds.), *Ming: Fifty Years that Changed China* (BP Exhibition, 2014).

34. T. Brook, 'Commerce: The Ming in the World', in Clunas and Harrison-Hall (eds.), *Ming*, p. 271.

35. G. Riello, *Cotton: The Fabric that Made the Modern World* (Cambridge, 2013), p. 67.

36. See R. Palat, *The Making of an Indian Ocean World-Economy, 1250–1650* (Basingstoke, 2015).

37. See L. Schick, *Un grand homme d'affaires au début du XVIe siècle: Jacob Fugger* (Paris, 1957), ch. 3.

38. See P. Jackson, *Mongols and the Islamic World: From Conquest to Conversion* (New Haven, 2017), pp. 90–93.

39. Ibid., p. 226.

40. D. Ludden, *Peasant History in South India* (Delhi, 1989), p. 42.

41. See H. A. R. Gibb, *Ibn Battuta: Travels in Asia and Africa, 1325–1354* [1929] (London, 1983), Introduction.

42. For a brilliant description, see J. Gommans, 'The Silent Frontier of South Asia, c.AD 1100–1800', *Journal of World History*, 9, 1 (1998), 1–23.

43. For the suggestion that the Ming use of rubies was a 'visual language of grandeur and status', see C. Clunas, 'Precious Stones and Ming Culture, 1400–1450', in C. Clunas, J. Harrison-Hall and Luk Yu-ping (eds.), *Ming China: Courts and Contacts, 1400–1450* (London, 2016).

44. Jackson, *Mongols*, pp. 234ff.

45. See Sheldon Pollock, 'The Transformation of Culture-Power in Indo-Europe, 1000–1300', *Medieval Encounters*, 10, 1–3 (2004), 247–78.

46. A. Reid, *Southeast Asia in the Age of Commerce 1450–1680*, vol. 2 (1993), p. 207.

47. Abulafia, *Great Sea*, pp. 362ff.

48. For some attempts, see S. R. Prange, 'The Contested Sea: Regimes of Maritime Violence in the Pre-Modern Indian Ocean', *Journal of Early Modern History*, 17, 1 (2013), 9–33.

49. See F. C. Lane, *Venice: A Maritime Republic* (Baltimore and London, 1973), p. 68.

50. Chen Dasheng and D. Lombard, 'Foreign Merchants in Maritime Trade in Quanzhou ('Zaitun')', in D. Lombard and J. Aubin (eds.), *Asian Merchants and Businessmen in the Indian Ocean and the China Sea* (New Delhi, 2000), p. 20.

51. A. C. Fong, ' "Together They Might Make Trouble": Cross-Cultural Interactions in Tang Dynasty Guangzhou, 618–907 CE', *Journal of World History*, 25, 4 (2014), 475–92.

52. See C. Baker, 'Ayutthaya Rising: From Land or Sea?', *Journal of South-east Asian Studies*, 34, 1 (2003), 41–62.

53. M. Collis, *Siamese White* [1936] (London, 1951), p. 47.

54. Deng Hui and Li Xin, 'The Asian Monsoons and Zheng He's Voyages to the Western Ocean', *Journal of Navigation*, 64, 2 (2011), 207–18.

55. See J. Horsburgh, *India Directory, or Directions for Sailing to and from the East Indies, China, New Holland [etc.]*, 3rd edn. (London, 1827), pp. 238ff.

56. See L. F. F. R. Thomaz, 'Melaka and Its Merchant Communities at the Turn of the Sixteenth Century', in Lombard and Aubin (eds.), *Asian Merchants*, pp. 25–39.

57. This was João de Barros, whose account was published in 1553. See P. E. De J. De Jong and H. L. A. Van Wijk, 'The Malacca Sultanate', *Journal of Southeast Asian History* 1, 2 (1960), 20–29.

58. C. N. Parkinson, *Trade in the Eastern Seas, 1793–1813* (Cambridge, 1937), p. 108.

59. G. Bouchon, 'A Microcosm: Calicut in the Sixteenth Century', in Lombard and Aubin (eds.), *Asian Merchants*, pp. 40–49.

60. J. Deloche, *Transport and Communications in India Prior to Steam Locomotion*, vol. 2: *Water Transport* (Delhi, 1994), p. 90.

61. W. Floor, *The Persian Gulf: A Political and Economic History of Five Port Cities 1500–1730* (Washington DC, 2006), ch. 1.

62. On this see the fascinating account in A. Villiers, *Sons of Sindbad* (London, 1940), of his voyage by dhow in the late 1930s.

63. See R. E. Margariti, *Aden and the Indian Ocean Trade* (Chapel Hill, 2007), pp. 38ff.

64. Ibid., p. 27.

65. Ibid., p. 207.

66. See S. Pradines, 'The Mamluk Fortifications of Egypt', *Mamluk Studies Review*, 19 (2016), 33ff.

67. For a description, see G. Christ, *Trading Conflicts: Venetian Merchants and Mamluk Officials in Late Medieval Alexandria* (Leiden, 2012), pp. 23–7.

68. See J. P. Cooper, *The Medieval Nile: Route, Navigation and Landscape in Islamic Egypt* (Cairo, 2014), ch. 9.

69. See G. Christ, 'Collapse and Continuity: Alexandria as a Declining City with a Thriving Port (Thirteenth to Sixteenth Centuries)', in W. Blockmans, M. Krom and J. Wubs-Mrozewicz (eds.), *The Routledge Handbook of Maritime Trade around Europe 1300–1600* (London, 2017), p. 124.

70. See F. J. Apellániz Ruiz de Galarreta, *Pouvoir et finance en Méditerranée pré-moderne: le deuxième état Mamelouk et le commerce des épices (1382–1517)* (Barcelona, 2009), esp. p. 42; Christ, *Trading Conflicts*, ch. 7.

71. Cooper, *Medieval Nile*, ch. 13.

72. G. Christ, 'Beyond the Network', in S. Conermann (ed.), *Everything is on the Move: The Mamluk Empire as a Node in (Trans-)Regional Networks* (Göttingen, 2014), p. 50.

73. See A. Sopracasa, 'Venetian Merchants and Alexandrian Officials (End of the Fifteenth-Beginning of the Sixteenth Century)', *Mamluk Studies Review*, 19 (2016).

74. Christ, *Trading Conflicts*, p. 49.

75. For this calculation, see *Encyclopaedia Islamica Online*, 'Alexandria'.

76. See P. Horden and N. Purcell, *The Corrupting Sea: A Study of Mediterranean History* (Oxford, 2000) ch. 6.

77. For this point, see W. Blockmans and J. Wubs-Mrozewicz, 'European Integration from the Seaside', in Blockmans et al. (eds.), *Maritime Trade around Europe*, pp. 448ff.

78. The classic study remains Lane, *Venice*.

79. A valuable recent study is M. Fusaro, *Political Economies of Empire in the Early Modern Mediterranean: The Decline of Venice and the Rise of England, 1450–1700* (Cambridge, 2015).

80. See R. C. Mueller, *The Venetian Money Market: Banks, Panics and the Public Debt, 1200–1500* (Baltimore, 1997), pp. 454ff.

81. See C. Shaw, 'Principles and Practice in the Civic Government of Fifteenth-Century Genoa', *Renaissance Quarterly*, 58 (2005), 45–90.

82. Apellániz, *Pouvoir et finance*, pp. 156ff.

83. See C. Taviani, 'The Genoese Casa di San Giorgio as a Micro-Economic and Territorial Nodal System', in Blockmans et al. (eds.), *Maritime Trade around Europe*.

84. See D. Coulon, *Barcelone et le grand commerce d'orient au moyen âge* (Barcelona, 2004); F. Fernandez-Armesto, *Barcelona* (London, 1991).

85. I have drawn on P. Russell, *Prince Henry the 'Navigator': A Life* (New Haven and London, 2000) for this account.

86. See G. Eekhout, 'Le Port de Bruges au moyen âge', in Société Scientifique de Bruxelles, *Les Ports ét leur fonction économique*, vol. 1 (Louvain, 1906), pp. 37–53; O. Gelderblom, *Cities of Commerce: The Institutional Foundations of International Trade in the Low Countries 1250–1650* (Princeton, 2013), pp. 16ff. The Beurs square is illustrated in Spufford, *Power and Profit*, p. 139.

87. See D. J. Harreld, *High Germans in the Low Countries* (Leiden, 2004), pp. 4–5.

88. Ibid., p. 2.

89. R. C. Hoffmann, 'Frontier Foods for Late Medieval Consumers: Culture, Economy, Ecology', *Environment and History*, 7, 2 (2001), 140ff.

90. Spufford, *Power and Profit*, pp. 386-8.

91. P. Dollinger, *The German Hansa* (Eng. trans., London, 1970), p. 111.

92. Ibid., pp. 187-9.

93. For Boston, see S. H. Rigby, ' "Sore Decay" and "Fair Dwellings": Boston and Urban Decline in the Later Middle Ages', *Midland History*, 10 (1985), 47-61; for King's Lynn, see K. Friedland and P. Richards (eds.), *Essays in Hanseatic History: The King's Lynn Symposium 1998* (Dereham, 2005).

94. The classic study is C. E. Hill, *The Danish Sound Dues and the Command of the Baltic* (Durham, NC, 1926). See ch. 2.

95. Dollinger, *German Hansa*, pp. 207ff.

96. See E. Lindberg, 'Club Goods and Inefficient Institutions: Why Danzig and Lübeck Failed in the Early Modern Period', *Economic History Review*, 62, 3 (2009), 604-28.

97. G. Milne, *The Port of Medieval London* (Stroud, 2003), ch. 4.

98. See H. C. Darby (ed.), *A New Historical Geography of England before 1600* (Cambridge, 1973), pp. 245-6.

99. Milne, *Medieval London*, pp. 91, 128, 149.

100. S. Thrupp, *The Merchant Class of Medieval London* [1948] (Ann Arbor, 1989), pp. 87ff.

101. A. A. Ruddock, *Italian Merchants and Shipping in Southampton 1270-1600* (Southampton, 1951), pp. 264-5.

102. For this see C. Dyer, *Making a Living in the Middle Ages: The People of Britain 850-1520* (London, 2003), p. 305.

103. See L. Benton, *Law and Colonial Cultures: Legal Regimes in World History, 1400-1900* (Cambridge, 2002), chs. 2 and 3.

104. F. Braudel, *The Wheels of Commerce* [1975] (Eng. trans., London, 1985), p. 405.

105. Ibid.

106. See E. S. Hunt and J. M. Murray, *A History of Business in Medieval Europe, 1200-1550* (Cambridge, 1999), pp. 154ff.; Spufford, *Power and Profit*, ch. 1.

107. This is brilliantly argued in S. R. Epstein, *Freedom and Growth* (London, 2000).

CHAPTER 2: COLUMBIAN PRELUDE

1. Adam Smith, *The Wealth of Nations*, vol. 2 (Everyman edn., n.d.), pp. 121-2.

2. S. M. Guérin, 'Forgotten Routes? Italy, Ifrīqiya and the Trans-Saharan Ivory Trade', *Al-Masāq*, 25, 1 (2013), 70-91.

3. T. Vorderstrasse, 'Trade and Textiles from Medieval Antioch', *Al-Masāq*, 22, 2 (2010), 153.

4. For a brilliant survey of their origins, see B. Cunliffe, *By Steppe, Desert and Ocean: The Birth of Eurasia* (Oxford, 2015).

5. See D. Buisseret (ed.), *Monarchs, Ministers and Maps: The Emergence of Cartography as a Tool of Government in Early Modern Europe* (Chicago and London, 1992).

6. See S. Mintz, *Sweetness and Power: The Place of Sugar in Modern History* (Harmondsworth, 1985), ch. 3; J. De Vries, *The Economy of Europe in an Age of Crisis, 1600-1750* (Cambridge, 1976), chs. 4 and 6.

7. The classic account of this is A. W. Crosby, *The Columbian Exchange: Biological and Cultural Consequences of 1492* (Westport, CT, 1972).

8. See Robert B. Marks, *China: Its Environment and History* (Lanham, MD, 2012), pp. 206, 170.

9. See Shuo Chen and James Kai-sing Kung, 'Of Maize and Men: The Effect of a New World Crop on Population and Economic Growth in China', *Journal of Economic Growth*, 21, 1 (2016), 71-99.

10. For a fascinating discussion of this, see J. C. McCann, *Maize and Grace: Africa's Encounter with a New World Food Crop 1500-2000* (Cambridge, MA, 2005), pp. 44-6.

11. See the hints in E. W. Evans and D. Richardson, 'Hunting for Rents: The Economics of Slaving in Pre-Colonial Africa', *Economic History Review*, 48, 4 (1995), 673.

12. R. Findlay and K. O'Rourke, National Bureau of Economic Research Working Paper, 'Commodity Market Integration 1500-2000', table 2, at http://venus.iere.go.kr/metadata/202821_w8579.pdf.

13. K. N. Chaudhuri, *The Trading World of Asia and the English East India Company 1660-1760* (Cambridge, 1978), p. 177.

14. Ibid., pp. 540-5.

15. See R. S. DuPlessis, *The Material Atlantic: Clothing, Commerce and Colonization in the Atlantic World, 1650-1800* (Cambridge, 2016).

16. Marks, *China*, p. 224. For a significantly lower estimate see the careful analysis in K. G. Deng, 'Foreign Silver, China's Economy and the Globalisation of the 16th to 19th Centuries', Global History and Maritime Asia Working and Discussion Paper Series, no. 4 (2007), available online.

17. See T. Andrade, *Lost Colony: The Untold Story of China's First Great Victory over the West* (Princeton, 2011), p. 14.

18. See E. M. Jacobs, *Merchant in Asia: The Trade of the Dutch East India Company during the Eighteenth Century* (Leiden, 2006).

19. See J. E. Inikori, *Africans and the Industrial Revolution in England* (Cambridge, 2002).

20. DuPlessis, *Material Atlantic*, p. 241.

21. L. Blussé, *Strange Company: Chinese Settlers, Mestizo Women and the Dutch in VOC Batavia* (Dordrecht, 1986), p. 26.

22. See B. Lemire, 'Revising the Historical Narrative: India, Europe and the Cotton Trade *c.*1300–1800', in G. Riello and P. Parthasarathi (eds.), *The Spinning World: A Global History of Cotton Textiles, 1200–1850* (Oxford, 2009).

23. See G. M. Theal, *Willem Adriaan van der Stel and Other Historical Sketches* (Cape Town, 1913), ch. 1.

24. See Kwee Hui Kian, 'The Rise of Chinese Commercial Dominance in Early Modern Southeast Asia', in Lin Yu-ju and M. Zelin (eds.), *Merchant Communities in Asia, 1600–1980* (London, 2015).

25. R. Ptak, *China's Seaborne Trade with South and Southeast Asia 1200–1750* (Aldershot, 1999).

26. See C. R. Boxer, *The Portuguese Seaborne Empire 1415–1825* (London, 1969), ch. 5.

27. D. Washbrook, 'India in the Early Modern World Economy: Modes of Production, Reproduction and Exchange', *Journal of Global History*, 2 (2007), 87–111, esp. 93 and 110.

28. Some of these disasters are chronicled in L. Colley, *The Ordeal of Elizabeth Marsh: A Woman in World History* (London, 2007). Marsh's husband was no less unlucky.

29. Inikori, *Africans*, p. 181.

30. Chaudhuri, *Trading World*, pp. 388 (tea), 547 (textiles).

31. See www.slavevoyages.org estimate.

32. J. De Vries, 'The Limits of Globalization in the Early Modern World', *Economic History Review*, 63, 3 (2010), 710–33, esp. 718.

33. DuPlessis, *Material Atlantic*, p. 240.

34. E. Murakami, 'A Comparison of the End of the Canton and Nagasaki Trade Control Systems', *Itinerario* 37, 3 (2013), 39–48.

35. M. B. Jansen, *The Making of Modern Japan* (Cambridge, MA, 2000), p. 260.

36. Quoted in A. Singer, *The Lion and the Dragon: The Story of the First British Embassy to the Court of the Emperor Qianlong in Peking, 1792–1794* (London, 1992), p. 99.

37. C. E. Kriger, '"Guinea Cloth": Production and Consumption of Cotton Textiles in West Africa before and during the Atlantic Slave Trade', in Riello and Parthasarathi (eds.), *The Spinning World*, pp. 105–26.

38. DuPlessis, *Material Atlantic*, p. 236.

39. Smith, *Wealth of Nations*, vol. 1, p. 394.

40. DuPlessis, *Material Atlantic*, ch. 4.

41. Smith, *Wealth of Nations*, vol. 2, p. 122.

42. See C. L. Brown, *Moral Capital: The Foundations of British Abolitionism* (Chapel Hill, 2006).

43. See C. Iannini, ' "The Itinerant Man": Crèvecoeur's Caribbean, Raynal's Revolution, and the Fate of Atlantic Cosmopolitanism', *William and Mary Quarterly*, 61 (2004), 208, 221-2.

44. See P. Cheney, *Revolutionary Commerce: Globalization and the French Monarchy* (Cambridge, MA, 2010).

45. R. Whatmore, *Republicanism and the French Revolution* (Oxford, 2000), p. 40.

46. Quoted in Ibid., p. 48.

47. Ibid., p. 56.

48. Baron de Montesquieu, *The Spirit of the Laws* [1748] (Eng. trans., New York, 1949), p. 316.

49. David Hume, 'Of Commerce', in S. Copley and A. Edgar (eds.), *David Hume: Selected Essays* (Oxford, 1993), p. 162.

50. Smith, *Wealth of Nations*, vol. 1, p. 436.

51. See A. von Oppen, *Terms of Trade and Terms of Trust: The History and Contexts of Pre-Colonial Market Production around the Upper Zambezi and Kasai* (Hamburg and Münster, 1993), pp. 49ff.

52. P. C. Perdue, *China Marches West: The Qing Conquest of Central Eurasia* (Cambridge, MA, 2005), offers a wonderful account.

53. See A. W. Knapp, *Cocoa and Chocolate: Their History from Plantation to Consumer* (London, 1920).

54. R. W. Unger, 'Shipping and Western European Economic Growth in the Late Renaissance: Potential Connections', *International Journal of Maritime History*, 18, 2 (2006), 101.

55. See D. Hancock, ' "A World of Business to Do": William Freeman and the Foundations of England's Commercial Empire, 1645-1707', *William and Mary Quarterly*, 57 (2000), 3-34.

56. R. S. Dunn, *Sugar and Slaves: The Rise of the Planter Class in the English West Indies, 1624-1713* (Chapel Hill, 1972), ch. 2.

57. See A. Borucki, D. Eltis and D. Wheat, 'Atlantic History and the Slave Trade to Spanish America', *American Historical Review*, 120, 2 (2015), 433-61.

58. Dunn, *Sugar and Slaves*, p. 72.

59. Unger, 'Shipping and Western European Economic Growth', 89-91.

60. For Bristol in the 1750s, see Sir Lewis Namier, *The Structure of Politics at the Accession of George III*, 2nd edn. (London, 1957), pp. 88–9.

61. C. Lesger, *The Rise of the Amsterdam Market and Information Exchange: Merchants, Commercial Expansion and Change in the Spatial Economy of the Low Countries, c.1550–1630* (Aldershot, 2006), pp. 214ff.; C. Wilson, *Anglo-Dutch Commerce and Finance in the Eighteenth Century* (Cambridge, 1941), ch. 1.

62. D. Ormrod, *The Rise of Commercial Empires: England and the Netherlands in the Age of Mercantilism, 1650–1770* (Cambridge, 2003), Table 2.1.

63. Ibid., p. 40.

64. Ibid., p. 276.

65. Ibid., Table 1.2.

66. The best recent study is P. Gauci, *Emporium of the World: The Merchants of London, 1660–1800* (London, 2007). For London's trades and industries, see M. Daunton, *Progress and Poverty: An Economic and Social History of Britain 1700–1850* (Oxford, 1995), pp. 138–40.

67. Wilson, *Anglo-Dutch Commerce*, p. 78.

68. C. R. Boxer, *The Golden Age of Brazil* (Berkeley, 1962), p. 312.

69. N. Zahedieh, 'Trade, Plunder and Economic Development in Early English Jamaica, 1655–89', *Economic History Review*, 39, 2 (1986), 205–22.

70. The myth of a large Crown revenue from Spanish America has been punctured by R. Grafe and A. Irigoin, 'A Stakeholder Empire: The Political Economy of Spanish Imperial Rule in America', *Economic History Review*, 65, 2 (2012), 609–51. For Spain's economic fortunes in this period, see R. Grafe, *Distant Tyranny: Markets, Power and Backwardness in Spain, 1650–1800* (Princeton, 2012), where backwardness is largely attributed to the failure of the state to centralize successfully.

71. For Spanish-American trade, see J. R. Fisher, *Economic Aspects of Spanish Imperialism in America, 1492–1810* (Liverpool, 1997), esp. chs. 4 and 6; for the Panama *galeones* see X. Lamikiz, 'Transatlantic Networks and Merchant Guild Rivalry in Colonial Trade with Peru, 1729–1780', *Hispanic American Historical Review*, 91, 2 (2011), 312.

72. P. H. Marks, 'Confronting a Mercantile Elite: Bourbon Reformers and the Merchants of Lima, 1765–1796', *The Americas*, 60, 4 (2004), 519–58. To Lima's dismay, merchants from Cadiz had been allowed to trade directly with Chile in the 1740s.

73. For a recent study of the city, see G. García, *Beyond the Walled City: Colonial Exclusion in Havana* (Oakland, CA, 2016), ch. 2.

74. For Charleston, see E. Hart, *Building Charleston: Town and Society in the Eighteenth-Century British Atlantic World* (Charlottesville, 2012).

75. T. Burnard and E. Hart, 'Kingston, Jamaica, and Charleston, South Carolina', *Journal of Urban History*, 39, 2 (2013), 214–34.

76. For an illuminating study, see S. Mentz, *The English Gentleman Merchant at Work: Madras and the City of London 1660–1740* (Copenhagen, 2005).

77. For an important recent study, see P. J. Stern, *The Company State: Corporate Sovereignty and the Early Modern Foundations of the British Empire in India* (Oxford, 2011).

78. See C. R. Boxer, *Francisco Vieira da Figueiredo: A Portuguese Merchant-Adventurer in South East Asia, 1624–1667* (The Hague, 1967).

79. Jacobs, *Merchant in Asia*, p. 231.

80. See Blussé, *Strange Company*, p. 19.

81. U. Bosma and R. Raben, *Being 'Dutch' in the Indies: A History of Creolisation and Empire, 1500–1920* (Singapore, 2008), p. 46.

82. Blussé, *Strange Company*, p. 74.

83. For Batavia's commercial decline, see L. Blussé, *Visible Cities: Canton, Nagasaki and Batavia and the Coming of the Americans* (Cambridge, MA, 2008), p. 64.

84. G. B. Souza, 'Opium and the Company: Maritime Trade and Imperial Finances on Java, 1684–1796', *Modern Asian Studies*, 43, 1 (2009), 113–33.

85. R. Van Niel, *Java's Northeast Coast 1740–1840* (Leiden, 2005), chs. 1 and 2.

86. J. Horsburgh, *India Directory, or Directions for Sailing to and from the East Indies, China, New Holland [etc.]*, 3rd edn. (London, 1827), p. 309.

87. L. Dermigny, *La Chine et l'Occident: le commerce à Canton au XVIIIe siècle, 1719–1833*, vol. 2 (Paris, 1964), p. 445.

88. Ibid.

89. I have relied for this account on the seminal work of Paul Van Dyke. See his *Merchants of Canton and Macao: Politics and Strategies in Eighteenth-Century Chinese Trade* (Hong Kong, 2012).

90. P. J. Marshall, *Bengal: The British Bridgehead – Eastern India 1740–1828* (Cambridge, 1987).

91. See O. Prakash, 'From Negotiation to Coercion: Textile Manufacturing in India in the Eighteenth Century', *Modern Asian Studies*, 41, 6 (2007), 1,331–68.

92. See R. C. Allen, *The British Industrial Revolution in Global Perspective* (Cambridge, 2009), pp. 128–9.

93. R. Davis, 'English Foreign Trade, 1700–1774', *Economic History Review*, 15, 2 (1962), 285–303.

CHAPTER 3: STEAM GLOBALIZATION

1. C. F. Adams Jr, 'The Railroad System', in C. F. Adams and H. Adams, *Chapters of Erie and Other Essays* [Boston, 1871] (New York, 1967), p. 354. C. F. Adams Jr (1835–1915), grandson and great-grandson of two American presidents, was a Boston patrician. He was later to serve as the respectable face of the Union Pacific Railroad, until he fell out with the tycoon Jay Gould.

2. These events can be followed in P. W. Schroeder, *The Transformation of European Politics, 1763–1848* (Oxford, 1994).

3. See M. E. Yapp, *Strategies of British India: Britain, Iran and Afghanistan, 1798–1850* (Oxford, 1980).

4. For a survey, see L. Bethell (ed.), *Spanish America after Independence c.1820–c.1870* (Cambridge, 1987).

5. The 'second slavery' is the subject of an extensive literature. See, for example, A. E. Kaye, 'The Second Slavery: Modernity in the Nineteenth-Century South and the Atlantic World', *Journal of Southern History*, 75, 3 (2009), 627–50.

6. H. Clay, *Speech of Henry Clay, in Defence of the American System, against the British Colonial System* (Washington DC, 1832), p. 18.

7. The classic account is H. Tinker, *A New System of Slavery: The Export of Indian Labour Overseas, 1830–1920* (London, 1974).

8. See B. W. Sheehan, *Seeds of Extinction: Jeffersonian Philanthropy and the American Indian* (Chapel Hill, 1973), pp. 20ff. For the highly ambiguous attitudes of many Enlightenment thinkers, see A. Pagden, *The Enlightenment and Why It Still Matters* (Oxford, 2013), pp. 139–42.

9. See C. A. Bayly, *Recovering Liberties: Indian Thought in the Age of Liberalism and Empire* (Cambridge, 2012), chs. 2 and 3.

10. A. E. Musson and E. Robinson, 'The Early Growth of Steam Power', *Economic History Review*, New Series, 11, 3 (1959), 418–39.

11. A. Nuvolari and B. Verspagen, 'Technical Choice, Innovation, and British Steam Engineering, 1800–50', *Economic History Review*, 62, 3 (2009), 685–710.

12. J. Tann and J. Aitken, 'The Diffusion of the Stationary Steam Engine from Britain to India 1790–1830', *Indian Economic and Social History Review*, 29, 2 (1992), 203.

13. See the lapidary judgement in N. Crafts, 'Productivity Growth in the Industrial Revolution', *Journal of Economic History*, 64, 2 (2004), 521–35.

14. G. N. von Tunzelmann, *Steam Power and British Industrialization to 1860* (Oxford, 1978), p. 295.

15. J. S. Lyons, 'Powerloom Profitability and Steam Power Costs: Britain in the 1830s', *Explorations in Economic History*, 24 (1987), 392–3.

16. These figures are drawn from M. G. Mulhall, *The Dictionary of Statistics* (London, 1892), p. 545.

17. Ibid., p. 546.

18. Tann and Aitken, 'Stationary Steam Engine'.

19. F. Mackey, *Steamboat Connections: Montreal to Upper Canada, 1816–1843* (Montreal and Kingston, 2000), ch. 1.

20. See Fellows of the Australian Academy of Technological Sciences and Engineering, *Technology in Australia 1788–1988* (online, 2000), ch. 12.

21. Tann and Aitken, 'Stationary Steam Engine'.

22. A. J. Bolton, 'Progress of Inland Steam-Navigation in North-East India from 1832', *Minutes of the Proceedings of the Institution of Civil Engineers*, 99 (1890), 330–42 (online).

23. See A. Odlyzko, 'Collective Hallucinations and Inefficient Markets: The British Railway Mania of the 1840s', www.dtc.umn.edu/~odlyzko/doc//hallucinations.pdf, 186.

24. O. Barak, 'Outsourcing: Energy and Empire in the Age of Coal, 1820–1911', *International Journal of Middle East Studies*, 47, 3 (2015), 428–29.

25. See V. İnal, 'The Eighteenth and Nineteenth Century Ottoman Attempts to Catch Up with Europe', *Middle East Studies*, 47, 5 (2011), 725–56.

26. For the terrors of the voyage, see W. D. Bernard and W. H. Hall, *A Narrative of the Voyages and Services of the Nemesis, from 1840 to 1843* (London, 1844).

27. See the fascinating discussion in Hsien-Chun Wang, 'Discovering Steam Power in China, 1840s–1860s', *Technology and Culture*, 51, 1 (2010), 31–54.

28. J. H. Clapham, *An Economic History of Modern Britain*, vol. 2: *Free Trade and Steel, 1850–1886* (Cambridge, 1932), p. 29.

29. Ibid., p. 82.

30. See R. Floud, *The British Machine Tool Industry, 1850–1914* (Cambridge, 1976).

31. For the argument that the Industrial Revolution sprang from a bourgeois culture sympathetic to innovation, see D. N. McCloskey, *Bourgeois Dignity: Why Economics Can't Explain the Modern World* (Chicago, 2010).

32. See *Minutes of the Proceedings of the Institution of Civil Engineers*, 29 (1870) (online).

33. The key argument in A. Malm, *Fossil Capital: The Rise of Steam Power and the Roots of Global Warming* (London, 2015).

34. See T. Balderston, 'The Economics of Abundance', *Economic History Review*, 63, 3 (2010), 569–90.

35. These figures are drawn from the *Encyclopaedia Britannica*, 1911 edition.

36. P. L. Cottrell, *British Overseas Investment in the Nineteenth Century* (London, 1975), p. 63.

37. V. Bignon, R. Esteves and A. Herranz-Loncán, 'Big Push or Big Grab? Railways, Government Activism, and Export Growth in Latin America, 1865–1913', *Economic History Review*, 68, 4 (2015), 1282.

38. The claim famously made in R. W. Fogel, *Railroads and American Economic Growth: Essays in Econometric History* (Baltimore, 1964).

39. P. A. David, 'Transport Innovation and Economic Growth: Professor Fogel on and off the Rails', *Economic History Review*, 22, 3 (1969), 506–25.

40. D. Donaldson and R. Hornbeck, 'Railroads and American Economic Growth: A "Market Access" Approach', *Quarterly Journal of Economics*, 131, 2 (May 2016), 799–858.

41. T. S. Berry, *Western Prices before 1861: A Study of the Cincinnati Market* (Cambridge, MA, 1943), p. 69.

42. See I. J. Kerr, 'Colonial India, Its Railways, and the Cliometricians', *Journal of Transport History*, 35, 1 (2014), 114–20.

43. Bignon, Esteves and Herranz-Loncán, 'Big Push or Big Grab?', 1279–81.

44. For a forensic study, see S. Sweeney, *Financing India's Imperial Railways, 1875–1914* (London, 2011).

45. F. Norris, *The Octopus: A Story of California* [1901] (Penguin edn., Harmondsworth, 1986), p. 11.

46. Charles Francis Adams, quoted in B. Marsden and C. Smith, *Engineering Empires: A Cultural History of Technology in Nineteenth-Century Britain* (Basingstoke, 2004), p. 169.

47. Quoted in I. F. Clarke, *The Pattern of Expectation 1644–2001* (London, 1979), p. 54.

48. D. Lardner, *The Steam Engine Explained and Illustrated* (London, 1840), p. 5.

49. W. H. G. Armytage, *A Social History of Engineering* (London, 1961), p. 74.

50. Quoted in Clarke, *Pattern*, p. 56.

51. M. Chevalier, *Système de la Méditerranée* (Paris, 1832), p. 37.

52. Ibid., p. 47.

53. R. to F. Cobden, 30 November 1836, in A. Howe (ed.), *The Letters of Richard Cobden*, vol. 1 (Oxford, 2007), p. 81.

54. R. Cobden, *England, Ireland, and America* [1835], 4th edn. (London, 1836), p. 11.

55. See A. Fyfe, *Steam-Powered Knowledge: William Chambers and the Business of Publishing, 1820–1860* (Chicago, 2012).

56. A. Anim-Addo, ' "Thence to the River Plate": Steamship Mobilities in the South Atlantic, 1842–1869', *Atlantic Studies*, 13, 1 (2016), 10.

57. *New York Daily Times*, 27 April 1852 (online).

58. See D. R. Headrick, *The Invisible Weapon* (Oxford and New York, 1991), p. 19.

59. Ibid., pp. 12–15.

60. Ibid., p. 22. For China and Australia, the times in 1900 were 80 and 100 minutes respectively.

61. See A. Nalbach, ' "The Software of Empire": Telegraphic News Agencies and Imperial Publicity, 1865–1914', in J. F. Codell (ed.), *Imperial Co-Histories: National Identities and the British and Colonial Press* (Madison, NJ, 2003).

62. Quoted in *Proceedings of the Colonial Conference 1894* (Ottawa, 1894), p. 89.

63. By the early twentieth century, Pender's group of companies controlled 40 per cent of the world's telegraph cables. See D. R. Headrick, The *Tentacles of Progress: Technology Transfer in the Age of Imperialism, 1850–1940* (Oxford and New York, 1988), p. 105.

64. D. P. Nickles, *Under the Wire: How the Telegraph Changed Diplomacy* (Cambridge, MA, 2003), p. 181.

65. S. M. Müller, 'From Cabling the Atlantic to Wiring the World', *Technology and Culture*, 57, 3 (2016), 507–26.

66. Nickles, *Under the Wire*, p. 180.

67. See V. Ogle, 'Whose Time Is It? The Pluralization of Time and the Global Condition, 1870s–1940s', *American Historical Review*, 118, 5 (2013), 1376–402.

68. See Nile Green, *Bombay Islam: The Religious Economy of the West Indian Ocean, 1840–1915* (Cambridge, 2011).

69. For the influence of the *haj*, see the important study by M. F. Laffan, *Islamic Nationhood and Colonial Indonesia* (London and New York, 2003).

70. In his *Oceana, or, England and Her Colonies* (London, 1886).

71. See J. M. Brown (ed.), *Mahatma Gandhi: The Essential Writings* (Oxford, 2008), pp. 68, 69, 83.

72. W. Woodruff, *Impact of Western Man* (London, 1966), p. 313.

73. Ibid., p. 264.

74. A. Maddison, *Contours of the World Economy, 1–2030 AD* (Oxford and New York, 2007), p. 43.

75. See Woodruff, *Impact*, p. 106.

76. R. Findlay and K. H. O'Rourke, *Power and Plenty: Trade, War, and the World Economy in the Second Millennium* (Princeton, 2007), p. 382.

77. G. J. Milne, 'Knowledge, Communications and the Information Order in Nineteenth-Century Liverpool', *International Journal of Maritime History*, 14, 1 (2002), 214.

78. R. Graham, *Britain and the Onset of Modernization in Brazil, 1850–1914* (Cambridge, 1972), esp. chs. 2, 3, 5, 7.

79. P. Winn, 'British Informal Empire in Uruguay in the Nineteenth Century', *Past and Present*, 73 (1976), 110, 112.

80. J. Adelman, *Republic of Capital: Buenos Aires and the Legal Transformation of the Atlantic World* (Stanford, 1999), chs. 9 and 10; R. Hora, *The Landowners of the Argentine Pampas* (Oxford, 2001), pp. 57ff.

81. London's role has been superbly described in D. Kynaston, *The City of London: Golden Years, 1890–1914* (London, 1995).

82. R. C. Michie, *The City of London: Continuity and Change, 1850–1990* (Basingstoke, 1992), ch. 2.

83. See S. D. Chapman, *The Rise of Merchant Banking* (London, 1984).

84. A. I. Bloomfield, *Short-Term Capital Movements under the Pre-1914 Gold Standard* (Princeton, 1963), p. 46.

85. Michie, *City of London*, p. 134.

86. Maddison, *Contours*, p. 224.

87. For the gold rushes, B. Mountford and S. Tuffnell (eds.), *A Global History of Gold Rushes* (Oakland, CA, 2018).

88. J. A. Mann, *The Cotton Trade of Great Britain* [1860] (reprint, London, 1968), p. 39.

89. Cobden, *England, Ireland, and America*, p. 11.

90. P. Baldwin, *Contagion and the State in Europe, 1830–1930* (Cambridge, 1999), p. 37.

91. K. D. Patterson, 'Cholera Diffusion in Russia, 1823–1923', *Social Science and Medicine*, 38, 9 (1994), 1171–91.

92. *Abstract of Proceedings and Reports of the International Sanitary Conference of 1866* (Bombay, 1867), pp. 16, 113.

93. J. A. Carrigan, *The Saffron Scourge: A History of Yellow Fever in Louisiana, 1796–1905* (Lafayette, LA, 1994).

94. See M. Echenberg, *Plague Ports: The Global Impact of Bubonic Plague, 1894–1901* (New York, 2007).

95. M. Harrison, *Contagion: How Commerce Has Spread Disease* (New Haven, 2012), p. 192.

96. L. Twrdek and K. Manzel, 'The Seed of Abundance and Misery: Peruvian Living Standards . . . 1820–1880', *Economics and Human Biology*, 8, 2 (2010), 145–52.

97. W. P. McGreevey, *An Economic History of Colombia, 1845–1930* (Cambridge, 1971), pp. 138ff.

98. See R. Owen, *The Middle East in the World Economy 1800–1914* (London, 1981), chs. 4 and 5.

99. C. Suter and H. Stamm, 'Coping with Global Debt Crises: Debt Settlements, 1820 to 1986', *Comparative Studies in Society and History*, 34, 4 (1992), 645–78.

100. For the importance of Paris as a financial centre, see Y. Cassis, *Capitals of Capital: The Rise and Fall of International Financial Centres, 1780–2005* (Cambridge, 2006), chs. 2 and 3.

101. Graphically described in I. Phimister, 'Corners and Company-Mongering: Nigerian Tin and the City of London, 1909–12', *Journal of Imperial and Commonwealth History*, 28, 2 (2000), 23–41; and Phimister, 'Frenzied Finance: Gold Mining in the Globalizing South, circa 1886–1896', in Mountford and Tuffnell (eds.), *Gold Rushes*, pp. 142–57.

102. J. A. Hobson, *The Evolution of Modern Capitalism* [1894], rev. edn. (London, 1926), p. 246.

103. G. R. Searle, *Corruption in British Politics, 1895–1930* (Oxford, 1987).

104. R. Austen, *African Economic History* (London and Portsmouth, NH, 1987), pp. 121–5.

105. A. Hochschild, *King Leopold's Ghost* (London, 1998).

106. See C. van Onselen, *Chibaro: African Mine Labour in Southern Rhodesia 1900–1933* (London, 1976), p. 50; I. Phimister, *Wangi Kolia* (Johannesburg, 1994).

107. B. Kidd, *Social Evolution* (London, 1894), p. 50.

108. R. McGregor, *Imagined Destinies: Aboriginal Australians and the Doomed Race Theory, 1880–1939* (Carlton, Victoria, 1997).

109. Quoted in R. Robinson and J. Gallagher, *Africa and the Victorians* (London, 1961), p. 5.

110. The classic account remains J. K. Fairbank, *Trade and Diplomacy on the China Coast: The Opening of the Treaty Ports, 1842–1854*, 2 vols. (Cambridge, MA, 1953).

111. See M. R. Auslin, *Negotiating with Imperialism: The Unequal Treaties and the Culture of Japanese Diplomacy* (Cambridge, MA, 2004), chs. 1–5.

112. For which see D. Omissi, *The Sepoy and the Raj* (Basingstoke, 1994).

113. See S. B. Saul, *Studies in British Overseas Trade, 1870–1914* (Liverpool, 1960).

114. D. Todd, 'A French Imperial Meridian, 1814–1870', *Past and Present*, 210 (2011), 155–86; and D. Todd, 'Transnational Projects of Empire in France, c.1815–c.1870', *Modern Intellectual History*, 12, 2 (2015), 265–93.

115. The advance of the United States as an empire is now best followed in A. G. Hopkins, *American Empire: A Global History* (Princeton, 2018), chs. 8 and 9.

116. Quoted in D. Gillard, *The Struggle for Asia, 1828–1914* (London, 1977), p. 103.

117. See A. Jersild, *Orientalism and Empire: North Caucasus Mountain Peoples and the Georgian Frontier, 1845–1917* (Montreal and Kingston, 2002).

118. See C. J. Colombos, *The International Law of the Sea*, 4th edn. (London, 1959), pp. 81–2.

119. This was Karl Kautsky's 'ultra-imperialism' against which Lenin raged in his *Imperialism: The Highest Stage of Capitalism* (London, 1917).

CHAPTER 4: OCEANS OF CHANGE

1. L. Paine, *The Sea and Civilization* (New York, 2015), p. 40.

2. For Joseph Conrad's description, see his *The Mirror of the Sea* (London, 1906), pp. 35, 95.

3. This has been brilliantly demonstrated in K. J. Banks, *Chasing Empire across the Sea: Communications and the State in the French Atlantic, 1713–1763* (Montreal, 2002).

4. A. Villiers, *Sons of Sindbad* (London, 1940).

5. H. J. Mackinder, 'The Geographical Pivot of History', *Geographical Journal*, 23, 4 (1904), 432.

6. 'The Interest of America in Sea Power, Present and Future', in A. Westcott (ed.), *Mahan on Naval Warfare* (Boston, 1919), p. 286.

7. C. Darwin, *Journal of Researches into the Geology and Natural History of the Various Countries Visited during the Voyage of HMS Beagle round the World . . .* [1843] (Everyman edn., London, 1906), p. 1.

8. J. Goodman, *The Rattlesnake: A Voyage of Discovery to the Coral Sea* (London, 2005).

9. H. M. Rozwadowski, 'Technology and Ocean-Scape: Defining the Deep Sea in the Mid-Nineteenth Century', *History and Technology*, 17, 3 (2001), 217–47.

10. J. Hyslop, ' "Ghostlike" Seafarers and Sailing Ship Nostalgia: The Figure of the Steamship Lascar in the British Imagination, *c.*1880–1960', *Journal for Maritime Research*, 16, 2 (2014), 212–28.

11. A. R. Wallace, *The Malay Archipelago* (London, 1869), ch. 28, for a description.

12 P. Machado, *Ocean of Trade: South Asian Merchants, Africa and the Indian Ocean, c.1750–1850* (Cambridge, 2014), chs. 3, 4 and 5. The British prohibited the slave trade after 1807, but slavery remained lawful in India until 1860.

13. R. G. Landen, *Oman since 1856* (Princeton, 1967), p. 111.

14. See G. Fox, *British Admirals and Chinese Pirates, 1832–1869* (London, 1940).

15. See J. B. Kelly, *Britain and the Persian Gulf, 1795–1880* (Oxford, 1968).

16. I. K. Steele, *The English Atlantic 1675–1740: An Exploration of Communication and Community* (Oxford, 1986).

17. For La Rochelle and Bordeaux, see B. Martinetti, *Les Négociants de la Rochelle au XVIIIe siècle* (Rennes, 2013); J.-P. Poussou, *Bordeaux et le Sud-Ouest au XVIIIe siècle* (Paris, 1983); P. Butel, *Les Négociants bordelais: L'Europe et les Îles au XVIIIe siècle* (Paris, 1974).

18. A. Roland, W. J. Bolster and A. Keyssar, *The Way of the Ship: America's Maritime History Reenvisioned, 1600–2000* (Hoboken, NJ, 2007), p. 194.

19. M. Maury, 'Maritime Interests of the South and West', *Southern Literary Messenger*, 11, 11 (November 1845), 655–8.

20. Quoted in J. H. Clapham, *An Economic History of Modern Britain: The Early Railway Age, 1820–1850* [1930], 2nd edn. (Cambridge, 1964) p. 506.

21. For the development of American coastal shipping, see R. G. Albion, *Square-Riggers on Schedule: The New York Sailing Packets to England, France and the Cotton Ports* (Princeton, 1938).

22. C. Capper, *The Port and Trade of London* (London, 1862), p. 309.

23. Roland, Bolster and Keyssar, *Way of the Ship*, p. 196.

24. Steele, *The English Atlantic*, pp. 170–73.

25. R. G. Albion, *The Rise of New York Port, 1815–1860* (New York, 1939), p. 52; R. C. McKay, *South Street: A Maritime History of New York* (New York, 1934), p. 161.

26. W. A. Fairburn, *Merchant Sail*, 6 vols. (Center Lovell, ME, 1945–55), vol. 2, pp. 1142, 1155; Albion, *Square-Riggers*, ch. 3.

27. P[arliamentary]. P[apers]. 1875, C.1167 Commercial Reports No. 4, p. 460: Report of Consul-General Archibald for New York, 1874.

28. P. de Rousiers and J. Charles, 'Le Port de Hambourg', in Société Scientifique de Bruxelles, *Les Ports et leur fonction économique*, vol. 3 (Louvain, 1908), p. 136.

29. Roland, Bolster, Keyssar, *Way of the Ship*, p. 196.

30. See L. Bethell, *The Abolition of the Brazilian Slave Trade* (Cambridge, 1970), pp. 370ff.

31. See J. McAleer, 'Looking East: St Helena, the South Atlantic and Britain's Indian Ocean World', *Atlantic Studies*, 13, 1 (2016), 78–98.

32. J. P. Delgado, *Gold Rush Port: The Maritime Archaeology of San Francisco's Waterfront* (Berkeley, 2009), pp. 41ff.

33. G. Blainey, *The Tyranny of Distance* (South Melbourne, Victoria, 1966), p. 195.

34. M'Culloch's *Commercial Dictionary*, new edn. (London, 1869), p. 1184.

35. L. L. Johnson and Z. Frank, 'Cities and Wealth in the South Atlantic: Buenos Aires and Rio de Janeiro before 1860', *Comparative Studies in Society and History*, 48, 3 (2006), 634–68.

36. R. Graham, *Britain and the Onset of Modernization in Brazil, 1850–1914* (Cambridge, 1968), ch. 2; D. C. M. Platt, *Latin America and British Trade, 1806–1914* (London, 1972), chs. 4, 6 and 7; J. Adelman, *Republic of Capital* (Stanford, 1999), chs. 9 and 10; P. Winn, 'British Informal Empire in Uruguay in the Nineteenth Century', *Past and Present*, 73 (1976), 110ff.

37. See R. G. Albion, 'Capital Movement and Transportation: British Shipping and Latin America, 1806–1914', *Journal of Economic History*, 11, 4 (1951), 361–74.

38. See C. Fyfe, *A History of Sierra Leone* (London, 1962).

39. Bethell, *Brazilian Slave Trade*, pp. 49, 104.

40. K. Mann, *Slavery and the Birth of an African City: Lagos, 1760–1900* (Bloomington, IN, 2007), p. 61.

41. Bethell, *Brazilian Slave Trade*, remains the classic account of this episode.

42. Lord Anson, *Voyage Round the World in 1740–1744* (Everyman edn., London, 1911), pp. 275–9, 317, 320.

43. See O. H. K. Spate, *The Pacific since Magellan*, vol. 3: *Paradise Found and Lost* (London, 1988), p. 173.

44. See R. Richards, *Honolulu: Centre of Trans-Pacific Trade* (Canberra, 2000).

45. Quoted in H. W. Bradley, 'Hawaii and the American Penetration of the Northeastern Pacific, 1800–1845', *Pacific Historical Review*, 12, 3 (1943), 282.

46. See D. Igler, 'Diseased Goods: Global Exchanges in the Eastern Pacific Basin, 1770–1850', *American Historical Review*, 109, 3 (2004), 693–719.

47 See E. Sinn, *Pacific Crossing: California Gold, Chinese Migration and the Making of Hong Kong* (Hong Kong, 2013).

48. For an authoritative account, see R. Holland, *Blue-Water Empire: The British in the Mediterranean since 1800* (London, 2012), chs. 2 and 3.

49. See F. E. Bailey, *British Policy and the Turkish Reform Movement: A Study in Anglo-Turkish Relations, 1826–1853* (Cambridge, MA, 1942).

50. F. Tabak, *The Waning of the Mediterranean, 1550–1870: A Geohistorical Approach* (Baltimore, 2008).

51. R. Owen, *The Middle East in the World Economy 1800–1914* (London, 1981), ch. 5.

52. V. J. Puryear, 'Odessa: Its Rise and International Importance, 1815–50', *Pacific Historical Review*, 3, 2 (1934), 193.

53. Ibid., 201.

54. A. Delis, 'From Lateen to Square Rig: The Evolution of the Greek-Owned Merchant Fleet and Its Ships in the Eighteenth and Nineteenth Centuries', *Mariner's Mirror*, 100, 1 (2014), 44–58.

55. G. Harlaftis and G. Kostelenos, 'International Shipping and National Economic Growth: Shipping Earnings and the Greek Economy in the Nineteenth Century', *Economic History Review*, 65, 4 (2012), 1,403–27.

56. See G. J. Milne, 'Maritime Liverpool', in J. Belchem (ed.), *Liverpool 800: Culture, Character and History* (Liverpool, 2006), p. 260.

57. See *The Black Sea Pilot* [1855], 3rd edn. (London, 1884), p. 5.

58. I have drawn on the classic article by G. S. Graham, 'The Ascendancy of the Sailing Ship, 1850–85', *Economic History Review*, 9, 1 (1956), 74–88.

59. See the sophisticated calculations in C. Brautaset and R. Grafe, 'The Quiet Transport Revolution', in Oxford University, *Discussion Papers in Economic and Social History*, no. 62 (2006), online.

60. See E. C. Smith, *A Short History of Naval and Marine Engineering* (Cambridge, 1937), pp. 18off.

61. See M. J. Daunton, *Coal Metropolis: Cardiff 1870–1914* (Leicester, 1977).

62. T. Boyns and S. Gray, 'Welsh Coal and the Informal Empire in South America, 1850–1913', *Atlantic Studies*, 13, 1 (2016), 65ff. The records of Cory Brothers are at the Glamorgan Archives.

63. See [US Navy Department], *Coaling, Docking, and Repairing Facilities of the Ports of the World* ... [1885], 3rd edn. (Washington DC, 1892).

64. See P. A. Shulman, *Coal and Empire: The Birth of Energy Security in Industrial America* (Baltimore, 2015), p. 85.

65. For a description, see J. Chalcraft, 'The Coal Heavers of Port Sa'id: State-Making and Worker Protest, 1869–1914', *International Labor and Working-Class History*, 60 (2001), 110–24.

66. For a brilliant evocation, see E. Newby, *The Last Grain Race* (London, 1956).

67. I have drawn on the excellent article by D. Kennerley, 'Stoking the Boilers: Firemen and Trimmers in British Merchant Ships, 1850–1950', *International Journal of Maritime History*, 20, 1 (2008), 191–220.

68. Hyslop, ' "Ghostlike" Seafarers'; M. Sherwood, 'Race, Nationality and Employment among Lascar Seamen, 1660 to 1945', *Journal of Ethnic and Migration Studies*, 17, 2 (1991), 233.

69. A. W. Kirkaldy, *British Shipping* (London, 1914), Appendix XVII. I have excluded US lake and river tonnage.

70. F. Harcourt, *Flagships of Imperialism: The P&O Company and the Politics of Empire from Its Origins to 1867* (Manchester, 2006); T. A. Bushell, *'Royal Mail': A Centenary History of the Royal Mail Line, 1839–1939* (London, 1939); F. E. Hyde, *Cunard and the North Atlantic 1840–1973: A History of Shipping and Financial Management* (London, 1975).

71. P.P. 1901 (300) Select Committee on Steamship Subsidies, *Report*, pp. 233ff.

72. Harcourt, *Flagships of Imperialism*, p. 214.

73. Chih-lung Lin, 'The British Dynamic Mail Contract on the North Atlantic: 1860–1900', *Business History*, 54, 5 (2012), 783–97.

74. See D. Keeling, 'Transatlantic Shipping Cartels and Migration between Europe and America, 1880–1914', *Essays in Economic and Business History*, 17, 1 (1999), 195–213.

75. Royal Commission on Shipping Rings, *Report*, P.P. 1909, xlvii, 4668, p. 12; Keeling, 'Shipping Cartels'.

76. Shipping Rings, *Report*, p. 78. However, six members of the Commission registered fierce opposition to this conclusion.

77. See R. Woodman, *A History of the British Merchant Navy*, vol. 4: *More Days, More Dollars: The Universal Bucket Chain, 1885–1920* (London, 2016), pp. 34–47.

78. B. Taylor, 'Tramp Shipping', in *Ships and Shipping*, vol. 2 (n.d. but *c.*1914), p. 264.

79. See G. Boyce, 'Edward Bates and Sons, 1897–1915: Tramping Operations in Recession and Recovery', *International Journal of Maritime History*, 23, 1 (2011), 13–50.

80. Woodruff, *Impact*, p. 272.

81. Calculated from Kirkaldy, *British Shipping*, Appendix, XVII.

82. See Y. Kaukiainen, 'Journey Costs, Terminal Costs and Ocean Tramp Freights: How the Price of Distance Declined from the 1870s to 2000', *International Journal of Maritime History*, 18, 2 (2006), 17–64, esp. 30.

83. For this argument, see R. Cohn, *Mass Migration Under Sail: European Immigration to the Antebellum United States* (Cambridge, 2009).

84. Woodruff, *Impact*, p. 260.

85. See B. Lubbock, *The Log of the 'Cutty Sark'*, 2nd edn. (Glasgow, 1945), p. 129.

86. D. A. Farnie, *East and West of Suez* (Oxford, 1969), p. 362.

87. Ibid., p. 751.

88. D. Kumar (ed.), *The Cambridge Economic History of India*, vol. 2: *c.1757–c.1970* (New Delhi, 1982), pp. 835–7.

89. A. J. Sargent, *Seaways of the Empire* (London, 1918), pp. 65ff.

90. J. Conrad, 'The End of the Tether' in his *Youth. A Narrative, and Two Other Stories* (Edinburgh and London, 1902), p. 189.

91. H. J. Schonfield, *The Suez Canal* (Harmondsworth, 1939), p. 111.

92. See the brilliantly suggestive remarks in Farnie, *Suez*, ch. 21.

93. See D. M. Williams and J. Armstrong, 'Changing Voyage Patterns in the Nineteenth Century: The Impact of the Steamship', *International Journal of Maritime History*, 22, 2 (2010), 151–70.

CHAPTER 5: AMERICAN GATEWAYS

1. A. Mackay, *The Western World: or Travels in the United States in 1846–47*, 2 vols. (Philadelphia, 1849), quoted in J. W. Reps, *Cities of the Mississippi* (Columbia, MO, and London, 1994), p. 106.

2. T. E. Redard, 'The Port of New Orleans: An Economic History, 1821–1860', PhD thesis, Louisiana State University (1985), Appendix II, Table 10 (available online).

3. R. G. Albion, *The Rise of New York Port, 1815–1860* (New York, 1939), p. 105.

4. D. Drake, *Remarks on the Importance of Promoting Literary and Social Concert in the Valley of the Mississippi* (1833), quoted in

E. Watts and D. Rachels (eds.), *The First West: Writing from the American Frontier, 1776–1860* (Oxford, 2002), p. 345.

5. S. P. Marler, *The Merchants' Capital* (Cambridge, 2013), p. 40.

6. F. Furstenberg, 'The Significance of the Trans-Appalachian Frontier in Atlantic History', *American Historical Review, 113*, 3 (June 2008), 673.

7. See D. W. Meinig, *The Shaping of America*, vol. 2: *Continental America, 1800–1867* (New Haven, 1993), p. 4. The Floridas were acquired piecemeal and later.

8. R. W. Van Alstyne, *The Rising American Empire* (Oxford, 1960), pp. 81, 86.

9. United States Census Office, *Agriculture of the United States in 1860* (Washington DC, 1864), p. 85; www.census.gov/library/publications/dec/1860b.html.

10. See W. Johnson, *Soul by Soul: Life Inside the Antebellum Slave Market* (Cambridge, MA, 1999).

11. A superb description is in R. Campanella, *Bienville's Dilemma: A Historical Geography of New Orleans* (Lafayette, LA, 2008).

12. For the Native American role in creating the site, see T. R. Kidder, 'Making the City Inevitable', in C. E. Colten (ed.), *Transforming New Orleans and Its Environs* (Pittsburgh, 2000).

13. T. N. Ingersoll, *Mammon and Manon in Early New Orleans: The First Slave Society in the Deep South, 1718–1819* (Knoxville, 1999), p. 254. Judah Benjamin from the city became the first openly Jewish US Senator.

14. N. Dessens, *From Saint-Domingue to New Orleans: Migration and Influences* (Gainesville, FL, 2007).

15. See D. T. Gleeson, *The Irish in the South, 1815–1877* (Chapel Hill, 2001), p. 53.

16. R. Campanella, 'An Ethnic Geography of New Orleans', *Journal of American History*, 94, 3 (2007), 704–15; Cabildo Museum, New Orleans.

17. Cabildo Museum, New Orleans.

18. See D. Grimsted, *American Mobbing, 1828–1861: Toward Civil War* (Oxford, 1998), p. 92.

19. U. B. Phillips, *Life and Labor in the Old South* (Boston, 1929), p. 151.

20. Theodore Clapp, *Autobiographical Sketches and Recollections* (Boston, 1858), p. 119.

21. Nicholas Trist to Virginia Randolph, 11 August 1822, University of North Carolina, Southern Historical Collection 02104, Nicholas Philip Trist Papers, 1.2, Folder 24 (online).

22. *De Bow's Review*, 16, 5 (1854): 'Yellow Fever in New Orleans' (online).

23. J. A. Carrigan, *The Saffron Scourge: A History of Yellow Fever in Louisiana, 1796–1905* (Lafayette, LA, 1994), pp. 4, 5, 7.

24. A. Kelman, *A River and Its City: The Nature of Landscape in New Orleans* (Berkeley, 2003), p. 88.

25. Amos Lefavour to J. Whitney, 30 March 1842, Library of Congress, Whitney and Burnham Papers, MSS 45450, Box 1.

26. See J. B. Rehder, *Delta Sugar: Louisiana's Vanishing Plantation Landscape* (Baltimore, 1999), p. 178.

27. See J. H. Moore, *Agriculture in Ante-Bellum Mississippi* [1958], 2nd edn. (Columbia, SC, 2010), ch. 1; M. J. Brazy, *American Planter: Stephen Duncan of Antebellum Natchez and New York* (Baton Rouge, 2006).

28. For an unflattering view of Natchez society in the 1850s, see F. L. Olmsted, *The Cotton Kingdom* [1861], ed. and introduced by A. M. Schlesinger, Modern Library edn. (New York, 1969), pp. 416–26.

29. See C. S. Aiken, *William Faulkner and the Southern Landscape* (Athens, GA, 2009), ch. 4.

30. *Agriculture of the United States in 1860*, p. 85.

31. Moore, *Ante-Bellum Mississippi*, pp. 69, 180. The white population had increased from 70,000 to 350,000.

32. See the fascinating study by R. Campanella, *Lincoln in New Orleans* (Lafayette, LA, 2010).

33. That the Cotton Kingdom was self-sufficient in foodstuffs has been reiterated forcefully in A. L. Olmstead and P. W. Rhode, 'Cotton, Slavery and the New History of Capitalism', *Explorations in Economic History*, 67 (2018), 13.

34. Redard, 'New Orleans', Appendix I, Table 3.

35. L. C. Hunter, *Steamboats on the Western Rivers* (Cambridge, MA, 1949), p. 59.

36. P. F. Paskoff, *Troubled Waters: Steamboat Disasters, River Improvements, and American Public Policy, 1821–1860* (Baton Rouge, 2007), p. 39.

37. Hunter, *Steamboats*, pp. 644–5.

38. See T. S. Berry, *Western Prices before 1861: A Study of the Cincinnati Market* (Cambridge, MA, 1943), p. 69.

39. Paskoff, *Troubled Waters*, p. 34.

40. Ibid., p. 159.

41. Olmstead and Rhode, 'Cotton, Slavery', 8.

42. W. W. Chenault and R. C. Reinders, 'The Northern-Born Community in New Orleans in the 1850s', *Journal of American History*, 51, 2 (1964), 232–47.

43. L. K. Salvucci and R. J. Salvucci, 'The Lizardi Brothers: A Mexican Family Business and the Expansion of New Orleans, 1825–1846', *Journal of Southern History*, 82, 4 (2016), 759–88.

44. W. Amory to Whitney and Burnham, 24 December 1842, Whitney and Burnham Papers, Box 1.

45. N. J. Dick and Co. to W. Newton Mercer, 8 April 1840. William Newton Mercer Papers, Howard-Tilton Library, Tulane University, MSS 64, Box 1.

46. For a classic account of the cotton factor, H. D. Woodman, *King Cotton and His Retainers: Financing and Marketing the Cotton Crop of the South, 1800–1925* (Lexington, KY, 1968).

47. J. H. Pease and W. H. Pease, 'The Economics and Politics of Charleston's Nullification Crisis', *Journal of Southern History*, 47, 3 (1981), 335–62.

48. E. L. Miller, *New Orleans and the Texas Revolution* (College Station, TX, 2004).

49. C. S. Urban, 'The Ideology of Southern Imperialism: New Orleans and the Caribbean, 1845–1860', *Louisiana Historical Quarterly*, 39, 1 (1956), 48–73.

50. On these, see M. Karp, *This Vast Southern Empire: Slaveholders at the Helm of American Foreign Policy* (Cambridge, MA, 2016), pp. 193, 197.

51. J. Majewski and T. W. Wahlstrom, 'Geography as Power: The Political Economy of Matthew Fontaine Maury', *Virginia Magazine of History and Biography*, 120, 4 (2012), 347.

52. Marler, *Merchants' Capital*, p. 43.

53. See Redard, 'New Orleans'.

54. See the map in J. Atack, F. Bateman, M. Haines and R. A. Margo, 'Did Railroads Induce or Follow Economic Growth? Urbanization and Population Growth in the American Midwest, 1850–1860', *Social Science History*, 34, 2 (2010), 176, 177.

55. *Agriculture of the United States in 1860*, p. 157.

56. J. F. Entz, *Exchange and Cotton Trade between England and the United States* (New York, 1840), p. 16 (online).

57. R. W. Fogel and S. L. Engerman, *Time on the Cross: The Economics of American Negro Slavery* (London, 1974), pp. 248–50; R. W. Fogel, *Without Consent or Contract: The Rise and Fall of American Slavery* (New York, 1989), p. 87. Of course, this concealed enormous differences in Southern incomes between slaves and free persons. Indeed, 'free' households in the South had incomes well above the average for

the US as a whole. See the income estimates in P. H. Lindert and J. G. Williamson, 'American Incomes 1774–1860', National Bureau of Economic Research Working Paper no. 18396 (2012), pp. 33, 36, at http://www.nber.org/papers/w18396.

58. L. Shore, *Southern Capitalists: The Ideological Leadership of an Elite, 1832–1885* (Chapel Hill, 1986), p. 48.

59. Moore, *Ante-Bellum Mississippi*, ch. 8.

60. For the claim, E. E. Baptist, *The Half Has Never Been Told: Slavery and the Making of American Capitalism* (New York, 2014), pp. 113, 126–7; and for the corrective, Olmstead and Rhode, 'Cotton, Slavery', 8–11.

61. J. Oakes, *The Ruling Race: A History of American Slaveholders* (New York, 1982, 1998), pp. 76–8. For the adverse effects of the 'shifting cultivation' practised in the South, and the ecological reasons behind it, see J. Majewski, *Modernizing a Slave Economy: The Economic Vision of the Confederate Nation* (Chapel Hill, 2009), ch. 2.

62. D. P. McNeilly, *The Old South Frontier: Cotton Plantations and the Formation of Arkansas Society* (Fayetteville, AR, 2000), pp. 7ff.

63. C. Woods, *Development Arrested: The Blues and Plantation Power in the Mississippi Delta* (London, 1998, 2017), p. 54.

64. See L. K. Ford, *Deliver Us from Evil: The Slavery Question in the Old South* (New York, 2009), pp. 508ff.

65. D. Brown, 'A Vagabond's Tale: Poor Whites, Herrenvolk Democracy, and the Value of Whiteness in the Late Antebellum South', *Journal of Southern History*, 79, 4 (2013), 799–840.

66. M. O'Brien, *Conjectures of Order: Intellectual Life and the American South, 1810–1860*, vol. 1 (Chapel Hill, 2004), p. 17.

67. Grimsted, *Mobbing*, p. 159.

68. Oakes, *Ruling Race*, p. 150.

69. See J. B. Stewart, 'The Emergence of Racial Modernity and the Rise of the White North, 1790–1840', *Journal of the Early Republic*, 18, 2 (1998), 182.

70. C. Phillips, *The Rivers Ran Backward: The Civil War and the Remaking of the American Middle Border* (Oxford, 2016), p. 20.

71. Shore, *Southern Capitalists*, p. 63.

72. See R. B. Kielbowicz, 'Modernization, Communication Policy, and the Geopolitics of News, 1820–1860', *Critical Studies in Mass Communication*, 3, 1 (1986), 30–32.

73. Marler, *Merchants' Capital*, pp. 122–3.

74. J. A. Nystrom, *New Orleans after the Civil War: Race, Politics, and a New Birth of Freedom* (Baltimore, 2010), p. 8.

75. For a recent recalculation of the damage, see P. F. Paskoff, 'Measure of War: A Quantitative Examination of the Civil War's Destructiveness in the Confederacy', *Civil War History*, 54, 1 (2008), 35–62.

76. Marler, *Merchants' Capital*, chs. 6 and 7.

77. J. J. Jackson, *New Orleans in the Gilded Age: Politics and Urban Progress 1880–1896* (Baton Rouge, 1969), pp. 4–21, 209.

78. B. I. Kaufman, 'New Orleans and the Panama Canal, 1900–1914', *Louisiana History*, 14, 4 (1973), 335, 344.

79. A. J. Sargent, *Seaports and Hinterlands* (London, 1938), p. 118.

80. Marler, *Merchants' Capital*, p. 230.

81. From 'Folly on Royal Street in the Raw Face of God' (1964); www.cnhs.org>ourpages>auto.

82. For an introduction, see W. J. Eccles, *France in America* (New York, 1972).

83. Montreal was built on an old Native American portage route. B. Rushforth, 'Insinuating Empire: Indians, Smugglers, and the Imperial Geography of Eighteenth-Century Montreal', in J. Gitlin, B. Berglund and A. Arenson (eds.), *Frontier Cities: Encounters at the Crossroads of Empire* (Philadelphia, 2012), p. 56.

84. The classic account is D. G. Creighton, *The Empire of the St Lawrence* [1937] (Toronto, 1956).

85. See for a 'contemporary' description E. Ross, *Beyond the River and the Bay* (Toronto, 1970).

86. H. A. Innis, *The Fur Trade in Canada* (Toronto, 1930), remains the authoritative account.

87. A. Greer, *The Patriots and the People: The Rebellion of 1837 in Rural Lower Canada* (Toronto, 1993).

88. See J. M. S. Careless, *The Union of the Canadas: The Growth of Canadian Institutions, 1841–1857* (Toronto, 1967).

89. G. P. de T. Glazebrook, *A History of Transportation in Canada*, vol. 1: *Continental Strategy to 1867* (Toronto, 1938, 1964), p. 84.

90. J. H. S. Reid, K. McNaught and H. S. Crowe (eds.), *A Source-Book of Canadian History: Selected Documents and Personal Papers* (Toronto, 1959), pp. 131ff.

91. See D. C. Masters, *The Reciprocity Treaty of 1854* [1937] (Toronto, 1963), pp. 122–3; *Semi-Centennial Report of the Montreal Board of Trade* (Montreal, 1893), p. 62.

92. J. Young, *Letters to the Hon. Francis Lemieux, Chief Commissioner Public Works . . .* (Montreal, 1855), p. 9.

93. See D. McCalla, *Planting the Province: The Economic History of Upper Canada, 1784–1870* (Toronto, 1993).

94. For Allan's career, see T. E. Appleton, *Ravenscrag: The Allan Royal Mail Line* (Toronto, 1974).

95. S. P. Day, *English America*, vol. 1 (1864), pp. 156ff.

96. See O. D. Skelton, *The Railway Builders* (Toronto, 1916); for a modern account, A. A. den Otter, *The Philosophy of Railways: The Transcontinental Railway Idea in British North America* (Toronto, 1997), ch. 4.

97. *Montreal in 1856* (Montreal, 1856), pp. 25, 30; see https://static.toronto publiclibrary.ca/da/pdfs/37131055411417d.pdf.

98. B.-M. Papillon, 'Montreal's Growth and Economic Changes in Quebec Province, 1851–1911', PhD thesis, Northwestern University (1986), available online, pp. 92ff.

99. D. McKeagan, 'Development of a Mature Securities Market in Montreal from 1817 to 1874', *Business History*, 51, 1 (2009), 59–76.

100. D. C. Masters, *The Rise of Toronto, 1850–1890* (Toronto, 1947), ch. 3; J. M. S. Careless, *Toronto to 1918* (Toronto, 1984).

101. See W. L. Morton, *Manitoba: A History* (Toronto, 1957), ch. 4.

102. K. Bourne, *Britain and the Balance of Power in North America, 1815–1908* (London, 1967).

103. 'A clever, most unprincipled party leader [who] had developed a system of political corruption that has demoralised the country' was one posthumous verdict. Quoted in G. T. Stewart, *The Origins of Canadian Politics* (Vancouver, 1986), p. 69.

104. D. G. Creighton, *John A. Macdonald: The Young Politician* (Toronto, 1952), offers a more sympathetic portrait of Macdonald.

105. P. B. Waite (ed.), *The Confederation Debates in the Province of Canada/1865* (Toronto, 1963), p. 101.

106. P. B. Waite, *The Life and Times of Confederation 1864–1867* (Toronto, 1962), ch. 10.

107. Den Otter, *Philosophy of Railways*, ch. 6.

108. See 'Donald Alexander Smith, 1st Baron Strathcona' and 'George Stephen', both in the *Dictionary of Canadian Biography* (online).

109. For the CPR, see H. A. Innis, *A History of the Canadian Pacific Railway* (Toronto, 1923); R. T. Naylor, *The History of Canadian Business, 1867–1914* [1975], new edn. (Toronto, 2006), vol. 1, ch. 8.

110. Figures in M. Q. Innis, *An Economic History of Canada* (Toronto, 1935), p. 286.

111. A. Dilley, *Finance, Politics, and Imperialism: Australia, Canada, and the City of London, c.1896–1914* (Basingstoke, 2012), p. 37.

112. Bodleian Library, MSS R. H. Brand, Box 26.

113. Dilley, *Finance*, p. 36.

114. For the growth of Montreal industries, see R. D. Lewis, 'A City Transformed: Manufacturing Districts and Suburban Growth in Montreal, 1850–1929', *Journal of Historical Geography*, 27, 1 (2001), 20–35.

115. Dilley, *Finance*, p. 57.

116. See United Nations Statistical Department, 'International Trade Statistics 1900–1960', at https://unstats.un.org/unsd/trade/imts/Historical%20data%201900-1960.pdf.

117. See G. Tulchinsky, 'The Montreal Business Community, 1837–1853', in D. S. Macmillan (ed.), *Canadian Business History: Selected Studies, 1497–1971* (Toronto, 1972).

118. D. MacKay, *The Square Mile: Merchant Princes of Montreal* (Vancouver, 1987).

119. Their careers can be traced in the *Dictionary of Canadian Biography*.

120. See 'Hugh Allan' in *Dictionary of Canadian Biography*.

121. See 'George Stephen' in *Dictionary of Canadian Biography*.

122. M. Slattery, 'Les Irlandais catholiques de Montréal', in G. Lapointe (ed.), *Société, culture et religion à Montréal, XIX–XX siècle* (Quebec, 1994), p. 44.

123. Den Otter, *Philosophy of Railways*, pp. 104–5.

124. See S. J. Potter, 'The Imperial Significance of the Canadian–American Reciprocity Proposals of 1911', *Historical Journal*, 47, 1 (2004), 81–100.

125. W. W. Swanson and P. C. Armstrong, *Wheat* (Toronto, 1930), pp. 214–16.

126. C. A. E. Goodhart, *The New York Money Market and the Finance of Trade, 1900–1913* (Cambridge, MA, 1969), Appendix 1.

127. A. Siegfried, *The Race Question in Canada* [Paris, 1906], pbk. edn. (Toronto, 1966), p. 185. For the Anglo-Protestants and their world, see M. W. Westley, *Remembrance of Grandeur: The Anglo-Protestant Elite of Montreal, 1900–1950* (Montreal, 1990).

128. J. Gilliland and S. Olson, 'Residential Segregation in an Industrializing City: A Closer Look', *Urban Geography*, 31, 1 (2010), 33.

129. The title of the famous novel by Hugh MacLennan (1945).

130. For Bourassa's career, see C. Murrow, *Henri Bourassa and French-Canadian Nationalism: Opposition to Empire* (Montreal, 1968).

131. For an accessible guide, see S. Mann Trofimenkoff, *The Dream of Nation: A Social and Intellectual History of Quebec* (Toronto, 1983), ch. 7.

132. D. Greasley and L. Oxley, 'A Tale of Two Dominions: Comparing the Macroeconomic Records of Australia and Canada since 1870', *Economic History Review*, 51, 2 (1998), 305ff.

133. W. A. Mackintosh, *The Economic Background to Dominion-Provincial Relations* [1939], pbk. edn. (Toronto, 1979), p. 89.

134. D. Baillargeon, 'La Crise ordinaire: les ménagères montréalaises et la crise des années trente', *Labour/Le Travail*, 30 (1992), 136.

135. See T. Copp, 'The Condition of the Working Class in Montreal, 1897–1920', in M. Horn and R. Sabourin (eds.), *Studies in Canadian Social History* (Toronto, 1974), p. 193.

136. Masters, *Toronto*, ch. 6.

137. J. Martin, 'How Toronto Became the Financial Capital of Canada', Rotman School of Management, University of Toronto, Case Study, (2012), p. 14.

138. A. R. M. Lower, 'Geographical Determinants in Canadian History', in R. Flenley (ed.), *Essays in Canadian History: Presented to George Mackinnan Wrong For His Eightieth Birthday* (Toronto, 1939).

139. *New York Daily Times (1850–1857)*, 27 March 1852 (online).

140. See N. M. Cool, 'Pelts and Prosperity: The Fur Trade and the Mohawk Valley, 1730–1776', *New York History*, 97, 2 (Spring 2016), 136.

141. See R. T. Aggarwala, ' "I Want a Packet to Arrive": Making New York City the Headquarters of British America, 1696–1783', *New York History*, 98, 1 (Winter 2017), 34ff.

142. See E. G. Burrows and M. Wallace, *Gotham: A History of New York City to 1898* (Oxford, 1998), ch. 22.

143. The classic account of New York's maritime assets is Albion, *The Rise of New York Port*.

144. See B. P. Murphy, *Building the Empire State: Political Economy in the Early Republic* (Philadelphia, 2015), pp. 208ff.

145. This figure was cited in J. D. B. De Bow, *The Industrial Resources, Etc., of the Southern and Western States* (1853). See P. S. Foner, *Business and Slavery: The New York Merchants and the Irrepressible Conflict* (Chapel Hill, 1941), p. 7.

146. W. Pencak and C. E. Wright (eds.), *New York and the Rise of American Capitalism* (New York, 1989), p. xii.

147. W. Cronon, *Nature's Metropolis: Chicago and the Great West* (New York, 1991), pp. 70, 77.

148. M. G. Myers, *The New York Money Market*, vol. 1: *Origins and Development* (New York, 1931), p. 104.

149. Cronon, *Nature's Metropolis*, p. 322.

150. See E. K. Spann, *The New Metropolis: New York City, 1840–1857* (New York, 1981), pp. 406, 408–9.

151. *New York Daily Times*, 10 March 1852 (online).

152. Foner, *Business and Slavery*, p. 4.

153. T. Kessner, *Capital City: New York City and the Men Behind America's Rise to Economic Dominance, 1860–1900* (New York, 2003), p. 31.

154. C. R. Geisst, *Wall Street: A History* (Oxford and New York, 1997), p. 57; Kessner, *Capital City*, pp. 31ff.

155. S. Beckert, *The Monied Metropolis: New York City and the Consolidation of the American Bourgeoisie, 1850–1896* (Cambridge, 2001), p. 410.

156. See S. Bruchey, *Enterprise: The Dynamic Economy of a Free People* (Cambridge, MA, 1990), p. 384.

157. The classic accounts are A. D. Chandler Jr, *The Railroads: The Nation's First Big Business* (New York, 1965), and A. D. Chandler Jr, *The Visible Hand: The Managerial Revolution in American Business* (Cambridge, MA, 1977), chs. 3, 4, 5; for a critique, R. R. John, 'Elaborations, Revisions, Dissents: Alfred D. Chandler, Jr.'s, *The Visible Hand* after Twenty Years', *Business History Review*, 71, 2 (1997), 151–200.

158. Beckert, *Monied Metropolis*, p. 141.

159. D. C. Hammack, 'Political Participation and Municipal Policy: New York City, 1870–1940', in T. Bender and C. E. Schorske (eds.), *Budapest and New York: Studies in Metropolitan Transformation, 1870–1930* (New York, 1994), p. 58.

160. J. Heffer, *Le Port de New York et le commerce extérieur américain (1860–1900)* (Paris, 1986), p. 7.

161. Ibid., p. 264.

162. E. Huntington, 'The Water Barriers of New York City', *Geographical Review*, 2, 3 (1916), 169–83.

163. The theme of A. M. Blake, *How New York Became American, 1890–1924* (Baltimore, 2006).

164. See Bender and Schorske (eds.), *Budapest and New York*, 'Introduction'.

165. N. Harris, 'Covering New York City: Journalism and Civic Identity in the Twentieth Century', in Bender and Schorske (eds.), *Budapest and New York*, pp. 258–60.

166. Bruchey, *Enterprise*, p. 382.

167. R. C. O. Matthews, C. H. Feinstein and J. C. Odling-Smee, *British Economic Growth 1856–1973* (Stanford, 1982), p. 433.

168. L. E. Davis and R. J. Cull, *International Capital Markets and American Economic Growth, 1820–1914* (Cambridge, 1994), p. 111.

169. See A. A. Stein, 'The Hegemon's Dilemma: Great Britain, the United States, and the International Economic Order', *International Organization*, 38, 2 (1984), 355–86.

170. F. W. Taussig, *Some Aspects of the Tariff Question* (Cambridge, MA, 1934), p. 139.

171. For this, see D. W. Meinig, *The Shaping of America, vol. 3. Transcontinental America, 1850–1915* (New Haven, 1998), p. 322.

172. See Goodhart, *New York Money Market*.

CHAPTER 6: A MARITIME *RAJ*

1. See S. Broadberry, J. Custodis and B. Gupta, 'India and the Great Divergence', *Explorations in Economic History*, 55, 1 (2015), 58–75.

2. See C. A. Bayly, *Rulers, Townsmen and Bazaars: North Indian Society in the Age of British Expansion, 1770–1870* (Cambridge, 1983), esp. ch. 7; for southern India, see D. Washbrook, 'South India 1770–1840: The Colonial Transition', *Modern Asian Studies*, 38, 3 (2004), 479–516, esp. 507ff.

3. D. Kumar (ed.), *The Cambridge Economic History of India* (hereafter *CEHI*), vol. 2 (Cambridge, 1982), p. 837.

4. See T. Roy, 'Trading Firms in Colonial India', *Business History Review*, 88, 1 (2014), 9–42.

5. See M. Adas, *The Burma Delta: Economic Development and Social Change on an Asian Rice Frontier* (Madison, WI, 1974) for a recent study, see S. Turnell, 'The Chettiars in Burma', www.econ.mq.edu.au/ Econ_docs/research_papers2/2005_research_papers/chettiar.pdf.

6. For their East African connections, see C. Markovits, Structure and Agency in the World of Asian Commerce in the Era of European Colonial Domination (c.1750–1950)', *Journal of the Economic and Social History of the Orient*, 50, 2/3 (2007), 114.

7. P.P. 1873 (C.820), Correspondence Respecting Sir Bartle Frere's Mission to the East Coast of Africa: Frere to Lord Granville, 7 May 1873.

8. P.P. 1871 (C.216), Return of H.M. Ships on Station, April and October, 1869 and 1870; J. B. Kelly, *Britain and the Persian Gulf, 1795–1880* (Oxford, 1968), p. 663.

9. Roy, 'Trading Firms', 9.

10. See G. Blake, *B.I. Centenary 1856–1956* (London, 1956), pp. 83, 159.

11. A. J. Sargent, *Seaways of the Empire* (London, 1918), ch. 3.

12. *Times of India* Digital Archive: I have drawn on accounts in the *Bombay Times and Journal of Commerce* for 18 and 29 July and 8 August 1846. Under two later editors, Lovat Fraser and Stanley Reed (the latter edited the paper from 1907 to 1923), the *Times of India* became one of India's two leading English-language newspapers, together with the Calcutta *Statesman*.

13. A. Farooqui, *Opium City: The Making of Early Victorian Bombay* (Gurgaon, 2006), p. 56.

14. See P. Nightingale, *Trade and Empire in Western India, 1784–1806* (Cambridge, 1970), p. 46.

15. See L. Subramanian, *Indigenous Capital and Imperial Expansion: Bombay, Surat and the West Coast* (Delhi, 1996); Farooqui, *Opium City*.

16. C. Markovits, 'The Political Economy of Opium Smuggling in Early Nineteenth Century India', *Modern Asian Studies*, 43, 1 (2009), 89–111.

17. *Bombay Times and Journal of Commerce*, 3 November 1838.

18. F. Broeze, 'The External Dynamics of Port City Morphology: Bombay 1815–1914', in I. Banga (ed.), *Ports and Their Hinterlands in India, 1700–1950* (New Delhi, 1992), p. 258.

19. D. E. Haynes, 'Market Formation in Khandesh, c.1820–1930', *Indian Economic and Social History Review*, 36, 3 (1999), 275–302.

20. S. Guha, 'Forest Polities and Agrarian Empires: The Khandesh Bhils, c.1700–1850', *Indian Economic and Social History Review*, 33, 2 (1996), 144.

21. See E. M. Gumperz, 'City-Hinterland Relations and the Development of a Regional Elite in Nineteenth Century Bombay', *Journal of Asian Studies*, 33, 4 (1974), 586.

22. See the fascinating account in H. Inagaki, 'The Rule of Law and Emergency in Colonial India', King's College London, PhD thesis, 2016; available online.

23. Calculated from S. M. Edwardes, *The Gazetteer of Bombay City and Island*, vol. 1 (Bombay, 1909), Appendix IV; T. E. Redard, 'The Port of New Orleans. An Economic History, 1821–1860', PhD phesis, Louisiana State University (1985), Appendix II, Table 10. Rupees converted at R10 = £1; dollars at $5 = £1.

24. See F. Broeze, 'Underdevelopment and Dependency: Maritime India during the Raj', *Modern Asian Studies*, 18, 3 (1984), 438ff.

25. *Bombay Times and Journal of Commerce*, 6 October 1849.

26. Ibid., 20 August 1845.

27. For the figures, *Bombay Times*, 12 March 1861.

28. In April 1861, seven for China, eight for London, forty-three for Liverpool. *Bombay Times*, 5 April 1861.

29. See I. J. Kerr, *Building the Railways of the Raj, 1850–1900* (Delhi, 1997), chs. 2, 3, 4.

30. For the best account, see A. K. Bagchi, *The Evolution of the State Bank of India: The Roots, 1806–1876*, Part II, *Diversity and Regrouping, 1860–1876* (Bombay, 1987), chs. 25–7.

31. W. W. Hunter (ed.), *Imperial Gazetteer of India*, vol. 2 (1881), p. 209.

32. *Times of India* (hereafter *TOI*), 17 July 1874. The *Bombay Times* had been renamed – significantly – in 1861.

33. *TOI*, 2 March 1878.

34. See *Materials towards a Statistical Account of the Town and Island of Bombay* (Bombay, 1894), vol. 2, Appendix II, pp. 522ff.

35. *TOI*, 18 January 1872.

36. Ibid., 12 August 1879.

37. Ibid., 29 June 1875.

38. Report of Chamber of Commerce, *TOI*, 2 November 1876.

39. See M. Vicziany, 'Bombay Merchants and Structural Changes in the Export Community, 1850 to 1880', in K. N. Chaudhuri and C. J. Dewey (eds.), *Economy and Society: Essays in Indian Economic and Social History* (Delhi, 1979), pp. 163–96.

40. *TOI*, 16 November 1874.

41. In fact, Jejeebhoy received a baronetcy – an inheritable title.

42. See *TOI*, 13 August 1877.

43. *TOI*, 28 June 1902.

44. J. S. Palsetia, 'Mad Dogs and Parsis: The Bombay Dog Riots of 1832', *Journal of the Royal Asiatic Society*, 3rd Series, 11, 1 (2001), 13–30.

45. M. Sharafi, 'A New History of Colonial Lawyering: Likhovski and Legal Identities in the British Empire', *Law and Social Inquiry*, 32, 4 (2007), 1070–71.

46. N. Green, *Bombay Islam: The Religious Economy of the West Indian Ocean, 1840–1915* (Cambridge, 2011), p. 121.

47. C. Dobbin, *Urban Leadership in Western India* (Oxford, 1972), p. 219.

48. *TOI*, 12 February 1889, reporting a speech in London by Sir Lepel Griffin.

49. See Green, *Bombay Islam*, p. 6; *Bombay Presidency Gazette*, vol. IX, part 2: Gujarati Population: Muslims and Parsis (Bombay, 1899).

50. Green, *Bombay Islam*, pp. 95, 97.

51. *TOI*, 17 November 1886.

52. See G. Johnson, *Provincial Politics and Indian Nationalism: Bombay and the Indian National Congress, 1880 to 1915* (Cambridge, 1973); R. I. Cashman, *The Myth of the Lokamanya* (Berkeley, 1975).

53. R. Chandavarkar, *The Origins of Industrial Capitalism in India* (Cambridge, 1994), p. 250.

54. See I. Klein, 'Urban Development and Death: Bombay City, 1870–1914', *Modern Asian Studies*, 20, 4 (1986), 725–54.

55. See A. H. Leith, *Report on the Sanitary State of the Island of Bombay* (Bombay, 1864).

56. A. R. Burnett-Hurst, *Labour and Housing in Bombay* (London, 1925), quoted in V. Anstey, *The Economic Development of India* (London, 1929), p. 499.

57. L.R.C. in *Journal of the Royal Statistical Society*, 89, 1 (1926), 155.

58. Klein, 'Urban Development', 745, 751.

59. S. B. Upadhyay, 'Communalism and Working Class: Riot of 1893 in Bombay City', *Economic and Political Weekly*, 24, 30 (1989), 69-75.

60. S. M. Edwardes, *The Gazetteer of Bombay City and Island* (Bombay, 1909), vol. 1, p. 448.

61. For this judgement, see N. Charlesworth, *Peasants and Imperial Rule: Agriculture and Agrarian Society in the Bombay Presidency, 1850–1935* (Cambridge, 1985).

62. See Gumperz, 'City-Hinterland Relations'.

63. C. Dobbin, 'Competing Elites in Bombay City Politics in the Mid-Nineteenth Century (1852–83)', in E. Leach and S. N. Mukherjee (eds.), *Elites in South Asia* (Cambridge, 1970), pp. 79–94.

64. See A. Seal, *The Emergence of Indian Nationalism* (Cambridge, 1971), pp. 226ff.

65. J. M. Brown, *Gandhi: Prisoner of Hope* (New Haven, 1990), offers an accessible introduction to an enormous literature. Gandhi had spent an unprofitable year in Bombay in 1891-2 looking for work as a barrister. See R. Guha, *Gandhi Before India* (London, 2013), ch. 3.

66. Two classic studies are D. Hardiman, *Peasant Nationalists of Gujarat: Kheda District, 1917–1934* (Delhi, 1981); S. Mehta, *The Peasantry and Nationalism: A Study of the Bardoli Satyagraha* (New Delhi, 1984), on Bardoli District.

67. See P. Kidambi, 'Nationalism and the City in Colonial India: Bombay, c.1890–1940', *Journal of Urban History*, 38, 5 (2012), 950–67. For Gandhi's ambiguous relations with the Parsi community, combining admiration and criticism, see D. Patel, 'Beyond Hindu–Muslim Unity: Gandhi, the Parsis and the Prince of Wales Riots of 1921', *Indian Economic and Social History Review*, 55, 2 (2018), 221–47.

68. For the arrival of Surendranath Banerjea from Calcutta to open a 'Moderates' Conference', see *TOI*, 1 November 1918.

69. See *Report of the Indian Taxation Enquiry Committee*, vol. 1 (Madras, 1925).

70. E. Thornton, *A Gazetteer of the Territories under the Government of the East-India Company* ... (1857), p. 173.

71. J. R. Martin, 'A Brief Topographical and Historical Notice of Calcutta', *The Lancet*, 50, 1,256 (1847), 330.

72. For Calcutta's origins, see R. Murphey, 'The City in the Swamp: Aspects of the Site and Early Growth of Calcutta', *Geographical Journal*, 130, 2 (1964), 241–56; F. Hasan, 'Indigenous Cooperation and the

Birth of a Colonial City: Calcutta, c.1698–1750', *Modern Asian Studies*, 26, 1 (1992), 65–82; K. Raj, 'The Historical Anatomy of a Contact Zone: Calcutta in the Eighteenth Century', *Indian Economic and Social History Review*, 48, 1 (2011), 55–82.

73. P. J. Marshall, 'The White Town of Calcutta under the Rule of the East India Company', *Modern Asian Studies*, 34, 2 (2000), 307–31.

74. For the shape of the city, see S. J. Hornsby, 'Discovering the Mercantile City in South Asia: The Example of Early Nineteenth-Century Calcutta', *Journal of Historical Geography*, 23, 2 (1997), 135–50.

75. For a contemporary description, see N. Allen, *The Opium Trade* (Boston, 1853), pp. 5–7 (available online).

76. From 4,670 chests (of 113 pounds) to more than 49,000. P.P. 1865 (94), *Opium: Return of Opium Exported . . . since the Year 1830 . . .*

77. See Z. Yalland, *Traders and Nabobs: The British in Cawnpore, 1765–1857* (Salisbury, 1987), pp. 100ff.

78. See T. Webster, 'An Early Global Business in a Colonial Context: The Strategies, Management, and Failure of John Palmer and Company of Calcutta, 1780–1830', *Enterprise and Society*, 6, 1 (2005), 98–133.

79. Hyde Clarke, *Colonization, Defence, and Railways in Our Indian Empire* (1857), p. 168 (online).

80. H. Mukherjee, *The Early History of the East Indian Railway, 1845–1879* (Calcutta, 1994).

81. Opium made up nearly 20 per cent of India's total exports by value in 1880–81, but had fallen to around 9 per cent a decade later. See Kumar (ed.), *CEHI*, vol. 2, p. 845.

82. The year 1888 was the first one in which tea imports from India and Sri Lanka exceeded those from China. G. G. Chisholm, *Handbook of Commercial Geography*, 7th edn. (1908), p. 127.

83. Kumar (ed.), *CEHI*, vol. 2, p. 844.

84. For an excellent description, see A. K. Bagchi, 'European and Indian Entrepreneurship in India, 1900–1930', in Leach and Mukherjee (eds.), *Elites in South Asia.*

85. See J. Forbes Munro, *Maritime Enterprise and Empire: Sir William Mackinnon and His Business Network, 1823–1893* (Woodbridge, 2003).

86. B. Gupta, 'Discrimination or Social Networks? Industrial Investment in Colonial India', *Journal of Economic History*, 74, 1 (2014), 146.

87. S. Sarkar, 'The City Imagined', in his *Writing Social History* (New Delhi, 1997), p. 164.

88. H. Leonard, *Report on the River Hooghly* (Calcutta, 1865), p. 8.

89. See Barun De, 'The History of Kolkata Port and the Hooghly River and Its Future', www.kolkataporttrust.gov.ind/showfile.php?layout= 1&lid=520.

90. See S. K. Munsi, *Geography of Transportation in Eastern India under the British Raj* (Calcutta, 1980), p. 113.

91. Ibid., pp. 83, 71.

92. *Imperial Gazetteer of India: Provincial Series, Bengal*, vol. 1 (Calcutta, 1909), p. 424.

93. See *Oxford Dictionary of National Biography*: 'Mackay, James Lyle, First Earl of Inchcape'.

94. Bagchi, 'European and Indian Entrepreneurship'.

95. See T. Bhattacharya, *The Sentinels of Culture: Class, Education and the Colonial Intellectual in Bengal, 1848–1885* (New Delhi, 2005), ch. 1: 'The Curious Case of the Bhadralok'.

96. The classic study is T. Raychaudhuri, *Europe Reconsidered: Perceptions of the West in Nineteenth-Century Bengal* (Delhi, 1989).

97. Risley to Curzon, 7 February 1904, quoted in D. Banerjee, *Aspects of Administration in Bengal–1898–1912* (New Delhi, 1980), p. 82.

98. Kipling's famous phrase. See his 'City of Dreadful Night, Jan.–Feb. 1888', in R. Kipling, *From Sea to Sea and Other Sketches: Letters of Travel*, vol. 2 (1919), pp. 201–69.

99. For a survey, see P. T. Nair, 'Civic and Public Services in Old Calcutta', in S. Chaudhuri (ed.), *Calcutta: The Living City*, vol. 1: *The Past* (Calcutta, 1990).

100. G. Stewart, *Jute and Empire: The Calcutta Jute Wallahs and the Landscapes of Empire* (Manchester, 1998), pp. 60ff.

101. R. K. Ray, *Urban Roots of Indian Nationalism: Pressure Groups and Conflict of Interests in Calcutta City Politics, 1875–1939* (New Delhi, 1979).

102. O. Goswami, 'Then Came the Marwaris', *Indian Economic and Social History Review*, 22, 3 (1985), 225–49 G. Oonk, 'The Emergence of Indigenous Industrialists in Calcutta, Bombay, and Ahmedabad, 1850–1947', *Business History Review*, 88, 1 (2014), 50ff.

103. Stewart, *Jute*, pp. 100ff.

104. O. Goswami, *Industry, Trade and Peasant Society: The Jute Economy of Eastern India, 1900–1947* (Delhi, 1991), p. 145.

105. Ibid., p. 146.

106. See the analysis in J. Gallagher, 'Congress in Decline. Bengal, 1930 to 1939', *Modern Asian Studies*, 7, 3 (1973), 589–645.

107. T. Robertson, *Report on the Administration and Working of Indian Railways* (Calcutta, 1903), p. 35.

108. R. Mukerjee, *The Changing Face of Bengal: A Study in Riverine Economy* (Calcutta, 1938), p. 195.

109. I have drawn on the account in T. Roy, *The Economic History of India 1857–1947* (New Delhi, 2000), esp. ch. 3; for a more recent analysis on similar lines, see B. Gupta, 'Falling Behind and Catching Up: India's Transition from a Colonial Economy', *Economic History Review*, 72, 3 (2019), 803–27.

110. League of Nations, *The Network of World Trade* (Geneva, 1942), pp. 99, 100.

111. See J. Chatterji, *The Spoils of Partition: Bengal and India, 1947–1967* (Cambridge, 2007).

112. T. Roy, 'The Transfer of Economic Power in Corporate Calcutta, 1950–1970', *Business History Review*, 91, 1 (2017), 7.

CHAPTER 7: FROM THE NANYANG TO THE YANGZI

1. See E. M. Jacobs, *Merchant in Asia: The Trade of the Dutch East India Company during the Eighteenth Century* (Leiden, 2006).

2. Raffles to Colonel Addenbrooke, 10 June 1819, in V. Harlow and F. Madden (eds.), *British Colonial Developments 1774–1834: Select Documents* (Oxford, 1953), p. 73; a fuller version can be found in C. E. Wurtzburg, *Raffles of the Eastern Isles* [1954] (Oxford, 1986), p. 520.

3. Raffles Memorandum 1819, Harlow and Madden (eds.), *Colonial Developments*, p. 76.

4. Wurtzburg, *Raffles*, pp. 631ff.

5. G. F. Bartle, 'Sir John Bowring and the Chinese and Siamese Commercial Treaties', *Bulletin of the John Rylands Library, Manchester*, 4, 2 (1962), 303. Bowring's bankers had been Jardine Matheson, the great opium merchant, and his son was a partner in the firm.

6. See G. S. Graham, *The China Station: War and Diplomacy, 1830–1860* (Oxford, 1978), p. 284.

7. *Singapore Free Press and Mercantile Advertiser*, 1 April 1847. The archive of the *Singapore Free Press*, *Straits Times* and other Singapore newspapers is available at http://eresources.nlb.gov.sg/newspapers.

8. See the graphic accounts in P. D. Coates, *The China Consuls: British Consular Officers, 1843–1943* (Hong Kong, 1988), chs. 1–6.

9. See A. R. Wallace, *The Malay Archipelago* [1869] (Oxford, 1986), chs. 10, 23 and 27.

10. Ibid., p. 32.

11. I have drawn on the fascinating account in S. Dobbs, 'The Singapore River, 1819-1869: Cradle of a Maritime Entrepot', *International Journal of Maritime History*, 13, 2 (2001), 95-118.

12. See the *China Sea Directory*, vol. 1 (1867), pp. 7, 272.

13. See A. Milner, 'Singapore's Role in Constituting a "Malay" Narrative', in N. Tarling (ed.), *Studying Singapore's Past* (Singapore, 2012), pp. 125-45.

14. M'Culloch's *Commercial Dictionary*, new edn. (London, 1869), p. 1285.

15. Figures from *Colonial Office List* (1865).

16. See Wong Lin Ken, 'Singapore: Its Growth as an Entrepot Port, 1819-1941', *Journal of Southeast Asian Studies*, 9, 1 (1978), Tables 1, 2, 3.

17. *China Directory*, p. 152.

18. M'Culloch's *Commercial Dictionary*, p. 1286.

19. Calculated from figures in M'Culloch's *Commercial Dictionary*, pp. 163, 881, 1289, 1350. During the American Civil War, and the 'cotton famine' it induced, Bombay's total trade doubled to reach some £70 million.

20. See, for example, the vehement defence of the opium trade in M'Culloch's *Commercial Dictionary*: 'Opium', pp. 977ff.

21. See 'Blue Book 1877', quoted in *Straits Times*, 19 October 1878.

22. *Straits Times*, 1 January 1870.

23. See the elaborate estimates of John Pender of the Eastern Telegraphic Company in the *Straits Times*, 26 February 1870.

24. Wong, 'Singapore', Table 10.

25. See Wong, 'Singapore', Tables 6, 7, 8.

26. *Straits Times*, 12 February 1870.

27. Ibid., 18 May 1872.

28. Wong, 'Singapore', 69.

29. *Straits Times*, 4 September 1875.

30. *Straits Times Overland Journal*, 27 May 1876.

31. W. G. Huff, *The Economic Growth of Singapore* (Cambridge, 1994), p. 52.

32. Quoted in J. Loadman, *Tears of the Tree: The Story of Rubber – A Modern Marvel* (Oxford and New York, 2005), p. 83.

33. Huff, *Singapore*, p. 182.

34. Stephanie Po-yin Chung, 'Surviving Economic Crises in Southeast Asia and Southern China: The History of Eu Yan Sang Business Conglomerates in Penang, Singapore and Hong Kong', *Modern Asian Studies*, 36, 3 (2002), 59.

35. Huff, *Singapore*, p. 154. By comparison, around 300,000 a year passed through Ellis Island in New York between 1892 and 1897, to reach nearly 900,000 in 1914.

36. I have drawn on G. L. Hicks (ed.), *Overseas Chinese Remittances from Southeast Asia, 1910–1940* (Singapore, 1993), based on studies by the Bank of Taiwan in 1914, 1942 and 1943, reflecting intense Japanese interest in China's financial resources.

37. *Straits Times*, 18 June 1904.

38. Ibid., 3 January 1913.

39. *Singapore Free Press*, 27 April 1920.

40. For the Straits Chinese, see Lee Poh Ping, *Chinese Society in Nineteenth Century Singapore* (Kuala Lumpur, 1978); M. R. Frost, 'Emporium in Imperio: Nanyang Networks and the Straits Chinese in Singapore, 1819–1914', *Journal of Southeast Asian Studies*, 36, 1 (2005), 29–66; for a contemporary account, see J. D. Vaughan, *The Manners and Customs of the Chinese of the Straits Settlements* (Singapore, 1879), pp. 3–6.

41. Lee, *Chinese Society*, pp. 72ff.

42. Quoted in Siew-Min Sai, 'Dressing Up Subjecthood: Straits Chinese, the Queue, and Contested Citizenship in Colonial Singapore', *Journal of Imperial and Commonwealth History*, 47, 3 (2019), 459.

43. The best account remains M. R. Godley, *The Mandarin-Capitalists from Nanyang: Overseas Chinese Enterprise in the Modernization of China 1893–1911* (Cambridge, 1981).

44. See C. M. Turnbull, 'The Malayan Connection', in Chan Lau Kit-ching and P. Cunich (eds.) *An Impossible Dream: Hong Kong University from Founding to Re-Establishment, 1910–1950* (New York, 2002).

45. Tzu-hui Celina Hung, '"There Are No Chinamen in Singapore"', *Journal of Chinese Overseas*, 5, 2 (2009), 260.

46. See D. P. S. Goh, 'Unofficial Contentions: The Postcoloniality of Straits Chinese Political Discourse in the Straits Settlements Legislative Council', *Journal of Southeast Asian Studies*, 41, 3 (2010), 483–507.

47. For Singapore's urban development, see R. Powell, 'The Axis of Singapore: South Bridge Road', in R. Bishop, J. Phillips and Wei-Wei Yeo (eds.), *Beyond Description: Singapore Space Historicity* (London, 2004); J. Beamish and J. Ferguson, *A History of Singapore Architecture: The Making of a City* (Singapore, 1985); N. Edwards, *The Singapore House and Residential Life 1819–1939* (Oxford, 1991).

48. B. S. A. Yeoh, *Contesting Space: Power Relations and the Urban Built Environment in Colonial Singapore* (Kuala Lumpur, 1996), pp. 46–8ff.

49. Ibid., p. 88.

50. See Michael Francis Laffan, *Islamic Nationhood and Colonial Indonesia: The Umma below the Winds* (London, 2003), pp. 149ff.

51. See the brilliant essay by Tim Harper, 'Singapore, 1915, and the Birth of the Asian Underground', *Modern Asian Studies*, 47, 6 (2013), 1782–811.

52. For this phrase, see Ibid., 1806.

53. 'Singapore and the Future of British Shipping at the Straits' by 'Imperium', *Straits Times*, 23 February 1903.

54. *Straits Times*, 10 December 1903.

55. Ibid., 24 October 1903.

56. Ibid., 21 January 1902.

57. See V. Anstey, *The Trade of the Indian Ocean* (London, 1929), p. 58.

58. See A. J. Sargent, *Seaways of the Empire* (London, 1918), pp. 26–7.

59. Huff, *Singapore*, p. 17.

60. I have followed the argument in Huei-Ying Kuo, *Networks beyond Empires: Chinese Business and Nationalism in the Hong Kong-Singapore Corridor, 1914–1941* (Leiden, 2014).

61. The best study of these early travails is C. Munn, *Anglo-China: Chinese People and British Rule in Hong Kong, 1841–1880* (Hong Kong, 2001, 2009).

62. S. Bard, *Traders of Hong Kong: Some Foreign Merchant Houses, 1841–1899* (Hong Kong, 1993).

63. I have drawn on the brilliant study by Elizabeth Sinn, *Pacific Crossing: California Gold, Chinese Migration, and the Making of Hong Kong* (Hong Kong, 2013); Chinese in America insisted on opium prepared in Hong Kong. See E. Sinn, 'Preparing Opium for America', *Journal of Chinese Overseas*, 1, 1 (2005), 16–42.

64. Ripon to Governor Robinson, 23 August 1894, in G. B. Endacott, *An Eastern Entrepôt: A Collection of Documents Illustrating the History of Hong Kong* (London, 1964).

65. Munn, *Anglo-China*, chs. 5, 6, 7.

66. The figure in 1898 was 44 per cent. Man-Houng Lin, 'Taiwan, Hong Kong, and the Pacific, 1895–1945', *Modern Asian Studies*, 44, 5 (2010), 1056ff.; Hui Po-keung, 'Comprador Politics and Middleman Capitalism', in Tak-Wing Ngo (ed.), *Hong Kong's History* (Hong Kong, 1999), p. 34.

67. E. J. Hardy, *John Chinaman at Home* (London, 1905) p. 25.

68. The authoritative account is D. R. Meyer, *Hong Kong as a Global Metropolis* (Cambridge, 2000).

69. A superb survey of China's treaty and other open ports is R. Nield, *China's Foreign Places: The Foreign Presence in China in the Treaty Port Era, 1840–1943* (Hong Kong, 2015).

70. See M. Elvin, *Another History: Essays on China from a European Perspective* (Broadway, New South Wales, 1996), ch. 4; Linda Cooke

Johnson, *Shanghai: From Market Town to Treaty Port, 1074–1858* (Stanford, 1995).

71. Cooke Johnson, *Shanghai*, pp. 94–6.

72. A brilliant portrait of this political and social evolution is R. Bickers, 'Shanghailanders: The Formation and Identity of the British Settler Community in Shanghai, 1843–1937', *Past and Present*, 159 (1998), 161–211.

73. For this description, see C. E. Darwent, *Shanghai: A Handbook For Travellers and Residents*, Shanghai (Shanghai, 1920); see also the beautifully illustrated P. Hibbard, *The Bund* (Hong Kong, 2007).

74. The classic study is Yen-p'ing Hao, *The Commercial Revolution in Nineteenth-Century China: The Rise of Sino-Western Mercantile Capitalism* (Berkeley and London, 1986).

75. H. B. Morse, *The Trade and Administration of the Chinese Empire* (London, 1908), p. 146.

76. A. L. McElderry, *Shanghai Old-Style Banks (Ch'ien-Chuang), 1800–1935: A Traditional Institution in a Changing Society* (Ann Arbor, MI, 1976), p. 50.

77. See R. Murphey, *Shanghai: Key to Modern China* (Cambridge, MA, 1953), p. 1.

78. See R. Bickers, *Britain in China* (Manchester, 1999), p. 125.

79. Quoted in F. Wakeman Jr and Wen-hsin Yeh (eds.), *Shanghai Sojourners* (Berkeley, 1992), p. 5.

80. For a superb description of (European) Shanghai society *c.*1919, see R. Bickers, *Empire Made Me: An Englishman Adrift in Shanghai* (London, 2003), ch. 3.

81. *North China Herald*, 5 December 1925.

82. Ibid., 25 October 1919, online.

83. See 'Shanghai in the Looking Glass' by 'M.E.T.', *North China Herald*, 20 September 1919, 763–5.

84. J. K. Fairbank, K. Frest Bruner and E. MacLeod Matheson (eds.), *The I.G. in Peking: Letters of Robert Hart: Chinese Maritime Customs, 1868–1907* (Cambridge, MA, 1975), vol.1, p. 15.

85. See H. van de Ven, *Breaking with the Past: The Maritime Customs Service and the Global Origins of Modernity in China* (New York, 2014).

86. *North China Herald*, 2 November 1929.

87. I have drawn on the fascinating account in A. Reinhardt, 'Navigating Imperialism in China: Steamship, Semicolony and Nation, 1860–1937', PhD dissertation, Princeton University (2002). Available online.

88. See Marie-Claire Bergère, *Shanghai: China's Gateway to Modernity* (Eng. trans., Stanford, 2009), ch. 10.

89. For the best recent account, see R. Bickers, *Out of China: How the Chinese Ended the Era of Western Domination* (London, 2017), chs. 1, 2 and 4.

90. See P. M. Coble Jr 'The Kuomintang Regime and the Shanghai Capitalists, 1927–29', *The China Quarterly*, 77 (1979), 1–24.

91. The classic account of this change is J. Osterhammel, 'Imperialism in Transition: British Business and the Chinese Authorities, 1931–37', *The China Quarterly*, 98 (June 1984), 260–80.

92. Quoted in N. Horesh, *Shanghai's Bund and Beyond: British Banks, Banknote Issuance, and Monetary Policy in China, 1842–1937* (New Haven, 2009), pp. 146ff.

93. See G. E. Hubbard, *Eastern Industrialization and Its Effect on the West* (London, 1938), p. 193.

94. See the advertisement of the 'Hong Kong and Whampoa Dock Company Limited', *China Mail*, 13 March 1930. Available online from Hong Kong Public Libraries at www.mmis.hkpl.gov.hk/old-hk-collection.

95. [British] Naval Intelligence Division, Geographical Handbooks Series, *China Proper*, vol. 3 (London, 1945), p. 325.

96. See *Hong Kong Daily Press*, 24 January 1930. Available as n.94.

97. 'Annual Report for 1930', *Hong Kong Daily Press*, 23 April 1931.

98. *China Mail*, 30 April 1930.

99. See T. Latter, 'Hong Kong's Exchange Rate Regimes in the Twentieth Century: The Story of Three Regime Changes', Hong Kong Institute for Monetary Research Working Paper no. 17/2004 (available online), pp. 15–16, 19.

100. S. Friedman in *Far East Survey* 8, 19 (27 September 1939), pp. 219–22. Quoted in L. F. Goodstadt, *Profits, Politics and Panics: Hong Kong's Banks and the Making of a Miracle Economy, 1935–1985* (Hong Kong, 2007), p. 42.

101. S. Tsang, *A Modern History of Hong Kong* (London and New York, 2004), pp. 107–8.

102. A. Maddison, *Contours of the World Economy, 1–2030 AD* (Oxford, 2007), pp. 164, 170.

103. S. L. Endicott, *Diplomacy and Enterprise: British China Policy 1933–1937* (Vancouver, 1975), p. 20.

104. A. Feuerwerker, *The Chinese Economy, 1912–1949* (Ann Arbor, MI, 1968), pp. 16–17.

CHAPTER 8: THE CRISIS OF THE METROPOLES

1. W. Woodruff, *Impact of Western Man* (London, 1966), p. 313.

2. R. Findlay and K. H. O'Rourke, *Power and Plenty: Trade, War, and the World Economy in the Second Millennium* (Princeton, 2007), p. 404.

3. A. Estevadeordal, B. Frantz and A. M. Taylor, 'The Rise and Fall of World Trade, 1870–1939', *Quarterly Journal of Economics*, 118, 2 (2003), 359.

4. D. Kumar (ed.), *Cambridge Economic History of India*, vol. 2: *c. 1757–c.1970* (Cambridge, 1982), pp. 834–7.

5. For these calculations, Woodruff, *Impact*, Tables IV/2 and IV/3.

6. I. Stone, *The Global Export of Capital from Great Britain, 1865–1914* (London, 1999), p. 411.

7. B. R. Mitchell, *European Historical Statistics 1750–1970*, pbk. edn. (London and Basingstoke, 1978), p. 47. The population of Europe, excluding Russia, in 1913 was about 350 million.

8. A. McKeown, 'Chinese Emigration in Global Context, 1850–1940', *Journal of Global History*, 5, 1 (2010), fig. 1.

9. S. S. Amrith, *Crossing the Bay of Bengal: The Furies of Nature and the Fortunes of Migrants* (Cambridge, MA, 2013), p. 118.

10. J. Belich, *Replenishing the Earth: The Settler Revolution and the Rise of the Anglo-World, 1783–1939* (Oxford, 2009), pp. 504, 507.

11. A. H. Jeeves, *Migrant Labour in South Africa's Mining Economy: The Struggle for the Gold Mines' Labour Supply 1890–1920* (Kingston and Montreal, 1985), Appendix One.

12. G. di Tella and D. C. M. Platt (eds.), *The Political Economy of Argentina 1880–1946* (London, 1986), p. 53; B. Sánchez-Alonso, 'Making Sense of Immigration Policy: Argentina, 1870–1930', *Economic History Review*, 66, 2 (2013), 608.

13. For this argument, see the classic work by Herbert Feis, *Europe: The World's Banker, 1870–1914* [1930], pbk. edn. (New York, 1965), p. 13.

14. Quoted in A. Offer, 'Empire and Social Reform', *Historical Journal*, 26, 1 (1983), 122ff. Lloyd George was Chancellor of the Exchequer.

15. J. M. Keynes, 'Great Britain's Foreign Investments', *New Quarterly* (February 1910), reprinted in E. Johnson (ed.), *The Collected Writings of John Maynard Keynes*, vol. XV (Cambridge, 1971), pp. 55–6.

16. H. J. Mackinder, 'Geographical Conditions Affecting the British Empire, 1: The British Islands', *Geographical Journal*, 33, 4 (1909), 474.

17. Tirpitz to Stosch, 21 December 1895, in Grand-Admiral Tirpitz, *My Memoirs* (Eng. trans., London, 1919), vol. 1, p. 61.

18. *The Memoirs of Count Witte* (Eng. trans., Garden City, NY, 1921), p. 122.

19. See M.-W. Serruys, 'The Port and City of Ostend', *International Journal of Maritime History*, 19, 2 (2007), 320.

20. R. Giffen, 'Some General Uses of Statistical Knowledge', *Journal of the Statistical Society of London* (Jubilee Volume, 1885), 100.

21. *Geographical Journal*, 12 (1898), 599–600.

22. *Economist*, 10 January 1914.

23. Ibid.

24. See A. G. Ford, *The Gold Standard, 1880–1914: Britain and Argentina* (Oxford, 1962), ch. 10.

25. For a brilliant analysis of these, see T. G. Otte, *July Crisis: The World's Descent into War, Summer 1914* (Cambridge, 2015).

26. H. N. Dickson, 'The Redistribution of Mankind', *Geographical Journal*, 42, 4 (1913), 383.

27. See G. G. Chisholm, 'The Free City of Danzig', *Geographical Journal*, 55, 4 (1920), 307. Chisholm was the leading British authority on commercial geography.

28. German-speaking 'Balts' had traditionally dominated Russia's Baltic provinces. See A. Henriksson, 'Riga', in M. F. Hamm (ed.), *The City in Late Imperial Russia* (Bloomington, IN, 1986), pp. 178–203.

29. See J. H. Bater, *St Petersburg: Industrialization and Change* (London and Montreal, 1976), pp. 213, 295.

30. I have drawn on the fascinating chapter by F. W. Skinner, 'Odessa and the Problem of Urban Modernization', in Hamm (ed.), *Late Imperial Russia*.

31. See F. Tabak, *The Waning of the Mediterranean* (Baltimore, 2008).

32. M'Culloch's *Commercial Dictionary*, new edn. (London, 1869), p. 1496.

33. See L. Sondhaus, 'Austria and the Adriatic: The Development of Habsburg Maritime Policy, 1797–1866', PhD thesis, University of Virginia, 1986 (online), pp. 179ff.

34. For example, *The Times*, 18 November 1876. Times Digital Archive.

35. See the *Economist*, 26 February 1921.

36. For which see the brilliant short history by Jan Morris, *Trieste and the Meaning of Nowhere* (London, 2006).

37. *Economist*, 24 December 1927, p. 7.

38. For living conditions in the city, see F. M. Snowden, *Naples in the Time of Cholera, 1884–1911* (Cambridge, 1995).

39. V. Zamagni, *The Economic History of Italy, 1860–1990* (Oxford, 1993), p. 124.

40. M. Theunissen, 'Le Port moderne de Gênes', in Société Scientifique de Bruxelles, *Les Ports et leur fonction économique*, vol. 3 (Louvain, 1908), p. 11.

41. Advertisement in *The Times*, 23 August 1879.

42. See M. E. Tonizzi, 'Economy, Traffic and Infrastructure in the Port of Genoa, 1861–1970', in G. Boyce and R. Gorski (eds.), *Resources and Infrastructures in the Maritime Economy, 1500–2000* [2002] (Liverpool Scholarship Online, 2019).

43. I have drawn on the gloomy appraisal in Theunissen, 'Gênes'.

44. See R. Lawton and R. Lee, *Population and Society in Western European Port-Cities c.1650–1939* (Liverpool, 2002), p. 75.

45. See R. J. B. Bosworth, *Italy, the Least of the Great Powers: Italian Foreign Policy before the First World War* (Cambridge, 1979), ch. 1.

46. A graphic display can be seen at the superb Musée d'histoire in Marseilles.

47. See J. T. Takeda, *Between Crown and Commerce: Marseille and the Early Modern Mediterranean*, (Baltimore, 2011), pp. 2, 10.

48. See P. Guiral, review of G. Rambert, *Marseille: la formation d'une grande cité moderne*, in *Géocarrefour*, 11, 3 (1935), 386–91.

49. See H. Blais and F. Deprest, 'The Mediterranean, a Territory between France and Colonial Algeria: Imperial Constructions', *European Review of History*, 19, 1 (2012), 53–7.

50. For the (largely urban) white *colon* society, see D. Rivet, *Le Maghreb à l'épreuve de la colonisation* (Paris, 2002), ch. 5.

51. G. Rambert, *Marseille: la Formation d'une grande cité moderne* (Paris, 1934), ch. 3.

52. G. Blondel, 'Le Port de Marseille', in Société Scientifique de Bruxelles, *Les Ports et leur fonction économique*, vol. 2 (Louvain, 1907), pp. 103–23.

53. M. Borutta, 'De la Méridionalité à la Méditerranée: le Midi de la France au temps de l'Algérie coloniale', *Cahiers de la Méditerranée*, 87 (2013), pp. 385–401.

54. See the *Economist*, 16 April 1910, p. 839.

55. See Ş. Pamuk and J. G. Williamson (eds.), *The Mediterranean Response to Globalization before 1950* (London and New York, 2000), pp. 4, 51.

56. Quoted in Blondel, 'Marseille', p. 123.

57. For Bremen, see L. Maischak, *German Merchants in the Nineteenth-Century Atlantic* (Cambridge, 2013).

58. A. Nicollet, 'André Siegfried et Le Havre', *Études Normandes*, 38, 2 (1989), 36–48. The famous political geographer was from one of these families.

59. For a superb portrait of the City, see D. Kynaston, *The City of London: Golden Years, 1890–1914* (London, 1995).

60. R. C. Michie, *The City of London* (London, 1992), p. 17.

61. *Economist*, 10 January 1914, p. 14.

62. A fascinating account can be found in L. Rodwell Jones, *The Geography of London River* (London, 1931), p. 26.

63. The figure for 1911 was 28,387 dockworkers. See G. Phillips and N. Whiteside, *Casual Labour: The Unemployment Question in the Port Transport Industry, 1880–1970* (Oxford, 1985), p. 41. The Liverpool figure was 26,946.

64. For this description I have drawn on Rodwell Jones, *London River*; J. Bird, *The Major Seaports of the United Kingdom* (London, 1963), chs. 14–17; and the contemporary account by G. Eeckhout, 'Le Port de Londres', in Société Scientifique, *Les Ports*, vol. 2, pp. 9–25.

65. The best modern study of Liverpool is J. Belchem (ed.), *Liverpool 800: Culture, Character and History* (Liverpool, 2006).

66. Described in Bird, *Seaports*, ch. 12.

67. T. Baines, *Liverpool in 1859* (Liverpool, 1859), p. 65.

68. See the plan in *Cox's Liverpool and Manchester Commercial Agents' Directory 1931–32* (Liverpool, 1932).

69. See P. de Rousiers, 'Les fonctions économiques de Liverpool', in Société Scientifique de Bruxelles, *Les Ports et leur Fonction économique*, vol. 1 (Louvain, 1906), pp. 95–110.

70. S. Marriner, *The Social and Economic Development of Merseyside* (London, 1982), p. 94.

71. See G. J. Milne, 'Maritime Liverpool', in Belchem (ed.), *Liverpool 800*, p. 305.

72. T. Lane, *Liverpool, City of the Sea* (Liverpool, 1997), pp. 61ff.

73. P. Waller, *Democracy and Sectarianism: A Political and Social History of Liverpool, 1868–1939* (Liverpool, 1981), p. 4.

74. See C. G. Pooley, 'Living in Liverpool: The Modern City', in Belchem (ed.), *Liverpool 800*, p. 214.

75. F. Neal, *Sectarian Violence: The Liverpool Experience, 1819–1914* (Manchester, 1988), pp. 224–43.

76. See J. Belchem and D. M. MacRaild, 'Cosmopolitan Liverpool', in Belchem (ed.), *Liverpool 800*, p. 375.

77. S. T. Bindoff, *The Scheldt Question to 1839* (London, 1945), ch. 9. The dues were finally redeemed in 1863.

78. *Economist*, 25 January 1913, pp. 9-11.
79. S. Moreels, M. Vandezande and K. Matthijs, 'Fertility in the Port City of Antwerp (1845-1920)', Working Paper for the Centre for Sociological Research, Leuven University, 2010 (available online), pp. 2, 3.
80. Reprinted in P. Gorceix (ed.), *La Belgique fin de siècle: Romans – Nouvelles – Théâtre* (Brussels, 1997), pp. 409-676.
81. For this portrait of Antwerp's commerce, see E. Dubois and M. Theunissen, 'Anvers et la vie économique nationale', in Sociáté Scientifique, *Les Ports*, vol. 1, pp. 111-49.
82. See J. Charles, 'Le Port de Rotterdam', in Société Scientifique, *Les Ports*, vol. 2, pp. 55-86.
83. T. Feys, *The Battle for the Migrants: The Introduction of Steamshipping on the North Atlantic and Its Impact on the European Exodus* (Liverpool Scholarship Online, 2019), p. 81.
84. For a detailed account, see A. Demangeon, 'Les relations de la France du nord avec l'Amérique', *Annales de Géographie*, 123 (1913), 227-44.
85. For Hamburg's complex constitutional arrangements, see R. J. Evans, *Death in Hamburg: Society and Politics in the Cholera Years 1830-1910* (Oxford, 1987), ch. 1.
86. *Economist*, 1 November 1913, 'Shipping and Trade of Hamburg'.
87. Evans, *Death in Hamburg*, p. 69.
88. N. Ferguson, *Paper and Iron: Hamburg Business and German Politics in the Era of Inflation, 1897-1927* (Cambridge, 1995), pp. 33, 205.
89. See Evans, *Death in Hamburg*, pp. 299ff.
90. L. Cecil, *Albert Ballin: Business and Politics in Imperial Germany, 1888-1918* (Princeton, 1967), p. 155.
91. Quoted in ibid.
92. J. M. Keynes, *The Economic Consequences of the Peace* (London, 1919), p. 1.
93. W. Ashworth, *A Short History of the International Economy, 1850-1950* (London, 1952), p. 63.
94. The best recent account of this can be found in A. Tooze, *The Deluge: The Great War and the Remaking of the Global Order, 1916-1931* (London, 2014).
95. M. Stopford, *Maritime Economics*, 2nd edn. (London, 1997), p. 54.
96. See L. Gall, G. Feldman, H. James, C.-L. Holtfrerich and H. E. Büschgen, *The Deutsche Bank 1870-1995* (Eng. trans., London, 1995), pp. 246-7.
97. For these developments, see League of Nations, *The Network of World Trade* (Geneva, 1941).
98. Sánchez-Alonso, 'Immigration Policy', 623.

99. The essential study is J. M. Atkin, *British Overseas Investment 1918–1931* (New York, 1977).

100. H. James, *The End of Globalization: Lessons from the Great Depression* (Cambridge, MA, 2001), pp. 48–9.

101. E. Staley, *World Economy in Transition: Technology versus Politics, Laissez Faire versus Planning, Power versus Welfare* (New York, 1939), p. 56.

102. W. M. Macmillan, *Warning from the West Indies* (London, 1936), issued as a 'Penguin Special' in 1938.

103. J. Iliffe, *A Modern History of Tanganyika* (Cambridge, 1979), p. 344.

104. For the West African case, see A. G. Hopkins, *An Economic History of West Africa* (London, 1973), pp. 254–67.

105. P. H. Lister, 'Regional Policies and Industrial Development on Merseyside 1930–60', in B. L. Anderson and P. J. M. Stoney (eds.), *Commerce, Industry and Transport: Studies in Economic Change on Merseyside* (Liverpool, 1983), p. 151; F. Broeze, 'The Political Economy of a Port City in Distress: Hamburg and National Socialism, 1933–1939', *International Journal of Maritime History*, 14, 2 (2002), 4.

106. For Montreal, see above, p. 197; D. Potts, 'Unemployed Workers in Adelaide: Assessing the Impact of the 1930s Depression', *Australian Historical Studies*, 19, 74 (1980), 125–31.

107. C. B. Schedvin, *Australia and the Great Depression* (Sydney, 1970), pp. 302–3; for Liverpool, see Marriner, *Merseyside*, p. 127; for Port Elizabeth, see G. Baines, 'A Progressive South African City? Port Elizabeth and Influx Control, ca. 1923–1953', *Journal of Urban History*, 31, 1 (2004), 75–100.

108. S. G. Sturmey, *British Shipping and World Competition* (London, 1962), ch. 5.

109. See D. Rothermund, *The Global Impact of the Great Depression, 1929–1939* (London and New York, 1996), ch. 10.

110. See P. Alhadeff, 'Dependency, Historiography and Objections to the Roca Pact', in C. Abel and C. M. Lewis (eds.), *Latin America, Economic Imperialism and the State: The Political Economy of the External Connection from Independence to the Present* (London, 1985), pp. 391–2.

111. See his lecture in *The World's Economic Crisis and the Way of Escape*, Halley Stewart Lecture 1931 (London, 1932), pp. 80–81.

112. M. J. Bonn, *Wandering Scholar* (London, 1948), pp. 318–19.

113. For these predictions, see M. J. Bonn, *The Crumbling of Empire: The Disintegration of World Economy* (London, 1938), ch. 6.

114. For a vigorous contemporary statement, see S. K. Datta, *Asiatic Asia* (London, 1932).

115. Staley, *World Economy in Transition*, pp. 34ff. Staley was drawing on the ideas in L. Mumford, *Technics and Civilization* (New York, 1934).

CHAPTER 9: LESSONS FROM SMYRNA

1. See E. Frangakis-Syrett, *The Commerce of Smyrna in the Eighteenth Century (1700–1820)* (Athens, 1992).

2. A. W. Kinglake, *Eothen: Traces of Travel brought Home from the East* [1844] (Nelson Classic edn., n.d.), p. 53.

3. M'Culloch's *Commercial Dictionary*, new edn. (London, 1869), p. 1308.

4. For the growth of trade, see R. Owen, *The Middle East the World Economy 1800–1914* (London, 1981), chs. 4 and 8.

5. A. Kitroeff, 'The Greek Diaspora in the Mediterranean and the Black Sea, as Seen through American Eyes (1815–1861)', in S. Vryonis Jr (ed.), *The Greeks and the Sea* (New York, 1993), p. 165.

6. See the superbly illustrated account in S. Zandi-Sayek, *Ottoman Izmir: The Rise of a Cosmopolitan Port 1840–1880* (Minneapolis, 2012).

7. M.-C. Smyrnelis, *Smyrne: la ville oubliée?* (Paris, 2006), p. 115.

8. See J. McCarthy, *Death and Exile: The Ethnic Cleansing of Ottoman Muslims, 1821–1922* (Princeton, 1995).

9. See M. Aksakal, *The Ottoman Road to War in 1914* (Cambridge, 2008), p. 48.

10. The classic study is M. Llewellyn Smith, *Ionian Vision: Greece in Asia Minor 1919–1922* (London, 1973).

11. For the American case, see J. Atack, F. Bateman, M. Haines and R. A. Margo, 'Did Railroads Induce or Follow Economic Growth? Urbanization and Population Growth in the American Midwest, 1850–1860', *Social Science History*, 34, 2 (2010), 171–97.

12. The 'Correlates of War' website lists around 290.

13. S. Doyle, *Crisis and Decline in Bunyoro: Population and Environment in Western Uganda 1860–1955* (Oxford and Athens, OH, 2006), offers a grim case study.

14. B. Etemad, *Possessing the World: Taking the Measurement, of Colonisation from the Eighteenth to the Twentieth Century* (Eng. trans., New York and Oxford, 2007), p. 94.

15. R. B. Marks, *China: Its Environment and History* (Lanham, MD, 2012), p. 229.

16. R. Nield, *China's Foreign Places: The Foreign Presence in China in the Treaty Port Era, 1840–1943* (Hong Kong, 2015), provides a wonderful survey of unfulfilled promise.

17. D. Hamer, 'Wellington on the Urban Frontier', in D. Hamer and R. Nicholls (eds.), *The Making of Wellington 1800–1914* (Wellington, 1990), pp. 227–52.

18. For the Colombian case, see E. Bassi, *An Aqueous Territory: Sailor Geographies and New Granada's Transimperial Greater Caribbean World* (Durham, NC, 2016). Colombia's 'nation-builders' sought to repudiate its Caribbean past.

19. See T. J. Wertenbaker, *Norfolk: Historic Southern Port* (Durham, NC, 1931, 1962), pp. 172ff.

20. See I. Bowman, *The Pioneer Fringe* (New York, 1931). For Brazil, see P. Monbeig, 'The Colonial Nucleus of Barão de Antonina, São Paulo', *Geographical Review*, 30, 2 (1940), 260–71.

21. See 'Aden le Volcan', *Le Monde*, 1 August 2017, pp. 2–4.

22. A. A. Sikainga, *'City of Steel and Fire': A Social History of Atbara, Sudan's Railway Town, 1906–1984* (Portsmouth, NH, 2002).

23. Ibid., p. 66.

24. See M. Frenz, 'Representing the Portuguese Empire: Goan Consuls in British East Africa, c.1910–1963', in E. Morier-Genoud and M. Cahen (eds.), *Imperial Migrations: Colonial Communities and Diaspora in the Portuguese World* (Basingstoke and New York, 2012), pp. 195–6.

25. Royal Institute of International Affairs, *World Agriculture: An International Survey* (London, 1932).

26. See R. C. Allen, *Farm to Factory: A Reinterpretation of the Soviet Industrial Revolution* (Princeton, 2003), ch. 1.

27. This change has been brilliantly described in R. Baldwin, *The Great Convergence* (Cambridge, MA, 2016).

28. See the 'Maritime Economy' supplement, *The Times*, 17 October 2018. Rotterdam, Antwerp, Hamburg and Los Angeles are the only non-Asian ports in the twenty largest.

29. See the trenchant analysis in A. Giridharadas, *Winners Take All: The Elite Charade of Changing the World* (London and New York, 2019), pp.146ff.

Further Reading

This is not intended as a full bibliography of the sources used in this book. The details of these can be found in the notes and references that accompany each chapter. It offers instead a selection of those books and articles that I found most useful, interesting or stimulating in writing this book.

I. GENERAL

There is an extraordinary range of material that provides an insight into the politics, society and culture of port cities in their global setting. It is especially rich for the nineteenth century and after. Newspapers, increasingly available in digital archives, are a vital source, although they reflect inevitably the bias of their owners. The *Times of India* (Bombay), *Straits Times* (Singapore), *China Mail* (Hong Kong) and *North China Herald* (Shanghai) can all be read online, as can the London *Times*, the *New York Times* and a selection of other British, Canadian and American newspapers. The *Economist* historical archive is also invaluable. Much material about trade and shipping can be found in the British Parliamentary Papers, also online. M'Culloch's *Commercial Dictionary* (I used the 'New Edition', ed. H. Reid (London 1869)) is an astonishing treasure trove of information about commodities, currencies and commercial practice, as well as individual ports around the world. G. Chisholm, *Handbook of Commercial Geography* (I used the 7th edition, London, 1908) combines a compendium of commodities with a brisk account of transport links and commercial conditions. M. G. Mulhall, *The Dictionary of Statistics* (London, 1892) also presents a mass of information, some reliable, some less so. A fascinating insight into the sailing-ship world can be gained from the various *Directories*, published in the nineteenth century to provide navigators with the most detailed instructions on winds, currents, landmarks, hazards like rocks and shoals, and entering ports. A classic example is J. Horsburgh, *India Directory, or Directions for Sailing to and from the East Indies, China, New Holland [etc.]* 3rd edn (London, 1827). It perhaps hardly needs saying that atlases of various periods convey much about the knowledge and expectations of their makers. They also indicate the most heavily used shipping routes, the spread of railways and the topography that facilitated or constricted the expansion of port city hinterlands. Much interesting material can be gleaned from the journals of the Royal Geographical Society of London (the *Geographical Journal*) and the American Geographical Society (the *Geographical Review*), especially for the period when geographers were happy to write descriptively. For recent scholarship on maritime history the place to turn first is the *International Journal of Maritime History*.

Port city history is not a new topic, although the recent popularity of global history has given it fresh impetus, and perhaps a livelier comparative dimension. French historians were among the first to give serious attention to the traffic between ports. F. Braudel, *The Mediterranean and the Mediterranean World in the Age of Phillip II* [1949] (Eng. trans, London, 1972), perhaps the most dazzling work by a twentieth-century historian, was soon followed by the monumental P. Chaunu, *Séville et l'Atlantique, 1504–1650* (11 volumes, Paris, 1955–60). In the English-speaking world, D. K. Basu (ed.), *The Rise and Growth of the Colonial Port Cities in Asia* (Santa Cruz, 1979) and F. Broeze (ed.), *Brides of the Sea: Port Cities of Asia from the 16th–20th Centuries* (Kensington, 1989) showed the possibilities. For its global setting, a still-valuable perspective can be found in H. Mackinder, *Democratic Ideals and Reality* (London, 1919), originally written to remind the peacemakers of geopolitical realities. A brilliant account of the (until then little acknowledged) role of trading diasporas is P. Curtin, *Cross-Cultural Trade in World History* (Cambridge, 1984). R. Findlay and K. H. O'Rourke, *Power and Plenty: Trade, War, and the World Economy in the Second Millennium* (Princeton, 2007) is a superb conspectus of the economic transition. A. G. Hopkins (ed.), *Globalization in World History*

(London, 2002) opened a new perspective. L. Paine, *The Sea and Civilization* (New York, 2015) presents a marvellous survey, strongest on the ancient and early modern world. J. Belich, *Replenishing the Earth: The Settler Revolution and the Rise of the Anglo-World, 1783–1939* (Oxford, 2009) is essential reading.

The World before Steam

B. Cunliffe, *By Steppe, Desert and Ocean: The Birth of Eurasia* (Oxford, 2015) is a generously illustrated account of Eurasia's early 'globalization'. V. Lieberman, *Strange Parallels: Southeast Asia in Global Context, c.800–1830*, 2 volumes (Cambridge, 2003, 2009) ranges far beyond South East Asia to consider India, China, Japan and Europe, offering a remarkable panorama of social and political change. F. Braudel, *Civilization and Capitalism, 15th–18th Century* [1967–79] (Eng. trans., London, 1981, 1982, 1984) is a brilliant account of the growth of a pre-modern world economy. A. Wink, *Al-Hind: The Making of the Indo-Islamic World*, 3 volumes (Leiden, 1990–2004) describes a world and its connections unfamiliar to most Western readers. For medieval Europe, P. Spufford, *Power and Profit: The Merchant in Medieval Europe* (London, 2002) can be read alongside S. R. Epstein, *Freedom and Growth: The Rise of States and Markets in Europe, 1300–1750* (London, 2000). M. Elvin, *The Pattern of the Chinese Past* (London, 1973) remains the definitive account of why Chinese economic growth had stalled by *c*.1300. The double impact of the Columbian voyages on Eurasia and the Americas is explored in A. W. Crosby, *The Columbian Exchange: The Biological and Cultural Consequences of 1492* (Westport, Conn., 1972). The new pattern of seaborne trade can be followed in two classic studies: R. Davis, *The Rise of the Atlantic Economies* (London, 1973) and H. Furber, *Rival Empires of Trade in the Orient, 1600–1800* (Minneapolis, 1976). The navigational challenges are described in I. K. Steele, *The English Atlantic 1675–1740* (Oxford, 1986) and C. N. Parkinson, *Trade in the Eastern Seas, 1793–1813* (Cambridge, 1937). J. H. Elliott, *Empires of the Atlantic World: Britain and Spain in America 1492–1830* (New Haven,

2006) supplies a much-needed comparative history. R. Drayton, *Nature's Government: Science, Imperial Britain and the 'Improvement' of the World* (New Haven, 2000) examines the role of contemporary scientists and savants. There remains no better introduction to the commercial mentality of the mid-eighteenth century than Adam Smith's combative *Wealth of Nations* [1776], to be found in innumerable editions.

2. THE AGE OF STEAM

The literature on industrialization and steam power is enormous. Accessible introductions include D. Landes, *The Unbound Prometheus: Technological Change and Industrial Development in Western Europe from 1750 to the Present* (Cambridge, 1969), E. A. Wrigley, *Continuity, Chance and Change: The Character of the Industrial Revolution in England* (Cambridge, 1988), R. C. Allen, *The British Industrial Revolution in Global Perspective* (Cambridge, 2009). N. Crafts, *British Economic Growth during the Industrial Revolution* (Oxford, 1985) warns against exaggerating its impact. A. Malm, *Fossil Capital: The Rise of Steam Power and the Roots of Global Warming* (London, 2016) explains the motives behind the shift from water power and denounces the technological determinism of much of the existing literature. Three books by Daniel Headrick describe the use Europeans put to their new technologies: *The Tools of Empire: Technology and European Imperialism in the Nineteenth Century* (New York, 1981); *The Tentacles of Progress: Technology Transfer in the Age of Imperialism, 1850–1940* (New York, 1988); *The Invisible Weapon: Telecommunications and International Politics, 1851–1945* (New York, 1991). W. Woodruff, *Impact of Western Man: A Study of Europe's Role in the World Economy 1750–1760* (London, 1966) is an invaluable compendium of hard information. H. Feis, *Europe, the World's Banker, 1870–1914* (New York, 1930) remains the definitive account of the capital transfers that lubricated the new world economy. London's central place is superbly described in D. Kynaston, *The City of London: Golden Years, 1890–1914* (London, 1995). The impact in the Middle East, not discussed in this book, is authoritatively covered in R. Owen, *The Middle East in the World Economy 1800–1914* (London, 1981). The (gradual) rise of the steamship can be followed in the classic article by G. S. Graham, 'The Ascendancy of the Sailing Ship 1850–85', *Economic History Review*, 9, 1 (1956), 74–88. J. Forbes Munro, *Maritime Enterprise and Empire: Sir William Mackinnon and His Business Network, 1823–1893* (Woodbridge, 2003) describes the growth of one of the great shipping enterprises of the era. D. A. Farnie, *East and West of Suez: The Suez Canal in History, 1854–1956* (Oxford, 1969) is a magisterial history of the changes brought by the faster connections between Europe and Asia. G. Blainey, *The Tyranny of Distance: How Distance Shaped Australia's History* (Melbourne, 1966) is a reminder that distance still mattered. M. Harrison, *Contagion: How Commerce Has Spread Disease* (New Haven, 2012) discusses the darker side of globalization. Life at sea has been the subject of a colossal imaginative literature. Joseph Conrad was the chronicler of the dying sailing ship era. Rudyard Kipling was *the* poet of the steamer: see his 'M'Andrew's Hymn' and 'Mulholland's Contract'. The sailing world of the East African dhow is marvellously evoked in A. Villiers, *Sons of Sindbad* (London, 1940).

3. NORTH AMERICA

D. W. Meinig on 'The Shaping of America: A Geographical Perspective on 500 Years of History', in four volumes, especially his *Continental America, 1800–1867* (New Haven, 1993), is fundamental. The rise of New Orleans can be followed in two excellent studies by R. Campanella, *Bienville's Dilemma: A Historical Geography of New Orleans* (Lafayette, LA, 2008) and *Lincoln in New Orleans: The 1828–1831 Flatboat Voyages and Their Place in History* (Lafayette, LA, 2010). The city's economy is authoritatively dealt with in S. Marler, *The Merchants' Capital: New Orleans and the Political Economy of the Nineteenth-Century South* (Cambridge, 2013). Few regions of the world have attracted more attention from historians. From a huge literature, I found J. Oakes, *The Ruling Race: A History of American Slaveholders* (New York, 1982, 1998) especially enlightening. The peculiar ethos of collective violence underpinning slavery in the South is forensically (and controversially) investigated in D. Grimsted, *American Mobbing, 1828–1861: Toward Civil War* (Oxford, 1998). The culture of slave society in the Deep South is brilliantly evoked in W. Johnson, *River of Dark Dreams: Slavery and Empire in the Cotton Kingdom* (Cambridge, 2013). F. L. Olmsted, later the designer of New York's Central Park, travelled through the South in the 1850s, keeping a copious diary. See his *The Cotton Kingdom* [1861] in A. M. Schlesinger (ed.), Modern Library edn (New York, 1969). C. S. Aitken, *William Faulkner and the Southern Landscape* (Athens, GA, 2009) is a fascinating study of northern Mississippi. The history of Canada is wonderfully served by the three-volume *Historical Atlas of Canada*, much more than an atlas. See especially volume 2, R. L. Gentilcore (ed.), *The Land Transformed, 1800–1891* (Toronto, 1993). The *Dictionary of Canadian Biography* (online) is far more than a dictionary. Every entry is a substantial history. Harold Adams Innis laid the groundwork for the study of a transcontinental Canadian economy. Much debated and critiqued, it remains foundational. See especially his *The Fur Trade in Canada: An Introduction to Canadian Economic History* (New Haven, 1930 and later editions). The classic account of merchant ambitions in Montreal is D. G. Creighton, *The Commercial Empire of the St Lawrence* [1937] (Toronto, 1956). See also G. Tulchinsky, *The River Barons: Montreal Businessmen and the Growth of Industry and Transportation, 1837–1853* (Toronto, 1977). A superb study of railway mania and its politics is A. A. den Otter, *The Philosophy of Railways: The Transcontinental Railway Idea in British North America* (Toronto, 1997). Montreal's divided culture and society are evoked in fiction in H. MacLennan, *Two Solitudes* (Toronto, 1945), a phrase that became a cliché. For New York, R. G. Albion's *The Rise of New York Port 1815–1860* (New York, 1939) is unrivalled. E. G. Burrows and M. Wallace, *Gotham: A History of New York City to 1898* (Oxford, 1998) is a close narrative, full of information. T. Kessner, *Capital City: New York City and the Men behind America's Rise to Economic Dominance, 1860–1900* (New York, 2003), S. Beckert, *The Monied Metropolis: New York City and the Consolidation of the American Bourgeoisie, 1850–1896* (Cambridge, 2001) and C. R. Geisst, *Wall Street: A History* (Oxford and New York, 1997) trace the place of finance. A classic of business history, A. D. Chandler Jr, *The Visible Hand: The Managerial Revolution in American Business* (Cambridge, 1977) explains the role of the giant corporation in New York's rise. The importance of New York's railway connections with the Midwest is explained in W. Cronon, *Nature's Metropolis: Chicago and the Great West* (New York, 1991).

4. THE MARITIME *RAJ*

T. Roy, *The Economic History of India 1857–1947* (New Delhi, 2000) is accessible and authoritative. A. Farooqui, *Opium City: The Making of Early Victorian Bombay* (Gurgaon, 2006) emphasizes the importance of opium exports to China in Bombay's commercial rise. P. Kidambi, *The Making of an Indian Metropolis: Colonial Governance and Public Culture in Bombay, 1890–1920* (Aldershot, 2007) is a recent scholarly history. R. Chandavarkar, *The Origins of Industrial Capitalism in India* (Cambridge, 1994) is a fundamental study of Bombay's cotton industry. N. Green, *Bombay Islam: The Religious Economy of the West Indian Ocean, 1840–1915* (Cambridge, 2011) explains Bombay's importance as an Islamic metropolis. Bombay's relations with its Presidency hinterland can be followed in G. Johnson, *Provincial Politics and Indian Nationalism: Bombay and the Indian National Congress, 1880 to 1915* (Cambridge, 1973) and D. Hardiman, *Peasant Nationalists of Gujarat: Kheda District 1917–1934* (Delhi, 1981). The agrarian setting is described in N. Charlesworth, *Peasants and Imperial Rule: Agriculture and Agrarian Society in the Bombay Presidency, 1850–1935* (Cambridge, 1985). I. J. Kerr, *Building the Railways of the Raj, 1850–1900* (Delhi, 1997) covers an essential subject. S. Chaudhuri (ed.), *Calcutta: The Living City*, Vol. 1: *The Past* (Calcutta, 1990) ranges over the social and cultural history of the city. P. Marshall, *Bengal: The British Bridgehead – Eastern India, 1740–1828* (Cambridge, 1987) covers the city's early history as a British outpost. G. Stewart, *Jute and Empire: The Calcutta Jute Wallahs and the Landscapes of Empire* (Manchester, 1998) describes British dominance over Calcutta's main industry and export. T. Raychaudhuri,

Europe Reconsidered: Perceptions of the West in Nineteenth-Century Bengal (Delhi, 1989) describes the ambiguities of Bengali response to alien Western culture. J. Gallagher, 'Congress in Decline: Bengal, 1930 to 1939', *Modern Asian Studies*, 7, 3 (1973) 589–645, reveals the political dilemma facing Hindu nationalists in interwar Bengal. J. Chatterji, *The Spoils of Partition: Bengal and India, 1947–1967* (Cambridge, 2007) discusses the results of Bengal's division at independence.

5. SOUTH EAST ASIA AND CHINA

The South East Asian setting has been superbly described in A. Reid, *Southeast Asia in the Age of Commerce, 1450–1680*, 2 vols. (New Haven, 1988, 1993). The role of the Dutch East India Company can be followed in E. M. Jacobs, *Merchant in Asia: The Trade of the Dutch East India Company during the Eighteenth Century* (Leiden, 2006). Singapore's 'founder', Stamford Raffles, is the subject of a large-scale biography by C. E. Wurtzburg, *Raffles of the Eastern Isles* [1954] (Oxford, 1986), though historians now take a more sceptical view of his status as a colonial hero. Alfred Russel Wallace, the contemporary and intellectual rival of Charles Darwin, spent many years in South East Asia. His *The Malay Archipelago* [1869] (Oxford, 1986) is a masterpiece of travel writing as well as natural history. C. M. Turnbull, *A History of Singapore, 1819–1975* (London and Kuala Lumpur, 1977) is an accessible history to be found in several later editions. Carl A. Trocki has written extensively on the importance of opium in South East Asian trade; see his *Opium and Empire: Chinese Society in Colonial Singapore, 1800–1910* (Ithaca NY, 1990), and his *Singapore: Wealth, Power and the Culture of Control* (Abingdon, 2006). W. G. Huff, *The Economic Growth of Singapore* (Cambridge, 1994) is essential reading. J. D. Vaughan, *The Manners and Customs of the Chinese of the Straits Settlements* [1879] (Kuala Lumpur, 1971) conveys a contemporary European view. M. R. Godley, *The Mandarin-Capitalists from Nanyang: Overseas Chinese Enterprise in the Modernization of China, 1893–1911* (Cambridge, 1981) explains the growing connection between Singapore and

Mainland Chinese in the period. From the voluminous literature on Hong Kong history, the best study of its early years as a colony is C. Munn, *Anglo-China: Chinese People and British Rule in Hong Kong, 1841–1880* (Hong Kong, 2001, 2009). E. Sinn, *Pacific Crossing: California Gold, Chinese Migration, and the Making of Hong Kong* (Hong Kong, 2013) explains Hong Kong's rise as the entrepôt of the China coast. S. Tsang, *A Modern History of Hong Kong* (London, 2004) is a comprehensive history. J. M. Carroll, *Edge of Empires: Chinese Elites and British Colonials in Hong Kong* (Hong Kong, 2007) brings out the social and cultural tensions of Hong Kong's peculiar location. D. Meyer, *Hong Kong as a Global Metropolis* (Cambridge, 2000) emphasizes Hong Kong's role as a primary financial centre. Robert Bickers is the pre-eminent historian of the foreign settlement in Shanghai. His pioneering article 'Shanghailanders: The Formation and Identity of the British Settler Community in Shanghai, 1843–1937', *Past and Present*, 159 (1998), 161–211, was followed up by *Empire Made Me: An Englishman Adrift in Shanghai* (London, 2003). H. B. Morse, *The Trade and Administration of the Chinese Empire* (London, 1908) is a contemporary account of how to make sense of the Middle Kingdom and negotiate its practices. Yen-p'ing Hao, *The Commercial Revolution in Nineteenth-Century China: The Rise of Sino-Western Mercantile Capitalism* (Berkeley and London, 1986) is the standard account of the role of the comprador. P. Hibbard, *The Bund, Shanghai* (Hong Kong, 2007) is a wonderfully illustrated history of Shanghai's 'main street'.

6. THE METROPOLES

R. Lawton and R. Lee (eds.), *Population and Society in Western European Port-Cities, c.1650–1939* (Liverpool, 2002) is a valuable survey. M. B. Miller, *Europe and the Maritime World: A Twentieth-Century History* (Cambridge, 2012) is essential reading. Modern studies of Europe's port cities are variable. London has been well served. R. C. Michie, *The City of London* (London, 1992) covers its commercial as well as financial functions. London's docklands are the subject of L. Rodwell Jones, *The Geography of London River*

(London, 1931). Both London and Liverpool docklands are dealt with commandingly in J. Bird, *The Major Seaports of the United Kingdom* (London, 1963). Liverpool's history has been superbly rendered in J. Belchem (ed.), *Liverpool 800: Culture, Character and History* (Liverpool, 2006). Hamburg is the subject of N. Ferguson, *Paper and Iron: Hamburg Business and German Politics in the Era of Inflation, 1897–1927* (Cambridge, 1995) and of R. J. Evans, *Death in Hamburg: Society and Politics in the Cholera Years 1830–1910* (Oxford, 1987). Jan Morris has written an atmospheric history of Trieste: *Trieste and the Meaning of Nowhere* (London, 2006). The decline and fall of the pre-1914 world economy have been brilliantly analysed in A. Tooze, *The Deluge: The Great War and the Remaking of the Global Order, 1916–1931* (London, 2014).

Index